Bernard Elison

Guy Fawkes in Ordsall Cave

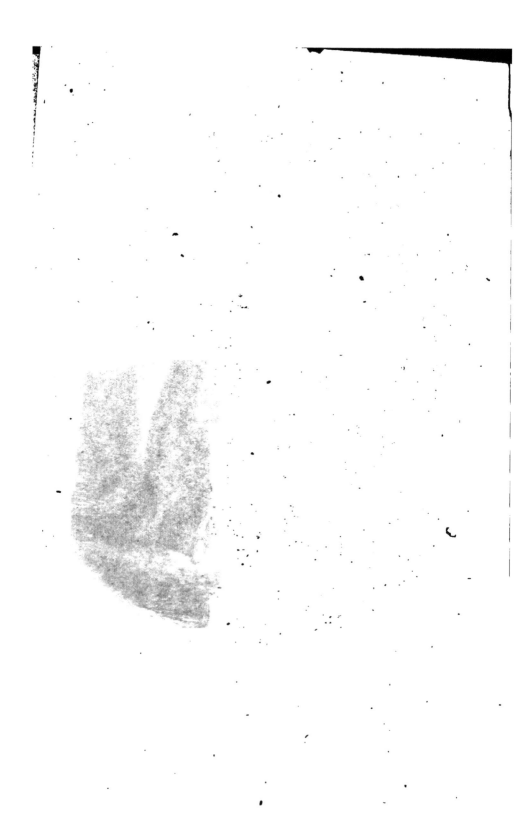

GUY FAWKES

OR

THE GUNPOWDER TREASON

AN HISTORICAL ROMANCE

BY

WILLIAM HARRISON AINSWORTH

"You shall swear by the blessed Trinity, and by the sacrament you now propose to receive, never to disclose directly or indirectly, by word or circumstance, the matter that shall be proposed to you to keep secret; nor desist from the execution thereof till the rest shall give you leave."—OATH OF THE CONSPIRATORS.

WITH ILLUSTRATIONS BY GEORGE CRUIKSHANK.

LONDON

GEORGE ROUTLEDGE AND SONS

BROADWAY, LUDGATE HILL

NEW YORK: 416 BROOME STREET

1878

BY W. HARRISON AINSWORTH.

Uniform with this Volume.

THE TOWER OF LONDON,
With Illustrations by GEORGE CRUIKSHANK.

WINDSOR CASTLE,
With Illustrations by GEORGE CRUIKSHANK.

ROOKWOOD,
With Illustrations by Sir JOHN GILBERT, R.A.

THE LANCASHIRE WITCHES,
With Illustrations by Sir JOHN GILBERT, R.A.

TO MRS. HUGHES.

KINGSTON LISLE, BERKS.

———◆———

My dear Mrs. Hughes,

You are aware that this Romance was brought to a close during my last brief visit at Kingston Lisle, when the time necessary to be devoted to it deprived me of the full enjoyment of your society, and, limiting my range—no very irksome restriction—to your own charming garden and grounds, prevented me from accompanying you in your walks to your favourite and beautiful downs. This circumstance, which will suffice to give it some interest in your eyes by associating it with your residence, furnishes me with a plea, of which I gladly avail myself, of inscribing it with your name, and of recording, at the same time, the high sense I entertain of your goodness and worth, the value I set upon your friendship—a friendship shared in common with some of the most illustrious writers of our time—and the gratitude I shall never cease to feel for attentions and kindnesses, little less than maternal, which I have experienced at your hands.

In the hope that you may long continue to diffuse happiness round your own circle, and contribute to the instruction and delight of the many attached friends with whom you maintain so active and so interesting a correspondence; and that you may live to see your grandsons fulfil their present promise, and tread in the footsteps of their high-minded and excellent-hearted father—and of *his* father! I remain

Your affectionate and obliged friend,

W. Harrison Ainsworth.

Kensal Manor House, Harrow Road,
July 26, 1841.

PREFACE.

The tyrannical measures adopted against the Roman Catholics in the early part of the reign of James the First, when the severe penal enactments against recusants were revived, and with additional rigour, and which led to the remarkable conspiracy about to be related, have been so forcibly and faithfully described by Doctor Lingard,* that the following extract from his history will form a fitting introduction to the present work,

"The oppressive and sanguinary code framed in the reign of Elizabeth, was re-enacted to its full extent, and even improved with additional severities. Every individual who had studied or resided, or should afterwards study or reside in any college or seminary beyond the sea, was rendered incapable of inheriting, or purchasing, or enjoying lands, annuities, chattels, debts, or sums of money, within the realm; and as missionaries sometimes eluded detection under the disguise of tutors, it was provided that no man should teach even the rudiments of grammar in public or in private, without the previous approbation of the diocesan.

"The execution of the penal laws enabled the king, by an ingenious comment, to derive considerable profit from his past forbearance. It was pretended that he had never forgiven the penalties of recusancy; he had merely forbidden them to be exacted for a time, in the hope that this indulgence would lead to conformity; but his expectations had been deceived; the obstinacy of the Catholics had grown with the lenity of the sovereign; and, as they were unworthy of further favour, they should now be left to the severity of the law. To their dismay, the legal fine of twenty pounds per lunar month was again demanded, and not only for the time to come, but for the whole period of the suspension; a demand which, by crowding thirteen payments into one, reduced many families of moderate incomes to a state of absolute beggary. Nor was this all. James was surrounded by numbers of his indigent countrymen. Their habits were expensive, their wants many, and their importunities incessant. To satisfy the more clamorous, a new expedient was devised. The king transferred to them his claims on some

* Vide *History of England*, vol. ix. New Edition.

of the more opulent recusants, against whom they were at
liberty to proceed by law, in his name, unless the sufferers
should submit to compound, by the grant of an annuity for
life, or the immediate payment of a considerable sum. This
was at a time when the jealousies between the two nations
had reached a height, of which, at the present day, we have
but little conception. Had the money been carried to the
royal coffers, the recusants would have had sufficient reason
to complain; but that Englishmen should be placed by their
king at the mercy of foreigners, that they should be stripped
of their property to support the extravagance of his Scottish
minions, this added indignity to injustice, exacerbated their
already wounded feelings, and goaded the most moderate
almost to desperation."

From this deplorable state of things, which is by no means
over-coloured in the above description, sprang the Gunpowder Plot.

The county of Lancaster has always abounded in Catholic
families, and at no period were the proceedings of the ecclesiastical commissioners more rigorous against them than at
that under consideration. Manchester, "the Goshen of this
Egypt," as it is termed by the fiery zealot, Warden Heyrick,
being the place where all the recusants were imprisoned, the
scene of the early part of this history has been laid in
that town and its immediate neighbourhood.

For the introduction of the munificent founder of the Blue-
Coat Hospital into a tale of this description I ought, perhaps,
to apologize; but if I should succeed by it in arousing my
fellow-townsmen to a more lively appreciation of the great
benefits they have derived from him, I shall not regret what
I have written.

In Viviana Radcliffe I have sought to portray the loyal and
devout Catholic, such as I conceive the character to have
existed at the period. In Catesby, the unscrupulous and
ambitious plotter, masking his designs under the cloak of
religion. In Garnet, the subtle, and yet sincere Jesuit. And
in Fawkes the gloomy and superstitious enthusiast. One
doctrine I have endeavoured to enforce throughout—TOLERA-
TION.

CONTENTS.

———

———

BOOK THE FIRST.

THE PLOT.

BOOK THE SECOND
THE DISCOVERY.

BOOK THE THIRD.
THE CONSPIRATORS.

GUY FAWKES.

Book the First.

THE PLOT.

Their searches are many and severe. They come either in the night or
early in the morning, and ever seek their opportunity, when the Catholics
are or would be best occupied, or are likely to be worse provided or look
for nothing. They willingliest come when few are at home to resist them,
that they may rifle coffers, and do what they list. They lock up the servants, and the mistress of the house, and the whole family, in a room by
themselves, while they, like young princes, go rifling the house at their
will.   *Letter to Verstegan, ap. Stonyhurst MSS.*

What a thing is it for a Catholic gentleman to have his house suddenly
beset on all sides with a number of men in arms, both horse and foot! and
not only his house and gardens, and such enclosed places all beset, but all
highways laid, for some miles near unto him, that none shall pass, but they
shall be examined! Then are these searches oft-times so rude and barbarous, that, if the doors be not opened in the instant they would enter, they
break open the doors with all violence, as if they were to sack a town of
enemies won by the sword.   *Father Gerard's MS.*

I.

AN EXECUTION IN MANCHESTER, AT THE BEGINNING OF THE SEVENTEENTH CENTURY.

MORE than two hundred and thirty-five years ago, or, to
speak with greater precision, in 1605, at the latter end of
June, it was rumoured one morning in Manchester that two
seminary priests, condemned at the late assizes under the
severe penal enactments then in force against the Papists,
were about to suffer death on that day. Attracted by the
report, large crowds flocked towards the place of execution,
which, in order to give greater solemnity to the spectacle, had
been fixed at the southern gate of the old Collegiate Church,
where a scaffold was erected. Near it was a large blood-

B

stained block, the use of which will be readily divined,
and adjoining the block, upon a heap of blazing coals, smoked
a caldron filled with boiling pitch, intended to receive the
quarters of the miserable sufferers.

The place was guarded by a small band of soldiers, fully
accoutred in corslets and morions, and armed with swords,
half-pikes, and calivers. Upon the steps of the scaffold stood
the executioner,—a square-built, ill-favoured personage,—
busied in arranging a bundle of straw upon the boards. He
was dressed in a buff jerkin, and had a long-bladed, two-
edged knife thrust into his girdle. Besides these persons,
there was a pursuivant,—an officer appointed by the Privy
Council to make search throughout the provinces for recusants, Popish priests, and other religious offenders. He
was occupied at this moment in reading over a list of suspected persons.

Neither the executioner nor his companions appeared in the
slightest degree impressed by the butcherly business about to
be enacted; for the former whistled carelessly as he pursued
his task, while the latter laughed and chatted with the crowd,
or jestingly pointed their matchlocks at the jackdaws wheeling
above them in the sunny air, or perching upon the pinnacles
and tower of the neighbouring fane. Not so the majority of
the assemblage. Most of the older and wealthier families in
Lancashire still continuing to adhere to the ancient faith of
their fathers, it will not be wondered at that many of their
dependents should follow their example. And, even of those
who were adverse to the creed of Rome, there were few who
did not murmur at the rigorous system of persecution adopted
towards its professors.

At nine o'clock the hollow rolling of a muffled drum was
heard at a distance. The deep bell of the church began to
toll, and presently afterwards the mournful procession was
seen advancing from the market-place. It consisted of a
troop of mounted soldiers, equipped in all respects like those
stationed at the scaffold, with their captain at their head, and
followed by two of their number with hurdles attached to
their steeds, on which were tied the unfortunate victims.
Both were young men—both apparently prepared to meet
their fate with firmness and resignation. They had been
brought from Radcliffe Hall—an old moated and fortified
mansion belonging to a wealthy family of that name, situated
where the close, called Pool Fold, now stands, and then recently converted into a place of security for recusants; the

two other prisons in Manchester—namely, the New Fleet on
Hunt's Bank, and the gaol on Salford Bridge—not being found
adequate to the accommodation of the numerous religious
offenders.

By this time the cavalcade had reached the place of execution. The soldiers drove back the throng with their pikes,
and cleared a space in front of the scaffold; when, just as
the cords that bound the limbs of the priests were unfastened,
a woman in a tattered woollen robe, with a hood partially
drawn over her face,—the features of which, so far as they
could be discerned, were sharp and attenuated,—a rope
girded round her waist, bare feet, and having altogether the
appearance of a Sister of Charity, sprang forward, and flung
herself on her knees beside them.

Clasping the hem of the garment of the nearest priest, she
pressed it to her lips, and gazed earnestly at him, as if imploring a blessing.

"You have your wish, daughter," said the priest, extending his arms over her. "Heaven and Our Lady bless you!"

The woman then turned towards the other victim, who
was audibly reciting the *Miserere.*

"Back, spawn of Antichrist!" interposed a soldier, rudely
thrusting her aside. "Don't you see you disturb the father's
devotions? He has enough to do to take care of his own
soul, without minding yours."

"Take this, daughter," cried the priest who had been first
addressed, offering her a small volume, which he took from
his vest, "and fail not to remember in your prayers the sinful soul of Robert Woodroofe, a brother of the Order of
Jesus."

The woman put out her hand to take the book; but before
it could be delivered to her it was seized by the soldier.

"Your priests have seldom anything to leave behind them,"
he shouted, with a brutal laugh, "except some worthless and
superstitious relic of a saint or martyr. What's this? Ah!
a breviary—a mass-book. I've too much regard for your
spiritual welfare to allow you to receive it," he added, about
to place it in his doublet.

"Give it her," exclaimed a young man, snatching it from
him, and handing it to the woman, who disappeared as soon
as she had obtained possession of it.

The soldier eyed the new-comer as if disposed to resent the
interference; but a glance at his apparel, which, though
plain, and of a sober hue, was rather above the middle class,

as well as a murmur from the crowd, who were evidently disposed to take part with the young man, induced him to stay his hand. He therefore contented himself with crying, "A recusant! a Papist!"

"I am neither recusant nor Papist, knave!" replied the other, sternly; "and I counsel you to mend your manners, and show more humanity, or you shall find I have interest enough to procure your dismissal from a service which you disgrace."

This reply elicited a shout of applause from the mob.

"Who is that bold speaker?" demanded the pursuivant from one of his attendants.

"Humphrey Chetham of Crumpsall," answered the man, "son to one of the wealthiest merchants of the town, and a zealous upholder of the true faith."

"He has a strange way of showing his zeal," rejoined the pursuivant, entering the answer in his note-book. "And who is the woman he befriended?"

"A half-crazed being called Elizabeth Orton," replied the attendant. "She was scourged and tortured during Queen Elizabeth's reign for pretending to the gift of prophecy, and was compelled to utter her recantation within yonder church. Since then she has never opened her lips."

"Indeed!" exclaimed the pursuivant: "I will engage to make her speak and to some purpose. Where does she live?"

"In a cave on the banks of the Irwell, near Ordsall Hall," replied the attendant. "She subsists on the chance contributions of the charitable; but she solicits nothing—and, indeed, is seldom seen."

"Her cave must be searched," observed the pursuivant; "it may be the hiding-place of a priest. Father Campion was concealed in such another spot at Stonor Park, near Henley-on-Thames, where he composed his ' *Decem Rationes;*' and, for a long time, eluded the vigilance of the commissioners. We shall pass it in our way to Ordsall Hall to-night, shall we not?"

The attendant nodded in the affirmative.

"If we surprise Father Oldcorne," continued the pursuivant, "and can prove that Sir William Radcliffe and his daughter, both of whom are denounced in my list, are harbourers and shelterers of recusants, we shall have done a good night's work."

At this moment, an officer advanced, and commanded the priests to ascend the scaffold.

As Father Woodroofe, who was the last to mount, reached the uppermost step, he turned round and cried in a loud voice, " Good people, I take you all to witness that I die in the true Catholic religion, and that I rejoice and thank God with all my soul, that He hath made me worthy to testify my faith therein by shedding my blood in this manner." He then advanced towards the executioner, who was busied in adjusting the cord round his companion's throat, and said, " God forgive thee—do thine office quickly ;" adding in a lower tone, " *Asperge me, Domine ; Domine, miserere mei!*"

And, amid the deep silence that ensued, the executioner performed his horrible task.

The execution over, the crowd began to separate slowly, and various opinions were expressed respecting the revolting and sanguinary spectacle just witnessed. Many, who condemned—and the majority did so—the extreme severity of the laws by which the unfortunate priests had just suffered, uttered their sentiments with extreme caution ; but there were some whose feelings had been too much excited for prudence, and who inveighed loudly and bitterly against the spirit of religious persecution then prevailing : while a few others of an entirely opposite persuasion looked upon the rigorous proceedings adopted against the Papists, and the punishment now inflicted upon their priesthood, as a just retribution for their own severities during the reign of Mary. In general, the common people entertained a strong prejudice against the Catholic party—for, as it has been shrewdly observed, " they must have some object to hate ; heretofore it was the Welsh, the Scots, or the Spaniards, but now in these latter times only the Papists ;" but in Manchester, near which, as has been already stated, so many old and important families, professing that religion, resided, the case was widely different ; and the mass of the inhabitants were favourably inclined towards them. It was the knowledge of this feeling that induced the commissioners, appointed to superintend the execution of the enactments against recusants, to proceed with unusual rigour in this neighbourhood.

The state of the Roman Catholic party at the period of this history was indeed most grievous. The hopes they had indulged of greater toleration on the accession of James the First had been entirely destroyed. The persecutions, suspended during the first year of the reign of the new monarch, were renewed with greater severity than ever; and though their present condition was deplorable enough, it was feared that worse remained in store for them. "They bethought themselves," writes Bishop Goodman, "that now their case was far worse than in the time of Queen Elizabeth; for they did live in some hope that after the old woman's life, they might have some mitigation, and even those who did then persecute them were a little more moderate, as being doubtful what times might succeed, and fearing their own case. But, now that they saw the times settled, having no hope of better days, but expecting that the uttermost rigour of the law should be executed, they became desperate: finding that by the laws of the kingdom their own lives were not secured, and for the carrying over of a priest into England it was no less than high treason. A gentlewoman was hanged only for relieving and harbouring a priest; a citizen was hanged only for being reconciled to the Church of Rome; besides, the penal laws were such, and so executed, that they could not subsist. What was usually sold in shops and usually bought, this the pursuivant would take away from them as being Popish and superstitious. One knight did affirm that in one term he gave twenty nobles in rewards to the door-keeper of the Attorney-General; another did affirm, that his third part which remained unto him of his estate did hardly serve for his expense in law to defend him from other oppressions; besides their children to be taken from home, to be brought up in another religion. So they did every way conclude that their estate was desperate; they could die but once, and their religion was more precious unto them than their lives. They did further consider their misery; how they were debarred in any course of life to help themselves. They could not practise law—they could not be citizens—they could have no office; they could not breed up their sons—none did desire to match with them; they had neither fit marriages for their daughters, nor nunneries to put them into: for those few which are beyond seas are not considerable in respect of the number of recusants, and none can be admitted into them without great sums of money, which they, being exhausted, could not supply. The Spiritual Court did not cease to molest them, to excommunicate them, then to imprison them; and thereby they were utterly disenabled to sue for their own." Such is a faithful picture of the state of the Catholic party at the commencement of the reign of James the First.

Pressed down by these intolerable grievances, is it to be wondered at that the Papists should repine,—or that some among their number, when all other means failed, should seek redress by darker measures? By a statute of Elizabeth, all who refused to conform to the established religion were subjected to a fine of twenty pounds a lunar month; and this heavy penalty, remitted, or rather suspended, on the accession of the new sovereign, was again exacted, and all arrears claimed. Added to this, James, whose court was thronged by a host of needy Scottish retainers, assigned to them a certain number of wealthy recusants, and empowered them to levy the fines—a privilege of which they were not slow to avail themselves. There were other pains and penalties provided for by the same statute, which were rigorously inflicted. To withdraw, or seek to withdraw another from the established religion, was accounted high treason, and punished accordingly; to hear mass involved a penalty of one hundred marks and a year's imprisonment; and to harbour a priest, under the denomination of a tutor, rendered the latter liable to a year's imprisonment, and his employer to a fine of ten pounds a month. Impressed with the belief that, in consequence of the unremitting persecutions which the Catholics underwent in Elizabeth's time, the religion would be wholly extirpated, Doctor Allen, a Lancashire divine, who afterwards received a cardinal's hat, founded a college at Douay, for the reception and education of those intending to take orders. From this university a number of missionary priests, or seminarists, as they were termed, were annually sent over to England; and it was against these persons, who submitted to every hardship and privation, to danger, and death itself, for the welfare of their religion, and in the hope of propagating its doctrines, that the utmost rigour of the penal enactments was directed. Among the number of seminarists despatched from Douay, and capitally convicted under the statute above mentioned, were the two priests whose execution has just been narrated.

As a portion of the crowd passed over the old bridge across the Irwell connecting Manchester with Salford, on which stood an ancient chapel erected by Thomas de Booth, in the reign of Edward the Third, and recently converted into a prison for recusants, they perceived the prophetess, Elizabeth Orton, seated upon the stone steps of the desecrated structure, earnestly perusing the missal given her by Father Woodroofe. A mob speedily collected round her; but, unconscious seemingly of their presence, the poor woman turned over leaf after leaf, and pursued her studies. Her hood was thrown back, and discovered her bare and withered neck, over which her dishevelled hair streamed in long sable elf locks. Irritated by her indifference, several of the by-standers, who had questioned her as to the nature of her studies, began to mock and jeer her, and endeavoured, by plucking her robe and casting little pebbles at her, to attract her attention. Roused at length by these annoyances, she arose ; and, fixing her large black eyes menacingly upon them, was about to stalk away, when they surrounded and detained her.

"Speak to us, Bess," cried several voices. "Prophesy—prophesy."

"I *will* speak to you," replied the poor woman, shaking her hand at them, "I *will* prophesy to you. And mark me, though ye believe not, my words shall not fall to the ground."

"A miracle ! a miracle !" shouted the by-standers. "Bess Orton, who has been silent for twenty years, has found her tongue at last."

"I have seen a vision, and dreamed a dream," continued the prophetess. "As I lay in my cell last night, meditating upon the forlorn state of our religion, and of its professors, methought nineteen shadowy figures stood before me—ay, nineteen—for I counted them thrice—and when I questioned them as to their coming,—for my tongue at first clove to the roof of my mouth, and my lips refused their office,—one of them answered, in a voice which yet rings in my ears, ' We are the chosen deliverers of our fallen and persecuted Church. To us is intrusted the rebuilding of her temples,—to our hands is committed the destruction of our enemies. The work will be done in darkness and in secret,—with toil and travail,—but it will at length be made manifest ; and when the hour is arrived, our vengeance will be terrible and exterminating.' With these words they vanished from my sight. Ah !" she exclaimed, suddenly starting, and passing her hand across her brow, as if to clear her sight, "it was no dream—no vision. I see one of them now."

"Where ? where ?" cried several voices.

The prophetess answered by extending her skinny arm towards some object immediately before her.

All eyes were instantly turned in the same direction, when they beheld a Spanish soldier—for such his garb proclaimed him—standing at a few paces' distance from them. He was wrapped in an ample cloak, with a broad-leaved steeple-crowned hat, decorated with a single green feather, pulled over his brows, and wore a polished-steel brigandine, trunk-hose, and buff boots drawn up to the knees. His arms consisted of a brace of petronels thrust into his belt, whence a long rapier depended. His features were dark as bronze, and well-formed, though strongly marked, and had an expression of settled sternness. His eyes were grey and penetrating, and shaded by thick beetle-brows; and his physiognomy was completed by a black peaked beard. His person was tall and erect, and his deportment soldier-like and commanding. Perceiving he had become an object of notice, the stranger cast a compassionate look at the prophetess, who still remained gazing fixedly at him, and throwing her a few pieces of money, strode away.

Watching his retreating figure till it disappeared from view, the crazed woman tossed her arms wildly in the air, and cried, in a voice of exultation, "Did I not speak the truth? —did I not tell you I had seen him? He is the deliverer of our Church, and is come to avenge the righteous blood which hath been this day shed."

"Peace, woman, and fly while there is yet time," cried the young man who had been designated as Humphrey Chetham. "The pursuivant and his myrmidons are in search of you."

"Then they need not go far to find me," replied the prophetess. "I will tell them what I told these people, that the day of bloody retribution is at hand,—that the avenger is arrived. I have seen him twice,—once in my cave, and once again here,—even where you stand."

"If you do not keep silence and fly, my poor creature," rejoined Humphrey Chetham, "you will have to endure what you suffered years ago,—stripes, and perhaps torture. Be warned by me—ah! it is too late. He is approaching."

"Let him come," replied Elizabeth Orton, "I am ready for him."

"Can none of you force her away?" cried Humphrey Chetham, appealing to the crowd; "I will reward you."

"I will not stir from this spot," rejoined the prophetess, obstinately; "I will testify to the truth."

The kind-hearted young merchant, finding any further attempt to preserve her fruitless, drew aside.

By this time, the pursuivant and his attendants had come up. "Seize her!" cried the former, "and let her be placed within this prison till I have reported her to the commissioners. If you will confess to me, woman," he added, in a whisper to her, "that you have harboured a priest, and will guide us to his hiding-place, you shall be set free."

"I know of no priests but those you have murdered," returned the prophetess, in a loud voice, "but I will tell you something that you wot not of. The avenger of blood is at hand. I have seen him. All here have seen him. And you shall see him—but not now—not now."

"What is the meaning of this raving?" demanded the pursuivant.

"Pay no heed to her talk," interposed Humphrey Chetham; "she is a poor crazed being, who knows not what she says. I will be surety for her inoffensive conduct."

"You must give me surety for yourself, sir," replied the pursuivant. "I have just learnt that you were last night at Ordsall Hall, the seat of that 'dangerous temporiser,'—for so he is designated in my warrant,—Sir William Radcliffe. And if report speaks truly, you are not altogether insensible to the charms of his fair daughter, Viviana."

"What is this to thee, thou malapert knave?" cried Humphrey Chetham, reddening, partly from anger, partly, it might be, from another emotion.

"Much, as you shall presently find, good Master Wolf-in-sheep's-clothing," retorted the pursuivant; "if you prove not a rank Papist at heart, then do I not know a true man from a false."

This angry conference was cut short by a piercing scream from the prophetess. Breaking from the grasp of her captors, who were about to force her into the prison, she sprang with a single bound upon the parapet of the bridge; and, utterly regardless of her dangerous position, turned, and faced the soldiers, who were struck mute with astonishment.

"Tremble!" she cried, in a loud voice, "tremble, ye evil-doers! Ye who have despoiled the house of God,—have broken his altars—scattered his incense,—slain his priests. Tremble, I say. The avenger is arrived. The bolt is in his hand. It shall strike king, lords, commons,—all! These are my last words,—take them to heart."

"Drag her off," roared the pursuivant, furiously.

"Use care—use gentleness, if ye are men," cried Humphrey Chetham.

"Think not you can detain me," cried the prophetess. "Avaunt, and tremble!"

So saying, she flung herself from the parapet.

The height from which she fell was about fifty feet.

Dashed into the air like jets from a fountain by the weight and force of the descending body, the water instantly closed over her. But she rose to the surface of the stream, about twenty yards below the bridge.

"She may yet be saved," cried Humphrey Chetham, who with the bystanders had hurried to the side of the bridge.

"You will only preserve her for the gallows," observed the pursuivant.

"Your malice shall not prevent my making the attempt," replied the young merchant. "Ha! assistance is at hand."

The exclamation was occasioned by the sudden appearance of the soldier in the Spanish dress, who rushed towards the left bank of the river, which was here, as elsewhere, formed of red sandstone rock, and following the course of the current, awaited the next appearance of the drowning woman. It did not occur till she had been carried a considerable distance down the stream, when the soldier, swiftly divesting himself of his cloak, plunged into the water, and dragged her ashore.

"Follow me," cried the pursuivant to his attendants. "I will not lose my prey."

But before he gained the bank of the river, the soldier and his charge had disappeared, nor could he detect any traces of them.

II.

ORDSALL CAVE.

AFTER rescuing the unfortunate prophetess from a watery grave in the manner just related, the soldier snatched up his cloak, and, taking his dripping burthen in his arms, hurried swiftly along the bank of the river, until he came to a large cleft in the rock, into which he crept, taking the prophetess with him, and thus eluded observation. In this retreat he continued upwards of two hours, during which time the poor creature, to whom he paid every attention that circumstances would admit, had so far recovered as to be able to speak. But it was evident that the shock had been too much for her, and that she was sinking fast. She was so faint that she could scarcely move; but she expressed a strong desire to

reach her cell before she breathed her last. Having described
its situation as accurately as she could to the soldier—who
before he ventured forth peeped out to reconnoitre—he again
raised her in his arms, and by her direction struck into a
narrow lane skirting the bank of the river.

Pursuing this road for about half a mile, he arrived at the
foot of a small knoll, covered by a clump of magnificent
beech-trees, and still acting under the guidance of the dying
woman, whose voice grew more feeble each instant, he mounted
it, and from its summit took a rapid survey of the surrounding
country. On the opposite bank of the river stood an old
hall, while further on, at some distance, he could perceive
through the trees the gables and chimneys of another ancient
mansion.

"Raise me up," said Elizabeth Orton, as he lingered on this
spot for a moment. "In that old house, which you see yonder,
Hulme Hall, I was born. I would willingly take one look at
it before I die."

"And the other hall, which I discern through the trees, is
Ordsall, is it not?" inquired the soldier.

"It is," replied the prophetess. "And now let us make
what haste we can. We have not far to go; and I feel I shall
not last long."

Descending the eminence, and again entering the lane, which
here made a turn, the soldier approached a grassy space, walled
in on either side by steep sandstone rocks. At the further
extremity of the enclosure, after a moment's search, by the
direction of his companion, he found, artfully concealed by
overhanging brushwood, the mouth of a small cave. He crept
into the excavation, and found it about six feet high, and of
considerable depth. The roof was ornamented with Runic
characters and other grotesque and half-effaced inscriptions,
while the sides were embelished with Gothic tracery, amid
which the letters I.H.S., carved in ancient church text, could
be easily distinguished. Tradition assigned the cell to the
priests of Odin, but it was evident that worshippers at other
and holier altars had more recently made it their retreat.
Its present occupant had furnished it with a straw pallet,
and a small wooden crucifix fixed in a recess in the wall.
Gently depositing her upon the pallet, the soldier took a seat
beside her on a stone slab at the foot of the bed. He next,
at her request, as the cave was rendered almost wholly dark
by the overhanging trees, struck a light, and set fire to a
candle placed within a lantern.

After a few moments passed in prayer, the recluse begged him to give her the crucifix that she might clasp it to her breast. This done, she became more composed, and prepared to meet her end. Suddenly, as if something had again disturbed her, she opened wide her glazing eyes, and starting up with a dying effort, stretched out her hands.

"I see him before them," she cried. "They examine him—they adjudge him! Ah! he is now in a dungeon! See, the torturers advance! He is placed on the rack—once—twice—thrice—they turn the levers! His joints snap in their sockets—his sinews crack! Mercy! he confesses! He is led to execution. I see him ascend the scaffold."

"Whom do you behold?" inquired the soldier listening to her in astonishment.

"His face is hidden from me," replied the prophetess; "but his figure is not unlike your own. Ha! I hear the executioner pronounce his name. How are you called?"

"GUY FAWKES," replied the soldier.

"It is the name I heard," rejoined Elizabeth Orton.

And, sinking backward, she expired.

Guy Fawkes gazed at her for some time, till he felt assured that the last spark of life had fled. He then turned away, and placing his hand upon his chin, became lost in deep reflection.

III.

ORDSALL HALL.

Soon after sunset, on the evening of the events previously related, the inmates of Ordsall Hall were disturbed and alarmed (for in those times of trouble any casual disturbance at night was sufficient to occasion alarm to a Catholic family) by a loud clamour for admittance from some one stationed at the farther side of the moat, then, as now, surrounding that ancient manorial residence. The drawbridge being raised, no apprehension was entertained of an attempt at forcible entrance on the part of the intruder, who, so far as he could be discerned in the deepening twilight, rendered yet more obscure by the shade of the trees under which he stood, appeared

to be a solitary horseman. Still, for fear of a surprise, it was
judged prudent by those inside the hall to turn a deaf ear to
the summons; nor was it until it had been more than once
repeated in a peremptory tone, that any attention was paid
to it. The outer gate was then cautiously opened by an old
steward and a couple of serving men, armed with pikes and
swords, who demanded the stranger's business, and were
answered that he desired to speak with Sir William Radcliffe.
The steward rejoined that his master was not at home, having
set out the day before for Chester: but that even if he were,
he would take it upon himself to affirm that no audience
would be given, on any pretence whatever, to a stranger at
such an unseasonable hour. To this the other replied, in a
haughty and commanding voice, that he was neither a stranger
to Sir William Radcliffe, nor ignorant of the necessity of
caution, though in this instance it was altogether superfluous;
and as, notwithstanding the steward's assertion to the contrary, he was fully persuaded his master *was* at home, he
insisted upon being conducted to him without further parley,
as his business would not brook delay. In vain the steward
declared he had spoken the truth. The stranger evidently
disbelieved him; but, as he could obtain no more satisfactory
answer to his interrogations, he suddenly shifted his ground,
and inquired whether Sir William's daughter, Mistress
Viviana, was likewise absent from home.

"Before I reply to the question, I must know by whom and
wherefore it is put?" returned the steward, evasively.

"Trouble not yourself further, friend, but deliver this letter
to her," rejoined the horseman, flinging a packet across the
moat. "It is addressed to her father, but there is no reason
why she should not be acquainted with its contents."

"Take it up, Olin Birtwissel," cried the steward, eyeing
the packet which had fallen at his feet suspiciously; "take
it up, I say, and hold it to the light, that I may consider it
well before I carry it to our young mistress. I have heard of
strange treacheries practised by such means, and care not to
meddle with it."

"Neither do I, good Master Heydocke," replied Birtwissel,
"I would not touch it for a twelvemonth's wages. It may
burst and spoil my good looks, and so ruin my fortunes with
the damsels. But here is Jeff Gellibronde, who, having no
beauty to lose, and being, moreover, afraid of nothing, will
pick it up for you."

"Speak for yourself, Olin," rejoined Gellibronde, in a surly tone. "I have no more fancy for a shattered limb, or a scorched face, than my neighbours."

"Dolts!" cried the stranger, who had listened to these observations with angry impatience, "if you will not convey my packet, which has nothing more dangerous about it than an ordinary letter, to your mistress, at least acquaint her that Mr. Robert Catesby, of Ashby St. Legers, is without, and craves an instant speech with her."

"Mr. Catesby!" exclaimed the steward, in astonishment. "If it be indeed your worship, why did you not declare yourself at once?"

"I may have as good reason for caution as yourself, Master Heydocke," returned Catesby, laughing.

"True," rejoined the steward; "but, methinks it is somewhat strange to find your worship here, when I am aware that my master expected to meet you, and certain other honourable gentlemen that you wot of, at a place in a clean opposite direction, Holywell, in Flintshire."

"The cause of my presence, since you desire to be certified of the matter, is simply this," replied Catesby, urging his steed towards the edge of the moat, while the steward advanced to meet him on the opposite bank, so that a few yards only lay between them; "I came round by Manchester," he continued, in a lower tone, "to see if any assistance could be rendered to the unfortunate fathers Woodroofe and Forshawe; but found on my arrival this morning that I was too late, as they had just been executed."

"Heaven have mercy on their souls!" ejaculated Heydocke, shuddering and crossing himself. "Yours was a pious mission, Mr. Catesby. Would it had been availing."

"I would so, too, with all my soul!" rejoined the other, fervently; "but fate ordained it otherwise. While I was in the town, I accidentally learnt from one, who informed me he had just parted with him, that your master was at home; and, fearing he might not be able to attend the meeting at Holywell, I resolved to proceed hither at nightfall, when my visit was not likely to be observed; having motives, which you may readily conjecture, for preserving the strictest secrecy on the occasion. The letter was prepared in case I should fail in meeting with him. And now that I have satisfied your scruples, good master steward, if Sir William be really within, I pray you lead me to him forthwith. If not your young mistress may serve my turn, for I have that to say which it imports one or other of them to know."

"In regard to my master," replied the steward, "he departed yesterday for Chester, on his way to join the pilgrimage to Saint Winifred's Well, as I have already assured your worship. And whoever informed you to the contrary, spoke falsely. But I will convey your letter and message to my young mistress, and on learning her pleasure as to receiving you, will instantly return and report it. These are dangerous times, your worship; dangerous times. A good Catholic knows not whom to trust, there are so many spoilers abroad."

"How, sirrah?" cried Catesby, angrily, "do you apply that observation to me?"

"Far be it from me," answered Heydocke, respectfully, "to apply any observation that may sound offensive to your worship, whom I know to be a most worthy gentleman, and as free from heresy as any in the kingdom. I was merely endeavouring to account for what may appear my over-caution in detaining you where you are till I learn my lady's pleasure. It is a rule in this house not to lower the drawbridge without orders after sunset; and I dare not, for my place, disobey it. Young Mr. Humphrey Chetham, of Crumpsall, was detained in the like manner no later than last night; and he is a visitor," he added, in a significant tone, "who is not altogether unwelcome to my mistress—ahem! But duty is no respecter of persons; and in my master's absence my duty is to protect his household. Your worship will pardon me."

"I will pardon anything but your loquacity and tediousness," rejoined Catesby, impatiently. "About your errand quickly."

"I am gone, your worship," returned the steward, disappearing with his companions.

Throwing the bridle over his horse's neck, and allowing him to drink his fill from the water of the moat, and afterwards, to pluck a few mouthfuls of the long grass that fringed its brink, Catesby abandoned himself to reflection. In a few moments, as the steward did not return, he raised his eyes, and fixed them upon the ancient habitation before him,—ancient, indeed, it was not at this time, having been in a great measure rebuilt by its possessor, Sir William Radcliffe, during the latter part of the reign of Elizabeth, in the rich and picturesque style of that period. Little could be distinguished of its projecting and retiring wings, its walls decorated with black and white chequer-work, the characteristic of the class of architecture to which it belonged, or of its magnificent embayed windows filled with stained glass; but the outline of its heavy roof, with its numerous gables, and groups of tall and elaborately-ornamented chimneys, might be distinctly traced in strong relief against the warm and still-glowing western sky.

Though much gone to decay, grievously neglected, and divided into three separate dwelling-houses, Ordsall Hall still retains much of its original character and beauty; and viewed at the magic hour above described, when the changes produced by the lapse of years cannot be detected, it presents much the same striking appearance that it offered to the gaze of Catesby. Situated on the north bank of the Irwell, which supplies the moat with a constant stream of fresh water, it commands on the south-west a beautiful view of the winding course of the river, here almost forming an island, of Trafford Park and its hall, of the woody uplands beyond it, and of the distant hills of Cheshire. The mansion itself is an irregular quadrangle, covering a considerable tract of ground. The gardens, once exquisitely laid out in the formal taste of Elizabeth's days, are also enclosed by the moat, surrounding (except in the intervals where it is filled up) a space of some acres in extent. At the period of this history, it was approached on the north-east by a noble avenue of sycamores, leading to within a short distance of its gates.

As Catesby surveyed this stately structure, and pondered upon the wealth and power of its owner, his meditations thus found vent in words:—" If I could but link Radcliffe to our cause, or win the hand of his fair daughter, and so bind him to me, the great attempt could not fail. She has refused me once. No matter. I will persevere till she yields. With Father Oldcorne to back my suit, I am assured of success. She is necessary to my purpose, and shall be mine."

Descended from an ancient Northamptonshire family, and numbering among his ancestry the well-known minister of the same name who flourished in the reign of Richard the Third, Robert Catesby,—at this time about forty,—had in his youth led a wild and dissolute life; and though bred in the faith of Rome, he had for some years abandoned its worship. In 1580, when the Jesuits, Campion and Parsons, visited England, he was reconciled to the Church he had quitted, and thenceforth became as zealous a supporter and promoter of its doctrines as he had heretofore been their bitter opponent. He was now actively engaged in all the

c

Popish plots of the period, and was even supposed to be connected with those designs of a darker dye which were set on foot for Elizabeth's destruction,—with Somerville's conspiracy,—with that of Arden and Throckmorton,—the latter of whom was his uncle on the maternal side,—with the plots of Bury and Savage,—of Ballard,—and of Babington. After the execution of the unfortunate Queen of Scots, he devoted himself to what was termed the Spanish faction, and endeavoured to carry out the schemes of a party, who, distrusting the vague promises of James, were anxious to secure the succession to a Catholic,—the Infanta of Spain, or the Duke of Parma. On the insurrection of the Earl of Essex, he took part with that ill-fated nobleman; and, though he escaped condign punishment for the offence, he was imprisoned and heavily fined.

From this time his career ran in darker channels. "Hunger starved for innovation," as he is finely described by Camden,—imbued with the fiercest religious fanaticism,—eloquent, wily, resolute,—able alike to delude the powerful and intimidate the weak,—he possessed all the ingredients of a conspirator. Associating with men like himself, of desperate character and broken fortunes, he was ever on the look-out for some means of retrieving his own condition, and redressing the wrongs of his Church. Well informed of the actual state of James's sentiments, when, on that monarch's accession, confident hopes were entertained by the Romanists of greater toleration for their religion, Catesby was the first to point out their mistake, and to foretell the season of terrible persecution that was at hand. On this persecution he grounded his hopes—hopes never realized, for the sufferers, amid all the grievances they endured, remained constant in their fidelity to the throne—of exciting a general insurrection among the Catholics.

Disappointed in this expectation,—disappointed, also, in his hopes of Spain, of France, and of aid from Rome, he fell back upon himself, and resolved upon the execution of a dark and dreadful project which he had long conceived, and which he could execute almost single-handed, without aid from foreign powers, and without the co-operation of his own party. The nature of this project, which, if it succeeded, would, he imagined, accomplish all or more than his wildest dreams of ambition or fanaticism had ever conceived, it will be the business of this history to develop. Without going further into detail at present, it may be mentioned that the success of the plot depended so entirely on its secrecy, and so well aware was its contriver of the extraordinary system of espionage carried on by the Earl of Salisbury and the Privy Council, that for some time he scarcely dared to trust it out of his keeping. At length, after much deliberation, he communicated it to five others, all of whom were bound to silence by an oath of unusual solemnity; and as it was necessary to the complete success of the conspiracy that its outbreak should be instantaneously followed by a rise on the part of the Catholics, he darkly hinted that a plan was on foot for their deliverance from the yoke of their oppressors, and counselled them to hold themselves in readiness to fly to arms at a moment's notice. But here again he failed. Few were disposed to listen to him; and of those who did, the majority returned for answer, "that their part was endurance, and that the only arms which Christians could use against lawful powers in their severity were prayers and tears."

Among the Popish party of that period, as in our own time, were ranked many of the oldest and most illustrious families in the kingdom,—families not less remarkable for their zeal for their religion than, as has before been observed, for their loyalty;—a loyalty afterwards approved in the disastrous reign of James the Second by their firm adherence to what they considered the indefeasible right of inheritance. Plots, indeed, were constantly hatched throughout the reigns of Elizabeth and James, by persons professing the religion of Rome; but in these the mass of the Catholics had no share. And even in the seasons of the bitterest persecution, when every fresh act of treason, perpetrated by some lawless and disaffected individual, was visited with additional rigour on their heads,—when the scaffold reeked with their blood, and the stake smoked with their ashes,—when their quarters were blackening on the gates and market-crosses of every city in the realm,—when their hearths were invaded, their religion proscribed, and the very name of Papist had become a byword,—even in those terrible seasons, as in the season under consideration, they remained constant in their fidelity to the crown.

From the troubled elements at work, some fierce and turbulent spirits were sure to arise,—some gloomy fanatics who, having brooded over their wrongs, real or imaginary, till they had lost all scruples of conscience, hesitated at no means of procuring redress. But it would be unjust to hold up such persons as representatives of the whole body of Catholics. Among the conspirators themselves there were redeeming shades. All were not actuated by the same atrocious motives. Mixed feelings induced Catesby to adopt the measure. Not so Guy Fawkes, who had already been leagued with the design. One idea alone ruled him. A soldier of fortune, but a stern religious enthusiast, he supposed himself chosen by Heaven for the redemption of his Church, and cared not what happened to himself, provided he accomplished his (as he conceived) holy design.

In considering the causes which produced the conspiracy about to be related, and in separating the disaffected party of the Papists from the temperate, due weight must be given to the influence of the priesthood. Of the Romish clergy there were two classes—the secular priests, and the Jesuits and missionaries. While the former, like the more moderate of the laity, would have been well-contented with toleration for their religion, the latter breathed nothing but revenge, and desired the utter subversion of the existing government, —temporal as well as ecclesiastical. Men, for the most part, of high intellectual powers, of untiring energy, and unconquerable fortitude, they were enabled by their zeal and ability te make many proselytes. By their means, secret correspondence was carried on with the different courts of Europe; and they were not without hope that, taking advantage of some favourable crisis, they should yet restore their Church to its former supremacy. To these persons,—who held as a maxim, "*Qui religionem Catholicam deserit regnandi jus omne amisit,*" —Catesby and his associates proved ready and devoted agents. Through their instrumentality, they hoped to accomplish the great work of their restoration. To Father Garnet, the provincial of the English Jesuits, of whom it will be necessary to speak more fully hereafter, the plot had been revealed by Catesby under the seal of confession; and, though it subsequently became a question whether he was justified in withholding a secret of such importance to the state, it is sufficient for the present purpose to say that he did withhold it. For the treasonable practices of the Jesuits and their faction some palliation may perhaps be found in the unrelenting persecution to which they were subjected; but if any excuse can be admitted for them, what opinion must be formed of the conduct of their temperate brethren? Surely, while the one is condemned, admiration may be mingled with the sympathy which must be felt for the unmerited sufferings of the other!

From the foregoing statement, it will be readily inferred that Sir William Radcliffe, a devout Catholic, and a man of large possessions, though somewhat reduced by the heavy fines imposed upon him as a recusant, must have appeared an object of importance to the conspirators; nor will it be wondered at that every means were used to gain him to their cause. Acting, however, upon the principles that swayed the well-disposed of his party, the knight resisted all these overtures, and refused to take any share in proceedings from which his conscience and loyalty alike revolted. Baffled, but not defeated, Catesby returned to the charge on a new point of assault. Himself a widower (or supposed to be so), he solicited the hand of the lovely Viviana Radcliffe, Sir William's only child, and the sole heiress of his possessions. But his suit in this quarter was also unsuccessful. The knight rejected the proposal, alleging that his daughter had no inclination to any alliance, inasmuch as she entertained serious thoughts of avowing herself to Heaven. Thus foiled, Catesby ostensibly relinquished his design.

Shortly before the commencement of this history, a pilgrimage to Saint Winifred's Well, in Flintshire, was undertaken by Father Garnet, the provincial of the Jesuits before mentioned, in company with several distinguished Catholic personages of both sexes, and to this ceremonial Sir William and his daughter were urgently bidden. The invitation was declined on the part of Viviana, but accepted by the knight, who, though unwilling to leave home at a period of so much danger, or to commit his daughter to any care but his own, even for so short a space, felt it to be his duty to give countenance by his presence to the ceremonial.

Accordingly, he departed for Chester on the previous day, as stated by the steward. And, though Catesby professed ignorance on the subject, and even affirmed he had heard to the contrary, it may be doubted whether he was not secretly informed of the circumstance, and whether his arrival, at this particular conjuncture, was not preconcerted.

Thus much in explanation of what is to follow. The course of Catesby's reflections was cut short by the return of the steward, who, informing him that he had his mistress's commands to admit him, immediately lowered the drawbridge for that purpose. Dismounting, and committing his steed to one of the serving-men, who advanced to take it, Catesby followed his conductor through a stone gateway, and crossing the garden, was ushered into a spacious and lofty hall, furnished with a long massy oak table, at the upper end of which was a raised dais. At one side of the chamber yawned a huge arched fireplace, garnished with enormous andirons, on which smouldered a fire composed of mixed turf and wood. Above the chimneypiece hung a suit of chain-armour, with the battle-axe, helmet, and gauntlets of Sir John Radcliffe, the first possessor of Ordsall who flourished in the reign of Edward the First: on the right, masking the entrance, stood a magnificent screen of carved oak.

Traversing this hall, Heydocke led the way to another large apartment; and placing lights on a Gothic-shaped table, offered a seat to the new-comer, and departed. The room in which Catesby was left was termed the Star-Chamber —a name retained to this day—from the circumstance of its ceiling being moulded and painted to resemble the heavenly vault when studded with the luminaries of night. It was terminated by a deeply-embayed window filled with stained glass of the most gorgeous colours. The walls, in some places, were hung with arras, in others wainscoted with dark lustrous oak, embellished with scrolls, ciphers, and fanciful designs. The mantelpiece was of the same solid material, curiously carved, and of extraordinary size. It was adorned with the armorial bearings of the family—two bends engrailed, and in chief a label of three—and other devices and inscriptions. The hearth was considerably raised above the level of the floor, and there was a peculiarity in the construction of the massive wooden pillars flanking it, that attracted the attention of Catesby, who rose with the intention of examining them more narrowly, when he was interrupted by the entrance of the lady of the mansion.

Advancing at a slow and dignified pace, Viviana Radcliffe courteously but gravely saluted her guest; and, without offering him her hand, motioned him to a chair, while she seated herself at a little distance. Catesby had seen her twice before; and whether the circumstances under which they now met might have caused some change in her demeanour he could not tell, but he thought her singularly altered. A year ago, she had been a lively, laughing girl of seventeen, with a bright brown skin, dark flowing tresses, and eyes as black and radiant as those of a gipsy. She was now a grave, collected woman, infinitely more beautiful, but wholly changed in character. Her complexion had become a clear, transparent white, and set off to great advantage her large, luminous eyes, and jetty brows. Her figure was tall and majestic; her features regular, delicately formed, and of the rarest and proudest class of beauty. She was attired in a dress of black wrought velvet, entirely without ornament, except the rosary at her girdle, with a small ebony crucifix attached to it. She wore a close-fitting cap, likewise of black velvet, edged with pearls, beneath which her raven tresses were gathered in such a manner as to display most becomingly the smooth and snowy expanse of her forehead. The gravity of her manner, not less than her charms of person, seem to have struck Catesby mute. He gazed on her in silent admiration for a brief space, utterly forgetful of the object of his visit, and the part he intended to play. During this pause she maintained the most perfect composure, and fixing her dark eyes full upon him, appeared to await the moment when he might choose to open the conversation.

Notwithstanding his age, and the dissolute and distracted life he had led, Catesby was still good-looking enough to have produced a favourable impression upon any woman easily captivated by manly beauty. The very expression of his marked and peculiar physiognomy,—in some degree an index to his character,—was sufficient to rivet attention; and the mysterious interest generally inspired by his presence was not diminished on further acquaintance with him. Though somewhat stern in their expression, his features were strikingly handsome, cast in an oval mould and clothed with the pointed beard and trimmed moustaches invariably met with in the portraits of Vandyck. His frame was strongly built, but well proportioned, and seemed capable of enduring the greatest fatigue. His dress was that of an ordinary gentleman of the period, and consisted of a doublet of quilted silk, of sober colour and stout texture; large trunk-hose swelling out at the hips; and buff boots, armed with spurs with immense rowels. He wore a high and stiffly-starched ruff round his throat; and his apparel was completed by a short cloak of brown cloth, lined with silk of a similar colour. His arms were rapier and poniard, and his high-crowned plumed hat, of the peculiar form then in vogue, and looped on the "leer-side" with a diamond clasp, was thrown upon the table.

Some little time having elapsed, during which he made no effort to address her, Viviana broke silence.

"I understood you desired to speak with me on a matter of urgency, Mr. Catesby," she remarked.

"I did so," he replied, as if aroused from a reverie; "and I can only excuse my absence of mind and ill manners, on the plea that the contemplation of your charms has driven all other matter out of my head."

"Mr. Catesby," returned Viviana, rising, "if the purpose of your visit be merely to pay unmerited compliments, I must at once put an end to it."

"I have only obeyed the impulse of my heart," resumed the other, passionately, "and uttered what involuntarily rose to my lips. But," he added, checking himself, "I will not offend you with my admiration. If you have read my letter to your father, you will not require to be informed of the object of my visit."

"I have not read it," replied Viviana, returning him the packet with the seal unbroken. "I can give no opinion on any matter of difficulty. And I have no desire to know any secret with which my father might not desire me to be acquainted."

"Are we overheard?" inquired Catesby, glancing suspiciously at the fireplace.

"By no one whom you would care to overhear us," returned the maiden.

"Then it is as I supposed," rejoined Catesby. "Father Oldcorne is concealed behind that mantelpiece?"

Viviana smiled an affirmative.

"Let him come forth, I pray you," returned Catesby. "What I have to say concerns him as much as yourself or your father; and I would gladly have his voice in the matter."

"You shall have it, my son," replied a reverend personage, clad in a priestly garb, stepping from out one side of the mantelpiece, which flew suddenly open, disclosing a recess curiously contrived in the thickness of the wall. "You shall have it," said Father Oldcorne, for he it was, approaching and extending his arms over him. "Accept my blessing and my welcome."

Catesby received the benediction with bowed head and bended knee.

"And now," continued the priest, "what has the bravest soldier of our Church to declare to its lowliest servant?"

Catesby then briefly explained, as he had before done to the steward, why he had taken Manchester in his route to

North Wales; and, after lamenting his inability to render any assistance to the unfortunate priests, he went on to state that he had accidentally learnt, from a few words let fall by the pursuivant to his attendant, that a warrant had been sent by the Earl of Salisbury for Sir William Radcliffe's arrest.

"My father's arrest!" exclaimed Viviana, trembling violently, "What—what is laid to his charge?"

"Felony," rejoined Catesby, sternly—"felony, without benefit of clergy—for so it is accounted by the present execrable laws of our land—in harbouring a Jesuit priest. If he is convicted of the offence, his punishment will be death —death on the gibbet, accompanied by indignities worse than those shown to a common felon."

"Holy Virgin!" ejaculated Father Oldcorne, lifting up his hands and raising his eyes to heaven.

"From what I gathered, the officers will visit this house to-night," continued Catesby.

"Our Lady be praised, they will not find him!" cried Viviana, who had been thrown into an agony of distress. "What is to be done in this frightful emergency, holy father?" she added, turning to the priest, with a supplicating look.

"Heaven only knows, dear daughter," replied Oldcorne. "You had better appeal for counsel to one who is more able to afford it than I am,—Mr. Catesby. Well aware of the crafty devices of our enemies, and having often eluded their snares himself, he may enable you to escape them. My own course is clear. I shall quit this roof at once, deeply and bitterly regretting that by entering it I have placed those whom I hold so dear, and from whom I have experienced so much kindness, in such fearful jeopardy."

"Oh, no, father!" exclaimed Viviana, "you shall not go."

"Daughter," replied Oldcorne, solemnly, "I have long borne the cross of Christ—have long endured the stripes inflicted upon me by the adversaries of our faith in patience; and my last actions and last breath shall testify to the truth of our holy religion. But, though I could endure aught on my own account, I cannot consent to bring misery and destruction upon others. Hinder me not, dear daughter. I will go at once."

"Hold, father!" interposed Catesby. "The step you would take may bring about what you are most anxious to avoid. If you are discovered and apprehended in this neighbourhood, suspicion will still attach to your protectors, and the secret of your departure will be wrung from some of the more timid of the household. Tarry where you are. Let the pursuivant make his search. I will engage to baffle his vigilance."

"He speaks the truth, dear father," returned Viviana. "You must not—shall not depart. There are plenty of hiding-places, as you know, within the mansion. Let them be as rigorous as they may in their search, they will not discover you."

"Whatever course you adjudge best for the security of others, I will pursue," rejoined Oldcorne, turning to Catesby. "Put me out of the question."

"My opinion has already been given, father," replied Catesby. "Remain where you are."

"But, if the officers should ascertain that my father is at Chester, and pursue him thither!" cried Viviana, suddenly struck by a new cause of alarm.

"A messenger must be immediately despatched after him to give him warning," returned Catesby.

"Will you be that messenger?" asked the maiden, eagerly.

"I would shed my heart's best blood to pleasure you," returned Catesby.

"Then I may count upon this service, for which, rest assured, I will not prove ungrateful," she rejoined.

"You may," answered Catesby. "And yet I would, on Father Oldcorne's account, that my departure might be delayed till to-morrow."

"The delay might be fatal," cried Viviana. "You must be in Chester before that time."

"Doubt it not," returned Catesby. "Charged with your wishes, the wind shall scarcely outstrip my speed."

So saying, he marched irresolutely towards the door, as if about to depart, when, just as he had reached it, he turned sharply round, and threw himself at Viviana's feet.

"Forgive me, Miss Radcliffe," he cried, "if I once again, even at a critical moment like the present, dare to renew my suit. I fancied I had subdued my passion for you, but your presence has awakened it with greater violence than ever."

"Rise, sir, I pray," rejoined the maiden, in an offended tone.

"Hear me, I beseech you," continued Catesby, seizing her hand. "Before you reject my suit, consider well that in these perilous seasons, when no true Catholic can call his life his own, you may need a protector."

"In the. event you describe, Mr. Catesby," answered Viviana, "I would at once fulfil the intention I have formed of devoting myself to Heaven, and retire to the convent of Benedictine nuns, founded by Lady Mary Percy, at Brussels.

"You would much more effectually serve the cause of your religion by acceding to my suit," observed Catesby, rising.

"How so?" she inquired.

"Listen to me, Miss Radcliffe," he rejoined, gravely, "and let my words be deeply graven upon your heart. In your hands rests the destiny of the Catholic Church."

"In mine!" exclaimed Viviana.

"In yours," returned Catesby. "A mighty blow is about to be struck for her deliverance."

"Ay, marry, is it," cried Oldcorne, with sudden fervour. "Redemption draweth nigh; the year of visitation approacheth to an end; and jubilation is at hand. England shall again be called a happy realm, a blessed country, a religious people. Those who knew the former glory of religion shall lift up their hands for joy to see it returned again. Righteousness shall prosper, and infidelity be plucked up by the root. False error shall vanish like smoke, and they which saw it shall say where is it become? The daughters of Babylon shall be cast down, and in the dust lament their ruin. Proud heresy shall strike her sail, and groan as a beast crushed under a cart-wheel. The memory of novelties shall perish with a crack, and as a ruinous house falling to the ground. Repent, ye seducers, with speed, and prevent the dreadful wrath of the Powerable. He will come as flame that burneth out beyond the furnace. His fury shall fly forth as thunder, and pitch upon their tops that malign him. They shall perish in his fury, and melt like wax before the fire."

"Amen!" ejaculated Catesby, as the priest concluded. "You have spoken prophetically, father."

"I have but recited a prayer transmitted to me by Father Garnet," rejoined Oldcorne.

"Do you discern any hidden meaning in it?" demanded Catesby.

"Yea, verily, my son," returned the priest. "In the *false error vanishing like* SMOKE,'—in the '*house perishing with a* CRACK,'—and in the '*fury flying forth as* THUNDER,'— I read the mode the great work shall be brought about."

"And you applaud the design?" asked Catesby, eagerly.

"*Non vero factum probo, sed eventum amo,*" rejoined the priest.

"The secret is safe in your keeping, father?" asked Catesby, uneasily.

"As if it had been disclosed to me in private confession," replied Oldcorne.

"Hum!" muttered Catesby. "Confessions of as much consequence to the state have ere now been revealed, father."

"A decree has been passed by his holiness, Clement VIII., forbidding all such revelations," replied Oldcorne. "And the question has been recently propounded by a learned brother of our order, Father Antonio Delrio, who, in his Magical Disquisitions, putteth it thus:—' Supposing a malefactor shall confess that he himself or some other has laid GUNPOWDER, or the like combustible matter, under a building——' "

"Ha!" exclaimed Catesby, starting.

" —' And, unless it be taken away,' " proceeded the priest, regarding him fixedly, " ' the whole house will be burnt, the prince destroyed, and as many as go into or out of the city will come to great mischief or peril !' "*

"Well!" exclaimed Catesby.

"The point then arises," continued Oldcorne, "whether the priest may make use of the secret thus obtained for the good of the government, and the averting of such danger; and, after fully discussing it, Father Delrio decides in the negative."

"Enough," returned Catesby.

"By whom is the blow to be struck?" asked Viviana, who had listened to the foregoing discourse in silent wonder.

"By me," answered Catesby. "It is for you to nerve my arm."

"You speak in riddles," she replied. "I understand you not."

"Question Father Oldcorne, then, as to my meaning," rejoined Catesby; "he will tell you that, allied to you, I could not fail in the enterprise on which I am engaged."

"It is the truth, dear daughter," Oldcorne asseverated.

"I will not inquire further into this mystery," returned Viviana, "for such it is to me. But, believing what you both assert, I answer, that willingly as I would lay down my life

* Confitetur maleficus se vel alium posuisse pulverem vel quid aliud sub tali limine, et nisi tollantur domum comburendam, principem interiturum, quotquot urbem egredienturque in magnam perniciem aut periculum venturos.—DELRIO Disq. Mag., lib. vi. cap. i. [Edit. 1600.]

for the welfare of our holy religion, persuading myself, as I do, that I have constancy enough to endure martyrdom for its sake,—I cannot consent to your proposal. Nay, if I must avouch the whole truth," she continued, blushing deeply, "my affections are already engaged, though to one with whom I can never hope to be united."

" You have your answer, my son," observed the priest.

Catesby replied with a look of the deepest mortification and disappointment; and, bowing coldly to Viviana, said, "I now depart to obey your behests, Miss Radcliffe."

" Commend me in all duty to my dear father," replied Viviana, " and believe that I shall for ever feel bound to you for your zeal."

" Neglect not all due caution, father," observed Catesby, glancing significantly at Oldcorne. " Forewarned, fore-armed."

" Doubt me not, my son," rejoined the Jesuit. " My prayers shall be for you.

> Gentem auferte perfidam
> Credentium de finibus,
> Ut Christo laudes debitas
> Persolvamus alacriter."

After receiving a parting benediction from the priest, Catesby took his leave. His steed was speedily brought to the door by the old steward; and mounting it, he crossed the drawbridge, which was immediately raised behind him, and hastened on his journey.

IV.

THE SEARCH.

IMMEDIATELY after Catesby's departure, Heydocke was summoned to his mistress's presence. He found her with the priest, and was informed that in all probability the house would be visited that night by the messengers of the Privy Council. The old steward received the intelligence as he might have done his death-warrant, and looked so bewildered and affrighted, that Viviana half repented having acquainted him with it.

"Compose yourself, Master Heydocke," she said, trying to reason him out of his fears; "the search may not take place. And if it does, there is nothing to be alarmed at. I am not afraid, you perceive."

"Nothing to be alarmed at, my dear young lady!" gasped the steward. "You have never witnessed a midnight search for a priest by these ruffianly catchpoles, as I have, or you would not say so. Father Oldcorne will comprehend my uneasiness, and excuse it. The miscreants break into the house like robbers, and treat its inmates worse than robbers would treat them. They have no regard for decency,—no consideration for sex,—no respect for persons. Not a chamber is sacred from them. If a door is bolted, they burst it open; a cabinet locked, they tarry not for the key. They pull down the hangings, thrust their rapier-points into the crevices of the wainscot, discharge their fire-arms against the wall, and sometimes threaten to pull down the house itself, if the object of their quest be not delivered to them. Their oaths, abominations, and menaces are horrible; and their treatment of females, even of your degree, honoured mistress, too barbarous to relate. Poor Lady Nevil died of the fright she got by such a visit at dead of night to her residence in Holborn. Mrs. Vavasour, of York, lost her senses; and many others whom I could mention have been equal sufferers. Nothing to be alarmed at! Heaven grant, my dear, dear young lady, that you may never be fatally convinced to the contrary!"

"Suppose my apprehensions are as great as your own, Master Heydocke," replied Viviana, who, though somewhat infected by his terrors, still maintained her firmness; "I do not see how the danger is to be averted by idle lamentations and misgivings. We must meet it boldly; and trust to Him who is our only safeguard in the hour of peril, for protection. Do not alarm the household, but let all retire to rest as usual."

"Right, daughter," observed the priest. "Preparations for resistance would only excite suspicion."

"Can you depend on the servants, in case they are examined?" asked Viviana of the steward, who by this time had partially recovered his composure.

"I think so," returned Heydocke; "but the threats of the officers are so dreadful, and their conduct so violent and outrageous, that I can scarcely answer for myself. I would not advise your reverence to remain in that hiding-place," he added, pointing to the chimney-piece; "they are sure to discover it."

"If not here, where shall I conceal myself?" rejoined Oldcorne, uneasily.

"There are many nooks in which your reverence might hide," replied the steward; "but the knaves are so crafty, and so well experienced in their vocation, that I dare not recommend any of them as secure. I would advise you to remain on the watch, and, in case of alarm, I will conduct you to the oratory in the north gallery, adjoining Mistress Viviana's sleeping-chamber, where there is a panel in the wall, known only to myself and my master, opening upon a secret passage running many hundred yards underground, and communicating with a small outbuilding on the other side of the moat. There is a contrivance in this passage, which I will explain to your reverence if need be, which will cut off any possibility of pursuit in that quarter."

"Be it so," replied the priest. "I place myself in your hands, good Master Heydocke, well assured of your fidelity. I shall remain throughout the night in this chamber, occupied in my devotions."

"You will suffer me to pray with you, father, I trust?" said Viviana.

"If you desire it, assuredly, dear daughter," rejoined Oldcorne; "but I am unwilling you should sacrifice your rest."

"It will be no sacrifice, father, for I should not slumber, even if I sought my couch," she returned. "Go, good Heydocke. Keep vigilant watch: and if you hear the slightest noise without, fail not to give us warning."

The steward bowed, and departed.

Some hours elapsed, during which nothing occurred to alarm Viviana and her companion, who consumed the time in prayer and devout conversation; when, just at the stroke of two—as the former was kneeling before her spiritual adviser, and receiving absolution for the slight offences of which a being so pure-minded could be supposed capable—a noise like the falling of a bar of iron was heard beneath the window. The priest turned pale, and cast a look of uneasiness at the maiden, who said nothing, but snatching up the light, and motioning him to remain quiet, hurried out of the room in search of the steward. He was nowhere to be found. In vain she examined all the lower rooms—in vain called to him by name. No answer was returned.

Greatly terrified, she was preparing to retrace her steps, when she heard the sound of muttered voices in the hall. Extinguishing her light, she advanced to the door, which was left ajar, and, taking care not to expose herself to observation, beheld several armed figures, some of whom bore dark lanterns, while others surrounded and menaced with their drawn swords the unfortunate steward. From their discourse she ascertained that, having thrown a plank across the moat, and concealed themselves within the garden until they had reconnoitred the premises, they had contrived to gain admittance unperceived through the window of a small back room, in which they had surprised Heydocke, who had fallen asleep on his post, and captured him. One amongst their number, who appeared to act as leader, and whom, from his garb, and the white wand he carried, Viviana knew must be a pursuivant, now proceeded to interrogate the prisoner. To every question proposed to him the steward shook his head; and, in spite of the threats of the examinant, and the blows of his followers, he persisted in maintaining silence.

"If we cannot make this contumacious rascal speak, we will find others more tractable," observed the pursuivant. "I will not leave any corner of the house unvisited; nor a soul within it unquestioned. Ah! here they come!"

As he spoke, several of the serving-men, with some of the female domestics, who had been alarmed by the noise, rushed into the hall, and on seeing it filled with armed men, were about to retreat, when they were instantly seized and detained. A scene of great confusion now ensued. The women screamed and cried for mercy, while the men struggled and fought with their captors. Commanding silence at length, the pursuivant proclaimed in the king's name that whoever would guide him to the hiding-place of Father Oldcorne, a Jesuit priest, whom it was known, and could be proved, was harboured within the mansion, should receive a free pardon and reward; while those who screened him, or connived at his concealment, were liable to fine, imprisonment, and even more severe punishment. Each servant was then questioned separately. But though all were more or less rudely dealt with, no information could be elicited.

Meanwhile, Viviana was a prey to the most intolerable anxiety. Unable to reach Father Oldcorne without crossing the hall, which she did not dare to attempt, she gave him up for lost; her sole hope being that, on hearing the cries of the domestics, he would provide for his own safety. Her anxiety was still farther increased when the pursuivant, having exhausted his patience by fruitless interrogatories, and satisfied his malice by frightening two of the females into fits, departed with a portion of his band to search the house, leaving the rest as a guard over the prisoners.

Viviana then felt that, if she would save Father Oldcorne, the attempt must be made without a moment's delay, and at any hazard. Watching her opportunity, when the troopers were occupied—some in helping themselves to such viands and liquors as they could lay hands upon—some in searching the persons of the prisoners for amulets and relics—while others, more humane, were trying to revive the swooning women, she contrived to steel unperceived across the lower end of the hall. Having gained the passage, she found to her horror that the pursuivant and his band were already within the star-chamber. They were sounding the walls with hammers and mallets, and from their exclamations, she learnt that they had discovered the retreat behind the fireplace, and were about to break it open.

"We have him," roared the pursuivant, in a voice of triumph. "The old owl's roost is here!"

Viviana, who stood at the door, drew in her breath, expecting that the next moment would inform her that the priest was made captive. Instead of this, she was delighted to find, from the oaths of rage and disappointment uttered by the troopers, that he had eluded them.

"He must be in the house, at all events," growled the pursuivant; "nor is it long since he quitted his hiding-place, as this cushion proves. We will not go away without him. And now, let us proceed to the upper chambers."

Hearing their footsteps approach, Viviana darted off, and quickly ascending the principal staircase, entered a long corridor. Uncertain what to do, she was about to proceed to her own chamber, and bar the door, when she felt her arm grasped by a man. With difficulty repressing a shriek, she strove to disengage herself, when a whisper told her it was the priest.

"Heaven be praised!" cried Viviana, "you are safe. How—how did you escape?"

"I flew up stairs on hearing the voices," replied Oldcorne. "But what has happened to the steward?"

"He is a prisoner," replied Viviana.

D

" All then is lost, unless you are acquainted with the secret panel he spoke of in the oratory," rejoined Oldcorne.

" Alas ! father, I am wholly ignorant of it," she answered. " But, come with me into my chamber; they will not dare to invade it."

" I know not that," returned the priest, despairingly. " These sacrilegious villains would not respect the sanctity of the altar itself."

" They come !" cried Viviana, as lights were seen at the foot of the stairs. " Take my hand—this way, father."

They had scarcely gained the room, and fastened the door, when the pursuivant and his attendants appeared in the corridor. The officer, it would seem, had been well instructed where to search, or was sufficiently practised in his duty, for he proceeded at once to several hiding-places in the different chambers which he visited. In one room he detected a secret staircase in the wall, which he mounted, and discovered a small chapel built in the roof. Stripping it of its altar, its statue of the Virgin, its crucifix, pix, chalice, and other consecrated vessels, he descended, and continued his search. Viviana's chamber was now the only one unvisited. Trying the door, and finding it locked, he tapped against it with his wand.

" Who knocks ?" asked the maiden.

" A state-messenger," was the reply. " I demand entrance in the King's name."

" You cannot have it," she replied. " It is my sleeping-chamber."

" My duty allows me no alternative," rejoined the pursuivant, harshly. " If you will not admit me quietly, I must use force."

" Do you know to whom you offer this rudeness ?" returned Viviana. " I am the daughter of Sir William Radcliffe."

" I know it," replied the pursuivant; " but I am not exceeding my authority. I hold a warrant for your father's arrest. And, if he had not been from home, I should have carried him to prison along with the Jesuit priest whom, I suspect, is concealed within your chamber. Open the door, I command you; and do not hinder me in the execution of my duty."

As no answer was returned to the application, the pursuivant commanded his men to burst open the door; and the order was promptly obeyed.

The chamber was empty.

On searching it, however, the pursuivant found a door concealed by the hangings of the bed. It was bolted on the other side, but speedily yielded to his efforts. Passing through it, he entered upon a narrow gallery, at the extremity of which his progress was stopped by another door, likewise fastened on the further side. On bursting it open, he entered a small oratory, wainscoted with oak, and lighted by an oriel window filled with stained glass, through which the newly-risen moon was pouring its full radiance, and discovered the object of his search.

" Father Oldcorne, I arrest you as a Jesuit and a traitor," shouted the pursuivant, in a voice of exultation. " Seize him !" he added, calling to his men.

" You shall not take him," cried Viviana, clinging despairingly to the priest, who offered no resistance, but clasped a crucifix to his breast.

" Leave go your hold, young mistress," rejoined the pursuivant, grasping Oldcorne by the collar of his vestment, and dragging him along ; " and rest thankful that I make you not, also, my prisoner."

" Take me; but spare him !—in mercy spare him !" shrieked Viviana.

" You solicit mercy from one who knows it not, daughter," observed the priest. " Lead on, sir. I am ready to attend you."

" Your destination is the New Fleet, father," retorted the pursuivant, in a tone of bitter raillery ; " unless you prefer the cell in Radcliffe Hall lately vacated by your saintly predecessor, Father Woodroofe."

" Help ! help !" shrieked Viviana.

" You may spare your voice, fair lady," sneered the pursuivant. " No help is at hand. Your servants are all prisoners."

The words were scarcely uttered, when a sliding panel in the wall flew open, and Guy Fawkes, followed by Humphrey Chetham, and another personage, sprang through the aperture, and presented a petronel at the head of the pursuivant.

V.

CHAT MOSS.

THE pursuivant was taken so completely unawares by the sudden appearance of Guy Fawkes and his companions, that he made no attempt at resistance. Nor were his attendants less confounded. Before they recovered from their surprise, Humphrey Chetham seized Viviana in his arms, and darting through the panel, called to the priest to follow him. Father Oldcorne was about to comply, when one of the soldiers, grasping the surcingle at his waist, dragged him forcibly backwards. The next moment, however, he was set free by Guy Fawkes, who, felling the man to the ground, and interposing himself between the priest and the other soldier, enabled the former to make good his retreat. This done, he planted himself in front of the panel, and with a petronel in each hand, menaced his opponents.

"Fly for your lives!" he shouted in a loud voice to the others. "Not a moment is to be lost. I have taken greater odds, and in a worse cause, and have not been worsted. Heed me not, I say. I will defend the passage till you are beyond reach of danger. Fly!—fly!"

"After them!" vociferated the pursuivant, stamping with rage and vexation; "after them instantly! Hew down that bold traitor. Show him no quarter. His life is forfeit to the king. Slay him as you would a dog!"

But the men, having no fire-arms, were so much intimidated by the fierce looks of Guy Fawkes, and the deadly weapons he pointed at their heads, that they hesitated to obey their leader's injunctions.

"Do you hear what I say to you, cravens?" roared the pursuivant. "Cut him down without mercy."

"They dare not move a footstep," rejoined Guy Fawkes, in a decisive tone.

"Recreants!" cried the pursuivant, foaming with rage, "is my prey to be snatched from me at the very moment I have secured it, through your cowardice? Obey me instantly, or, as Heaven shall judge me, I will denounce you to my Lord Derby and the commissioners as aiders and abettors in Father Oldcorne's escape!—and you well know what your punishment will be if I do so. What!—are you afraid of one man?"

"Our pikes are no match for his petronels," observed the foremost soldier, sullenly.

"They are not," rejoined Guy Fawkes; "and you will do well not to compel me to prove the truth of your assertion. As to you, Master Pursuivant," he continued, with a look so stern that the other quailed before it, "unwilling as I am to shed blood, I shall hold your life, if I am compelled to take it, but just retribution for the fate you have brought upon the unfortunate Elizabeth Orton."

"Ha!" exclaimed the pursuivant, starting. "I thought I recognised you. You are the soldier in the Spanish garb who saved that false prophetess from drowning."

"I saved her only for a more lingering death," rejoined Guy Fawkes.

"I know it," retorted the pursuivant. "I found her dead body when I visited her cell on my way hither, and gave orders to have it interred without coffin or shroud in that part of the burial-ground of the Collegiate Church in Manchester reserved for common felons."

"I know not what stays my hand," rejoined Guy Fawkes, fiercely. "But I am strongly tempted to give you a grave beside her."

"I will put your daring to the proof!" cried the pursuivant, snatching a pike from one of his followers, and brandishing it over his head. "Throw down your arms, or you die!"

"Back!" exclaimed Guy Fawkes, presenting a petronel at him, "or I lodge a bullet in your brain."

"Be advised by me, and rush not on certain destruction, good Master Pursuivant," said the foremost soldier, plucking his mantle. "I see by his bloodthirsty looks that the villain is in earnest."

"I hear footsteps," cried the other soldier; "our comrades are at hand."

"Then it is time for me to depart," cried Guy Fawkes, springing through the secret door, and closing it after him.

"Confusion!" exclaimed the pursuivant; "but he shall not escape. Break open the panel."

The order was promptly obeyed. The men battered the stout oak board, which was of great thickness, with their pikes, but it resisted every effort, nor was it until the arrival of a fresh band of soldiers with lights, mallets, chisels, and other implements suitable to the purpose, that it could be forced open. This accomplished, the pursuivant, commanding his attendants to follow him, dashed through the aperture.

As they proceeded singly along the narrow passage, the roof became so low that they were compelled to adopt a stooping posture. In this manner they hurried on until their further progress was stopped by a massive stone door, which appeared to descend from above by some hidden contrivance, no trace of bolt or other fastening being discernible. The flag fitted closely in channels in the walls, and had all the appearance of solid masonry. After examining this obstacle for a moment, the pursuivant was convinced that any attempt to move it would be impracticable, and muttering a deep execration, he gave the word to return.

"From the course it appears to take," he observed, "this passage must communicate with the garden,—perhaps with the further side of the moat. We may yet secure them, if we use despatch."

To return to the fugitives. On arriving at the point where the stone door was situated, which he discovered by the channels in the wall above mentioned, Guy Fawkes searched for an iron ring, and, having found it, drew it towards him, and the ponderous flag slowly dropped into its place. He then groped his way cautiously along in the dark, until his foot encountered the top of a ladder, down which he crept, and landed on the floor of a damp deep vault. Having taken the precaution to remove the ladder, he hastened onwards for about fifty yards, when he came to a steep flight of stone steps, distinguishable by a feeble glimmer of light from above, and mounting them, emerged through an open trap-door into a small building situated at the western side of the moat, where, to his surprise and disappointment, he found the other fugitives.

"How comes it you are here?" he exclaimed, in a reproachful tone. "I kept the wolves at bay thus long, to enable you to make good your retreat."

"Miss Radcliffe is too weak to move," replied Humphrey Chetham; "and I could not persuade Father Oldcorne to leave her."

"I care not what becomes of me," said the priest. "The sooner my painful race is run the better. But I cannot—will not abandon my dear charge thus."

"Think not of me, father, I implore you," rejoined Viviana, who had sunk overpowered with terror and exhaustion. "I shall be better soon. Master Chetham, I am assured, will remain with me till our enemies have departed, and I will then return to the hall."

" Command me as you please, Miss Radcliffe," replied Humphrey Chetham. " You have but to express a wish to insure its fulfilment on my part."

" Oh! that you had suffered Mr. Catesby to tarry with us till the morning, as he himself proposed, dear daughter," observed the priest, turning to Viviana.

" Has Catesby been here?" inquired Guy Fawkes, with a look of astonishment.

" He has," replied Oldcorne. " He came to warn us that the hall would be this night searched by the officers of state; and he also brought word that a warrant had been issued by the Privy Council for the arrest of Sir William Radcliffe."

" Where is he now?" demanded Fawkes, hastily.

" On the way to Chester, whither he departed in all haste, at Viviana's urgent request, to apprise her father of his danger," rejoined the priest.

" This is strange!" muttered Guy Fawkes. " Catesby here, and I not know it!"

" He had a secret motive for his visit, my son," whispered Oldcorne, significantly.

" So I conclude, father," replied Fawkes, in the same tone.

" Viviana Radcliffe," murmured Humphrey Chetham, in low and tender accents, " something tells me that this moment will decide my future fate. Emboldened by the mysterious manner in which we have been brought together, and you, as it were, have been thrown upon my protection, I venture to declare the passion I have long indulged for you; —a passion which, though deep and fervent as ever agitated human bosom, has hitherto, from the difference of our rank, and yet more from the difference of our religious opinions, been without hope. What has just occurred,—added to the peril in which your worthy father stands, and the difficulties in which you yourself will necessarily be involved,—makes me cast aside all misgiving, and perhaps with too much presumption, but with a confident belief that the sincerity of my love renders me not wholly undeserving of your regard, earnestly solicit you to give me a husband's right to watch over and defend you."

Viviana was silent. But even by the imperfect light the young merchant could discern that her cheek was covered with blushes.

" Your answer?" he cried, taking her hand.

"You must take it from my lips, Master Chetham," interposed the priest; "Viviana Radcliffe never can be yours."

"Be pleased to let her speak for herself, reverend sir," rejoined the young merchant, angrily.

"I represent her father, and have acquainted you with his determination," rejoined the priest. "Appeal to her, and she will confirm my words."

"Viviana, is this true?" asked Chetham. "Does your father object to your union with me?"

Viviana answered by a deep sigh, and gently withdrew her hand from the young merchant's grasp.

"Then there is no hope for me?" cried Chetham.

"Alas! no," replied Viviana; "nor for me—of earthly affection. I am already dead to the world."

"How so?" he asked.

"I am about to vow myself to Heaven," she answered.

"Viviana!" exclaimed the young man, throwing himself at her feet, "reflect!—oh! reflect, before you take this fatal—this irrevocable step."

"Rise, sir," interposed the priest, sternly; "you plead in vain. Sir William Radcliffe will never wed his daughter to a heretic. In his name I command you to desist from further solicitation."

"I obey," replied Chetham, rising.

"We lose time here," observed Guy Fawkes, who had been lost for a moment in reflection. "I will undertake to provide for your safety, father. But, what must be done with Viviana? She cannot be left here. And her return to the hall would be attended with danger."

"I will not return till the miscreants have quitted it," said Viviana.

"Their departure is uncertain," replied Fawkes. "When they are balked of their prey they sometimes haunt a dwelling for weeks."

"What will become of me?" cried Viviana, distractedly.

"It were vain, I fear, to entreat you to accept an asylum with my father at Clayton Hall, or at my own residence at Crumpsall," said Humphrey Chetham.

"Your offer is most kind, sir," replied Oldcorne, "and is duly appreciated. But Viviana will see the propriety—on every account—of declining it."

"I do; I do," she acquiesced.

"Will you entrust yourself to my protection?" observed Fawkes.

"Willingly," replied the priest, answering for her. "We shall find some place of refuge," he added, turning to Viviana, "where your father can join us, and where we can remain concealed till this storm has blown over."

"I know many such," rejoined Fawkes, "both in this county and in Yorkshire, and will guide you to one."

"My horses are at your service," said Humphrey Chetham. "They are tied beneath the trees in the avenue. My servant shall bring them to the door," and, turning to his attendant, he gave him directions to that effect. "I was riding hither an hour before midnight," he continued, addressing Viviana, "to offer you assistance, having accidentally heard the pursuivant mention his meditated visit to Ordsall Hall to one of his followers, when, as I approached the gates, this person," pointing to Guy Fawkes, "crossed my path, and seizing the bridle of my steed, demanded whether I was a friend to Sir William Radcliffe. I answered in the affirmative, and desired to know the motive of his inquiry. He then told me that the house was invested by a numerous band of armed men, who had crossed the moat by means of a plank, and were at that moment concealed within the garden. This intelligence, besides filling me with alarm, disconcerted all my plans, as I hoped to have been beforehand with them—their inquisitorial searches being generally made at a late hour, when all the inmates of a house intended to be surprised are certain to have retired to rest. While I was bitterly reproaching myself for my dilatoriness, and considering what course it would be best to pursue, my servant, Martin Heydocke, son to your father's old steward, who had ridden up at the stranger's approach, informed me that he was acquainted with a secret passage communicating beneath the moat with the hall. Upon this, I dismounted; and fastening my horse to a tree, ordered him to lead me to it without an instant's delay. The stranger, who gave his name as Guy Fawkes, and professed himself a stanch Catholic, and a friend of Father Oldcorne, begged permission to join us, in a tone so earnest that I at once acceded to his request. We then proceeded to this building, and after some search discovered the trap-door. Much time was lost, owing to our being unprovided with lights, in the subterranean passage; and it was more than two hours before we could find the ring connected with the stone door, the mystery of which Martin explained to us. This delay we feared would render our scheme abortive, when, just as we reached the panel, we heard your shrieks. The spring was touched, and—you know the rest."

"And shall never forget it," replied Viviana, in a tone of the deepest gratitude.

At this juncture, the tramp of horses was heard at the door; and the next moment it was thrown open by the younger Heydocke, who, with a look, and in a voice of the utmost terror, exclaimed, "They are coming!—they are coming!"

"The pursuivant?" cried Guy Fawkes.

"Not him alone, but the whole gang," rejoined Martin. "Some of them are lowering the drawbridge, while others are crossing the plank. Several are on horseback, and I think I discern the pursuivant amongst the number. They have seen me, and are hurrying in this direction." -

As he spoke, a loud shout corroborated his statement.

"We are lost!" exclaimed Oldcorne.

"Do not despair, father," rejoined Guy Fawkes. "Heaven will not abandon its faithful servants. The Lord will deliver us out of the hands of these Amalekites."

"To horse, then, if you would indeed avoid them," urged Humphrey Chetham. "The shouts grow louder. Your enemies are fast approaching."

"Viviana," said Guy Fawkes, "are you willing to fly with us?"

"I will do anything rather than be left to those horrible men," she answered.

Guy Fawkes then raised her in his arms, and sprang with his lovely burthen upon the nearest charger. His example was quickly followed by Humphrey Chetham, who, vaulting on the other horse, assisted the priest to mount behind him. While this took place, Martin Heydocke darted into the shed, and instantly bolted the door.

It was a beautiful moonlight night, almost as bright as day, and the movements of each party were fully revealed to the other. Guy Fawkes perceived at a glance that they were surrounded; and, though he had no fears for himself, he was full of apprehension for the safety of his companion. While he was debating with himself as to the course it would be best to pursue, Humphrey Chetham shouted to him to turn to the left, and started off in that direction. Grasping his fair charge, whom he had placed before him on the saddle, firmly with his left arm, and wrapping her in his ample cloak, Guy Fawkes drew his sword, and striking spurs into his steed, followed in the same track.

The little fabric which had afforded them temporary shelter, it has already been mentioned, was situated on the west of the hall, at a short distance from the moat, and was screened from observation by a small shrubbery. No sooner did the fugitives emerge from this cover, than loud outcries were raised by their antagonists, and every effort was made to intercept them. On the right, galloping towards them on a light but swift courser, taken from Sir William Radcliffe's stables, came the pursuivant, attended by half-a-dozen troopers, who had accommodated themselves with horses in the same manner as their leader. Between them and the road leading to Manchester, were stationed several armed men on foot. At the rear, voices proclaimed that others were in full pursuit; while in front, a fourth detachment menaced them with their pikes. Thus beset on all sides, it seemed scarcely possible to escape. Nothing daunted, however, by the threats and vociferations with which they were received, the two horsemen boldly charged this party. The encounter was instantaneous. Guy Fawkes warded off a blow, which, if it had taken effect, must have robbed Viviana of life, and struck down the fellow who aimed it. At the same moment his career was checked by another assailant, who, catching his bridle with the hook of his pike, commanded him to surrender. Fawkes replied by cleaving the man's staff asunder, and, having thus disembarrassed himself, was about to pursue his course, when he perceived that Humphrey Chetham was in imminent danger from a couple of soldiers who had stopped him, and were trying to unhorse his companion. Riding up to them, Guy Fawkes, by a vigorous and well-directed attack, speedily drove them off; and the fugitives, being now unimpeded, were enabled to continue their career.

The foregoing occurrences were witnessed by the pursuivant with the utmost rage and vexation. Pouring forth a torrent of threats and imprecations, he swore he would never rest till he had secured them, and urging his courser to its utmost speed, commanded his men to give chase.

Skirting a sluice, communicating between the Irwell and the moat, Humphrey Chetham, who, as better acquainted with the country than his companions, took the lead, proceeded along its edge for about a hundred yards, when he suddenly struck across a narrow bridge covered with sod, and entered the open fields. Hitherto Viviana had remained silent. Though fully aware of the risk she had run, she gave no sign of alarm—not even when the blow was aimed against her life; and it was only on conceiving the danger in some degree past, that she ventured to express her gratitude.

"You have displayed so much courage," said Guy Fawkes,

in answer to her speech, " that it would be unpardonable to deceive you. Our foes are too near us, and too well mounted, to make it by any means certain we shall escape them,—unless by stratagem."

" They are within a hundred yards of us," cried Humphrey Chetham, glancing fearfully backwards. " They have possessed themselves of your father's fleetest horses; and, if I mistake not, the rascally pursuivant has secured your favourite barb."

" My gentle Zayda!" exclaimed Viviana. " Then indeed we are lost. She has not her match for speed."

" If she bring her rider to us alone, she will do us good service," observed Guy Fawkes, significantly.

The same notion, almost at the same moment, occurred to the pursuivant. Having witnessed the prowess displayed by Guy Fawkes in his recent attack on the soldiers, he felt no disposition to encounter so formidable an opponent single-handed; and, finding that the high-mettled barb on which he was mounted, by its superior speed and fiery temper, would inevitably place him in such a dilemma, he prudently resolved to halt, and exchange it for a more manageable steed.

This delay was of great service to the fugitives, and enabled them to get considerably ahead. They had now gained a narrow lane, and tracking it, speedily reached the rocky banks of the Irwell. Galloping along a foot-path that followed the serpentine course of the stream for a quarter of a mile, they arrived at a spot marked by a bed of osiers, where Humphrey Chetham informed them there was a ford.

Accordingly, they plunged into the river, and while stemming the current, which here ran with great swiftness, and rose up above the saddles, the neighing of a steed was heard from the bank they had quitted. Turning at the sound, Viviana beheld her favourite courser on the summit of a high rock. The soldier to whom Zayda was entrusted had speedily, as the pursuivant foresaw, distanced his companions, and chose this elevated position to take sure aim at Guy Fawkes, against whom he was now levelling a caliver. The next moment a bullet struck against his brigandine, but without doing him any injury. The soldier, however, did not escape so lightly. Startled by the discharge, the fiery barb leaped from the precipice into the river, and throwing her rider, who was borne off by the rapid stream, swam towards the opposite bank which she reached just as the others were landing. At the sound of her mistress's voice she stood still, and allowed

Humphrey Chetham to lay hold of her bridle; and Viviana declaring she was able to mount her, Guy Fawkes, who felt that such an arrangement was most likely to conduce to her safety, and who was, moreover, inclined to view the occurrence as a providential interference in their behalf, immediately assisted her into the saddle.

Before this transfer could be effected, the pursuivant and his attendants had begun to ford the stream. The former had witnessed the accident that had befallen the soldier from a short distance; and, while he affected to deplore it, internally congratulated himself on his prudence and foresight. But he was by no means so well satisfied when he saw how it served to benefit the fugitives.

"That unlucky beast!" he exclaimed. "Some fiend must have prompted me to bring her out of the stable. Would she had drowned herself instead of poor Dickon Duckesbury, whom she hath sent to feed the fishes. With her aid, Miss Radcliffe will doubtless escape. No matter. If I secure Father Oldcorne, and that black-visaged trooper in the Spanish garb, who, I'll be sworn, is a secret intelligencer of the pope, if not of the devil, I shall be well contented. I'll hang them both on a gibbet higher than Haman's."

And muttering other threats to the same effect, he picked his way to the opposite shore. Long before he reached it, the fugitives had disappeared; but on climbing the bank, he beheld them galloping swiftly across a well-wooded district steeped in moonlight, and spread out before his view, and inflamed by the sight he shouted to his attendants, and once more started in pursuit.

Cheered by the fortunate incident above related, which, in presenting her with her own steed in a manner so surprising and unexpected, seemed almost to give her assurance of deliverance, Viviana, inspirited by the exercise, felt her strength and spirits rapidly revive. At her side rode Guy Fawkes, who ever and anon cast an anxious look behind, to ascertain the distance of their pursuers, but suffered no exclamation to escape his lips. Indeed, throughout the whole affair, he maintained the reserve belonging to his sombre and taciturn character, and neither questioned Humphrey Chetham as to where he was leading them, nor proposed any deviation from the route he had apparently chosen. To such remarks as were addressed to him, Fawkes answered in monosyllables; and it was only when occasion required, that he volunteered any observation or advice. He seemed to surrender himself to chance. And perhaps, if his bosom could have been examined, it would have been found that he considered himself a mere puppet in the hands of destiny.

In other and calmer seasons, he might have dwelt with rapture on the beautiful and varied country through which they were speeding, and which from every knoll they mounted, every slope they descended, every glade they threaded, intricacy pierced, or tangled dell tracked, presented new and increasing attractions. The charming district since formed into a park by the Traffords, from whom it derives its present designation, was at this time—though part of the domain of that ancient family—wholly unenclosed. Old Trafford Hall lies (for it is still in existence) more than a mile nearer to Manchester, a little to the east of Ordsall Hall; but the modern residence of the family is situated in the midst of the lovely region through which the fugitives were riding.

But, though the charms of the scene, heightened by the gentle medium through which they were viewed, produced little effect upon the iron nature of Guy Fawkes, they were not without influence on his companions, especially Viviana. Soothed by the stillness of all around her, she almost forgot her danger; and surrendering herself to the dreamy enjoyment generally experienced in contemplating such a scene at such an hour, suffered her gaze to wander over the fair woody landscape before her, till it was lost in the distant moonlit wolds.

From the train of thought naturally awakened by this spectacle, she was roused by the shouts of the pursuers; and, glancing timorously behind her, beheld them hurrying swiftly along the valley they had just quitted. From the rapidity with which they were advancing, it was evident they were gaining upon them, and she was about to urge her courser to greater speed, when Humphrey Chetham laid his hand upon the rein to check her.

"Reserve yourself till we gain the brow of this hill," he remarked; "and then put Zayda to her mettle. We are not far from our destination."

"Indeed!" exclaimed Viviana. "Where is it?"

"I will show it to you presently," he answered.

Arrived at the summit of the high ground, which they had been for some time gradually ascending, the young merchant pointed out a vast boggy tract, about two miles off, in the vale beneath them.

"That is our destination," he said.

"Did I not hold it impossible you could trifle with me at such a time as this, I should say you were jesting," rejoined Viviana. "The place you indicate, unless I mistake you, is Chat Moss, the largest and most dangerous marsh in Lancashire."

"You do not mistake me, neither am I jesting, Viviana," replied the young merchant, gravely. "Chat Moss *is* the mark at which I aim."

"If we are to cross it, we shall need a Will-o'-the-wisp to guide us, and some friendly elf to make firm the ground beneath our steeds," rejoined Viviana, in a slightly sarcastic tone.

"Trust to me and you shall traverse it in safety," resumed Humphrey Chetham.

"I would sooner trust myself to the pursuivant and his band, than venture upon its treacherous surface," she replied.

"How is this, young sir?" interposed Guy Fawkes, sternly. "Is it from heedlessness or rashness that you are about to expose us to this new danger?—which, if Viviana judges correctly, and my own experience of such places inclines me to think she does so—is greater than that which now besets us."

"If there is any danger I shall be the first to encounter it, for I propose to act as your guide," returned Humphrey Chetham, in an offended tone. "But the treacherous character of the marsh constitutes our safety. I am acquainted with a narrow path across it, from which the deviation of a foot will bring certain death. If our pursuers attempt to follow us their destruction is inevitable. Viviana may rest assured I would not needlessly expose so dear a life as hers. But it is our best chance of safety."

"Humphrey Chetham is in the right," observed the priest. "I have heard of the path he describes; and if he can guide us along it, we shall effectually baffle our enemies."

"I cry you mercy, sir," said Viviana. "I did not apprehend your meaning. But I now thankfully resign myself to your care."

"Forward, then," cried the young merchant. And they dashed swiftly down the declivity.

Chat Moss, towards which they were hastening, though now drained, in part cultivated, and traversed by the busiest and most-frequented railroad in England, or the world, was, within the recollection of many of the youngest of the present generation, a dreary and almost impassable waste. Surveyed from the heights of Dunham, whence the writer has often gazed upon it, envying the plover her wing to skim over its broad expanse, it presented with its black boggy soil, striped like a motley garment, with patches of grey, tawny, and dunnish red, a singular and mysterious appearance. Conjecture fixes this morass as the site of a vast forest, whose immemorial and Druid-haunted groves were burnt by the Roman invaders; and seeks to account for its present condition by supposing that the charred trees—still frequently found within its depths—being left where the conflagration had placed them, had choked up its brooks and springs, and so reduced it to a general swamp. Drayton, however, in the following lines from the Faerie Land, places its origin as far back as the Deluge:

——Great Chat Moss at my fall
Lies full of turf and marl, her unctuous mineral;
And blocks as black as pitch, with boring augurs found,
There at the General Flood supposed to be drown'd.

But the former hypothesis appears the more probable. A curious description of Chat Moss, as it appeared at the time of this history, is furnished by Camden, who terms it "a swampy tract of great extent, a considerable part of which was carried off in the last age by swollen rivers with great danger whereby the rivers were infected, and great quantities of fish died. Instead thereof is now a valley watered by a small stream, and many trees were discovered thrown down, and lying flat, so that one may suppose when the ground lay neglected, and the waste water of brooks was not drained off into the open valleys, or their courses stopped by neglect or desolation, all the lower grounds were turned into swamps (which we call *mosses*), or into pools. If this was the case, no wonder so many trees are found covered, and, as it were, buried in such places all over England, but especially here. For the roots being loosened by too excessive wet, they must necessarily fall down and sink in so soft a soil. The people hereabouts search for them with poles and spits, and after marking the place, dig them up and use them for firing, for they are like torches, equally fit to burn and to give light, which is probably owing to the bituminous earth that surrounds them, whence the common people suppose them firs, though Cæsar denies that there were such trees in Britain."

But, though vast masses of the bog had been carried off by the Irwell and the Mersey, as related by Camden, the general appearance of the waste—with the exception of the valley and the small stream—was much the same as it continued to our own time. Its surface was more broken and irregular, and black gaping chasms and pits filled with water and slime as dark-coloured as the turf whence it flowed, pointed out the spots where the swollen and heaving swamp had burst its bondage. Narrow paths, known only to the poor turf-cutters and other labourers who dwelt upon its borders, and gathered fuel with poles and spits in the manner above described, intersected it at various points. But as they led in many cases to dangerous and deep gulfs, to dismal quagmires and fathomless pits; and, moreover, as the slightest departure from the proper track would have whelmed the traveller in an oozy bed, from which, as from a quick-sand, he would have vainly striven to extricate himself—it was never crossed without a guide, except by those familiar with its perilous courses. One painful circumstance connected with the history of Chat Moss remains to be recorded —namely, that the attempt made to cultivate it by the great historian Roscoe—an attempt since carried out, as has already been shown, with complete success—ended in a result ruinous to the fortunes of that highly-gifted person, who, up to the period of this luckless undertaking, was as prosperous as he was meritorious.

By this time the fugitives had approached the confines of the marsh. An accident, however, had just occurred, which nearly proved fatal to Viviana, and owing to the delay it occasioned, brought their pursuers into dangerous proximity with them. In fording the Irwell, which, from its devious course, they were again compelled to cross, about a quarter of a mile below Barton, her horse missed its footing, and precipitated her into the rapid current. In another instant she would have been borne away, if Guy Fawkes had not flung himself into the water, and seized her before she sank. Her affrighted steed, having got out of its depth, began to swim off, and it required the utmost exertion on the part of Humphrey Chetham, embarrassed as he was by the priest, to secure it. In a few minutes all was set to rights, and Viviana was once more placed on the saddle, without having sustained further inconvenience than was occasioned by her dripping apparel. But those few minutes, as has been just stated, sufficed to bring the pursuivant and his men close

E

upon them; and as they scrambled up the opposite bank, the
plunging and shouting behind them told that the latter had
entered the stream.

"Yonder is Baysnape," exclaimed Humphrey Chetham,
calling Viviana's attention to a ridge of high ground on the
borders of the waste. "Below it lies the path by which I
propose to enter the moss. We shall speedily be out of the
reach of our enemies."

"The marsh at least will hide us," answered Viviana, with
a shudder. "It is a terrible alternative."

"Fear nothing, dear daughter," observed the priest. "The
saints, who have thus marvellously protected us, will continue
to watch over us to the end, and will make the path over yon
perilous waste as safe as the ground on which we tread."

"I like not the appearance of the sky," observed Guy
Fawkes, looking uneasily upwards. "Before we reach the
spot you have pointed out, the moon will be obscured. Will
it be safe to traverse the moss in the dark?"

"It is our only chance," replied the young merchant,
speaking in a low tone, that his answer might not reach
Viviana's ears; "and after all, the darkness may be serviceable. Our pursuers are so near, that if it were less gloomy,
they might hit upon the right track. It will be a risk to us
to proceed, but certain destruction to those who follow. And
now let us make what haste we can. Every moment is precious."

The dreary and fast darkening waste had now opened upon
them in all its horrors. Far as the gaze could reach appeared
an immense expanse, flat almost as the surface of the ocean,
and unmarked, so far as could be discerned in that doubtful
light, by any trace of human footstep or habitation. It was
a stern and sombre prospect, and calculated to inspire terror
in the stoutest bosom. What effect it produced on Viviana
may be easily conjectured. But her nature was brave and
enduring, and, though she trembled so violently as scarcely
to be able to keep her seat, she gave no utterance to her fears.
They were now skirting that part of the morass since denominated, from the unfortunate speculation previously alluded to,
"Roscoe's Improvements." This tract was the worst and
most dangerous portion of the whole moss. Soft, slabby,
and unsubstantial, its treacherous beds scarcely offered secure
footing to the heron that alighted on them. The ground
shook beneath the fugitives as they hurried past the edge of the
groaning and quivering marsh. The plover, scared from its

nest, uttered its peculiar and plaintive cry; the bittern shrieked; the other night-fowl poured forth their doleful notes; and the bull-frog added its deep croak to the ominous concert. Behind them came the thundering tramp and loud shouts of their pursuers. Guy Fawkes had judged correctly. Before they reached Baysnape the moon had withdrawn behind a rack of clouds, and it had become profoundly dark. Arrived at this point, Humphrey Chetham called to them to turn off to the right.

"Follow singly," he said, "and do not swerve a hair's breadth from the path. The slightest deviation will be fatal. Do you, sir," he added to the priest, "mount behind Guy Fawkes, and let Viviana come next after me. If I should miss my way, do not stir for your life."

The transfer effected, the fugitives turned off to the right, and proceeded at a cautious pace along a narrow and shaking path. The ground trembled so much beneath them, and their horses' feet sank so deeply in the plashy bog, that Viviana demanded, in a tone of some uneasiness, if he was sure he had taken the right course?

"If I had not," replied Humphrey Chetham, "we should ere this have found our way to the bottom of the morass."

As he spoke, a floundering plunge, accompanied by a horrible and quickly-stifled cry, told that one of their pursuers had perished in endeavouring to follow them.

"The poor wretch is gone to his account," observed Viviana, in a tone of commiseration. "Have a care!—have a care, lest you share the same fate."

"If I can save you, I care not what becomes of me," replied the young merchant. "Since I can never hope to possess you, life has become valueless in my eyes."

"Quicken your pace," shouted Guy Fawkes, who brought up the rear. "Our pursuers have discovered the track, and are making towards us."

"Let them do so," replied the young merchant. "They can do us no farther injury."

"That is false!" cried the voice of a soldier from behind. And, as the words were uttered, a shot was fired, which, though aimed against Chetham, took effect upon his steed. The animal staggered, and his rider had only time to slide from his back when he reeled off the path, and was ingulfed in the marsh.

Hearing the plunge of the steed, the man fancied he had hit his mark, and hallooed in an exulting voice to his companions. But his triumph was of short duration. A ball from the petronel of Guy Fawkes pierced his brain, and, dropping from his saddle, he sank, together with his horse, which he dragged along with him into the quagmire.

"Waste no more shot," cried Humphrey Chetham; "the swamp will fight our battles for us. Though I grieve for the loss of my horse, I may be better able to guide you on foot."

With this, he seized Viviana's bridle, and drew her steed along at a quick pace, but with the greatest caution. As they proceeded, a light like that of a lantern was seen to rise from the earth, and approach them.

"Heaven be praised!" exclaimed Viviana: "some one has heard us, and is hastening to our assistance."

"Not so," replied Humphrey Chetham. "The light you behold is an *ignis fatuus*. Were you to trust yourself to its delusive gleam, it would lead you to the most dangerous parts of the moss."

"And, as if to exhibit its real character, the little flame, which hitherto had burnt as brightly and steadily as a wax-candle, suddenly appeared to dilate, and assuming a purple tinge, emitted a shower of sparks, and then flitted rapidly over the plain.

"Woe to him that follows it!" cried Humphrey Chetham.

"It has a strange unearthly look," observed Viviana, crossing herself. "I have much difficulty in persuading myself it is not the work of some malignant sprite."

"It is only an exhalation of the marsh," replied Chetham. "But see! others are at hand."

Their approach, indeed, seemed to have disturbed all the weird children of the waste. Lights were seen trooping towards them in every direction; sometimes stopping, sometimes rising in the air, now contracting, now expanding, and when within a few yards of the travellers, retreating with inconceivable swiftness.

"It is a marvellous and incomprehensible spectacle," remarked Viviana.

"The commonfolk hereabouts affirm that these Jack-o'-lanterns, as they term them, always appear in greater numbers when some direful catastrophe is about to take place," rejoined the young merchant.

"Heaven avert it from us," ejaculated Viviana.

"It is an idle superstition," returned Chetham. "But we must now keep silence," he continued, lowering his voice, and stopping near the charred stump of a tree, left, it would seem, as a mark. "The road turns here; and, unless our pursuers know it, we shall now quit them for ever. We must not let a sound betray the course we are about to take."

Having turned this dangerous corner in safety, and conducted his companions as noiselessly as possible for a few yards along the cross path, which being narrower was consequently more perilous than the first, Humphrey Chetham stood still, and, imposing silence upon the others, listened to the approach of their pursuers. His prediction was speedily and terribly verified. Hearing the movement in advance, but unable to discover the course taken by the fugitives, the unfortunate soldiers, fearful of losing their prey, quickened their pace, in the expectation of instantly overtaking them. They were fatally undeceived. Four only of their number, besides their leader, remained—two having perished in the manner heretofore described. The first of these, disregarding the caution of his comrade, laughingly urged his horse into a gallop, and, on passing the mark, sunk as if by magic, and before he could utter a single warning cry, into the depths of the morass. His disappearance was so instantaneous, that the next in order, though he heard the sullen plunge, was unable to draw in the rein, and was likewise ingulfed. A third followed; and a fourth, in his efforts to avoid their fate, backed his steed over the slippery edge of the path. Only one now remained. It was the pursuivant, who, with the prudence that characterized all his proceedings, had followed in the rear. He was so dreadfully frightened, that, adding his shrieks to those of his attendants, he shouted to the fugitives, imploring assistance in the most piteous terms, and promising never again to molest them, if they would guide him to a place of safety. But his cries were wholly unheeded; and he perhaps endured in those few minutes of agony as much suffering as he had inflicted on the numerous victims of his barbarity. It was indeed an appalling moment. Three of the wretched men had not yet sunk, but were floundering about in the swamp, and shrieking for help. The horses, as much terrified as their riders, added their piercing cries to the half-suffocated yells. And, as if to make the scene more ghastly, myriads of dancing lights flitted towards them, and throwing an unearthly glimmer over this part of the morass, fully revealed their struggling figures. Moved by compassion for the poor wretches, Viviana implored Humphrey Chetham to assist them, and, finding him immovable, she appealed to Guy Fawkes.

"They are beyond all human aid," the latter replied.

" Heaven have mercy on their souls !" ejaculated the priest.
" Pray for them, dear daughter. Pray heartily, as I am
about to do." And he recited in an audible voice the Romish
formula of supplication for those *in extremis*.

Averting her gaze from the spectacle, Viviana joined fervently in the prayer.

By this time two of the strugglers had disappeared. The
third, having freed himself from his horse, contrived for
some moments, during which he uttered the most frightful
cries, to keep his head above the swamp. His efforts were
tremendous, but unavailing, and served only to accelerate his
fate. Making a last desperate plunge towards the bank
where the fugitives were standing, he sank above the chin.
The expression of his face, shown by the ghastly glimmer of
the fen-fires, as he was gradually swallowed up, was horrible.

" *Requiem æternam dona eis, Domine*," exclaimed the
priest.

" All is over," cried Humphrey Chetham, taking the bridle
of Viviana's steed, and leading her onwards. " We are free
from our pursuers."

" There is one left," she rejoined, casting a look backwards.

" It is the pursuivant," returned Guy Fawkes, sternly.
" He is within shot," he added, drawing his petronel.

" Oh, no—no !—in pity spare him !" cried Viviana. " Too
many lives have been sacrificed already."

" He is the cause of all the mischief," answered Guy
Fawkes, unwillingly replacing the petronel in his belt, " and
may live to injure you and your father."

" I will hope not," rejoined Viviana ; " but spare him !—
oh, spare him !"

" Be it as you please," replied Guy Fawkes. " The marsh,
I trust, will not be so merciful."

With this, they slowly resumed their progress. On hearing their departure, the pursuivant renewed his cries in
a more piteous tone than ever ; but, in spite of the entreaties
of Viviana, nothing could induce her companions to lend him
assistance.

For some time they proceeded in silence, and without
accident. As they advanced, the difficulties of the path
increased, and it was fortunate that the moon, emerging from
the clouds in which, up to this moment, she had been
shrouded, enabled them to steer their course in safety. At
length, after a tedious and toilsome march for nearly half a

mile, the footing became more secure, the road widened, and they were able to quicken their pace. Another half mile landed them upon the western bank of the morass. Viviana's first impulse was to give thanks to Heaven for their deliverance, nor did she omit in her prayer a supplication for the unfortunate beings who had perished.

Arrived at the point now known as Rawson Nook, they entered a lane, and proceeded towards Astley Green, where perceiving a cluster of thatched cottages among the trees, they knocked at the door of the first, and speedily obtained admittance from its inmates, a turf-cutter and his wife. The man conveyed their steeds to a neighbouring barn, while the good dame offered Viviana such accommodation and refreshment as her humble dwelling afforded. Here they tarried till the following evening, as much to recruit Miss Radcliffe's strength, as for security.

At the young merchant's request, the turf-cutter went in the course of the day to see what had become of the pursuivant. He was nowhere to be found. But he accidentally learned from another hind, who followed the same occupation as himself, that a person answering to the officer's description had been seen to emerge from the moss near Baysnape at daybreak, and take the road towards Manchester. Of the unfortunate soldiers nothing but a steel cap and a pike, which the man brought away with him, could be discovered.

After much debate, it was decided that their safest plan would be to proceed to Manchester, where Humphrey Chetham undertook to procure them safe lodgings at the Seven Stars—an excellent hostel, kept by a worthy widow, who, he affirmed, would do anything to serve him. Accordingly, they set out at nightfall—Viviana taking her place before Guy Fawkes, and relinquishing Zayda to the young merchant and the priest. Shaping their course through Worsley, by Monton Green and Pendleton, they arrived in about an hour within sight of the town, which then—not a tithe of its present size, and unpolluted by the smoky atmosphere in which it is now constantly enveloped—was not without some pretensions to a picturesque appearance. Crossing Salford Bridge, they mounted Smithy Bank, as it was then termed, and proceeding along Cateaton-street, and Hanging Ditch, struck into Whithing (now Withy) Grove, at the right of which, just where a few houses were beginning to straggle up Shude Hill, stood, and still stands, the comfortable hostel of the Seven Stars. Here they stopped, and were warmly welcomed

by its buxom mistress, Dame Sutcliffe. Muffled in Guy
Fawkes's cloak, the priest gained the chamber to which he
was ushered unobserved. And Dame Sutcliffe, though her
Protestant notions were a little scandalized at her dwelling
being made the sanctuary of a Popish priest, promised, at
the instance of Master Chetham, whom she knew to be no
favourer of idolatry in a general way, to be answerable for
his safety.

VI.

THE DISINTERMENT.

HAVING seen every attention shown to Viviana by the hostess
—who, as soon as she discovered that she had the daughter
of Sir William Radcliffe of Ordsall, under her roof, bestirred
herself in right earnest for her accommodation—Humphrey
Chetham, notwithstanding the lateness of the hour—it was
past midnight—expressed his determination to walk to his
residence at Crumpsall, to put an end to any apprehension
which might be entertained by the household at his prolonged
absence.

With this view, he set forth; and Guy Fawkes, who seemed
to be meditating some project which he was unwilling to disclose to the others, quitted the hostel with him, bidding the
chamberlain sit up for him, as he should speedily return.
They had not gone far when he inquired the nearest way to
the Collegiate Church, and was answered that they were then
proceeding towards it, and in a few moments should arrive at
its walls. He next asked the young merchant whether he
could inform him which part of the churchyard was allotted
to criminals. Humphrey Chetham, somewhat surprised by
the question, replied, "At the north-west, near the charnel,"
adding, "I shall pass within a short distance of the spot, and
will point it out to you."

Entering Fennel-street, at the end of which stood an
ancient cross, they soon came in sight of the church. The
moon was shining brightly, and silvered the massive square
tower of the fane, the battlements, pinnacles, buttresses, and
noble eastern window, with its gorgeous tracery. While Guy
Fawkes paused for a moment to contemplate this reverend and
beautiful structure, two venerable personages, having long

snowy beards, and wrapped in flowing mantles edged with sable fur, passed the end of the street. One of them carried a lantern, though it was wholly needless, as it was bright as day; and as they glided stealthily along, there was something so mysterious in their manner, that it greatly excited the curiosity of Guy Fawkes, who inquired from his companion if he knew who they were.

"The foremost is the warden of Manchester, the famous Doctor Dee," replied Humphrey Chetham, "divine, mathematician, astrologer—and, if report speaks truly, conjuror."

"Is that Doctor Dee?" cried Guy Fawkes, in astonishment.

"It is," replied the young merchant: "and the other in the Polish cap is the no less celebrated Edward Kelley, the doctor's assistant, or, as he is ordinarily termed, his seer."

"They have entered the churchyard," remarked Guy Fawkes. "I will follow them."

"I would not advise you to do so," rejoined the other. "Strange tales are told of them. You may witness that it is not safe to look upon."

The caution, however, was unheeded. Guy Fawkes had already disappeared, and the young merchant, shrugging his shoulders, proceeded on his way towards Hunt's Bank.

On gaining the churchyard, Guy Fawkes perceived the warden and his companion creeping stealthily beneath the shadow of a wall in the direction of a low fabric, which appeared to be a bone-house, or charnel, situated at the north-western extremity of the church. Before this building grew a black and stunted yew-tree. Arrived at it, they paused, and looked round to see whether they were observed. They did not, however, notice Guy Fawkes, who had concealed himself behind a buttress. Kelley then unlocked the door of the charnel, and brought out a pickaxe and mattock. Having divested himself of his cloak, he proceeded to shovel out the mould from a new-made grave at a little distance from the building. Doctor Dee stood by, and held the lantern for his assistant.

Determined to watch their proceedings, Guy Fawkes crept towards the yew-tree, behind which he ensconced himself. Kelley, meanwhile, continued to ply his spade with a vigour that seemed almost incomprehensible in one so far stricken in years, and of such infirm appearance. At length he paused, and kneeling within the shallow grave, endeavoured to drag something from it. Doctor Dee knelt to assist him.

After some exertion, they drew forth the corpse of a female, which had been interred without coffin, and apparently in the habiliments worn during life. A horrible suspicion crossed Guy Fawkes. Resolving to satisfy his doubts at once, he rushed forward, and beheld in the ghastly lineaments of the dead the features of the unfortunate prophetess, Elizabeth Orton.

VII.

DOCTOR DEE.

"How now, ye impious violaters of the tomb! ye worse than famine-stricken wolves, that rake up the dead in church-yards!" cried Guy Fawkes, in a voice of thunder, to Doctor Dee and his companion; who, startled by his sudden appearance, dropped the body, and retreated to a short distance. "What devilish rites are ye about to enact, that ye thus profane the sanctity of the grave?"

"And who art thou that darest thus to interrupt us?" demanded Dee, sternly.

"It matters not," rejoined Fawkes, striding towards them. "Suffice it you are both known to *me.* You, John Dee, warden of Manchester, who deserve to be burnt at the stake for your damnable practices, rather than hold the sacred office you fill; and you, Edward Kelley, his associate, who boast of familiar intercourse with demons, and, unless fame belies you, have purchased the intimacy at the price of your soul's salvation. I know you both. I know, also, whose body you have disinterred—it is that of the ill-fated prophetess, Elizabeth Orton. And if you do not instantly restore it to the grave whence you have snatched it, I will denounce you to the authorities of the town."

"Knowing thus much, you should know still more," retorted Doctor Dee, "namely, that I am not to be lightly provoked. You have no power to quit the churchyard—nay, not so much as to move a limb without my permission."

As he spoke, he drew from beneath his cloak a small phial, the contents of which he sprinkled over the intruder. Its effect was wonderful and instantaneous. The limbs of Guy Fawkes stiffened where he stood. His hand remained immovably fixed upon the pommel of his sword, and he seemed transformed into a marble statue.

"You will henceforth acknowledge and respect my power," he continued. "Were it my pleasure, I could bury you twenty fathoms deep in the earth beneath our feet; or, by invoking certain spirits, convey you to the summit of yon lofty tower," pointing to the church, "and hurl you from it headlong. But I content myself with depriving you of motion, and leave you in possession of sight and speech, that you may endure the torture of witnessing what you cannot prevent."

So saying, he was about to return to the corpse with Kelley, when Guy Fawkes exclaimed, in a hollow voice:

"Set me free, and I will instantly depart."

"Will you swear never to divulge what you have seen?" demanded Dee, pausing.

"Solemnly," he replied.

"I will trust you, then," rejoined the Doctor;—"the rather that your presence interferes with my purpose."

Taking a handful of loose earth from an adjoining grave, and muttering a few words, that sounded like a charm, he scattered it over Fawkes. The spell was instantly broken. A leaden weight seemed to be removed from his limbs. His joints regained their suppleness, and with a convulsive start, like that by which a dreamer casts off a nightmare, he was liberated from his preternatural thraldom.

"And now, begone!" cried Doctor Dee, authoritatively.

"Suffer me to tarry with you a few moments," said Guy Fawkes, in a deferential tone. "Heretofore, I will freely admit, I regarded you as an impostor; but now I am convinced you are deeply skilled in the occult sciences, and would fain consult you on the future."

"I have already said that your presence troubles me," replied Doctor Dee. "But if you will call upon me at the College to-morrow, it may be I will give you further proofs of my skill."

"Why not now, reverend sir?" urged Fawkes. "The question I would ask is better suited to this dismal spot and witching hour than to daylight and the walls of your study."

"Indeed!" exclaimed Dee. "Your name?"

"Guy Fawkes," replied the other.

"Guy Fawkes!" echoed the Doctor, starting. "Nay, then, I guess the nature of the question you would ask."

"Am I then known to you, reverend sir?" inquired Fawkes, uneasily.

"As well as to yourself—nay, better," answered the Doctor. "Bring the lantern hither, Kelley," he continued, addressing his companion. "Look!" he added, elevating the light so as to throw it upon the countenance of Fawkes: "it is the very face,—the bronzed and strongly-marked features,—the fierce black eye,—the iron frame, and foreign garb of the figure we beheld in the show-stone."

"It is," replied Kelley. "I could have singled him out amid a thousand. He looked thus as we tracked his perilous course, with his three companions, the priest, Chetham, and Viviana Radcliffe, across Chat Moss."

"How have you learned this?" cried Guy Fawkes, in amazement.

"By the art that reveals all things," answered Kelley.

"In proof that your thoughts are known to me," observed Dee, "I will tell you the inquiry you would make before it is uttered. You would learn whether the enterprise on which you are engaged will succeed."

"I would," replied Fawkes.

"Yet more," continued Dee. "I am aware of the nature of the plot, and could name to you all connected with it."

"Your power is, indeed, wonderful," rejoined Fawkes in an altered tone. "But will you give me the information I require?"

"Hum!" muttered Dee.

"I am too poor to purchase it," proceeded Fawkes, "unless a relic I have brought from Spain has any value in your eyes."

"Tush!" exclaimed Dee, angrily. "Do you suppose I am a common juggler, and practise my art for gain?"

"By no means, reverend sir," said Fawkes. "But I would not willingly put you to trouble, without evincing my gratitude."

"Well, then," replied Dee, "I will not refuse your request. And yet I would caution you to beware how you pry into the future. You may repent your rashness when it is too late."

"I have no fear," rejoined Fawkes. "Let me know the worst."

"Enough," answered Dee. "And now listen to me. That carcass having been placed in the ground without the holy rites of burial being duly performed, I have power over it. And, as the witch of Endor called up Samuel, as is recorded in Holy Writ,—as Erichtho raised up a corpse to reveal to Sextus Pompeius the event of the Pharsalian war,—as Elisha breathed life into the nostrils of the Shunamite's son,—as Alcestis was invoked by Hercules,—and as the dead maid was brought back to life by Apollonius Thyaneus,—so I, by certain powerful incantations, will allure the soul of the prophetess, for a short space, to its former tenement, and compel it to answer my questions. Dare you be present at this ceremony?"

" I dare," replied Fawkes.

" Follow me, then," said Dee. " You will need all your courage."

Muttering a hasty prayer, and secretly crossing himself, Guy Fawkes strode after him towards the grave. By the Doctor's directions, he, with some reluctance, assisted Kelley to raise the corpse, and convey it to the charnel. Dee followed, bearing the lantern, and, on entering the building, closed and fastened the door.

The chamber in which Guy Fawkes found himself was in perfect keeping with the horrible ceremonial about to be performed. In one corner lay a mouldering heap of skulls, bones, and other fragments of mortality; in the other a pile of broken coffins, emptied of their tenants, and reared on end. But what chiefly attracted his attention, was a ghastly collection of human limbs, blackened with pitch, girded round with iron hoops, and hung, like meat in a shambles, against the wall. There were two heads, and, though the features were scarcely distinguishable, owing to the liquid in which they had been immersed, they still retained a terrific expression of agony. Seeing his attention directed to these revolting objects, Kelley informed him they were the quarters of the two priests who had recently been put to death, which had been left there previously to being placed on the church-gates. The implements, and some part of the attire used by the executioner in his butcherly office, were scattered about, and mixed with the tools of the sexton; while in the centre of the room stood a large wooden frame supported by trestles. On this frame, stained with blood and smeared with pitch, showing the purpose to which it had been recently put, the body was placed. This done, Doctor Dee set down the lantern beside it; and, as the light fell upon its livid features, sullied with earth, and exhibiting traces of decay, Guy Fawkes was so appalled by the sight that he half repented of what he had undertaken.

Noticing his irresolution, Doctor Dee said, " You may yet retire if you think proper."

" No," replied Fawkes, rousing himself ; " I will go through
with it."

" It is well," replied Dee.   And he extinguished the light.

An awful silence now ensued, broken only by a low murmur
from Doctor Dee, who appeared to be reciting an incantation.
As he proceeded, his tones became louder, and his accents
those of command.   Suddenly, he paused, and seemed to
await a response.   But, as none was made, greatly to the
disappointment of Guy Fawkes, whose curiosity, notwithstanding his fears, was raised to the highest pitch, he cried,
" Blood is wanting to complete the charm."

" If that is all, I will speedily supply the deficiency," replied Guy Fawkes ; and, drawing his rapier, he bared his left
arm, and pricked it deeply with the point of the weapon.

" I bleed now," he cried.

" Sprinkle the corpse with the ruddy current," rejoined
Doctor Dee.

" Your commands are obeyed," replied Fawkes.   " I have
placed my hand on its breast, and the blood is flowing upon
it."

Upon this the Doctor began to mutter an incantation in a
louder and more authoritative tone than before.   Presently,
Kelley added his voice, and they both joined in a sort of
chorus, but in a jargon wholly unintelligible to Guy Fawkes.

All at once a blue flame appeared above their heads, and,
slowly descending, settled upon the brow of the corpse, light-
ing up the sunken cavities of the eyes, and the discoloured
and distorted features.

" The charm works," shouted Doctor Dee.

" She moves! she moves !" exclaimed Guy Fawkes.   " She
is alive !"

" Take off your hand," cried the Doctor, " or mischief may
ensue."   And he again continued his incantation.

" Down on your knees !" he exclaimed, at length, in a terrible voice.   " The spirit is at hand."

There was a rushing sound, and a stream of dazzling light-
ning shot down upon the corpse, which emitted a hollow
groan.   In obedience to the Doctor's commands, Guy Fawkes
had prostrated himself on the ground ; but he kept his gaze
steadily fixed on the body, which, to his infinite astonishment,
slowly arose, until it stood erect upon the frame.   There it
remained perfectly motionless, with the arms close to the
sides, and the habiliments torn and dishevelled.   The blue
light still retained its position upon the brow, and commu-

nicated a horrible glimmer to the features. The spectacle was so dreadful that Guy Fawkes would fain have averted his eyes, but he was unable to do so. Doctor Dee and his companion, meanwhile, continued their invocations, until, as it seemed to Fawkes, the lips of the corpse moved, and an awful voice exclaimed, " Why have you called me ?"

" Daughter !" replied Doctor Dee, rising, " in life thou wert endowed with the gift of prophecy. In the grave, that which is to come must be revealed to thee. We would question thee."

" Speak, and I will answer," replied the corpse.

" Interrogate her, my son," said Dee, addressing Fawkes, " and be brief, for the time is short. So long only as that flame burns have I power over her."

" Spirit of Elizabeth Orton," cried Guy Fawkes, " if indeed thou standest before me, and some demon hath not entered thy frame to delude me,—by all that is holy, and by every blessed saint, I adjure thee to tell me whether the scheme on which I am now engaged for the advantage of the Catholic Church will prosper ?"

" Thou art mistaken, Guy Fawkes," returned the corpse. " Thy scheme is not for the advantage of the Catholic Church."

" I will not pause to inquire wherefore," continued Fawkes. " But grant that the means are violent and wrongful, will the end be successful ?"

" The end will be death," replied the corpse.

" To the tyrant—to the oppressors ?" demanded Fawkes.

" To the conspirators," was the answer.

" Ha !" ejaculated Fawkes.

" Proceed, if you have aught more to ask," cried Doctor Dee. " The flame is expiring."

" Shall we restore the fallen religion ?" demanded Fawkes.

But before the words could be pronounced the light vanished, and a heavy sound was heard, as of the body falling on the frame.

" It is over," said Doctor Dee.

" Can you not summon her again ?" asked Fawkes, in a tone of deep disappointment. I had other questions to ask."

." Impossible," replied the Doctor. " The spirit is fled, and will not be recalled. We must now commit the body to the earth. And this time it shall be more decently interred."

"My curiosity is excited—not satisfied," said Guy Fawkes. "Would it were to occur again."

"It is ever thus," replied Doctor Dee. "We seek to know that which is interdicted—and quench our thirst at a fountain that only inflames our curiosity the more. Be warned, my son. You are embarked on a perilous enterprise, and if you pursue it, it will lead you to certain destruction."

"I cannot retreat," rejoined Fawkes, "and would not if I could. I am bound by an oath too terrible to be broken."

"I will absolve you of your oath, my son," said Doctor Dee, eagerly.

"You cannot, reverend sir," replied Fawkes. "By no sophistry could I clear my conscience of the ties imposed upon it. I have sworn never to desist from the execution of this scheme, unless those engaged in it shall give me leave. Nay, so resolved am I, that if I stood alone I would go on."

As he spoke, a deep groan issued from the corpse.

"You are again warned, my son," said Dee.

"Come forth," said Guy Fawkes, rushing towards the door, and throwing it open. "This place stifles me."

The night has already been described as bright and beautiful. Before him stood the Collegiate Church bathed in moonlight. He gazed abstractedly at this venerable structure for a few moments, and then returned to the charnel, where he found Doctor Dee and Kelley employed in placing the body of the prophetess in a coffin, which they had taken from a pile in the corner. He immediately proffered his assistance, and in a short space the task was completed. The coffin was then borne towards the grave, at the edge of which it was laid while the burial-service was recited by Dr. Dee. This ended, it was laid into its shallow resting place, and speedily covered with earth.

When all was ready for their departure, the Doctor turned to Fawkes, and, bidding him farewell, observed:

"If you are wise, my son, you will profit by the awful warning you have this night received."

"Before we part, reverend sir, replied Fawkes, "I would ask if you know of other means whereby an insight may be obtained into the future?"

"Many, my son," replied Dee. "I have a magic glass, in which, with due preparation, you may behold exact representations of coming events. I am now returning to the College, and if you will accompany me, I will show it to you."

The offer was eagerly accepted, and the party quitted the churchyard.

VIII.

THE MAGIC GLASS.

THE old College of Manchester occupied, as is well-known, the site of the existing structure, called after the benevolent individual by whom that admirable charity was founded, and whom we have ventured to introduce in this history—the Chetham Hospital. Much, indeed, of the ancient building remains; for though it was considerably repaired and enlarged, being "very ruinous and in great decay," at the time of its purchase in 1654, by the feoffees under Humphrey Chetham's will, from the sequestrators of the Earl of Derby's estates, still the general character of the fabric has been preserved, and several of its chambers retained. Originally built on the foundation of a manor-house, denominated the Baron's Hall—the abode of the Grelleys and the De la Warrs, lords of Manchester—the College continued to be used as the residence of the warden and fellows of the Collegiate Church until the reign of Edward the First, when that body was dissolved. On the accession, however, of Mary, the college was re-established; but the residence of the ecclesiastical body being removed to a house in Deansgate, the building was allowed to become extremely dilapidated, and was used partly as a prison for recusants and other offenders, and partly as a magazine for powder. In this state Doctor Dee found it when he succeeded to the wardenship in 1595, and preferring it, notwithstanding its ruinous condition, to the house appointed for him elsewhere, took up his abode within it.

Situated on a high rock, overhanging the river Irk—at that time a clear stream, remarkable for the excellence of its fish—and constructed entirely of stone, the old College had then, and still has to a certain extent, a venerable and monastic appearance. During Dee's occupation of it, it became a sort of weird abode in the eyes of the vulgar, and many a timorous look was cast at it by those who walked at eventide on the opposite bank of the Irk. Sometimes the curiosity of the watchers was rewarded by beholding a few sparks issue from the chimney, and now and then the red reflection of a fire might be discerned through the window. But generally nothing could be perceived, and the building seemed as dark and mysterious as its occupant.

One night, however, a loud explosion took place—so loud indeed that it shook the whole pile to its foundation, dislodged one or two of the chimneys, and overthrew an old wall, the stones of which rolled into the river beneath. Alarmed by the concussion, the inhabitants of Hunt's Bank rushed forth, and saw, to their great alarm, that the wing of the college occupied by Doctor Dee was in flames. Though many of them attributed the circumstance to supernatural agency, and were fully persuaded that the enemy of mankind was at that instant bearing off the conjuror and his assistant, and refused to interfere to stop the conflagration, others more humane and less superstitious, hastened to lend their aid to extinguish the flames. On reaching the College, they could scarcely credit their senses on finding that there was no appearance of fire; and they were met by the Doctor and his companion at the gates, who informed them that their presence was unnecessary, as all danger was over. From that night Doctor Dee's reputation as a wizard was firmly established.

At the period of this history, Doctor Dee was fast verging on eighty, having passed a long life in severe and abstruse study. He had travelled much, had visited most of the foreign courts, where he was generally well received, and was profoundly versed in mathematics, astronomy, the then popular science of judicial astrology, and other occult learning. So accurate were his calculations esteemed, that he was universally consulted as an oracle. For some time he resided in Germany, where he was invited by the Emperor, Charles the Fifth, and retained by his brother and successor, Ferdinando. He next went to Louvain, where his reputation had preceded him; and from thence to Paris, where he lectured at the schools on geometry, and was offered a professorship of the university, but declined it. On his return to England in 1551, he was appointed one of the instructors of the youthful monarch, Edward the Sixth, who presented him with an annual pension of a hundred marks. This he was permitted to commute for the rectory of Upton-upon-Severn, which he retained until the accession of Mary, when being charged with devising her Majesty's destruction by enchantments—certain waxen images of the Queen having been found within his abode—he was thrown into prison, rigorously treated, and kept in durance for a long period. At length, from want of sufficient proof against him, he was liberated.

Dee shared the common fate of all astrologers: he was

alternately honoured and disgraced. His next patron was Lord Robert Dudley (afterwards the celebrated Earl of Leicester), who it is well-known was a firm believer in the superstitious arts to which Dee was addicted, and by whom he was employed, on the accession of Elizabeth, to erect a scheme to ascertain the best day for her coronation. His prediction was so fortunate that it procured him the favour of the Queen, from whom he received many marks of regard. As it is not needful to follow him through his various wanderings, it may be sufficient to mention, that in 1564, he proceeded to Germany on a visit to the Emperor Maximilian, to whom he dedicated his "*Monas Hieroglyphica;*" that in 1571 he fell grievously sick in Lorrain, whither two physicians were despatched to his aid by Elizabeth; and that on his recovery he returned to his own country, and retired to Mortlake, where he gathered together a vast library, comprising the rarest and most curious works on all sciences, together with a large collection of manuscripts.

While thus living in retirement, he was sought out by Edward Kelley, a native of Worcestershire, who represented himself as in possession of an old book of magic, containing forms of invocation, by which spirits might be summoned and controlled, as well as a ball of ivory, found in the tomb of a bishop who had made great progress in hermetic philosophy, which was filled with the powder of projection. These treasures Kelley offered to place in the hands of the Doctor on certain conditions which were immediately acquiesced in, and thenceforth Kelley became a constant inmate in his house, and an assistant in all his practices. Shortly afterwards they were joined by a Polish nobleman, Albert de Laski, Palatine of Suabia, whom they accompanied to Prague, at the instance of the Emperor Rodolph the Second, who desired to be initiated into their mysteries. Their reception at this court was not such as to induce a long sojourn at it; and Dee having been warned by his familiar spirits to sell his effects and depart, complied with the intimation, and removed to Poland. The same fate attended him here. The nuncio of the Pope denounced him as a sorcerer, and demanded that he should be delivered up to the Inquisition. This was refused by the monarch; but Dee and his companion were banished from his dominions, and compelled to fly to Bohemia, where they took refuge in the castle of Trebona, belonging to Count Rosenberg. Shortly afterwards, Dee and Kelley separated, the magical instruments being delivered to the former, who bent his course homewards; and on his arrival in London was warmly welcomed by the Queen. During his absence, his house at Mortlake had been broken open by the populace, under the pretence of its being the abode of a wizard, and rifled of its valuable library and manuscripts— a loss severely felt by its owner. Some years were now passed by Dee in great destitution, during which he prosecuted his studies with the same ardour as before, until at length in 1595, when he was turned seventy, fortune again smiled upon him, and he was appointed to the wardenship of the College of Manchester, whither he repaired, and was installed in great pomp.

But his residence in this place was not destined to be a tranquil one. His reputation as a dealer in the black art had preceded him, and rendered him obnoxious to the clergy, with whom he had constant disputes, and a feud subsisted between him and the fellows of his church. It has already been mentioned that he refused to occupy the house allotted him, but preferred taking up his quarters in the old dilapidated College. Various reasons were assigned by his enemies for this singular choice of abode. They affirmed—and with some reason—that he selected it because he desired to elude observation—and that his mode of life, sufficiently improper in a layman, was altogether indecorous in an ecclesiastic. By the common people he was universally regarded as a conjuror—and many at first came to consult him; but he peremptorily dismissed all such applicants; and, when seven females, supposed to be possessed, were brought to him that he might exercise his power over the evil spirits, he refused to interfere. He also publicly examined and rebuked a juggler named Hartley, who pretended to magical knowledge. But these things did not blind his enemies, who continued to harass him to such a degree, that he addressed a petition to James the First, entreating to be brought to trial, when the accusations preferred against him might be fully investigated and his character cleared. The application, and another to the like effect addressed to Parliament, were disregarded. Dee had not been long established in Manchester when he was secretly joined by Kelley, and they recommenced their search after the grand secret—passing the nights in making various alchymical experiments, or in fancied conferences with invisible beings.

Among other magical articles possessed by Doctor Dee was a large globe of crystal which he termed the Holy Stone, because he believed it had been brought him by "angelical ministry;" and "in which," according to Meric Casaubon, "and out of which, by persons qualified for it, and admitted to the sight of it, all shapes and figures mentioned in every action were seen, and voices heard." The same writer informs us it was "round-shaped, of a pretty bigness, and most like unto crystal." Dee himself declared to the Emperor Rodolph, "that the spirits had brought him a stone of that value that no earthly kingdom was of such worthiness as to be compared to the virtue and dignity thereof." He was in the habit of daily consulting this marvellous stone, and recording the visions he saw therein, and the conferences he held through it with the invisible world.

Followed by Guy Fawkes and Kelley, the Doctor took his way down Long Mill Gate, and stopping at an arched gateway on the left, near which, on the site of the modern structure, stood the public school, founded a century before by Hugh Oldham, Bishop of Exeter—he unlocked a small wicket, and entered a spacious court, surrounded on one side by high stone walls, and on the other by a wing of the College.

Conducting his guest to the principal entrance of the building, which lay at the farther end of the court, Doctor Dee ushered him into a large chamber, panelled with oak, and having a curiously-moulded ceiling, ornamented with grotesque sculpture. This room, still in existence, and now occupied by the master of the school, formed Doctor Dee's library. Offering Fawkes a chair, the Doctor informed him that when all was ready, Kelley should summon him, and, accompanied by his assistant, he withdrew. Half an hour elapsed before Kelley returned. Motioning Guy Fawkes to follow him, he led the way through several intricate passages to a chamber which was evidently the magician's sacred retreat. In a recess on one side stood a table, covered with cabalistic characters and figures, referring to the celestial influences. On it was placed the holy stone, diffusing such a glistening radiance as is emitted by the pebble called cat's-eye. On the floor a wide circle was described, in the rings of which magical characters, resembling those on the table, were traced. In front stood a brasier, filled with flaming coals; and before it hung a heavy black curtain, appearing to shroud some mystery from view.

Desiring Fawkes to place himself in the centre of the circle, Doctor Dee took several ingredients from a basket handed

him by Kelley, and cast them into the brasier. As each herb
or gum was ignited, the flame changed its colour; now
becoming crimson, now green, now blue, while fragant or
noxious odours loaded the atmosphere. These suffumigations
ended, Dee seated himself on a chair near the table, whither
he was followed by Kelley, and commanding Fawkes not to
move a footstep, as he valued his safety, he waved his wand,
and began in a solemn tone to utter an invocation. As he
continued, a hollow noise was heard overhead, which gradually
increased in loudness, until it appeared as if the walls were
tumbling about their ears.

"The spirits are at hand!" cried Dee. "Do not look behind you, or they will tear you in pieces."

"As he spoke, a horrible din was heard, as of mingled
nowling, shrieking, and laughter. It was succeeded by a low
faint strain of music, which gradually died away, and then all
was silent.

"All is prepared," cried Dee. "Now what would you
behold?"

"The progress of the great enterprise," replied Fawkes.

Doctor Dee waved his wand. The curtains slowly unfolded,
and Guy Fawkes perceived as in a glass a group of dark
figures; amongst which he noticed one in all respects resembling himself. A .priest was apparently proposing an
oath, which the others were uttering.

"Do you recognise them?" said Doctor Dee.

"Perfectly," replied Fawkes.

"Look again," said Dee.

As he spoke the figures melted away, and a new scene was
presented on the glass. It was a gloomy vault, filled with
barrels, partly covered with fagots and billets of wood.

"Have you seen enough?" demanded Dee.

"No," replied Fawkes, firmly. "I have seen what is past.
I would behold that which is to come."

"Look again, then," rejoined the Doctor, waving his
wand.

For an instant the glass was darkened, and nothing could
be discerned except the lurid flame and thick smoke arising
from the brasier. The next moment an icy chill shot through
the frame of Guy Fawkes as he beheld a throng of skeletons
arranged before him. The bony fingers of the foremost of
the grisly assemblage were pointed towards an indistinct
object at its feet. As this object gradually became more de-
fined, Guy Fawkes perceived that it was a figure resembling

himself, stretched upon the wheel, and writhing in the agonies of torture.

He uttered an exclamation of terror, and the curtains were instantly closed.

Half an hour afterwards, Guy Fawkes quitted the College, and returned to the Seven Stars.

IX.

THE PRISON ON SALFORD BRIDGE.

On the following morning, Guy Fawkes had a long and private conference with Father Oldcorne. The priest appeared greatly troubled by the communication made to him, but he said nothing, and was for some time lost in reflection, and evidently weighing within himself what course it would be best to pursue. His uneasiness was not without effect on Viviana Radcliffe, and she ventured at last to inquire whether he apprehended any new danger.

"I scarcely know what I apprehend, dear daughter," he answered. "But circumstances have occurred which render it impossible we can remain longer in our present asylum with safety. We must quit it at nightfall."

"Is our retreat then discovered?" inquired Viviana, in alarm.

"Not as yet, I trust," replied Oldcorne;" "but I have just ascertained from a messenger that the pursuivant, who we thought had departed for Chester, is still lingering within the town. He has offered a large reward for my apprehension, and having traced us to Manchester, declares he will leave no house unsearched till he finds us. He has got together a fresh band of soldiers, and is now visiting every place he thinks likely to afford us shelter."

"If this is the case," rejoined Viviana, "why remain here a single moment? Let us fly at once."

"That would avail nothing—or rather, it would expose us to fresh risk, dear daughter," replied Oldcorne. "Every approach to the town is guarded, and soldiers are posted at the corners of the streets, who stop and examine each suspected person."

"Heaven protect us?" exclaimed Viviana.

"But this is not all," continued the priest. "By some inexplicable and mysterious means, the designs of certain of the most assured friends of the Catholic cause have come to the knowledge of our enemies, and the lives and safeties of many worthy men will be endangered: amongst others, that of your father."

"You terrify me!" cried Viviana.

"The rack shall force nothing from me, father," said Fawkes, sternly.

"Nor from me, my son," rejoined Oldcorne. "I have that within me which will enable me to sustain the bitterest agonies that the persecutors of our Church can inflict."

"Nor shall it force aught from me," added Viviana. "For, though you have trusted me with nothing that can implicate others, I plainly perceive some plot is in agitation for the restoration of our religion, and I more than suspect Mr. Catesby is its chief contriver."

"Daughter!" exclaimed Oldcorne, uneasily.

"Fear nothing, father," she rejoined. "As I have said, the rack shall not force me to betray you. Neither should it keep me silent when I feel that my counsel—such as it is—may avail you. The course you are pursuing is a dangerous and fatal one; dangerous to yourselves, and fatal to the cause you would serve. Do not deceive yourselves. You are struggling hopelessly and unrighteously, and Heaven will never assist an undertaking which has its aim in the terrible waste of life you meditate."

Father Oldcorne made no reply, but walked apart with Guy Fawkes; and Viviana abandoned herself to sorrowful reflection.

Shortly after this, the door was suddenly thrown open, and Humphrey Chetham rushed into the room. His looks were full of apprehension, and Viviana was at no loss to perceive that some calamity was at hand.

"What is the matter?" she cried, rising.

"The pursuivant and his men are below," he replied. "They are interrogating the hostess, and are about to search the house; I managed to pass them unperceived."

"We will resist them to the last," said Guy Fawkes drawing a petronel.

"Resistance will be in vain," rejoined Humphrey Chetham. "They more than treble our number."

"Is there no means of escape?" asked Viviana.

"None whatever," replied Chetham. "I hear them on the stairs. The terrified hostess has not dared to deny you, and is conducting them hither."

"Stand back!" cried Guy Fawkes, striding towards the door, "and let me alone confront them. That accursed pursuivant has escaped me once. But he shall not do so a second time."

"My son," said Oldcorne, advancing towards him; "preserve yourself, if possible. Your life is of consequence to the great cause. Think not of us—think not of revenging yourself upon this caitiff. But think of the high destiny for which you are reserved. That window offers a means of retreat. Avail yourself of it. Fly—Fly!"

"Ay, fly!" repeated Viviana. "And you, Humphrey Chetham—your presence here can do no good. Quick!—they come!"

"Nothing should induce me to quit you at such a moment, Viviana," replied Chetham, "but the conviction that I may be able to liberate you, should these miscreants convey you to prison."

"Fly!—fly, my son," cried Oldcorne. "They are at the door."

Thus urged, Guy Fawkes reluctantly yielded to Oldcorne's entreaties and sprang through the window. He was followed by Chetham. Viviana darted to the casement, and saw that they had alighted in safety on the ground, and were flying swiftly up Shude Hill. Meanwhile, the pursuivant had reached the door, which Chetham had taken the precaution to fasten, and was trying to burst it open. The bolts offered but a feeble resistance to his fury, and the next moment he dashed into the room, at the head of a band of soldiers.

"Seize them!" he cried. "Ha!" he added, glancing round the room with a look of disappointment, "where are the others? Where is the soldier in the Spanish garb? Where is Humphrey Chetham? Confess at once, dog!" he continued, seizing the priest by the throat, "or I will pluck the secret from your breast."

"Do not harm him," interposed Viviana. "I will answer the question. They are fled."

"Fled!" echoed the pursuivant, in consternation. "How?"

"Through that window," replied Viviana.

"After them!" cried the pursuivant to some of his attendants. "Take the soldier, dead or alive! And now," he continued, as his orders were obeyed, "you, Father Oldcorne, Jesuit and traitor; and you, Viviana Radcliffe, his shelterer and abettor, I shall convey you both to the prison on Salford Bridge. Seize them, and bring them along."

"Touch me not," rejoined Viviana, pushing the men aside, who rudely advanced to obey their leader's command. "You have no warrant for this brutality. I am ready to attend you. Take my arm, father."

Abashed at this reproof, the pursuivant stalked out of the room. Surrounded by the soldiers, Viviana and the priest followed. The sad procession was attended by crowds to the very door of the prison, where, by the pursuivant's commands, they were locked in separate cells.

The cell in which Viviana was confined was a small chamber at the back of the prison, and on the upper story. It had a small grated window overlooking the river. It has already been mentioned that this prison was originally a chapel built in the reign of Edward the Third, and had only recently been converted into a place of security for recusants. The chamber allotted to Viviana was contrived in the roof, and was so low that she could scarcely stand upright in it. It was furnished with a chair, a small table, and a straw pallet.

The hours passed wearily with Viviana as they were marked by the deep-toned clock of the Collegiate Church, the tall tower of which fronted her window. Oppressed by the most melancholy reflections, she was for some time a prey almost to despair. On whatever side she looked, the prospect was equally cheerless, and her sole desire was that she might find a refuge from her cares in the seclusion of a convent. For this she prayed,—and she prayed also that Heaven would soften the hearts of her oppressors, and enable those who suffered to endure their yoke with patience. In the evening provisions were brought her, and placed upon the table, together with a lamp, by a surly-looking gaoler. But Viviana had no inclination to eat, and left them untouched. Neither could she prevail upon herself to lie down on the wretched pallet, and she therefore determined to pass the night in the chair.

After some hours of watchfulness, her eyelids closed, and she continued to slumber until she was aroused by a slight noise at the window. Starting at the sound, she flew towards it, and perceived in the gloom the face of a man. She would have uttered a loud cry, when the circumstances of her situation rushed to her mind, and the possibility that it might be a friend checked her. The next moment satisfied her that she had acted rightly. A voice, which she recognised as that of Humphrey Chetham, called to her by name in a low tone, bidding her fear nothing, as he was come to set her free.

"How have you managed to reach this window?" asked Viviana.

"By a rope ladder," he answered. "I contrived in the darkness to clamber upon the roof of the prison from the parapets of the bridge, and, after securing the ladder to a projection, dropped the other end into a boat, rowed by Guy Fawkes, and concealed beneath the arches of the bridge. If I can remove this bar so as to allow you to pass through the window, dare you descend the ladder?"

"No," replied Viviana, shuddering. "My brain reels at the mere idea."

"Think of the fate you will escape," urged Chetham.

"And what will become of Father Oldcorne?" asked Viviana. "Where is he?"

"In the cell immediately beneath you," replied Chetham.

"Can you not liberate him?" she continued.

"Assuredly, if he will risk the descent," answered Chetham, reluctantly.

"Free him first," rejoined Viviana, "and at all hazards I will accompany you."

The young merchant made no reply, but disappeared from the window. Viviana strained her gaze downwards; but it was too dark to allow her to see anything. She, however, heard a noise like that occasioned by a file; and shortly afterwards a few muttered words informed her that the priest was passing through the window. The cords of the ladder shook against the bars of her window,—and she held her breath for fear. From this state of suspense she was relieved in a few minutes by Humphrey Chetham, who informed her that Oldcorne had descended in safety, and was in the boat with Guy Fawkes.

"I will fulfil my promise," replied Viviana, trembling: "but I fear my strength will fail me."

"You had better find death below than tarry here," replied Humphrey Chetham, who as he spoke was rapidly filing through the iron bar. "In a few minutes this impediment will be removed."

The young merchant worked hard, and in a short time the stout bar yielded to his efforts.

"Now, then," he cried, springing into the room, "you are free."

"I dare not make the attempt," said Viviana; "my strength utterly fails me."

"Nay, then," he replied, "I will take the risk upon myself. You must not remain here."

So saying, he caught her in his arms, and bore her through the window.

With some difficulty, and no little risk, he succeeded in gaining a footing on the ladder. This accomplished, he began slowly to descend. When half-way down, he found he had overrated his strength, and he feared he should be compelled to quit his hold; but, nerved by his passion, he held on, and making a desperate effort, completed the descent in safety.

X.

THE FATE OF THE PURSUIVANT.

ASSISTED by the stream, and plying his oars with great rapidity, Guy Fawkes soon left the town far behind him; nor did he relax his exertions until checked by Humphrey Chetham. He then ceased rowing, and directed the boat towards the left bank of the river.

"Here we propose to land," observed the young merchant to Viviana. "We are not more than a hundred yards from Ordsall Cave, where you can take refuge for a short time, while I proceed to the Hall, and ascertain whether you can return to it with safety."

"I place myself entirely in your hands," she replied; "but I fear such a course will be to rush into the very face of danger. Oh! that I could join my father at Holywell! With him I should feel secure."

"Means may be found to effect your wishes," returned Humphrey Chetham; "but, after the suffering you have recently endured, it will scarcely be prudent to undertake so long a journey without a few hours' repose. To-morrow,— or the next day,—you may set out."

"I am fully equal to it now," rejoined Viviana, eagerly; "and any fatigue I may undergo will not equal my present anxiety. You have already done so much for me, that I venture to presume still further upon your kindness. Provide some means of conveyance for me and for Father Old-corne to Chester, and I shall for ever be beholden to you."

*Guy Fawkes and Humphrey Chetham rescuing Father
Oldcorne & Viviana Radcliffe from the Pursuivant.*

"I will not only do what you desire, Viviana, if it be possible," answered Chetham; "but, if you will allow me, I will serve as your escort."

"And I, also," added Guy Fawkes.

"All I fear is, that your strength may fail you," continued the young merchant, in a tone of uneasiness.

"Fear nothing, then," replied Viviana. "I am made of firmer material than you imagine. Think only of what *you* can do, and doubt not my ability to do it, also."

"I ever deemed you of a courageous nature, daughter," observed Oldcorne; "but your resolution surpasses my belief."

By this time the boat had approached the shore. Leaping upon the rocky bank, the young merchant assisted Viviana to land, and then performed the same service for the priest. Guy Fawkes was the last to disembark; and, having pulled the skiff aground, he followed the others, who waited for him at a short distance. The night was profoundly dark, and the path they had taken, being shaded by large trees, was scarcely discernible. Carefully guiding Viviana, who leaned on him for support, the young merchant proceeded at a slow pace, and with the utmost caution. Suddenly, they were surprised and alarmed by a vivid blaze of light bursting through the trees on the left.

"Some building must be on fire!" exclaimed Viviana.

"It is Ordsall Hall,—it is your father's residence," cried Humphrey Chetham.

"It is the work of that accursed pursuivant, I will be sworn," said Guy Fawkes.

"If it be so, may Heaven's fire consume him!" rejoined Oldcorne.

"Alas! alas!" cried Viviana, bursting into tears, "I thought myself equal to every calamity; but this new stroke of fate is more than I can bear."

As she spoke, the conflagration evidently increased. The sky was illumined by the red reflection of the flames; and as the party hurried forward to a rising ground, whence a better view could be obtained of the spectacle, they saw the dark walls of the ancient mansion apparently wrapped in the devouring element.

"Let us hasten thither," cried Viviana, distractedly.

"I and Guy Fawkes will fly there," replied the young merchant, "and render all the assistance in our power. But, first, let me convey you to the cave."

More dead than alive, Viviana suffered herself to be borne

in that direction. Making his way over every impediment, Chetham soon reached the excavation; and depositing his lovely burthen upon the stone couch, and leaving her in charge of the priest, he hurried with Guy Fawkes towards the Hall.

On arriving at the termination of the avenue, they found, to their great relief, that it was not the main structure, but an out-building which was in flames, and from its situation the young merchant conceived it to be the stables. As soon as they made this discovery, they slackened their pace, being apprehensive, from the shouts and other sounds that reached them, that some hostile party might be among the assemblage. Crossing the drawbridge—which was fortunately lowered—they were about to shape their course towards the stables, which lay at the further side of the Hall, when they perceived the old steward, Heydocke, standing at the doorway and wringing his hands in distraction. Humphrey Chetham immediately called to him.

"I should know that voice!" cried the old man, stepping forward. "Ah! Mr. Chetham, is it you? You are arrived at a sad time, sir—a sad time—to see the old house, where I have dwelt, man and boy, sixty years and more, in flames. But one calamity has trodden upon the heels of another. Ever since Sir William departed for Holywell nothing has gone on right—nothing whatever. First, the house was searched by the pursuivant and his gang; then my young mistress disappeared; then it was rifled by these plunderers; and now, to crown all, it is on fire, and will speedily be burnt to the ground."

"Say not so," replied the young merchant. "The flames have not yet reached the Hall; and, if exertion is used, they may be extinguished without further mischief."

"Let those who have kindled them extinguish them," replied Heydocke, sullenly. "I will not raise hand more."

"Who are the incendiaries?" demanded Fawkes.

"The pursuivant and his myrmidons," replied Heydocke. "They came here to-night; and after ransacking the house under pretence of procuring further evidence against my master, and carrying off everything valuable they could collect,—plate, jewels, ornaments, money, and even wearing-apparel,—they ended by locking up all the servants,—except myself, who managed to elude their vigilance,—in the cellar, and setting fire to the stables."

"Wretches!" exclaimed Humphrey Chetham.

"Wretches, indeed!" repeated the steward. "But this is not all the villany they contemplate. I had concealed myself in the store-room, under a heap of lumber, and in searching for me they chanced upon a barrel of gunpowder——"

"Well!" interrupted Guy Fawkes.

"Well, sir," pursued Heydocke, "I heard the pursuivant remark to one of his comrades, 'This is a lucky discovery. If we can't find the steward, we'll blow him and the old house to the devil.' Just then some one came to tell him I was hidden in the stables, and the whole troop adjourned thither. But being balked of their prey, I suppose, they wreaked their vengeance in the way you perceive."

"No doubt," rejoined Humphrey Chetham. "But they shall bitterly rue it. I will myself represent the affair to the commissioners."

"It will be useless," groaned Heydocke. "There is no law to protect the property of a Catholic."

"Where is the barrel of gunpowder you spoke of?" asked Guy Fawkes, as if struck by a sudden idea.

"The villains took it with them when they quitted the store-room," replied the steward. "I suppose they have got it in the yard."

"They have lighted a fire which shall be quenched with their blood," rejoined Fawkes, fiercely. "Follow me. I may need you both."

So saying, he darted off, and turning the corner, came in front of the blazing pile. Occupying one side of a large quadrangular court, the stables were wholly disconnected with the Hall, and though the fire burnt furiously, yet as the wind carried the flames and sparks in a contrary direction, it was possible the latter building might escape if due precaution were taken. So far, however, from this being the case, it seemed the object of the bystanders to assist the progress of the conflagration. Several horses, saddled and bridled, had been removed from the stable, and placed within an open cowhouse. To these Guy Fawkes called Chetham's attention, and desired him and the old steward to secure some of them. Hastily giving directions to Heydocke, the young merchant obeyed,—sprang on the back of the nearest courser, and seizing the bridles of two others, rode off with them. His example was followed by Heydocke, and one steed only was left. Such was the confusion and clamour prevailing around, that the above proceeding passed unnoticed.

Guy Fawkes, meanwhile, ensconcing himself behind the

court-gate, looked about for the barrel of gunpowder. For some time he could discover no trace of it. At length, beneath a shed, not far from him, he perceived a soldier seated upon a small cask, which he had no doubt was the object he was in search of. So intent was the man upon the spectacle before him, that he was wholly unaware of the approach of an enemy; and creeping noiselessly up to him, Guy Fawkes felled him to the ground with a blow from the heavy butt-end of his petronel. The action was not perceived by the others; and carrying the cask out of the yard, Fawkes burst in the lid, and ascertained that the contents were what they had been represented. He then glanced around, to see how he could best execute his purpose.

On the top of the wall adjoining the stables he beheld the pursuivant, with three or four soldiers, giving directions and issuing orders. Another and lower wall, forming the opposite side of the quadrangle, and built on the edge of the moat, approached the scene of the fire, and on this, Guy Fawkes, with the barrel of gunpowder on his shoulder, mounted. Concealing himself behind a tree, which overshadowed it, he watched a favourable moment for his enterprise.

He had not to wait long. Prompted by some undefinable feeling, which caused him to rush upon his destruction, the pursuivant ventured upon the roof of the stables, and was followed by his companions. No sooner did this occur, than Guy Fawkes dashed forward, and hurled the barrel with all his force into the midst of the flames, throwing himself at the same moment into the moat. The explosion was instantaneous and tremendous;—so loud as to be audible even under the water. Its effects were terrible. The bodies of the pursuivant and his companions were blown into the air, and carried to the further side of the moat. Of those standing before the building, several were destroyed, and all more or less injured. The walls were thrown down by the concussion, and the roof and its fiery fragments projected into the moat. An effectual stop was put to the conflagration; and, when Guy Fawkes rose to the boiling and agitated surface of the water, the flames were entirely extinguished. Hearing groans on the opposite bank of the moat, he forced his way through the blazing beams, which were hissing near him; and snatching up a still burning fragment, hastened in the direction of the sound. In the blackened and mutilated object that met his gaze, he recognised the pursuivant. The dying wretch also recognised him, and attempted to speak;

but in vain—his tongue refused its office, and with a horrible attempt at articulation, he expired.

Alarmed by the explosion, the domestics,—who, it has already been mentioned, were confined in the cellar,—were rendered so desperate by their fears, that they contrived to break out of their prison, and now hastened to the stables to ascertain the cause of the report. Leaving them to assist the sufferers, whose dreadful groans awakened some feelings of compunction in his iron breast, Guy Fawkes caught the steed, —which had broken its bridle and rushed off, and now stood shivering, shaking, and drenched in moisture near the draw-bridge,—and, mounting it, galloped towards the cave.

At its entrance, he was met by Humphrey Chetham and Oldcorne, who eagerly inquired what had happened.

Guy Fawkes briefly explained.

"It is the hand of Heaven manifested by your arm, my son," observed the priest. "Would that it had stricken the tyrant and apostate prince by whom our Church is persecuted! But his turn will speedily arrive."

"Peace, father!" cried Guy Fawkes, sternly.

"I do not lament the fate of the pursuivant," observed Humphrey Chetham. "But this is a frightful waste of human life—and in such a cause!"

"It is the cause of Heaven, young sir," rejoined the priest, angrily.

"I do not think so," returned Chetham; "and but for my devotion to Viviana, I would have no further share in it."

"You are at liberty to leave us, if you think proper," retorted the priest, coldly.

"Nay, say not so, father," interposed Viviana, who had been an unobserved listener to the foregoing discourse. "You owe your life—your liberty, to Mr. Chetham."

"True, daughter," replied the priest. "I have been too hasty, and entreat his forgiveness."

"You have it, reverend sir," rejoined the young merchant. "And now, Master Heydocke," he added, turning to the steward, "you may return to the Hall with safety. No one will molest you more, and your presence may be needed."

"But my young mistress," said Heydocke.

"I am setting out for Holywell to join my father," replied Viviana. "You will receive our instructions from that place."

"It is well," returned the old man, bowing respectfully. "Heaven shield us from further misfortune!"

G

Humphrey Chetham having assisted Viviana into the saddle, and the rest of the party having mounted, they took the road to Chester, while Heydocke returned to the Hall.

XI.

THE PILGRIMAGE TO SAINT WINIFRED'S WELL.

EARLY on the following morning, the party, who had ridden hard, and had paused only for a short time at Knutsford to rest their steeds, approached the ancient and picturesque city of Chester. Skirting its high, and then partly fortified walls, above which appeared the massive tower of the venerable cathedral, they passed through the east gate, and proceeding along the street deriving its name from that entrance, were about to halt before the door of a large hostel, called the Saint Werburgh's Abbey, when, to their great surprise, they perceived Catesby riding towards them.

"I thought I could not be mistaken," cried the latter, as he drew near and saluted Viviana. "I was about to set out for Manchester with a despatch to you from your father, Miss Radcliffe, when this most unexpected and fortunate encounter spares me the journey. But may I ask why I see you here, and thus attended?" he added, glancing uneasily at Humphrey Chetham.

A few words from Father Oldcorne explained all. Catesby affected to bend his brow, and appear concerned at the relation. But he could scarcely repress his satisfaction.

"Sir William Radcliffe *must* join us now," he whispered to the priest.

"He must—he *shall*," replied Oldcorne, in the same tone.

"Your father wishes you to join him at Holt, Miss Radcliffe," remarked Catesby, turning to her, "whence the pilgrimage starts to-morrow for Saint Winifred's Well. There are already nearly thirty devout persons assembled."

"Indeed!" replied Viviana. "May I inquire their names?"

"Sir Everard and Lady Digby," replied Catesby; "the Lady Anne Vaux and her sister, Mrs. Brooksby; Mr. Ambrose Rookwood and his wife, the two Winters, Tresham, Wright, Fathers Garnet and Fisher, and many others, in all probability unknown to you. The procession started ten days ago from Gothurst, in Buckinghamshire, Sir Everard Digby's residence, and proceeded from thence by slow stages to Norbrook and Haddington, at each of which houses it halted for some days. Yesterday, it reached Holt, and starts, as I have just told you, to-morrow for Holywell. If you are so disposed, you will be able to attend it."

"I will gladly do so," replied Viviana. "And since I find it is not necessary to hurry forward, I will rest myself for a short time here."

So saying, she dismounted, and the whole party entered the hostel. Viviana withdrew to seek a short repose, and glance over her father's letter, while Catesby, Guy Fawkes, and Oldcorne, were engaged in deep consultation. Humphrey Chetham, perceiving that his attendance was no further required, and that he was an object of suspicion and dislike to Catesby,—for whom he also entertained a similar aversion, —prepared to return. And when Viviana made her appearance, he advanced to bid her farewell.

"I can be of no further service to you, Viviana," he said, in a mournful tone; "and as my presence might be as unwelcome to your father, as it seems to be to others of your friends, I will now take my leave."

"Farewell, Mr. Chetham," she replied. "I will not attempt to oppose your departure; for, much as I grieve to lose you—and that I do so these tears will testify—I feel that it is for the best. I owe you much—more—far more than I can ever repay. It would be unworthy in me, and unfair to you, to say that I do not, and shall not ever feel the deepest interest in you; that, next to my father, there is no one whom I regard—nay, whom I love so much."

"Love! Viviana?" echoed the young merchant, trembling.

"Love, Mr. Chetham," she continued, turning very pale; "since you compel me to repeat the word. I avow it boldly, because"—and her voice faltered—"I would not have you suppose me ungrateful, and because I never can be yours."

"I will not attempt to dissuade you from the fatal determination you have formed of burying your charms in a cloister," rejoined Humphrey Chetham. "But, oh! if you do love me, why condemn yourself — why condemn me to hopeless misery?"

"I will tell you why," replied Viviana. "Because you are not of my faith: and because I never will wed a heretic."

"I am answered," replied the young merchant, sadly.

"Mr. Chetham," interposed Oldcorne, who had approached

them unperceived; "it is in your power to change Viviana's determination."

"How?" asked the young merchant, starting.

"By being reconciled to the Church of Rome."

"Then it will remain unaltered," replied Chetham, firmly.

"And, if Mr. Chetham would consent to this proposal, *I* would not," said Viviana. "Farewell," she added, extending her hand to him, which he pressed to his lips. "Do not let us prolong an interview so painful to us both. The best wish I can desire for you is, that we may never meet again."

Without another word, and without hazarding a look at the object of his affections, Chetham rushed out of the room, and mounting his horse, rode off in the direction of Manchester.

"Daughter," observed Oldcorne, as soon as he was gone, "I cannot too highly approve of your conduct, or too warmly applaud the mastery you display over your feelings. But——" and he hesitated.

"But what, father?" cried Viviana, eagerly. "Do you think I have done wrong in dismissing him."

"By no means, dear daughter," replied the priest. "You have acted most discreetly. But you will forgive me if I urge you—nay, implore you not to take the veil; but rather to bestow your hand upon some Catholic gentleman——"

"Such as Mr. Catesby," interrupted Viviana, glancing in the direction of the individual she mentioned, who was watching them narrowly from the further end of the room.

"Ay, Mr. Catesby," repeated Oldcorne, affecting not to notice the scornful emphasis laid on the name. "None more fitting could be found, nor more worthy of you. Our Church has not a more zealous servant and upholder; and he will be at once a father and a husband to you. Such a union would be highly profitable to our religion. And, though it is well for those whose hearts are burthened with affliction, and who are unable to render any active service to their faith, to retire from the world, it behoves every sister of the Romish Church to support it at a juncture like the present, at any sacrifice of personal feeling."

"Urge me no more, father," replied Viviana, firmly. "I will make every sacrifice for my religion, consistent with principle and feeling. But I will not make this; neither am I required to make it. And I beg you will entreat Mr. Catesby to desist from further importunity."

Oldcorne bowed and retired. Nor was another syllable exchanged between them prior to their departure.

Crossing the old bridge over the Dee, then defended at each extremity by a gate and tower, the party took the road to Holt, where they arrived in about an hour. The recent conversation had thrown a restraint over them, which was not removed during the journey. Habitually taciturn, as has already been remarked, Guy Fawkes seemed gloomier and more thoughtful than ever; and though he rode by the side of Viviana, he did not volunteer a remark, and scarcely appeared conscious of her presence. Catesby and Oldcorne kept aloof, and it was not until they came in sight of the little town which formed their destination that the former galloped forward, and striking into the path on the right, begged Viviana to follow him. A turn in the road shortly afterwards showed them a large mansion screened by a grove of beech-trees.

"That is the house to which we are going," observed Catesby.

And as he spoke, they approached a lodge, the gates of which being opened by an attendant, admitted them to the avenue.

Viviana's heart throbbed with delight at the anticipated meeting with her father; but she could not repress a feeling of anxiety at the distressing intelligence she had to impart to him. As she drew near the house, she perceived him walking beneath the shade of the trees with two other persons; and quickening her pace, sprang from her steed, and almost before he was aware of it was in his arms.

"Why do I see you here so unexpectedly, my dear child?" cried Sir William Radcliffe, as soon as he had recovered from the surprise which her sudden appearance occasioned him. "Mr. Catesby only left this morning, charged with a letter entreating you to set out without delay,—and now I behold you. What has happend?"

Viviana then recounted the occurrences of the last few days.

"It is as I feared," replied Sir William, in a desponding tone. "Our oppressors will never cease till they drive us to desperation."

"They will not!" rejoined a voice behind him. "Well may we exclaim with the prophet—'How long, O Lord, shall I cry, and thou wilt not hear? Shall I cry out to thee suffering violence, and thou wilt not save? Why hast thou showed

me iniquity and grievance, to see rapine and injustice before
me? Why lookest thou upon them that do unjust things,
and holdest thy peace when the wicked devoureth the man
that is more just than himself?'"

Viviana looked in the direction of the speaker, and beheld
a man in a priestly garb, whose countenance struck her forcibly. He was rather under the middle height, of a slight
spare figure, and in age might be about fifty. His features,
which in his youth must have been pleasing, if not handsome, and which were still regular, were pale and emaciated;
but his eye was dark, and of unusual brilliancy. A single
glance at this person satisfied her it was Father Garnet, the
provincial of the English Jesuits; nor was she mistaken in
her supposition.

Of this remarkable person, so intimately connected with
the main events of the history about to be related, it may be
proper to offer some preliminary account. Born at Nottingham in 1554, in the reign of Queen Mary, and of obscure
parentage, Henry Garnet was originally destined to the
Protestant Church, and educated, with a view to taking
orders, at Winchester School, whence it was intended he
should be removed in due course to Oxford. But this design
was never carried into effect. Influenced by motives into
which it is now scarcely worth while inquiring, and which
have been contested by writers on both sides of the question,
Garnet proceeded from Winchester to London, where he
engaged himself as corrector of the press to a printer of law-
books, named Tottel, in which capacity he became acquainted
with Sir Edward Coke and Chief Justice Popham, — one
of whom was afterwards to be the leading counsel against
him, and the other his judge. After continuing in this
employment for two years, during which he had meditated a
change in his religion, he went abroad, and travelling first to
Madrid, and then to Rome, saw enough of the Catholic
priesthood to confirm his resolution, and in 1575 he assumed
the habit of a Jesuit. Pursuing his studies with the utmost
zeal and ardour at the Jesuits' College, under the celebrated
Bellarmine, and the no less celebrated Clavius, he made such
progress that, upon the indisposition of the latter, he was
able to fill the mathematical chair. Nor was he less skilled
in philosophy, metaphysics, and divinity; and his knowledge
of Hebrew was so profound that he taught it publicly in the
Roman schools.

To an enthusiastic zeal in the cause of the religion he had

espoused, Garnet added great powers of persuasion and eloquence,—a combination of qualities well fitting him for the
office of a missionary priest; and undismayed by the dangers
he would have to encounter, and eager to propagate his doctrines, he solicited to be sent on this errand to his own
country. At the instance of Father Parsons, he received an
appointment to the mission of 1586, and he secretly landed
in England in the same year. Braving every danger, and
shrinking from no labour, he sought on all hands to make
proselytes to the ancient faith, and to sustain the wavering
courage of its professors. Two years afterwards on the imprisonment of the Superior of the Jesuits, being raised to that
important post, he was enabled to extend his sphere of action;
and redoubling his exertions in consequence, he so well discharged his duties, that it was mainly owing to him that the
Catholic party was kept together during the fierce persecutions of the latter end of Elizabeth's reign.

Compelled to personate various characters, as he travelled
from place to place, Garnet had acquired a remarkable facility
for disguise; and such was his address and courage, that he
not unfrequently imposed upon the very officers sent in pursuit of him. Up to the period of Elizabeth's demise, he had
escaped arrest; and, though involved in the treasonable
intrigue with the King of Spain, and other conspiracies, he
procured a general pardon under the great seal. His office
and profession naturally brought him into contact with the
chief Catholic families throughout the kingdom; and he
maintained an active correspondence with many of them by
means of his various agents and emissaries. The great object
of his life being the restoration of the fallen religion, to
accomplish this, as he conceived, great and desirable end,
he was prepared to adopt any means, however violent or
obnoxious. When, under the seal of confession, Catesby
revealed to him his dark designs, so far from discouraging
him, all he counselled was caution. Having tested the disposition of the wealthier Romanists to rise against their
oppressors, and finding a general insurrection, as has before
been stated, impracticable, he gave every encouragement and
assistance to the conspiracy forming among the more desperate and discontented of the party. At his instigation, the
present pilgrimage to Saint Winifred's Well was undertaken,
in the hope that, when so large a body of the Catholics were
collected together, some additional aid to the project might
be obtained.

One of the most mysterious and inexplicable portions of Garnet's history is that relating to Anne Vaux. This lady, the daughter of Lord Vaux of Harrowden, a rigid Catholic nobleman, and one of Garnet's earliest patrons and friends, on the death of her father in 1595, attached herself to his fortunes,—accompanied him in all his missions,—shared all his privations and dangers,—and, regardless of calumny or reproach, devoted herself entirely to his service. What is not less singular, her sister, who had married a Catholic gentleman named Brooksby, became his equally zealous attendant. Their enthusiasm produced a similar effect on Mr. Brooksby; and wherever Garnet went, all three accompanied him.

By his side, on the present occasion, stood Sir Everard Digby. Accounted one of the handsomest, most accomplished, and best-informed men of his time, Sir Everard, at the period of this history only twenty-four, had married, when scarcely sixteen, Maria, heiress of the ancient and honourable family of Mulshoe, with whom he obtained a large fortune, and the magnificent estate of Gothurst, or Gaythurst, in Buckinghamshire. Knighted by James the First at Belvoir Castle, on his way from Scotland to London, Digby, who had once formed one of the most brilliant ornaments of the court, had of late, in a great degree, retired from it. "Notwithstanding," writes Father Greenway, "that he had dwelt much in the Queen's court, and was in the way of obtaining honours and distinction by his graceful manners and rare parts, he chose rather to bear the cross with the persecuted Catholics, *et vivere abjectus in domo Domini*, than to sail through the pleasures of a palace and the prosperities of the world, to the shipwreck of his conscience and the destruction of his soul." Having only when he completed his minority professed the Catholic religion, he became deeply concerned at its fallen state, and his whole thoughts were bent upon its restoration. This change in feeling was occasioned chiefly, if not altogether, by Garnet, by whom his conversion had been accomplished.

Sir Everard Digby was richly attired in a black velvet doublet, with sleeves slashed with white satin, and wore a short mantle of the same material, similarly lined. He had the enormous trunk-hose, heretofore mentioned, as the distinguishing peculiarity of the custom of the period, and wore black velvet shoes, ornamented with white roses. An ample ruff encircled his throat. His hat was steeple-crowned, and somewhat broader in the leaf than was ordinarily worn, and shaded with a plume of black feathers. His hair was raven black, and he wore a pointed beard, and moustaches. His figure was tall and stately, and his features grave and finely formed.

By this time the group had been joined by the others, and a friendly greeting took place. Guy Fawkes was presented by Catesby to Sir William Radcliffe and Sir Everard Digby. To Garnet he required no introduction, and Father Oldcorne was known to all. After a little further conversation, the party adjourned to the house, which belonged to a Welsh Catholic gentleman named Griffiths, who though absent at the time, had surrendered it to the use of Sir Everard Digby and his friends.

On their entrance, Viviana was introduced by her father to Lady Digby, who presided as hostess, and welcomed her with great cordiality. She was then conducted to her own room, where she was speedily joined by Sir William; and they remained closeted together till summoned to the principal meal of the day. At the table, which was most hospitably served, Viviana found, in addition to her former companions, a large assemblage, to most of whom she was a stranger, consisting of Anne Vaux, Mr. Brooksby and his wife, Ambrose Rookwood, two brothers named Winter, two Wrights, Francis Tresham,—persons of whom it will be necessary to make particular mention hereafter,—and several others, in all amounting to thirty.

The meal over, the company dispersed, and Viviana and her father, passing through an open window, wandered forth upon a beautiful and spreading lawn, and thence under the shade of the beech-trees. They had not been long here, anxiously conferring on recent events, when they perceived Garnet and Catesby approaching.

"Father, dear father!" cried Viviana, hastily, "I was about to warn you; but I have not time to do so now. Some dark and dangerous plot is in agitation to restore our religion. Mr. Catesby is anxious to league you with it. Do not—do not yield to his solicitations!"

"Fear nothing on that score, Viviana," replied Sir William; "I have already perplexities enow without adding to them."

"I will leave you, then," she replied. And, as soon as the others came up, she made some excuse for withdrawing, and returned to the house. The window of her chamber com-

manded the avenue, and from it she watched the group. They
remained for a long time pacing up and down, in earnest
conversation. By-and-by they were joined by Oldcorne and
Fawkes. Then came a third party, consisting of the Winters
and Wrights; and, lastly, Sir Everard Digby and Tresham
swelled the list.

The assemblage was then harangued by Catesby, and the
most profound attention paid to his address. Viviana kept
her eye fixed upon her father's countenance, and from its
changing expression inferred what effect the speech produced
upon him. At its conclusion, the assemblage separated in
little groups; and she perceived, with great uneasiness, that
Father Garnet passed his arm through that of her father,
and led him away. Some time elapsed, and neither of them
reappeared.

"My warning was in vain; he *has* joined them!" she
exclaimed.

"No, Viviana!" cried her father's voice behind her, "I
have *not* joined them. Nor *shall* I do so."

"Heaven be praised!" she exclaimed, flinging her arms
around his neck.

Neither of them were aware that they were overheard by
Garnet, who had noiselessly followed Sir William into the
room, and muttered to himself, "For all this, he *shall* join
the plot, and she *shall* wed Catesby."

He then coughed slightly, to announce his presence; and,
apologizing to Viviana for the intrusion, told her he came
to confess her previously to the celebration of mass, which
would take place that evening, in a small chapel in the house.
Wholly obedient to the command of her spiritual advisers,
Viviana instantly signified her assent; and, her father having
withdrawn, she laid open the inmost secrets of her heart to
the Jesuit. Severely reprobating her love for a heretic, before
he would give her absolution, Garnet enjoined her, as a penance, to walk barefoot to the holy well on the morrow, and to
make a costly offering at the shrine of the saint. Compliance
being promised to his injunction, he pronounced the absolution, and departed.

Soon after this, mass was celebrated by Garnet, and the
sacrament administered to the assemblage.

An hour before daybreak, the party again assembled in the
chapel, where matins were performed; after which, the female
devotees, who were clothed in snow-white woollen robes, with
wide sleeves and hoods, and having large black crosses woven

in front, retired for a short time, and reappeared, with their feet bared, and hair unbound. Each had a large rosary attached to the cord that bound her waist.

Catesby thought Viviana had never appeared so lovely as in this costume; and as he gazed at her white and delicately formed feet, her small rounded ankles, her dark and abundant tresses falling in showers almost to the ground, he became more deeply enamoured than before. His passionate gaze was, however, unnoticed, as the object of it kept her eyes steadily fixed on the ground. Lady Digby, who was a most beautiful woman, scarcely appeared to less advantage; and, as she walked side by side with Viviana in the procession, the pair attracted universal admiration from all who beheld them.

Everything being at last in readiness, and the order of march fully arranged, two youthful choristers, in surplices, chanting a hymn to Saint Winifred, set forth. They were followed by two men bearing silken banners, on one of which was displayed the martyrdom of the saint whose shrine they were about to visit, and on the other a lamb carrying a cross; next came Fathers Oldcorne and Fisher, each sustaining a large silver crucifix; next, Garnet alone, in the full habit of his order; next, the females, in the attire before described, and walking two and two; next, Sir Everard Digby and Sir William Radcliffe; and lastly, the rest of the pilgrims, to the number of fourteen. These were all on foot. But at the distance of fifty paces behind them rode Guy Fawkes and Catesby, at the head of twenty well-armed and well-mounted attendants, intended to serve as a guard in case of need.

In such order, this singular procession moved forward at a slow pace, taking its course along a secluded road leading to the ridge of hills extending from the neighbourhood of Wrexham to Mold, and from thence, in an almost unbroken chain, to Holywell.

Along these heights, whence magnificent views were obtained of the broad estuary of the Dee and the more distant ocean, the train proceeded without interruption; and though the road selected was one seldom traversed, and through a country thinly peopled, still, the rumour of the pilgrimage having gone abroad, hundreds were stationed at different points to behold it. Some expressions of disapprobation were occasionally manifested by the spectators; but the presence of the large armed force effectually prevented any interference.

Whenever such a course could be pursued, the procession took its way over the sward. Still the sufferings of the females were severe in the extreme; and before Viviana had proceeded a mile, her white, tender feet were cut and bruised by the sharp flints over which she walked; every step she took leaving a bloody print behind it. Lady Digby was in little better condition. But such was the zeal by which they, in common with all the other devotees following them, were animated, that not a single murmur was uttered.

Proceeding in this way, they reached at mid-day a small stone chapel on the summit of the hill overlooking Plas-Newydd, where they halted, and devotions being performed, the females bathed their lacerated limbs in a neighbouring brook, after which they were rubbed with a cooling and odorous ointment. Thus refreshed, they again set forward, and halting a second time at Plas-Isaf, where similar religious ceremonies were observed, they rested for the day at a lodging prepared for their reception in the vicinity of Mold.

The night being passed in prayer, early in the morning they commenced their march in the same order as before. When Viviana first set her feet to the ground, she felt as if she were treading on hot iron, and the pain was so excruciating, that she could not repress a cry.

"Heed not your sufferings, dear daughter," observed Garnet, compassionately; "the waters of the holy fountain will heal the wounds both of soul and body."

Overcoming her agony by a powerful effort, she contrived to limp forward; and the whole party was soon after in motion. Halting for two hours at Pentre-Terfyn, and again at Skeviog, the train, towards evening, reached the summit of the hill overlooking Holywell, at the foot of which could be seen the ruins of Basingwerk Abbey, and the roof of the ancient chapel erected over the sacred spring. At this sight, those who were foremost in the procession fell on their knees; and the horsemen dismounting, imitated their example. An earnest supplication to Saint Winifred was then poured forth by Father Garnet, in which all the others joined, and a hymn in her honour chanted by the choristers.

Their devotions ended, the whole train arose, and walked slowly down the deep descent. As they entered the little town, which owes its name and celebrity to the miraculous spring rising within it, they were met by a large concourse of people, who had flocked from Flint and the other neighbouring places to witness the ceremonial. Most of the inhabitants of Holywell, holding their saintly patroness in the deepest veneration, viewed this pilgrimage to her shrine as a proper tribute of respect, while those of the opposite faith were greatly impressed by it. As the procession advanced, the crowd divided into two lines to allow it passage, and many fell on their knees imploring a blessing from Garnet, which he in no instance refused. When within a hundred yards of the sacred well, they were met by a priest, followed by another small train of pilgrims. A Latin oration having been pronounced by this priest, and replied to in the same language by Garnet, the train was once more put in motion, and presently reached the ancient fabric built over the sacred fountain.

The legend of Saint Winifred is so well known, that it is scarcely necessary to repeat it. For the benefit of the uninformed, however, it may be stated that she flourished about the middle of the seventh century, and was the daughter of Thewith, one of the chief lords of Wales. Devoutly educated by a monk named Beuno, who afterwards received canonization, she took the veil, and retired to a small monastery (the ruins of which still exist), built by her father near the scene of her subsequent martyrdom. Persecuted by the addresses of Caradoc, son of Alan, Prince of Wales, she fled from him to avoid his violence. He followed, and inflamed by fury at her resistance, struck off her head. For this atrocity, the earth instantly opened and swallowed him alive, while from the spot where the head had fallen gushed forth a fountain of unequalled force and purity, producing more than a hundred tons a minute. The bottom of this miraculous well is strewn with pebbles streaked with red veins, in memory of the virgin saint from whose blood it sprung. On its margin grows an odorous moss, while its gelid and translucent waters are esteemed a remedy for many disorders. Winifred's career did not terminate with her decapitation. Resuscitated by the prayers of Saint Beuno, she lived many years a life of the utmost sanctity, bearing, as a mark of the miracle performed in her behalf, a narrow crimson circle round her throat.

Passing the chapel adjoining the well built in the reign of Henry the Seventh by his mother, the pious Countess of Richmond, the pilgrims came to the swift clear stream rushing from the well. Instead of ascending the steps leading to the edifice built over the spring, they plunged into the stream, and crossing it entered a structure by a doorway on the further side. Erected by the Countess of Richmond at the

same period as the chapel, this structure, quadrangular in
form, and of great beauty, consists of light clustered pillars
and mouldings, supporting the most gorgeous tracery and
groining, the whole being ornamented with sculptured bosses,
pendent capitals, fretwork, niches, and tabernacles.   In the
midst is a large stone basin, to receive the water of the fountain, around which the procession now grouped, and as soon
as all were assembled, at the command of Father Garnet they
fell on their knees.

It was a solemn and striking sight to see this large group
prostrated around that beautiful fountain, and covered by
that ancient structure,—a touching thing to hear the voice
of prayer mingling with the sound of the rushing water.
After this, they all arose.   A hymn was then chanted, and
votive offerings made at the shrine of the saint.   The male
portion of the assemblage then followed Garnet to the chapel,
where further religious rites were performed, while the female
devotees, remaining near the fountain, resigned themselves
to the care of several attendants of their own sex, who, having
bathed their feet in the water, applied some of the fragrant
moss above described to the wounds; and, such was the faith
of the patients, or the virtue of the application, that in a
short time they all felt perfectly restored, and able to join
their companions in the chapel.   In this way the evening was
spent; and it was not until late that they finished their
devotions, and departed to the lodgings provided for them
in the town.

Impressed with a strange superstitious feeling, which he
could scarcely acknowledge to himself, Guy Fawkes determined to pass the night near the well.   Accordingly, without
communicating his intention to his companions, he threw
a small knapsack over his shoulder, containing a change of
linen, and a few articles of attire, and proceeded thither.

It was a brilliant moonlight night, and, as the radiance,
streaming through the thin clustered columns of the structure, lighted up its fairy architecture, and fell upon the clear
cold waves of the fountain, revealing the blood-streaked
pebbles beneath, the effect was inexpressibly beautiful.   So
charmed was Guy Fawkes by the sight that he remained for
some time standing near the edge of the basin, as if fasci-
nated by the marvellous spring that boiled up and sparkled
at his feet.   Resolved to try the efficacy of the bath, he threw
off his clothes and plunged into it.   The water was cold as
ice; but on emerging from it he felt wonderfully refreshed.

Having dressed himself, he wrapped his cloak around him, and, throwing himself on the stone floor, placed the knapsack under his head, and grasping a petronel in his right hand, to be ready in case of a surprise, disposed himself to slumber.

Accustomed to a soldier's couch, he soon fell asleep. He had not long closed his eyes when he dreamed that from out of the well a female figure, slight and unsubstantial as the element from which it sprang, arose. It was robed in what resembled a nun's garb; but so thin and vapoury, that the very moonlight shone through it. From the garments of the figure, as well as from the crimson circle round its throat, he knew that it must be the patroness of the place, the sainted Winifred, that he beheld. He felt no horror, but the deepest awe. The arm of the figure was raised,—its benignant regards fixed upon him,—and, as soon as it gained the level of the basin, it glided towards him.

XII.

THE VISION.

BEFORE daybreak on the following morning, Garnet, who had been engaged in earnest conference with Catesby during the whole of the night, repaired to the sacred spring for the purpose of bathing within it, and performing his solitary devotions at the shrine of the saint. On ascending the steps of the structure, he perceived Guy Fawkes kneeling beside the fountain, apparently occupied in prayer; and, being unwilling to disturb him, he paused. Finding, however, after the lapse of a few minutes, that he did not move, he advanced towards him, and was about to lay his hand upon his shoulder, when he was arrested by the very extraordinary expression of his countenance. His lips were partly open, but perfectly motionless, and his eyes, almost starting from their sockets, were fixed upon the boiling waters of the spring. His hands were clasped, and his look altogether was that of one whose faculties were benumbed by awe or terror.

Aware of the fanatical and enthusiastical character of Fawkes, Garnet had little doubt that, by keeping long vigil at the fountain, he had worked himself into such a state of over-excitement as to imagine he beheld some preternatural appearance; and it was with some curiosity that he awaited the result. Glancing in the same direction, his eye rested upon the bottom of the well, but he could discern nothing except the glittering and blood-streaked pebbles, and the reflection of the early sunbeams that quivered on its steaming surface. At length, a convulsion passed over the frame of the kneeler, and heaving a deep sigh he arose. Turning to quit the spring, he confronted Garnet, and demanded, in a low voice:

"Have you likewise seen the vision, father?"

Garnet made no reply, but regarded him steadfastly.

"Has the blessed Winifred appeared to you, I say?" continued Fawkes.

"No," answered Garnet; "I am but just come hither. It is for you, my son,—the favoured of Heaven,—for whom such glorious visions are reserved. I have seen nothing. How did the saint manifest herself to you?"

"In her earthly form," replied Fawkes; "or rather, I should say, in the semblance of the form she bore on earth. Listen to me, father. I came hither last night to make my couch beside the fountain. After plunging into it, I felt marvellously refreshed, and disposed myself to rest on that stone. Scarcely had my eyes closed when the saintly virgin appeared to me. Oh, father, it was a vision of seraphic beauty, such as the eye of man hath seldom seen!"

"And such only as it is permitted the elect of Heaven to see," observed Garnet.

"Alas! father," rejoined Guy Fawkes, "I can lay little claim to such an epithet. Nay, I begin to fear that I have incurred the displeasure of Heaven."

"Think not so, my son," replied Garnet, uneasily. "Relate your vision, and I will interpret it to you."

"Thus then it was, father," returned Fawkes. "The figure of the saint arose from out the well, and gliding towards me laid its finger upon my brow. My eyes opened, but I was as one oppressed with a nightmare, unable to move. I then thought I heard my name pronounced by a voice so wondrously sweet that my senses were quite ravished. Fain would I have prostrated myself, but my limbs refused their office. Neither could I speak, for my tongue was also enchained."

"Proceed, my son," observed Garnet; "I am curious to know what ensued."

"Father," replied Guy Fawkes, "if the form I beheld was that of Saint Winifred,—and that it was so, I cannot doubt, —the enterprise on which we are engaged will fail. It is *not* approved by Heaven. The vision warned me to desist."

"You cannot desist, my son," rejoined Garnet, sternly. "Your oath binds you to the project."

"True," replied Fawkes; "and I have no thought of abandoning it. But I am well assured it will not be successful."

"Your thinking so, my son, will be the most certain means of realizing your apprehensions," replied Garnet, gravely. "But let me hear the exact words of the spirit. You may have misunderstood them."

"I cannot repeat them precisely, father," replied Fawkes; "but I could not misapprehend their import, which was the deepest commiseration for our forlorn and fallen Church, but a positive interdiction against any attempt to restore it by bloodshed. 'Suffer on,' said the spirit; 'bear the yoke patiently, and in due season God will avenge your wrongs, and free you from oppression. You are thus afflicted that your faith may be purified. But if you resort to violence, you will breed confusion, and injure, not serve, the holy cause on which you are embarked.' Such, father, was the language of the saint. It was uttered in a tone so tender and sympathizing, that every word found an echo in my heart, and I repented having pledged myself to the undertaking. But, when I tell you that she added that all concerned in the conspiracy should perish, perhaps you may be deterred from proceeding further."

"Never!" returned Garnet. "Nor will I suffer any one engaged in it to retreat. What matter if a few perish, if the many survive? Our blood will not be shed in vain, if the true religion of God is restored. Nay, as strongly as the blessed Winifred herself resisted the impious ravisher, Caradoc, will I resist all inducements to turn aside from my purpose. It may be that the enterprise *will* fail. It may be that we *shall* perish. But if we die thus, we shall die as martyrs, and our deaths will be highly profitable to the Catholic religion."

"I doubt it," observed Fawkes.

"My son," said Garnet, solemnly, "I have ever looked upon you as one destined to be the chief agent in the great work of redemption. I have thought that, like Judith, you were chosen to destroy the Holofernes who oppresses us.

H

Having noted in you a religious fervour and resolution admirably fitting you for the task, I thought, and still think, you expressly chosen by Heaven for it. But, if you have any misgiving, I beseech you to withdraw from it. I will absolve you from your oath; and, enjoining you only to strictest secrecy, will pray you to depart at once, lest your irresolution should be communicated to the others."

"Fear nothing from me, father," rejoined Fawkes. "I have no irresolution, no wavering, nor shall any engaged with us be shaken by my apprehension. You have asked me what I saw and heard, and I have told you truly. But I will speak of it no more."

"It will be well to observe silence, my son," answered Garnet; "for though you, like myself, are unnerved, its effect on others might be injurious. But you have not yet brought your relation to an end. How did the figure disappear?"

"As it arose, father," replied Fawkes. "Uttering in a sweet but solemn voice, which yet rings in my ears, the words, 'Be warned!' it glided back to the fountain, whose waves as it approached grew still, and gradually melted from my view."

"But when I came hither, you appeared to be gazing at the spring," said Garnet. "What did you then behold?"

"My first impulse on awakening about an hour ago," replied Fawkes, "was to prostrate myself before the fountain, and to entreat the intercession of the saint who had thus marvellously revealed herself to me. As I prayed, methought its clear lucid waters became turbid, and turned to the colour of blood"

"It is a type of the blood of slaughtered brethren of our faith, which has been shed by our oppressors," rejoined Garnet.

"Rather of our own, which shall be poured forth in this cause," retorted Fawkes. "No matter. I am prepared to lose the last drop of mine."

"And I," said Garnet; "and, I doubt not, like those holy men who have suffered for their faith, that we shall both win a crown of martyrdom."

"Amen!" exclaimed Fawkes. "And you think the sacrifice we are about to offer will prove acceptable to God?"

"I am convinced of it, my son," answered Garnet. "And I take the sainted virgin, from whose blood this marvellous spring was produced, to witness that I devote myself unhesitatingly to the project, and that I firmly believe it will profit our Church."

As he spoke, a singular circumstance occurred, which did not fail to produce an impression on both parties,—especially Guy Fawkes. A violent gust of wind, apparently suddenly aroused, whistled through the slender columns of the structure, and catching the surface of the water, dashed it in tiny waves against their feet.

"The saint is offended," observed Fawkes.

"It would almost seem so," replied Garnet, after a pause. "Let us proceed to the chapel, and pray at her shrine. We will confer on this matter hereafter. Meantime, swear to me that you will observe profound secrecy respecting this vision."

"I swear," replied Guy Fawkes.

At this moment, another and more violent gust agitated the fountain.

"We will tarry here no longer," said Garnet. "I am not proof against these portents of ill."

So saying, he led the way to the chapel. Here they were presently joined by several of the female devotees, including Viviana, Anne Vaux, and Lady Digby. Matins were then said, after which various offerings were made at the shrine of the saint. Lady Digby presented a small tablet set in gold, representing on one side the martyrdom of Saint Winifred, and on the other the Salutation of Our Lady. Anne Vaux gave a small enamelled cross of gold; Viviana a girdle of the same metal, with a pendant sustaining a small Saint John's head surrounded with pearls.

"Mine will be a poor soldier's offering," said Guy Fawkes, approaching the shrine, which was hung around with the crutches, staves, and bandages of those cured by the healing waters of the miraculous spring. "This small silver scallop-shell, given me by a pilgrim, who died in my arms near the chapel of Saint James of Compostella, in Spain, is the sole valuable I possess."

"It will be as acceptable as a more costly gift, my son," replied Garnet, placing it on the shrine.

Of all the offerings then made, that silver scallop-shell is the only one preserved.

XIII.

THE CONSPIRATORS.

On Viviana's return from her devotions, she found her father in the greatest perturbation and alarm. The old steward, Heydocke, who had ridden express from Ordsall Hall, had just arrived, bringing word that the miserable fate of the pursuivant and his crew had aroused the whole country; that officers, attended by a strong force, and breathing vengeance, were in pursuit of Sir William Radcliffe and his daughter; that large sums were offered for the capture of Guy Fawkes and Father Oldcorne; that most of the servants were imprisoned; that he himself had escaped with great difficulty; and that, to sum up this long catalogue of calamities. Master Humphrey Chetham was arrested, and placed in the New Fleet. "In short, my dear young mistress," concluded the old man, "as I have just observed to Sir William, all is over with us, and there is nothing left but the grave."

"What course have you resolved upon, dear father?" inquired Viviana, turning anxiously to him.

"I shall surrender myself," he answered. "I am guilty of no crime, and can easily clear myself from all imputation."

"You are mistaken," she replied. "Do not hope for justice from those who know it not. But, while the means of escape are allowed you, avail yourself of them."

"No, Viviana," replied Sir William Radcliffe, firmly; "my part is taken. I shall abide the arrival of the officers. For you, I shall entrust you to the care of Mr. Catesby."

"You cannot mean this, dear father," she cried, with a look of distress. "And if you do, I will never consent to such an arrangement."

"Mr. Catesby is strongly attached to you, child," replied Sir William, "and will watch over your safety as carefully as I could do myself."

"He may be attached to me," rejoined Viviana, "though I doubt the disinterestedness of his love. But nothing can remove my repugnance to him. Forgive me, therefore, if, in this one instance, I decline to obey your commands. I dare not trust myself with Mr. Catesby."

"How am I to understand you?" inquired Sir William.

"Do not ask me to explain, dear father," she answered, "but imagine I must have good reason for what I say. Since you are resolved upon surrendering yourself, I will go into captivity with you. The alternative is less dreadful than that you have proposed."

"You distract me, child," cried the knight, rising and pacing the chamber in great agitation. "I cannot bear the thought of your imprisonment. Yet if I fly, I appear to confess myself guilty."

"If your worship will entrust Mistress Viviana with me," interposed the old steward, "I will convey her whithersoever you direct,—will watch over her day and night,—and, if need be, die in her defence."

"Thou wert ever a faithful servant, good Heydocke," rejoined Sir William, extending his hand kindly to him, "and art as true in adversity as in prosperity."

"Shame to me if I were not," replied Heydocke, pressing the knight's fingers to his lips and bathing them in his tears. "Shame to me if I hesitated to lay down my life for a master to whom I owe so much."

"If it is your pleasure, dear father," observed Viviana, "I will accompany Master Heydocke; but I would far rather be permitted to remain with you." ·

"It would avail nothing," replied Sir William; "we should be separated by the officers. Retire to your chamber, and prepare for instant departure; and, in the meanwhile, I will consider what is best to be done."

"Your worship's decision must be speedy," observed Heydocke; "I had only a few hours' start of the officers. They will be here ere long."

"Take this purse," replied Sir William, "and hire three of the fleetest horses you can procure, and station yourself at the outskirts of the town, on the road to Saint Asaph. You understand ?"

"Perfectly," replied Heydocke. And he departed to execute his master's commands, while Viviana withdrew to her own chamber.

Left alone, the knight was perplexing himself as to where he should shape his course, when he was interrupted by the sudden entrance of Catesby and Garnet.

"We have just met your servant," Sir William," said the former, "and have learnt the alarming intelligence he has brought."

"What is your counsel in this emergency, father?" said Radcliffe, appealing to Garnet.

"Flight—instant flight, my son," was the answer.

"My counsel is resistance," said Catesby. "We are here assembled in large numbers, and are well armed. Let us await the arrival of the officers, and see whether they will venture to arrest you."

"They will arrest us all, if they have force sufficient to do so," replied Garnet; "and there are many reasons, as you well know, why it is desirable to avoid any disturbance at present."

" True," replied Catesby. " What say you then," he continued, addressing Radcliffe, " to our immediate return to
Holt, where means may be found to screen you till this storm
has blown over ?"

Sir William having assented to the proposal, Catesby instantly departed to acquaint the others, and, as soon as
preparations could be made, and horses procured, the whole
party composing the pilgrimage quitted Holywell, and ascending the hill at the back of the town, took the direction
of Mold, where they arrived, having ridden at a swift pace,
in about half an hour. From thence they proceeded, without accident or interruption, to the mansion they had recently
occupied near Holt. On reaching it all the domestics were
armed, and certain of their number stationed at the different
approaches to the house to give the alarm in case of the
enemy's appearance. But as nothing occurred during the
night, the fears of Sir William and his friends began in some
degree to subside.

About noon, on the following day, as Guy Fawkes, who
ever since the vision at Saint Winifred's Well had shunned
all companionship, walked forth beneath the avenue alone,
he heard a light step behind him, and, turning, beheld
Viviana. Gravely bowing, he was about to pursue his
course, when quickening her pace, she was instantly by his
side.

" I have a favour to solicit," she said.

" There is none I would refuse you," answered Fawkes,
halting ; " but, though I have the will, I may not have the
power to grant your request."

" Hear me, then," she replied, hurriedly. " Of all my father's
friends—of all who are here assembled, you are the only
one I dare trust—the only one from whom I can hope for
assistance."

" I am at once flattered and perplexed by your words,
Viviana," he rejoined ; nor can I guess whither they tend.
But speak freely. If I cannot render you aid, I can at least
give you counsel."

" I must premise, then," said Viviana, " that I am aware,
from certain obscure hints let fall by Father Oldcorne, that
you, Mr. Catesby, and others are engaged in a dark and
dangerous conspiracy."

" Viviana Radcliffe," returned Guy Fawkes, sternly, " you
have once before avowed your knowledge of this plot. I will
not attempt disguise with you. A project is in agitation for

the deliverance of our fallen Church; and since you have become acquainted with its existence—no matter how—you must be bound by an oath of secrecy, or," and his look grew darker, and his voice sterner, "I will not answer for your life."

"I will willingly take the oath on certain conditions," said Viviana.

"You must take it unconditionally," rejoined Fawkes.

"Hear me out," said Viviana. "Knowing that Mr. Catesby and Father Garnet are anxious to induce my father to join this conspiracy, I came hither to implore you to prevent him from doing so."

"Were I even willing to do this—which I am not," replied Fawkes, "I have not the power. Sir William Ratcliffe would be justly indignant at any interference on my part."

"Heed not that," replied Viviana. "You, I fear, are linked to this fearful project beyond the possibility of being set free. But he is not. Save him! save him!"

"I will take no part in urging him to join it," replied Fawkes. "But I can promise nothing further."

"Then, mark me," she returned; "if further attempts are made by any of your confederates to league him with their plot, I myself will disclose all I know of it."

"Viviana," rejoined Fawkes, in a threatening tone, "I again warn you that you endanger your life."

"I care not," she rejoined; "I would risk twenty lives, if I possessed them, to preserve my father."

"You are a noble-hearted lady," replied Fawkes, unable to repress the admiration inspired by her conduct; "and if I can accomplish what you desire, I will. But I see not how it can be done."

"Everything is possible to one of your resolution," replied Viviana.

"Well, well," replied Fawkes, a slight smile crossing his rugged features; "the effort at least shall be made."

"Thanks! thanks!" ejaculated Viviana; and, overcome by her emotion, she sank half fainting into his arms.

While he held her thus, debating within himself whether he should convey her to the house, Garnet and Catesby appeared at the other end of the avenue. Their surprise at the sight was extreme; nor was it less when Viviana, opening her eyes as they drew near, uttered a slight cry and disappeared.

"This requires an explanation," said Catesby, glancing fiercely at Fawkes.

"You must seek it, then, of the lady," rejoined the latter, moodily.

"It will be easily explained, I have no doubt," interposed Garnet. "Miss Ratcliffe was seized with a momentary weakness, and her companion offered her support."

"That will scarcely suffice for me," cried Catesby.

"Let the subject be dropped for the present," rejoined Garnet, authoritatively. "More important matter claims our attention. We came to seek you, my son," he continued, addressing Fawkes. "All those engaged in the great enterprise are about to meet in a summer-house in the garden."

"I am ready to attend you," replied Fawkes. "Will Sir William Radcliffe be there?"

"No," replied Garnet; "he has not yet joined us. None will be present at this meeting but the sworn conspirators."

With this, the trio took their way towards the garden, and proceeding along a walk edged with clipped yew-trees, came to the summer-house—a small circular building overrun with ivy and creepers, and ornamented in front by two stone statues on pedestals. Here they found Sir Edward Digby, Ambrose Rookwood, Francis Tresham, Thomas and Robert Winter, John and Christopher Wright, awaiting their arrival.

The door being closed and bolted, Garnet, placing himself in the midst of the assemblage, said, "Before we proceed further, I will again administer the oath to all present." Drawing from his vest a primer, and addressing Sir Everard Digby, he desired him to kneel, and continued thus in a solemn tone: "You shall swear by the Blessed Trinity, and by the sacrament you propose to receive, never to disclose directly nor indirectly, by word or circumstance, the matter that shall be proposed to you to keep secret, nor desist from the execution thereof, until the rest shall give you leave."

"I swear," replied Digby, kissing the primer.

The oath was then taken in like manner by the others. This done, Catesby was about to address the meeting, when Tresham, glancing uneasily at the door, remarked: "Are you assured we have no eavesdroppers?"

"I will keep watch without," rejoined Fawkes, "if you have any fears."

"It were better," replied Robert Winter. "We cannot be too cautious. But if you go forth, you will not be able to take part in the discussion."

"My part is to act, not to talk," rejoined Fawkes, marching towards the door. And shutting it after him, he took up his position outside.

Upon this Catesby commenced a long and inflammatory harangue, in which he expatiated with great eloquence and fervour on the wrongs of the Catholic party, and the deplorable condition of their Church. "It were easy to slay the tyrant by whom we are oppressed," he said, in conclusion; "but his destruction would be small gain to us. We must strike deeper, to hew down the baneful stock of heresy. All our adversaries must perish with him, and in such a manner as shall best attest the vengeance of Heaven. Placed beneath the Parliament-house, a mine of powder shall hurl its heretical occupants into the air—nor shall any one survive the terrible explosion. Are we all agreed to this plan?"

All the conspirators expressed their assent except Sir Everard Digby.

"Before I give my concurrence to the measure," observed the latter, "I would fain be resolved by Father Garnet whether it is lawful to destroy some few of our own faith with so many heretics."

"Unquestionably, my son," replied Garnet. "As in besieging a city we have a right to kill all within it, whether friends or enemies, so in this case we are justified in destroying the innocent with the guilty, because their destruction will be advantageous to the Catholic cause."

"I am satisfied," replied Digby.

"As to the tyrant and apostate James," continued Garnet, "he is excommunicated, and his subjects released from their allegiance. I have two breves sent over by his holiness Pope Clement VIII. three years ago, one directed to the clergy, and the other to the nobility of this realm, wherein, alluding to Queen Elizabeth, it is expressly declared that, 'so soon as that miserable woman should depart out of this life, none shall be permitted to ascend the throne, how near soever in proximity of blood, unless they are such as will not only tolerate the Catholic faith, but in every way support it. By this brief, James is expressly excluded. He has betrayed, not supported the Church of Rome. Having broken his word with us, and oppressed our brethren more rigorously even than his predecessor, the remorseless Elizabeth, he is unworthy longer to reign and must be removed."

"He must," reiterated the conspirators.

"The Parliament-house being the place where all the mischief done us has been contrived by our adversaries, it is fitting that it should be the place of their chastisement," remarked Catesby.

"Doubtless," rejoined Ambrose Rookwood.

" Yet if the blow we meditate should miscarry," observed Thomas Winter, " the injury to the Catholic religion will be so great, that not only our enemies, but our very friends will condemn us."

" There is no chance of miscarriage, if we are true to each other," returned Catesby, confidently. " And if I suspected any one of treachery, I would plunge my sword into his bosom, were he my brother."

" You would do wrong to act thus on mere suspicion," remarked Tresham, who stood near him.

" In a case like this, he who gives the slightest ground for doubt would merit death," replied Catesby, sternly; " and I would slay him."

" Hum !" exclaimed Tresham, uneasily.

" Mr. Catesby will now perhaps inform us what has been done to carry the project into effect?" inquired Sir Everard Digby.

" A small habitation has been taken by one of our confederates, Mr. Thomas Percy, immediately adjoining the Parliament-house," replied Catesby, " from the cellar of which it is proposed to dig a mine through the wall of the devoted building, and to deposit within it a sufficient quantity of gunpowder and other combustibles to accomplish our purpose. This mine must be digged by ourselves, as we can employ no assistants, and will be a laborious and dangerous task. But I for one will cheerfully undertake it."

" And I," said the elder Wright.

" And I," cried several others.

" Supposing the mine digged, and the powder deposited," observed Ambrose Rookwood, " whose hand will fire the train ?"

" Mine !" cried Guy Fawkes, throwing open the door. As soon as he had spoken, he retired and closed it after him.

" He will keep his word," remarked Garnet. " He is of a nature so resolute that he would destroy himself with the victims rather than fail. Catiline was not a bolder conspirator than Guy Fawkes."

" Well, gentlemen," observed Catesby, " we are now at the latter end of July. All must be ready against the meeting of Parliament in November."

" There is some likelihood, I hear, that the meeting of the House will be prorogued till February," remarked Tresham.

" So much the better," rejoined Catesby, " it will give us more time for preparation."

"So much the worse, I think," cried Ambrose Rookwood. "Delays are ever dangerous, and doubly dangerous in a case like ours."

"I am far from desiring to throw any impediment in the way of our design," observed Sir Everard Digby, "but I would recommend before we proceed to this terrible extremity, that one last effort should be made to move the King in our behalf."

"It is useless," replied Catesby. "So far from toleration, he meditates severer measures against us; and, I am well assured, if Parliament is allowed to meet, such laws will be passed as will bring all of us within premunire. No, no. We have no hope from James, nor his ministers."

"Nor yet from France or Spain," observed Thomas Winter. "In my conference with the Constable Velasco, at Bergen, I received assurances of the good-will of Philip towards us, but no distinct promise of interference in our behalf. The Archduke Albert is well disposed, but he can render no assistance. We must depend upon ourselves."

"Ay, marry, must we," replied Catesby, "and fortunate is it that we have devised a plan by which we can accomplish our purpose unaided. We only require funds to follow up with effect the blow we shall strike."

"My whole fortune shall be placed at your disposal," replied Sir Everard Digby.

"Part of mine has already been given," said Tresham, "and the rest shall follow."

"Would I had aught to peril in the matter except my life," said Catesby. "I would throw everything upon the stake."

"You do enough in venturing thus much, my son," rejoined Garnet. "To you the whole conduct of the enterprise is committed."

"I live for nothing else," replied Catesby, "and if I see it successful, I shall have lived long enough."

"Cannot Sir William Radcliffe be induced to join us?" asked Rookwood. "He would be an important acquisition, and his wealth would prove highly serviceable."

"I have sounded him," answered Catesby. "But he appears reluctant."

"Be not satisfied with one attempt," urged Christopher Wright. "The jeopardy in which he now stands may make him change his mind."

"I am loth to interrupt the discussion," returned Garnet, "but I think we have tarried here long enough. We will

meet again at midnight, when I hope to introduce Sir William
Radcliffe to you as a confederate."

The party then separated, and Garnet went in search of the
knight.

Ascertaining that he was in his own chamber, he proceeded
thither, and found him alone. Entering at once upon the
subject in hand, Garnet pleaded his cause with so much zeal
that he at last wrung a reluctant consent from the listener.
Scarcely able to conceal his exultation, he then proposed to
Sir William to adjourn with him to the private chapel in the
house, where, having taken the oath, and received the sacrament upon it, he should forthwith be introduced to the conspirators, and the whole particulars of the plot revealed to
him. To this the knight, with some hesitation, agreed. As
they traversed a gallery leading to the chapel, they met
Viviana. For the first time in his life Radcliffe's gaze sank
before his daughter, and he would have passed her without
speaking had she not stopped him.

"Father! dear father!" she cried, "I know whither you
are going—and for what purpose. Do not—do not join
them."

Sir William Radcliffe made no reply, but endeavoured
gently to push her aside.

She would not, however, be repulsed, but prostrating herself before him, clasped his knees, and besought him not to
proceed.

Making a significant gesture to Sir William, Garnet walked
forward.

"Viviana," cried the knight, sternly, "my resolution is
taken. I command you to retire to your chamber."

So saying, he broke from her, and followed Garnet. Clasping her hands to her brow, Viviana gazed for a moment with
a frenzied look after him, and then rushed from the gallery.

On reaching the chapel, Sir William, who had been much
shaken by this meeting, was some minutes in recovering his
composure. Garnet employed the time in renewing his arguments, and with so much address that he succeeded in quieting
the scruples of conscience which had been awakened in the
knight's breast by his daughter's warning.

"And now, my son," he said, "since you have determined
to enrol your name in the list of those sworn to deliver their
Church from oppression, take this primer in your hand, and
kneel down before the altar, while I administer the oath
which is to unite you to us."

Garnet then advanced towards the altar, and Sir William

was about to prostrate himself upon a cushion beside it, when the door was suddenly thrown open, and Guy Fawkes strode into the chapel.

"Hold!" he exclaimed, grasping Radcliffe's right arm, and fixing his dark glance upon him; "you shall not take that oath."

"What mean you?" cried Garnet, who, as well as the knight, was paralyzed with astonishment at this intrusion. "Sir William Radcliffe is about to join us."

"I know it," replied Fawkes; "but it may not be. He has no heart in the business, and will lend it no efficient assistance. We are better without him than with him."

As he spoke, he took the primer from the knight's hand, and laid it upon the altar.

"This conduct is inexplicable," cried Garnet, angrily. "You will answer for it to others, as well as to me."

"I will answer for it to all," replied Guy Fawkes. "Let Sir William Radcliffe declare before me and before Heaven, that he approves the measure, and I am content he should take the oath."

"I cannot belie my conscience by saying so," replied the knight, who appeared agitated by conflicting emotions.

"Yet you have promised to join us," cried Garnet, reproachfully.

"Better break that promise than a solemn oath," rejoined Guy Fawkes, sternly. "Sir William Radcliffe, there are reasons why you should not join this conspiracy. Examine your inmost heart and it will tell you what they are."

"I understand you," replied the knight.

"Get hence," cried Garnet, unable to control his indignation, or I will pronounce our Church's most terrible malediction against you."

"I shall not shrink from it, father," rejoined Fawkes, humbly, but firmly, "seeing I am acting rightly."

"Undeceive yourself, then, at once," returned Garnet, "and learn that you are thwarting our great and holy purpose."

"On the contrary," replied Fawkes, "I am promoting it, by preventing one from joining it who will endanger its success."

"You are a traitor!" cried Garnet, furiously.

"A traitor!" exclaimed Guy Fawkes, his eye blazing with fierce lustre, though his voice and demeanour were unaltered —"I who have been warned thrice—twice by the dead—and lastly by a vision from heaven, yet still remain firm to my purpose—I who have voluntarily embraced the most dangerous and difficult part of the enterprise—I, who would suffer the utmost extremity of torture, rather than utter a word that should reveal it—a traitor! No, father, I am none. If you think so, take this sword and at once put an end to your doubts."

There was something so irresistible in the manner of Guy Fawkes, that Garnet remained silent.

"Do with me what you please," continued Fawkes; "but do not compel Sir William Radcliffe to join the conspiracy. He will be fatal to it."

"No one shall compel me to join it," replied the knight.

"Perhaps it is better thus," returned Garnet, after a pause, during which he was buried in reflection. "I will urge you no further, my son. But before you depart you must swear not to divulge what you have just learnt."

"Willingly," replied the knight.

"There is another person who must also take that oath," said Guy Fawkes, having accidentally become acquainted with as much as yourself."

And stepping out of the chapel, he immediately afterwards returned with Viviana.

"You will now understand why I would not allow Sir William to join the conspiracy," he observed to Garnet.

"I do," replied the latter, gloomily.

The oath administered, the knight and his daughter quitted the chapel, accompanied by Guy Fawkes. Viviana was profuse in her expressions of gratitude, nor was her father less earnest in his acknowledgments.

A few hours after this, Sir William Radcliffe informed Sir Everard Digby that it was his intention to depart immediately, and, though the latter attempted to dissuade him by representing the danger to which he would be exposed, he continued inflexible. The announcement surprised both Catesby and Garnet, who were present when it was made, and added their entreaties to those of Digby—but without effect. Catesby's proposal to serve as an escort was likewise refused by Sir William, who said he had no fears, and when questioned as to his destination, he returned an evasive answer. This sudden resolution of the knight, coupled with his refusal to join the plot, alarmed the conspirators, and more than one expressed fears of treachery. Sir Everard Digby, however, was not of the number, but asserted that Radcliffe was a man of the highest honour, and he would answer for his secrecy with his life.

"Will you answer for that of his daughter?" demanded Tresham.

"*I* will," replied Fawkes.

"To put the matter beyond a doubt," observed Catesby. " I will set out shortly after him, and follow him unobserved till he halts for the night, and ascertain whether he stops at any suspicious quarter."

"Do so, my son," replied Garnet.

"It is needless," observed Sir Everard Digby; "but do as you please."

By this time, Radcliffe's horses being brought round by Heydocke, he and his daughter took a hasty leave of their friends. When they had been gone a few minutes, Catesby called for his steed; and, after exchanging a word or two with Garnet, rode after them. He had proceeded about a couple of miles along a cross-road leading to Nantwich, which he learnt from some cottagers was the route taken by the party before him, when he heard the tramp of a horse in the rear, and, turning at the sound, beheld Guy Fawkes. Drawing in the bridle, he halted till the latter came up, and angrily demanded on what errand he was bent.

"My errand is the same as your own," replied Fawkes. "I intend to follow Sir William Radcliffe, and, if need be, defend him."

Whatever Catesby's objections might be to this companion-ship, he did not think fit to declare them, and, though evidently much displeased, suffered Guy Fawkes to ride by his side without opposition.

Having gained the summit of the mountainous range extending from Malpas to Tottenhall, whence they beheld the party whose course they were tracking enter a narrow lane at the foot of the hill, Catesby, fearful of losing sight of them, set spurs to his steed. Guy Fawkes kept close beside him, and they did not slacken their pace until they reached the lane.

Having proceeded along it for a quarter of a mile, they were alarmed by the sudden report of fire-arms, followed by a loud shriek, which neither of them doubted was uttered by Viviana. Again dashing forward, on turning a corner of the road, they beheld the party surrounded by half a dozen troopers. Sir William Radcliffe had shot one of his assailants, and, assisted by Heydocke, was defending himself bravely against the others. With loud shouts, Catesby and Guy Fawkes galloped towards the scene of strife. But they were too late. A bullet pierced the knight's brain; and he

no sooner fell, than, regardless of himself, the old steward
flung away his sword, and threw himself, with the most
piteous lamentations, on the body.

Viviana, meanwhile, had been compelled to dismount, and
was in the hands of the troopers. On seeing her father's
fate, her shrieks were so heart-piercing, that even her captors
were moved to compassion. Fighting his way towards her,
Catesby cut down one of the troopers, and snatching her
from the grasp of the other, who was terrified by the furious
assault, placed her on the saddle beside him, and striking
spurs into his charger at the same moment, leapt the hedge,
and made good his retreat.

This daring action, however, could not have been accomplished without the assistance of Guy Fawkes, who warded
off with his rapier all the blows aimed at him and his lovely
charge. While thus engaged, he received a severe cut on the
head, which stretched him senseless and bleeding beneath his
horse's feet.

XIV.

THE PACKET.

ON recovering from the effects of the wound he had received
from the trooper, Guy Fawkes found himself stretched upon
a small bed in a cottage, with Viviana and Catesby watching
beside him. A thick fold of linen was bandaged round his
head, and he was so faint from the great effusion of blood he
had sustained, that after gazing vacantly around him for a
few minutes, and but imperfectly comprehending what he
beheld, his eyes closed, and he relapsed into insensibility.
Restoratives being applied, he revived in a short time, and,
in answer to his inquiries how he came thither, was informed
by Catesby that he had been left for dead by his assailants,
who, contenting themselves with making the old steward
prisoner, had ridden off in the direction of Chester.

"What has become of Sir William Radcliffe?" asked the
wounded man in a feeble voice.

Catesby raised his finger to his lips, and Fawkes learnt the
distressing nature of the question he had asked by the agonizing cry that burst from Viviana. Unable to control her
grief, she withdrew, and Catesby then told him that the body
of Sir William Radcliffe was lying in an adjoining cottage,

whither it had been transported from the scene of the conflict; adding that it was Viviana's earnest desire that it should be conveyed to Manchester to the family vault in the Collegiate Church; but that he feared her wish could not be safely complied with. A messenger, however, had been despatched to Holt; and Sir Everard Digby, and Fathers Garnet and Oldcorne, were momentarily expected, when some course would be decided upon for the disposal of the unfortunate knight's remains.

"Poor Viviana!" groaned Fawkes. "She has now no protector."

"Rest easy on that score," rejoined Catesby. "She shall never want one while I live."

The wounded man fixed his eyes, now blazing with red and unnatural light, inquiringly upon him, but he said nothing.

"I know what you mean," continued Catesby; "you think I shall wed her, and you are in the right. I shall. The marriage is essential to our enterprise; and the only obstacle to it is removed."

Fawkes attempted to reply, but his parched tongue refused its office. Catesby arose, and carefully raising his head, held a cup of water to his lips. The sufferer eagerly drained it, and would have asked for more; but seeing that the request would be refused, he left it unuttered.

"Have you examined my wound?" he said, after a pause.

Catesby answered in the affirmative.

"And do you judge it mortal?" continued Fawkes. "Not that I have any fear of Death. I have looked him in the face too often for that. But I have somewhat on my mind which I would fain discharge before my earthly pilgrimage is ended."

"Do not delay it then," rejoined the other. "Knowing I speak to a soldier, and a brave one, I do not hesitate to tell you your hours are numbered."

"Heaven's will be done!" exclaimed Fawkes, in a tone of resignation. "I thought myself destined to be one of the chief instruments of the restoration of our holy religion. But I find I was mistaken. When Father Garnet arrives, I beseech you let me see him instantly. Or, if he should not come speedily, entreat Miss Radcliffe to grant me a few moments in private."

"Why not unburthen yourself to me?" returned Catesby, distrustfully. "In your circumstances I should desire no

better confessor than a brother soldier—no other crucifix
than a sword-hilt."

"Nor I," rejoined Fawkes. "But this is no confession
I am about to make. What I have to say relates to others,
not to myself."

"Indeed!" exclaimed Catesby. "Then there is the more
reason why it should not be deferred. I hold it my duty to
tell you that the fever of your wound will, in all probability,
produce delirium. Make your communication while your
senses remain to you. And whatever you enjoin shall be
rigorously fulfilled."

"Will you swear this?" cried Fawkes, eagerly. But before
an answer could be returned, he added, in an altered tone,
"No—no—it cannot be."

"This is no time for anger," rejoined Catesby, sternly,
"or I should ask whether you doubt the assurance I have
given you?"

"I doubt nothing but your compliance with my request,"
returned Fawkes. "And oh! if you hope to be succoured
at your hour of need, tell Miss Radcliffe I desire to speak
with her."

"The message will not need to be conveyed," said Viviana,
who had noiselessly entered the room; "she is here."

Guy Fawkes turned his gaze in the direction of the voice;
and, notwithstanding his own deplorable condition, he was
filled with concern at the change wrought in her appearance
by the terrible shock she had undergone. Her countenance
was as pale as death—her eyes, from which no tears would
flow, as is ever the case with the deepest distress, were glassy
and lustreless—her luxuriant hair hung in dishevelled masses
over her shoulders—and her attire was soiled and disordered.

"You desire to speak with me," she continued, advancing
towards the couch of the wounded man.

"It must be alone," he replied.

Viviana glanced at Catesby, who reluctantly arose, and
closed the door after him. "We are alone now," she said.

"Water! water!" gasped the sufferer, "or I perish." His
request being complied with, he continued in a low solemn
voice, "Viviana, you have lost the dearest friend you had on
earth, and you will soon lose one who, if he had been spared,
would have endeavoured, as far as he could, to repair the loss.
I say not this to aggravate your distress, but to prove the
sincerity of my regard. Let me conjure you with my dying
breath, not to wed Mr. Catesby."

"Fear it not," replied Viviana. "I would rather endure death than consent to do so."

"Be upon your guard against him, then," continued Fawkes. "When an object is to be gained, he suffers few scruples to stand in his way."

"I am well aware of it," replied Viviana; "and on the arrival of Sir Everard Digby, I shall place myself under his protection."

"Should you be driven to extremity," said Fawkes, taking a small packet from the folds of his doublet, "break open this; it will inform you what to do. Only promise me you will not have recourse to it till all other means have failed."

Viviana took the packet, and gave the required promise.

"Conceal it about your person, and guard it carefully," continued Fawkes; "for you know not when you may require it. And now, having cleared my conscience, I can die easily. Let me have your prayers."

Viviana knelt down by the bedside, and poured forth the most earnest supplications in his behalf.

"Perhaps," she said, as she arose, "and it is some consolation to think so—you may be saved by death from the commission of a great crime, which would for ever have excluded you from the joys of heaven."

"Say rather," cried Guy Fawkes, whose brain began to wander, "which would have secured them to me. Others will achieve it; but I shall have no share in their glory or their reward."

"Their reward will be perdition in this world and in the next," rejoined Viviana. "I repeat, that though I deeply deplore your condition, I rejoice in your delivery from this sin. It is better—far better—to die thus, than by the hands of the common executioner."

"What do I see?" cried Guy Fawkes, trying to raise himself, and sinking back again instantly upon the pillow. "Elizabeth Orton rises before me. She beckons me after her—I come!—I come!"

"Heaven pity him!" cried Viviana. "His senses have left him!"

"She leads me into a gloomy cavern," continued Fawkes, more wildly; "but my eyes are like the wolf's, and can penetrate the darkness. It is filled with barrels of gunpowder. I see them ranged in tiers, one above another. Ah! I know where I am now. It is the vault beneath the Parliament-house. The King and his nobles are assembled in the

hall above. Lend me a torch, that I may fire the train, and
blow them into the air. Quick! quick! I have sworn their
destruction, and will keep my oath. What matter if I perish
with them? Give me the torch, I say, or it will be too late.
Is the powder damp that it will not kindle? And see! the
torch is expiring—it is gone out! Distraction!—to be baffled
thus! Why do you stand and glare at me with your stony
eyes? Who are those with you? Fiends!—no! they are
armed men. They seize me—they drag me before a grave
assemblage. What is that hideous engine? The rack!—
Bind me on it—break every limb—ye shall not force me to
confess—ha! ha! I laugh at your threats—ha! ha!"

"Mother of mercy! release him from this torture!" cried
Viviana.

"So! ye have condemned me," continued Fawkes, "and will
drag me to execution. Well, well, I am prepared. But what a
host is assembled to see me! Ten thousand faces are turned
towards me, and all with one abhorrent bloodthirsty expression. And what a scaffold! Get it done quickly, thou
butcherly villain. The rope is twisted round my throat in
serpent folds. It strangles me—ah!"

"Horror!" exclaimed Viviana. "I can listen to this no
longer. Help, Mr. Catesby, help!"

"The knife is at my breast—it pierces my flesh—my heart
is torn forth—I die! I die!" And he uttered a dreadful groan.

"What has happened?" cried Catesby, rushing into the
room. "Is he dead?"

"I fear so," replied Viviana; "and his end has been a
fearful one."

"No—no," said Catesby; "his pulse still beats—but
fiercely and feverishly. You had better not remain here
longer, Miss Radcliffe. I will watch over him. All will soon
be over."

Aware that she could be of no further use, Viviana cast a
look of the deepest commiseration at the sufferer, and retired.
The occupant of the cottage, an elderly female, had surrendered all the apartments of her tenement, except one small
room, to her guests, and she was therefore undisturbed. The
terrible event which had recently occurred, and the harrowing
scene she had just witnessed, were too much for Viviana, and
her anguish was so intense, that she began to fear her reason
was deserting her. She stood still,—gazed fearfully round,
as if some secret danger environed her,—clasped her hands
to her temples, and found them burning like hot iron,—and

then, alarmed at her own state, knelt down, prayed, and wept. Yes! she wept, for the first time, since her father's destruction, and the relief afforded by those scalding tears was inexpressible.

From this piteous state she was aroused by the tramp of horses at the door of the cottage, and the next moment Father Garnet presented himself.

"How uncertain are human affairs!" he said, after a sorrowful greeting had passed between them. "I little thought, when we parted yesterday, we should meet again so soon, and under such afflicting circumstances."

"It is the will of Heaven, father," replied Viviana, "and we must not murmur at its decrees, but bear our chastening as we best may."

"I am happy to find you in such a comfortable frame of mind, dear daughter. I feared the effect of the shock upon your feelings. But I am glad to find you bear up against it so well."

"I am surprised at my own firmness, father," replied Viviana. "But I have been schooled in affliction. I have no tie left to bind me to the world, and shall retire from it, not only without regret, but with eagerness."

"Say not so, dear daughter," replied Garnet. "You have, I trust, much happiness in store for you; and when the sharpness of your affliction is worn off, you will view your condition in a more cheering light."

"Impossible!" she cried, mournfully. "Hope is wholly extinct in my breast. But I will not contest the point. Is not Sir Everard Digby with you?"

"He is not, daughter," replied Garnet, "and I will explain to you wherefore. Soon after your departure yesterday, the mansion we occupied at Holt was attacked by a band of soldiers, headed by Miles Topcliffe, one of the most unrelenting of our persecutors; and though they were driven off with some loss, yet, as there was every reason to apprehend they would return with fresh force, Sir Everard judged it prudent to retreat; and accordingly he and his friends, with all their attendants, except those he has sent with me, have departed for Buckinghamshire."

"Where, then, is Father Oldcorne?" inquired Viviana.

"Alas! daughter," rejoined Garnet, "I grieve to say he is a prisoner. Imprudently exposing himself during the attack, he was seized and carried off by Topcliffe and his myrmidons."

"How true is the saying that misfortunes never come single !" sighed Viviana. "I seem bereft of all I hold dear."

"Sir Everard has sent four of his trustiest servants with me," remarked Garnet. "They are well armed, and will attend you wherever you chose to lead them. He has also furnished me with a sum of money for your use."

"He is most kind and considerate," replied Viviana. "And now, father," she faltered, "there is one subject which it is necessary to speak upon; and, though I shrink from it, it must not be postponed."

"I guess what you mean, daughter," said Garnet, sympathizingly; "you allude to the interment of Sir William Radcliffe. Is the body here ?"

"It is in an adjoining cottage," replied Viviana, in a broken voice. "I have already expressed my wish to Mr. Catesby to have it conveyed to Manchester, to our family vault."

"I see not how that can be accomplished, dear daughter," replied Garnet; "but I will confer with Mr. Catesby on the subject. "Where is he ?"

"In the next room, by the couch of Guy Fawkes, who is dying," said Viviana.

"Dying !" echoed Garnet, starting. "I heard he was dangerously hurt, but did not suppose the wound would prove fatal. Here is another grievous blow to the good cause."

At this moment the door was opened by Catesby.

"How is the sufferer ?" asked Garnet.

"A slight change for the better appears to have taken place," answered Catesby. "His fever has in some degree abated, and he has sunk into a gentle slumber."

"Can he be removed with safety ?" inquired Garnet: "for, I fear, if he remains here, he will fall into the hands of Topcliffe and his crew, who are scouring the country in every direction." And he recapitulated all he had just stated to Viviana.

Catesby was for some time lost in reflection.

"I am fairly perplexed as to what course it will be best to pursue," he said. "Dangers and difficulties beset us on every side. I am inclined to yield to Viviana's request, and proceed to Manchester."

"That will be rushing into the very face of danger," observed Garnet.

"And, therefore, may be the safest plan," replied Catesby. "Our adversaries will scarcely suspect us of so desperate a step."

"Perhaps you are in the right, my son," returned Garnet, after a moment's reflection. "At all events, I bow to your judgment."

"The plan is too much in accordance with my own wishes to meet with any opposition on my part," observed Viviana.

"Will you accompany us, father?" asked Catesby; "or do you proceed to Gothurst?"

"I will go with you, my son. Viviana will need a protector. And, till I have seen her in some place of safety, I will not leave her."

"Since we have come to this determination," rejoined Catesby, "as soon as the needful preparations can be made, and Guy Fawkes has had some hours' repose, we will set out. Under cover of night we can travel with security; and, by using some exertion, may reach Ordsall Hall, whither, I presume, Viviana would choose to proceed, in the first instance, before daybreak."

"I am well mounted, and so are my attendants," replied Garnet; "and, by the provident care of Sir Everard Digby, each of them has a led horse with him."

"That is well," said Catesby. "And now, Viviana, may I entreat you to take my place for a short time by the couch of the sufferer? In a few hours everything shall be in readiness."

He then retired with Garnet, while Viviana proceeded to the adjoining chamber, where she found Guy Fawkes still slumbering tranquilly.

As the evening advanced, he awoke, and appeared much refreshed. While he was speaking, Garnet and Catesby approached his bedside, and he seemed overjoyed at the sight of the former. The subject of the journey being mentioned to him, he at once expressed his ready compliance with the arrangement, and only desired that the last rites of his Church might be performed for him before he set out.

Garnet informed him that he had come for that very purpose; and as soon as they were left alone, he proceeded to the discharge of his priestly duties, confessed and absolved him, giving him the viaticum and the extreme unction. And, lastly, he judged it expedient to administer a powerful opiate, to lull the pain of his wound on the journey.

This done, he summoned Catesby, who, with two of the attendants, raised the couch on which the wounded man was stretched, and conveyed him to the litter. So well was this managed, that Fawkes sustained no injury, and little inconvenience, from the movement. Two strong country vehicles had been procured : the one containing the wounded man's litter, the other the shell, which had been hastily put together, to hold the remains of the unfortunate Sir William Radcliffe. Viviana being placed in the saddle, and Catesby having liberally rewarded the cottagers who had afforded them shelter, the little cavalcade was put in motion. In this way they journeyed through the night ; and shaping their course through Tarporley, Northwich, and Altringham, arrived at daybreak in the neighbourhood of Ordsall Hall.

XV.

THE ELIXIR.

On beholding the well-remembered roof and gables of the old mansion peeping from out the grove of trees in which it was embosomed, Viviana's heart died away within her. The thought that her father, who had so recently quitted it in the full enjoyment of health, and of every worldly blessing, should be so soon brought back a corpse, was almost too agonizing for endurance. Reflecting, however, that this was no season for the indulgence of grief, but that she was called upon to act with firmness, she bore up resolutely against her emotion.

Arrived within a short distance of the Hall, Catesby caused the little train to halt under the shelter of the trees, while he rode forward to ascertain that they could safely approach it. As he drew near, everything proclaimed that the hand of the spoiler had been there. Crossing the drawbridge, he entered the court, which bore abundant marks of the devastation recently committed. Various articles of furniture, broken, burnt, or otherwise destroyed, were lying scattered about. The glass in the windows was shivered; the doors forced from their hinges; the stone-copings of the walls pushed off; the flower-beds trampled upon; the moat itself was in some places choked up with rubbish, while in others its surface was covered with floating pieces of timber.

Led by curiosity, Catesby proceeded to the spot where the stables had stood. Nothing but a heap of blackened ruins met his gaze. Scarcely one stone was standing on another. The appearance of the place was so desolate and disheartening, that he turned away instantly. Leaving his horse in a shed, he entered the house. Here, again, he encountered fresh ravages. The oak-panels and skirting-boards were torn from the walls; the ceilings pulled down; and the floor lay inch-deep in broken plaster and dust. On ascending to the upper rooms he found the same disorder. The banisters of the stairs were broken; the bedsteads destroyed; the roof partially untiled. Every room was thickly strewn with leaves torn from valuable books, with fragments of apparel, and other articles, which the searchers not being able to carry off had wantonly destroyed.

Having contemplated this scene of havoc for some time, with feelings of the bitterest indignation, Catesby descended to the lowest story; and, after searching ineffectually for the domestics, was about to depart, when, turning suddenly, he perceived a man watching him from an adjoining room. Catesby instantly called to him; but, seeing that the fellow disregarded his assurances, and was about to take to his heels, he drew his sword, and threatened him with severe punishment if he attempted to fly. Thus exhorted, the man—who was no other than the younger Heydocke—advanced towards him; and throwing himself at his feet, begged him in the most piteous terms to do him no injury.

"I have already told you I am a friend," replied Catesby, sheathing his sword.

"Ah! Mr. Catesby, is it you I behold?" cried Martin Hey-docke, whose fears had hitherto prevented him from noticing the features of the intruder. "What brings your worship to this ill-fated house?"

"First let me know if there is any enemy about?" replied Catesby.

"None that I am aware of," rejoined Martin. "Having ransacked the premises, and done all the mischief they could, as you perceive, the miscreants departed the day before yesterday, and I have seen nothing of them since, though I have been constantly on the watch. The only alarm I have had was that occasioned by your worship just now."

"Are you alone here?" demanded Catesby.

"No, your worship," answered Martin. "There are several of the servants concealed in a secret passage under the house. But they are so terrified by what has lately happened, that they never dare show themselves, except during the night-time."

"I do not wonder at it," replied Catesby.

"And now may I inquire whether your worship brings any

tidings of Sir William Radcliffe and Mistress Viviana ?" rejoined Martin. " I hope no ill has befallen them. My father,
old Jerome Heydocke, set out to Holywell a few days ago, to
apprise them of their danger, and I have not heard of them
since."

" Sir William Radcliffe is dead," replied Catesby. " The
villains have murdered him. Your father is a prisoner."

" Alas ! alas !" cried the young man, bursting into tears ;
" these are fearful times to live in. What will become of
us all ?"

" We must rise against the oppressor," replied Catesby,
sternly. " Bite the heel that tramples upon us."

" We must," rejoined Martin. " And if my poor arm could
avail, it should not be slow to strike."

" Manfully resolved !" cried Catesby, who never lost an
opportunity of gaining a proselyte. " I will point out to you
a way by which you may accomplish what you desire. But
we will talk of this hereafter. Hoard up your vengeance till
the fitting moment for action arrives."

He then proceeded to explain to the young man, who was
greatly surprised by the intelligence, that Viviana was at
hand, and that the body of Sir William had been brought
thither for interment in the family vault at the Collegiate
Church. Having ascertained that there was a chamber, which,
having suffered less than the others, might serve for Viviana's
accommodation, Catesby returned to the party.

A more melancholy cavalcade has been seldom seen than
now approached the gates of Ordsall Hall. First rode
Viviana, in an agony of tears, for her grief had by this time
become absolutely uncontrollable, with Catesby on foot,
leading her horse. Next came Garnet, greatly exhausted
and depressed ; his eyes cast dejectedly on the ground. Then
came the litter, containing Guy Fawkes ; and lastly, the
vehicle with the body of Sir William Radcliffe. On arriving
at the gate, Viviana was met by two female servants, whom
Martin Heydocke had summoned from their hiding places ;
and as soon as she had dismounted, she was supported, for
she was scarcely able to walk unaided, to the chamber destined for her reception. This done, Catesby proceeded, with
some anxiety, to superintend the removal of Fawkes, who
was perfectly insensible. His wound had bled considerably
during the journey ; but the effusion had stopped when the
faintness supervened. He was placed in one of the lower
rooms till a sleeping-chamber could be prepared for him.
The last task was to attend to the remains of the late un-

fortunate possessor of the mansion. By Catesby's directions a large oak table, once occupying the great hall, was removed to the Star Chamber, already described as the principal room of the house; and, being securely propped up—for, like the rest of the furniture, it had been much damaged by the spoilers, though, being of substantial material, it offered greater resistance to their efforts—the shell containing the body was placed upon it.

"Better he should lie thus," exclaimed Catesby, when the melancholy office was completed, "than live to witness the wreck around him. Fatal as are these occurrences," he added, pursuing the train of thought suggested by the scene, "they are yet favourable to my purpose. The only person who could have prevented my union with Viviana Radcliffe—her father—lies there. Who would have thought, when she rejected my proposal a few days ago, in this very room, how fortune would conspire—and by what dark and inscrutable means—to bring it about! Fallen as it is, this house is not yet fallen so low, but I can reinstate it. Its young mistress mine, her estates mine—for she is now inheritress of all her father's possessions—the utmost reach of my ambition were gained, and all but *one* object of my life—for which I have dared so much, and struggled so long—achieved!"

"What are you thinking of my son?" asked Garnet, who had watched the changing expression of his sombre countenance—"what are you thinking of?" he said, tapping him on the shoulder.

"Of that which is never absent from my thoughts, Father —the great design," replied Catesby; "and of the means of its accomplishment, which this sad scene suggests."

"I do not understand you, my son," rejoined the other.

"Does not Radcliffe's blood cry aloud for vengeance?" continued Catesby; "and think you his child will be deaf to the cry? No, father, she will no longer tamely submit to wrongs that would steel the gentlest bosom, and make firm the feeblest arm, but will gᵣ hand and heart with us in our project. Viviana must be mine," he added, altering his tone; "*ours* I should say—for, if she is mine, all the vast possessions that have accrued to her by her father's death shall be devoted to the furtherance of the mighty enterprise."

"I cannot think she will refuse you now, my son," replied Garnet.

"She *shall not* refuse me father," rejoined Catesby. "The time has gone by for idle wooing."

"I will be no party to forcible measures, my son," returned

Garnet, gravely. "As far as persuasion goes, I will lend you every assistance in my power, but nothing further."

"Persuasion is all that will be required, I am assured, father," answered Catesby, hastily, perceiving he had committed himself too far. "But let us now see what can be done for Guy Fawkes."

"Would there was any hope of his life!" exclaimed Garnet, sighing deeply. "In losing him, we lose the bravest of our band."

"We do," returned Catesby. "And yet he has been subject to strange fancies of late."

"He has been appalled, but never shaken," rejoined Garnet. "Of all our number, you and he were the only two upon whom I could rely. When he is gone, you will stand alone."

Catesby made no reply, but led the way to the chamber where the wounded man lay. He had regained his consciousness, but was too feeble to speak. After such restoratives as were at hand had been administered, Catesby was about to order a room to be fitted up for him, when Viviana, whose anxiety for the sufferer had overcome her affliction, made her appearance. On learning Catesby's intentions, she insisted upon Fawkes being removed to the room allotted to her, which had not been dismantled like the rest. Seeing it was in vain to oppose her, Catesby assented, and the sufferer was accordingly carried thither, and placed within the bed—a large antique piece of furniture, hung with faded damask curtains. The room was one of the oldest in the house, and at the further end stood a small closet, approached by an arched doorway, and fitted up with a hassock and crucifix, which, strange to say, had escaped the ravages of the searchers.

Placed within the couch, Guy Fawkes began to ramble as before about the conspiracy; and, fearing his ravings might awaken the suspicion of the servants, Catesby would not suffer any of them to come near him, but arranged with Garnet to keep watch over him by turns. By degrees, he became more composed; and, after dozing a little, opened his eyes, and, looking round, inquired anxiously for his sword. At first Catesby, who was alone with him at the time, hesitated in his answer, but seeing he appeared greatly disturbed, he showed him that his hat, gauntlets, and rapier were lying by the bedside.

"I am content," replied the wounded man, smiling faintly;

"that sword has never left my side, waking or sleeping, for twenty years. Let me grasp it once more—perhaps for the last time."

Catesby handed him the weapon. He looked at it for a few moments, and pressed the blade to his lips.

"Farewell, old friend!" he said, a tear gathering in his eye, "farewell! Catesby," he added, as he resigned the weapon to him, "I have one request to make. Let my sword be buried with me."

"It shall," replied Catesby, in a voice suffocated by emotion, for the request touched him where his stern nature was most accessible: "I will place it by you myself."

"Thanks!" exclaimed Fawkes. And soon after this, he again fell into a slumber.

His sleep endured for some hours; but his breathing grew fainter and fainter, so that at the last it was scarcely perceptible. A striking change had likewise taken place in his countenance, and these signs convinced Catesby he had not long to live. While he was watching him with great anxiety, Viviana appeared at the door of the chamber and beckoned him out. Noiselessly obeying the summons, and following her along the gallery, he entered a room where he found Garnet.

"I have called you to say that a remedy has been suggested to me by Martin Heydocke," observed Viviana, "by which I trust Guy Fawkes may yet be saved."

"How?" asked Catesby, eagerly.

"Doctor Dee, the warden of Manchester, of whom you must have heard," she continued, "is said to possess an elixir of such virtue, that a few drops of it will snatch him who drinks them from the very jaws of death."

"I should not have suspected you of so much credulity, Viviana," replied Catesby; "but grant that Doctor Dee possesses this marvellous elixir—which for my own part I doubt—how are we to obtain it?"

"If you will repair to the college, and see him, I doubt not he will give it you," rejoined Viviana.

Catesby smiled incredulously.

"I have a claim upon Doctor Dee," she persisted, "which I have never enforced. I will now use it. Show him this token," she continued, detaching a small ornament from her neck; "tell him you bring it from me, and I am sure he will comply with your request."

"Your commands shall be obeyed, Viviana," replied

Catesby; "but I frankly confess I have no faith in the remedy."

"It is at least worth the trial, my son," observed Garnet. "Doctor Dee is a wonderful person, and has made many discoveries in medicine, as in other sciences, and this marvellous specific may, for aught we know, turn out no imposture."

"If such is your opinion," replied Catesby, "I will set out at once. If it is to be tried at all, it must be without delay. The poor sufferer is sinking fast."

"Go, then," cried Viviana, "and Heaven speed your mission! If you could prevail upon Doctor Dee to visit the wounded man in person, I should prefer it. Besides, I have another request to make of him—but that will do hereafter. Lose not a moment now."

"I will fly on the wings of the wind," replied Catesby. "Heaven grant that when I return the object of our solicitude may not be past all human aid!"

With this, he hurried to an out-building in which the horses were placed, and choosing the strongest and fleetest from out their number, mounted, and started at full gallop in the direction of Manchester; nor did he relax his speed until he reached the gates of the ancient college. Hanging the bridle of his smoking steed to a hook in the wall, he crossed the large quadrangular court; and finding the principal entrance open, passed the lofty room now used as the refectory, ascended the flight of stone stairs that conducts the modern visitor to the library, and was traversing the long galleries communicating with it, and now crowded with the learning of ages, bequeathed by the benevolence of his rival, Humphrey Chetham, when he encountered a grave but crafty-looking personage, in a loose brown robe and Polish cap, who angrily demanded his business.

Apologising for the intrusion, Catesby was about to explain, when a small oak door near them was partly opened, and an authoritative voice, from within, exclaimed, "Do not hinder him, Kelley; I know his business, and will see him."

The seer made no further remark, but pointing to the door, Catesby at once comprehended that it was Dee's voice he had heard; and, though somewhat startled by the intimation that he was expected, entered the room. He found the Doctor surrounded by his magical apparatus, and slowly returning to the chair he had just quitted.

Without looking behind him to see whom he addressed, Dee continued, "I have just consulted my show-stone, and know why you are come hither. You bring a token from Viviâna Radcliffe."

"I do," replied Catesby, in increased astonishment. "It is here."

"It is needless to produce it," replied Dee, still keeping his back towards him. "I have seen it already. Kelley," he continued, "I am about to set out for Ordsall Hall immediately. You must accompany me."

"Amazement!" cried Catesby. "Is the purpose of my visit then really known to your reverence?"

"You shall hear," rejoined Dee, facing him. "You have a friend who is at the point of death, and having heard that I possess an elixir of wonderful efficacy, are come in quest of it."

"True," replied Catesby, utterly confounded.

"The name of that friend," pursued Dee, regarding him fixedly, "is Guy Fawkes,—your own, Robert Catesby."

"I need no more to convince me, reverend sir," rejoined Catesby, trembling, in spite of himself, "that all I have heard of your wonderful powers falls far short of the truth."

"You are but just in time," replied Dee, bowing gravely in acknowledgment of the compliment. "Another hour, and it would have been too late."

"Then you think he will live!" cried Catesby, eagerly.

"I am sure of it," replied Dee, "provided——"

"Provided what?" interrupted Catesby. "Is there aught I can do to insure his recovery?"

"No," replied Dee, sternly. "I am debating within myself whether it is worth while reviving him for a more dreadful fate."

"What mean you, reverend sir?" asked Catesby, a shade passing over his countenance.

"You understand my meaning, and therefore need no explanation," replied Dee. "Return to Ordsall Hall, and tell Miss Radcliffe I will be there in an hour. Bid her have no further fear. If the wounded man breathes when I arrive, I will undertake to cure him. Add further, that I know the other request she desires to make of me, and that it is granted before it is asked. Farewell, sir, for a short time."

On reaching the court, Catesby expanded his chest, shook his limbs, and exclaimed, "At length, I breathe freely. The atmosphere of that infernal chamber smelt so horribly of sulphur that it almost stifled me. Well, if Doctor Dee has not dealings with the devil, man never had! However, if he cures Guy Fawkes, I care not whence the medicine comes from."

As he descended Smithy Bank, and was about to cross the old bridge over the Irwell, he perceived a man riding before him, who seemed anxious to avoid him. Struck by this person's manner, he urged his horse into a quicker pace, and being better mounted of the two, soon overtook him, when to his surprise he found it was Martin Heydocke.

"What are you doing here, sirrah?" he demanded.

"I have been sent by Mistress Viviana with a message to Mr. Humphrey Chetham," replied the young man, in great confusion.

"Indeed!" exclaimed Catesby, angrily. "And how dared you convey a message to him, without consulting me on the subject?"

"I was not aware you were my master," replied Martin, sulkily. "If I owe obedience to any one, it is to Mr. Chetham, whose servant I am. But if Mistress Viviana gives me a message to deliver, I will execute her commands, whoever may be pleased or displeased."

"I did but jest, thou saucy knave," returned Catesby, who did not desire to offend him. "Here is a piece of money for thee. Now, if it be no secret, what was Miss Radcliffe's message to thy master?"

"I know not what her letter contained," replied Martin; "but his answer was, that he would come to the Hall at midnight."

"It is well I ascertained this," thought Catesby, and he added aloud, "I understood your master had been arrested and imprisoned."

"So he was," replied Martin; "but he had interest enough with the commissioners to procure his liberation."

"Enough," replied Catesby; and striking spurs into his charger, he dashed off.

A quarter of an hour's hard riding brought him to the Hall, and, on arriving there, he proceeded at once to the wounded man's chamber, where he found Viviana and Garnet.

"Have you succeeded in your errand?" cried the former, eagerly. "Will Doctor Dee come, or has he sent the elixir?"

"He will bring it himself," replied Catesby.

Viviana uttered an exclamation of joy, and the sound appeared to reach the ears of the sufferer, for he stirred, and groaned faintly.

"Doctor Dee desired me to tell you," continued Catesby, drawing Viviana aside, and speaking in a low tone, "that your other request was granted."

Viviana looked surprised, and as if she did not clearly understand him.

"Might he not refer to Humphrey Chetham?" remarked Catesby, somewhat maliciously.

"Ah! you have learnt from Martin Heydocke that I have written to him," returned Viviana, blushing deeply. "What I was about to ask of Doctor Dee had no reference to Humphrey Chetham. It was to request permission to privately inter my father's remains in our family vault in the Collegiate Church. But how did he know I had any request to make?"

"That passes my comprehension," replied Catesby, "unless he obtained his information from his familiar spirits."

Shortly after this, Doctor Dee and Kelley arrived at the Hall. Catesby met them at the gate, and conducted them to the wounded man's chamber. Coldly saluting Garnet, whom he eyed with suspicion, and bowing respectfully to Viviana, the Doctor slowly advanced to the bedside. He gazed for a short time at the wounded man, and folded his arms thoughtfully upon his breast. The eyes of the sufferer were closed, and his lips slightly apart, but no breath seemed to issue from them. His bronzed complexion had assumed the ghastly hue of death, and his strongly-marked features had become fixed and rigid. His black hair, stiffened and caked with blood, escaped from the bandages around his head, and hung in elf locks on the pillow. It was a piteous spectacle; and Doctor Dee appeared much moved by it.

"The worst is over," he muttered; "why recal the spirit to its wretched tenement?"

"If you can save him, reverend sir, do not hesitate," implored Viviana.

"I am come hither for that purpose," replied Dee; "but I must have no other witness to the experiment except yourself and my attendant Kelley."

"I do not desire to be present, reverend sir," replied Viviana; "but I will retire into that closet, and pray that your remedy may prevail."

"My prayers for the same end shall be offered in the adjoining room," observed Garnet; and taking Catesby's arm, who seemed spell-bound by curiosity, he dragged him away.

K

The door closed, and Viviana withdrew into the closet, where she knelt down before the crucifix. Doctor Dee seated himself on the bedside; and taking a gourd-shaped bottle, filled with a clear sparkling liquid, from beneath his robe, he raised it to his eyes with his left hand, while he placed his right, on the wrist of the wounded man. In this attitude he continued for a few seconds, while Kelley, with his arms folded, likewise kept his gaze fixed on the phial. At the expiration of that time, Dee, who had apparently counted the pulsations of the sufferer, took out the glass stopper from the bottle, the contents of which diffused a pungent odour around; and wetting a small piece of linen with it, applied it to his temples. He then desired Kelley to raise his head, and poured a few drops down his throat. This done, he waited a few minutes, and repeated the application.

"Look!" he cried to Kelley. "The elixir already begins to operate. His chest heaves. His limbs shiver. That flush upon the cheek, and that dampness upon the brow, denote that the animal heat is restored. A third draught will accomplish the cure."

"I can already feel his heart palpitate," observed Kelley, placing his hand on the patient's breast.

"Heaven be praised!" ejaculated Viviana, who had suspended her devotions to listen.

"Hold him tightly," cried Dee to his assistant, "while I administer the last draught. He may injure himself by his struggles."

Kelley obeyed, and twined his arms tightly round the wounded man. And fortunate it was that the precaution was taken, for the elixir was no sooner poured down his throat than his chest began to labour violently, his eyes opened, and, raising himself bolt-upright, he struggled violently to break from the hold imposed upon him. This he would have effected, if Dee had not likewise lent his aid to prevent him.

"This is, indeed, a wonderful sight," cried Viviana, who had quitted the closet, and now gazed on, in awe and astonishment. "I can never be sufficiently thankful to you, reverend sir."

"Give thanks to Him to whom alone they are due," replied Dee. "Summon your friends. They may now resume their posts. My task is accomplished."

Catesby and Garnet being called into the room, could scarcely credit their senses when they beheld Guy Fawkes, who, by this time had ceased struggling, reclining on Kelley's shoulder, and, except a certain wildness in the eye and cadaverousness of hue, looking as he was wont to do.

XVI.

THE COLLEGIATE CHURCH AT MANCHESTER.

BIDDING Kelley remain with Guy Fawkes, Doctor Dee signified to Viviana that he had a few words to say to her in private before his departure, and leading the way to an adjoining room, informed her that he was aware of her desire to have her father's remains interred in the Collegiate Church, and that, so far from opposing her inclinations, he would willingly accede to them, only recommending as a measure of prudence that the ceremonial should be performed at night, and with as much secrecy as possible. Viviana thanked him in a voice of much emotion for his kindness, and entirely acquiesced in his suggestion of caution. At the same time she could not help expressing her surprise that her thoughts should be known to him. "Though, indeed," she added, "after the wonderful exhibition I have just witnessed of your power, I can scarcely suppose that any limits are to be placed to it."

"Few things are hidden from me," replied Dee, with a gratified smile; "even the lighter matters of the heart, in which I might be supposed to take little interest, do not altogether elude my observation. In reference to this, you will not, I am sure, be offended with me, Viviana, if I tell you I have noticed with some concern the attachment that has arisen between you and Humphrey Chetham."

Viviana uttered an exclamation of surprise, and a deep blush suffused her pallid cheeks.

"I am assuming the privilege of an old man with you, Viviana," continued Dee, in a graver tone, "and I may add, of an old friend, for your lamented mother was one of my dearest and best friends, as you perchance called to mind, when you sent me to-day, by Mr. Catesby, the token I gave her years ago. You have done unwisely in inviting Humphrey Chetham to come hither to-night."

"How so?" she faltered.

"Because, if he keeps his appointment, fatal consequences

K 2

may ensue," answered Dee. "Your message has reached
the ears of one from whom, most of all, you should have
concealed it."

"Mr. Catesby has heard of it, I know," replied Viviana.
"But you do not apprehend any danger from him?"

"He is Chetham's mortal foe," rejoined Dee, "and will
slay him, if he finds an opportunity."

"You alarm me," she cried. "I will speak to Mr. Catesby
on the subject, and entreat him, as he values my regard, to
offer no molestation to his fancied rival."

"*Fancied* rival!" echoed Dee, raising his brows contemptuously. "Do you seek to persuade me that you do not love
Humphrey Chetham?"

"Assuredly not," replied Viviana. "I freely acknowledge
my attachment to him. It is as strong as my aversion to
Mr. Catesby. But the latter is aware that the suit of his
rival is as hopeless as his own."

"Explain yourself, I pray you," said Dee.

"My destiny is the cloister—and this he well knows," she
rejoined. "As soon as my worldly affairs can be arranged,
I shall retire to the English nunnery at Brussels, where I
shall vow myself to Heaven."

"Such is your present intention," replied Dee. "But you
will never quit your own country."

"What shall hinder me?" asked Viviana, uneasily.

"Many things," returned Dee. "Amongst others, this
meeting with your lover."

"Call him not by that name, I beseech you, reverend sir,"
she rejoined. "Humphrey Chetham will never be other to
me than a friend."

"It may be," answered Dee. "But your destiny is *not* the
cloister."

"For what am I reserved, then?" demanded Viviana,
trembling.

"All I dare tell you," he returned, "all it is needful for
you to know is, that your future career is mixed up with
that of Guy Fawkes. But do not concern yourself about
what is to come. The present is sufficient to claim your
attention."

"True," replied Viviana; "and my first object shall be
to despatch a messenger to Humphrey Chetham to prevent
him from coming hither."

"Trouble yourself no further on that score," returned Dee.
"I will convey the message to him. As regards the funeral,

it must take place without delay. I will be at the south porch of the chuch with the keys at midnight, and Robert Burnell, the sexton, and another assistant on whom I can depend, shall be in attendance. Though it is contrary to my religious opinions and feelings to allow a Romish priest to perform the service, I will not interfere with Father Garnet. I owe your mother a deep debt of gratitude, and will pay it to her husband and her child."

"Thanks!—in *her* name, thanks!" cried Viviana, in a voice suffocated by emotion.

"And now," continued Dee, "I would ask you one further question. My art has made me acquainted that a plot is hatching against the King and his Government by certain of the Catholic party. Are you favourable to the design?"

"I am not," replied Viviana, firmly. "Nor can you regard it with more horror than myself."

"I was sure of it," returned Dee. "Nevertheless, I am glad to have my supposition confirmed from your own mouth."

With this, he moved towards the door, but Viviana arrested his departure.

"Stay, reverend sir," she cried, with a look of great uneasiness; "if you are in possession of this dread secret, the lives of my companions are in your power. You will not betray them? Or, if you deem it your duty to reveal the plot to those endangered by it, you will give its contrivers timely warning?"

"Fear nothing," rejoined Dee. "I cannot, were I so disposed, interfere with the fixed purposes of fate. The things revealed by my familiar spirits never pass my lips. They are more sacred than the disclosures made to a priest of your faith at the confessional. The bloody enterprise on which these zealots are bent will fail. I have warned Fawkes; but my warning, though conveyed by the lips of the dead, and by other means equally terrible, was unavailing. I would warn Catesby and Garnet, but they would heed me not. Viviana Ratcliffe," he continued, in a solemn voice, "you questioned me just now about the future. Have you courage to make the same demand from your dead father? If so, I will compel his corpse to answer you."

"Oh! no—no," cried Viviana, horror-stricken; "not for worlds would I commit so impious an act. Gladly as I would know what fate has in store for me, nothing should induce me to purchase the knowledge at so dreadful a price."

· "Farewell, then," rejoined Dee. "At midnight, at the south porch of the Collegiate Church, I shall expect you."

So saying, he took his departure; and, on entering the gallery, he perceived Catesby hastily retreating.

"Aha!" he muttered. "We have had a listener here. Well, no matter. What he has heard may prove serviceable to him."

He then returned to the chamber occupied by Guy Fawkes, and finding he had dropped into a deep and tranquil sleep, motioned Kelley, who was standing by the bedside watching his slumbers, with folded arms, to follow him, and, bowing gravely to Garnet, quitted the Hall.

As he crossed the court, on his way to the drawbridge, Catesby suddenly threw himself in his path, and laying his hand upon his sword, cried in a menacing voice: "Doctor Dee, neither you nor your companion shall quit the Hall till you have solemnly sworn not to divulge aught pertaining to the plot, of which you have so mysteriously obtained information."

"Is this my recompense for rescuing your comrade from the jaws of death, sir?" replied Dee, sternly.

"The necessity of the case must plead its excuse," rejoined Catesby. "My own safety, and the safety of those leagued with me, require that I should be peremptory in my demand. Did I not owe you a large debt of gratitude for your resuscitation of Guy Fawkes, I would have insured your secrecy with your life. As it is, I will be content with your oath."

"Fool!" exclaimed Dee, "stand aside, or I will compel you to do so."

"Think not to terrify me by idle threats," returned Catesby. "I willingly acknowledge your superior skill—as, indeed, I have good reason to do—in the science of medicine; but I have no faith in your magical tricks. A little reflection has shown me how the knowledge I at first thought so wonderful was acquired. You obtained it by means of Martin Heydocke, who, mounted on a swift steed, reached the college before me. He told you of the object of my visit—of Viviana's wish to have her father interred in the Collegiate Church—of her message to Humphrey Chetham. You were, therefore, fully prepared for my arrival, and at first, I must confess, completely imposed upon me. Nay, had I not overheard your conversation just now with Viviana, I might have remained your dupe still. But your allusion to Chetham's visit awakened my suspicions, and, on reconsidering the matter, the whole trick flashed upon me."

"What more?" demanded Dee, his brow lowering and his eyes sparkling with rage.

"Thus much," returned Catesby. "I have your secret, and you have mine. And though the latter is the more important, inasmuch as several lives hang upon it, whereas a conjuror's worthless reputation is alone dependent on the other, yet both must be kept. Swear, then, not to reveal the plot, and in my turn, I will take any oath you choose to dictate not to disclose the jugglery I have detected."

"I will make no terms with you," returned Dee: "and if I do not reveal your damnable plot, it is not from consideration of you or your associates, but because the hour for its disclosure is not yet arrived. When full proof of your guilt can be obtained, then rest assured it will be made known—though not by me. Not one of your number shall escape—not one."

Catesby again laid his hand upon his sword, and seemed from his looks to be meditating the destruction of the Doctor and his assistant. But they appeared wholly unconcerned at his glances.

"What you have said concerning Martin Heydocke is false —as false as your own foul and bloody scheme," pursued Dee. "I have neither seen, nor spoken with him."

"But your assistant, Edward Kelley, has," retorted Catesby, "and that amounts to the same thing."

"For the third and last time I command you to stand aside," cried Dee, in a tone of concentrated anger.

Catesby laughed aloud.

"What if I refuse?" he said in a jeering voice.

Doctor Dee made no answer: but, suddenly drawing a small phial from beneath his robe, cast its contents in his opponent's face. Blinded by the spirit, Catesby raised his hand to his eyes, and while in this condition a thick cloth was thrown over his head from behind, and, despite his resistance, he was borne off, and bound with a strong cord to an adjoining tree.

Half an hour elapsed, during which he exhausted his fury in vain outcries for assistance, and execrations and menaces against Dee and his companion. At the expiration of that time, hearing steps approaching, he called loudly to be released, and was answered by the voice of Martin Heydocke.

"What! is it your worship I behold?" cried Martin, in a tone of affected commiseration. "Mercy on us! what has happened? Have the rascally searchers been here again?"

"Hold your peace, knave, and unbind me," rejoined Catesby, angrily. "I shrewdly suspect," he added, as his commands were obeyed, and the cord twined around his arms unfastened, and the cloth removed—"I shrewdly suspect," he said, fixing a stern glance upon Martin, which effectually banished the smile from his demure countenance, "that you have had some share in this business."

"What! I, your worship?" exclaimed Martin. "Not the slightest, I assure you. It was by mere chance I came this way, and, perceiving some one tied to a tree, was about to take to my heels, when, fancying I recognised your worship's well-formed legs, I ventured forward."

"You shall become more intimately acquainted with my worship's boots, rascal, if I find my suspicions correct," rejoined Catesby. "Have you the effrontery to tell me you have never seen this rope and this cloth before?"

"Certes, I have, your worship," replied Martin. "May the first hang me, and the last serve as my winding-sheet, if I speak not the truth! Ah, now I look again," he added, pretending to examine them. "It must be a horse-cloth and halter from the stable. Peradventure, I *have* seen them."

"That I will be sworn you have, and used them too," rejoined Catesby. "I am half inclined to tie you to the tree in my place. But where is your employer?—where is Doctor Dee?"

"Doctor Dee is *not* my employer," answered Martin, "neither do I serve him. Mr. Humphrey Chetham, as I have already told your worship, is my master. As to the Doctor, he left the Hall some time since. Father Garnet thought you had accompanied him on the road. I have seen nothing of him. Of a truth, I have not."

Catesby reflected a moment, and then strode towards the Hall; while Martin, with a secret smile, picked up the halter and cloth, and withdrew to the stable.

Repairing to the chamber of the wounded man, Catesby found Garnet seated by his couch, and related what had occurred. The Jesuit listened with profound attention to the recital, and on its conclusion observed:

"I am sorry you have offended Doctor Dee, my son. He might have proved a good friend. As it is, you have made him a dangerous enemy."

"He was not to be trusted, father," returned Catesby. "But if you have any fears of him, or Kelley, I will speedily set them at rest."

"No violence, my son," rejoined Garnet. "You will only increase the mischief you have already occasioned. I do not think Dee will betray us. But additional circumspection will be requisite. Tarry here while I confer with Viviana on this subject. She has apparently some secret influence with the Doctor, and may be prevailed upon to exert it in our behalf."

It was long before Garnet returned. When he reappeared, his looks convinced Catesby that the interview had not proved satisfactory.

"Your imprudence has placed us in a perilous position, my son," he observed. "Viviana refuses to speak to Doctor Dee on the subject, and strongly reprobates your conduct."

Catesby's brow lowered.

"There is but one course to pursue," he muttered, rising; "our lives or his must be sacrificed. I will act at once."

"Hold!" exclaimed Garnet, authoritatively. "Wait till to-morrow; and, if aught occurs in the interim to confirm your suspicions, do as you think proper. I will not oppose you."

"If I forbear so long," returned Catesby, "it will not be safe to remain here."

"I will risk it," said Garnet, "and I counsel you to do the same. You will not leave Viviana at this strait."

"I have no such thoughts," replied Catesby. "If I go, she goes too."

"Then it will be in vain, I am sure, to endeavour to induce her to accompany you till her father is interred," observed Garnet.

"True," replied Catesby; "I had forgotten that. We shall meet the hoary juggler at the church, and an opportunity may occur for executing my purpose there. Unless he will swear at the altar not to betray us, he shall die by my hand."

"An oath in such a case would be no security, my son," returned Garnet; "and his slaughter and that of his companion would be equally inefficacious, and greatly prejudicial to our cause. If he means to betray us, he has done so already. But I have little apprehension. I do not think him well affected towards the Government; and I cannot but think, if you had not thus grossly insulted him, he would have favoured rather than opposed our design. If he was aware of the plot, and adverse to it, what need was there to exert his skill in behalf of our dying friend, who, but for him, would have been, ere this, a lump of lifeless clay? No, no, my son. You are far too hasty in your judgment. Nor am I less surprised at your injustice. Overlooking the great benefit conferred upon us, because some trifling scheme has been thwarted, you would requite our benefactor by cutting his throat."

"Your rebuke is just, father," returned Catesby. "I have acted heedlessly. But I will endeavour to repair my error."

"Enough, my son," replied Garnet. "It will be advisable to go well armed to the church to-night, for fear of a surprise. But I shall not absent myself on that account."

"Nor I," rejoined Catesby.

The conversation was then carried on, on other topics, when they were interrupted by the entrance of Viviana, who came to consult them about the funeral. It was arranged— since better could not be found—that the vehicle used to bring thither the body of the unfortunate knight should transport it to its last home. No persuasions of Garnet could induce Viviana to relinquish the idea of attending the ceremony; and Catesby, though he affected the contrary, secretly rejoiced at her determination.

Night came, and all was in readiness. Viviana to the last indulged in a hope that Humphrey Chetham would arrive in time to attend the funeral with her; but, as he did not appear, she concluded he had received Doctor Dee's warning. Martin Heydocke was left in charge of Guy Fawkes, who still continued to slumber deeply, and, when within half an hour of the appointed time, the train set out.

They were all well mounted, and proceeded at a slow pace along the lane skirting the west bank of the Irwell. The night was profoundly dark; and, as it was not deemed prudent to carry torches, some care was requisite to keep in the right road. Catesby rode first, and was followed by Garnet and Viviana, after whom came the little vehicle containing the body. The rear was brought up by three of the servants sent by Sir Everard Digby; a fourth acting as driver of the sorry substitute for a hearse. Not a word was uttered by any of the party. In this stealthy manner was the once-powerful and wealthy Sir William Radcliffe, the owner of the whole district through which they were passing, conveyed to the burial-place of his ancestors!

In shorter time than they had allowed themselves for the journey, the melancholy cavalcade reached Salford Bridge, and crossing it at a quick pace, as had been previously arranged by Catesby, arrived without molestation or notice (for no one was abroad in the town at that hour) at the southern gate of the Collegiate Church, where, it may be remembered, Guy Fawkes had witnessed the execution of the two seminary priests, and on the spikes of which their heads and dismembered bodies were now fixed. An old man here presented himself, and, unlocking the gate, informed them he was Robert Burnell, the sexton. The shell was then taken out, and borne on the shoulders of the servants towards the church, Burnell leading the way. Garnet followed; and as soon as Catesby had committed the horses to the care of the driver of the carriage, he tendered his arm to Viviana, who could scarcely have reached the sacred structure unsupported.

Doctor Dee met them at the church porch, as he had appointed, and, as soon as they had passed through it, the door was locked. Addressing a few words in an undertone to Viviana, but not deigning to notice either of her companions, Dee directed the bearers of the body to follow him, and proceeded towards the choir.

The interior of the reverend and beautiful fane was buried in profound gloom, and the feeble light diffused by the sexton's lantern only made the darkness more palpable. On entering the broad and noble nave nothing could be seen of its clustered pillars, or of the exquisite pointed arches, enriched with cinquefoil and quatrefoil, enclosing blank shields, which they supported. Neither could its sculptured cornice; its clerestory windows; its upper range of columns, supporting demi-angels playing on musical instruments; its moulded roof crossed by transverse beams, enriched in the interstices with sculptured ornaments, be distinguished. Most of these architectural glories were invisible; but the very gloom in which they were shrouded was imposing. As the dim light fell upon pillar after pillar as they passed, revealing their mouldings, piercing a few feet into the side aisles, and falling upon the grotesque heads, the embattled ornaments and grotesque tracery of the arches, the effect was inexpressibly striking.

Nor were the personages inappropriate to the sombre scene. The reverend figure of Dee, with his loose, flowing robes and long white beard; the priestly garb and grave aspect of Garnet; the soldier-like bearing of Catesby, his armed heel and rapier-point clanking upon the pavement; the drooping figure of Viviana, whose features were buried in her kerchief, and whose sobs were distinctly audible; the strangely-fashioned coffin, and the attendants by whom it was borne; —all constituted a singular, and, at the same time, deeply-interesting picture.

Approaching the magnificent screen terminating the nave, they passed through an arched gateway within it, and entered the choir. The west end of this part of the church was assigned as the burial-place of the ancient and honourable family, the head of which was about to be deposited within it, and was designated from the circumstance, the "Radcliffe chancel." A long slab of grey marble, in which a brass plate, displaying the armorial bearings of the Radcliffes, was inserted, had been removed, and the earth thrown out of the cavity beneath it. Kelley, who had assisted in making the excavation, was standing beside it, leaning on a spade, with a lantern at his feet. He drew aside as the funeral train approached, and the shell was deposited at the edge of the grave.

Picturesque and striking as was the scene in the nave, it fell far short of that now exhibited. The choir of the Collegiate Church at Manchester may challenge comparison with any similar structure. Its thirty elaborately-carved stalls, covered with canopies of the richest tabernacle work, surmounted by niches, mouldings, pinnacles, and perforated tracery, and crowned with a richly-sculptured cornice; its side aisles, with their pillars and arches; its moulded ceiling rich in the most delicate and fairy tracery; its gorgeous altar-screen of carved oak; and its magnificent eastern window, then filled with stained glass, form a *coup-d'œil* of almost unequalled splendour and beauty. Few of these marvels could now be seen. But such points of the pinnacles and hanging canopies of the stalls, of the façades of the side-aisles, and of the fretted roof, as received any portion of the light, came in with admirable effect.

"All is prepared, you perceive," observed Dee to Viviana. "I will retire while the ceremony is performed." And gravely inclining his head, he passed through an arched door in the south aisle, and entered the chapter-house.

Garnet was about to proceed with the service appointed by the Romish Church for the burial of the dead, when Viviana, uttering a loud cry, would have fallen, if Catesby had not flown to her assistance, and borne her to one of the stalls. Recovering her self-possession the next moment, she entreated him to leave her; and while the service proceeded, she knelt down and prayed fervently for the soul of the departed.

Placing himself at the foot of the body, Garnet sprinkled it with holy water, which he had brought with him in a small silver consecrated vessel. He then recited the *De Profundis*, the *Miserere*, and other antiphons and prayers; placed incense in a burner, which he had likewise brought with him, and having lighted it, bowed reverently towards the altar, sprinkled the body thrice with holy water, at the sides, at the head, and the feet; and then walking round it with the incense-burner, dispersed its fragrant odour over it. This done, he recited another prayer, pronounced a solemn benediction over the place of sepulture, and the body was lowered into it.

The noise of the earth falling upon the shell aroused Viviana from her devotions. She looked towards the grave, but could see nothing but the gloomy group around it, prominent among which appeared the tall figure of Catesby. The sight was too much for her, and, unable to control her grief, she fainted. Meanwhile, the grave was rapidly filled, all lending their aid to the task; and nothing was wanting but to restore the slab to its original position. By the united efforts of Catesby, Kelley, and the sexton, this was soon accomplished, and the former, unaware of what had happened, was about to proceed to Viviana, to tell her all was over, when he was arrested by a loud knocking at the church door, accompanied by a clamorous demand for admittance.

"We are betrayed!" exclaimed Catesby. "It is as I suspected. Take care of Viviana, father. I will after the hoary impostor, and cleave his skull! Extinguish the lights —quick! quick!"

Garnet hastily complied with these injunctions, and the choir was plunged in total darkness. He then rushed to the stalls, but could nowhere find Viviana. He called her by name, but received no answer, and was continuing his fruitless search, when he heard footsteps approaching, and the voice of Catesby exclaimed:

"Follow me with your charge, father."

"Alas! my son, she is not here," replied Garnet. "I have searched each stall as carefully as I could in the dark. I fear she has been spirited away."

"Impossible!" cried Catesby. And he ran his hand along the row of sculptured seats, but without success. "She is indeed gone!" he exclaimed, distractedly. "It was here I left her—nay, here I beheld her at the very moment the lights were extinguished. Viviana!—Viviana!"

But all was silent.

"It is that cursed magician's handiwork!" he continued, striking his forehead in despair.

"Did you find him?" demanded Garnet.

"No," replied Catesby. "The door of the chapter-house was locked inside. The treacherous villain did well to guard against my fury."

"You provoked his resentment, my son," rejoined Garnet. "But this is not a season for reproaches. Something must be done. Where is Kelley?"

At the suggestion, Catesby instantly darted to the spot where the seer had stood. He was not there. He then questioned the servants, whose teeth were chattering with fright, but they had neither heard him depart, nor could tell anything about him; and perceiving plainly from their trepidation that these men would lend no aid, even if they did not join the assailants, he returned to communicate his apprehensions to Garnet.

During all this time the knocking and vociferations at the door had continued with increased violence, and reverberated in hollow peals along the roof and aisles of the church.

The emergency was a fearful one. Catesby, however, had been too often placed in situations of peril, and was too constitutionally brave, to experience much uneasiness for himself; but his apprehensions lest Garnet should be captured, and the sudden and mysterious disappearance of Viviana, almost distracted him. Persuading himself she might have fallen to the ground, or that he had overlooked the precise spot where he had left her, he renewed his search, but with no better success than before; and he was almost beginning to believe that some magic might have been practised to cause her disappearance, when it occurred to him that she had been carried off by Kelley.

"Fool that I was, not to think of that before!" he exclaimed. "I have unintentionally aided their project by extinguishing the lights. But now that I am satisfied she is gone, I can devote my whole energies to the preservation of Garnet. They shall not capture us so easily as they anticipate."

With this, he approached the priest, and grasping his hand drew him noiselessly along. They had scarcely passed through the arched doorway in the screen, and set foot within the nave, when the clamour without ceased. The next moment a thundering crash was heard; the door burst open, and a number of armed figures bearing torches, with drawn swords in their hands, rushed with loud vociferations into the church.

"We must surrender, my son," cried Garnet. "It will be useless to contend against that force."

"But we may yet escape them," rejoined Catesby. And glancing hastily round he perceived a small open door in the wall at the right, and pointing it out to the priest, hurried towards it.

On reaching it, they found it communicated with a flight of stone steps, evidently leading to the roof.

"Saved! saved!" cried Catesby, triumphantly. "Mount first, father. I will defend the passage."

The pursuers, who saw the course taken by the fugitives, set up a loud shout, and ran as swiftly as they could in the same direction, and by the time the latter had gained the door they were within a few yards of it. Garnet darted up the steps; but Catesby lingered to make fast the door, and thus oppose some obstacle to the hostile party. His efforts, however, were unexpectedly checked, and, on examination, he found it was hooked to the wall at the back. Undoing the fastening, the door swung to, and he instantly bolted it. Overjoyed at his success, and leaving his pursuers, who at this moment arrived, to vent their disappointment in loud menaces, he hastened after Garnet. Calling loudly to him, he was answered from a small dark chamber on the right, into which the priest had retreated.

"We have but prolonged our torture," groaned Garnet. "I can find no outlet. Our foes will speedily force an entrance, and we must then fall into their hands."

"There must be some door opening upon the roof, father," rejoined Catesby. "Mount as high as you can, and search carefully. I will defend the stairs, and will undertake to maintain my post against the whole rout."

Thus urged, Garnet ascended the steps. After the lapse of a few minutes, during which the thundering at the door below increased, and the heavy blows of some weighty implement directed against it were distinctly heard, he cried:

"I have found a door, but the bolts are rusty—I cannot move them."

"Use all your strength, father," shouted Catesby, who, having planted himself with his drawn sword at an advantageous point, was listening with intense anxiety to the exertions of the assailing party. "Do not relax your efforts for a moment."

"It is in vain, my son," rejoined Garnet, in accents of despair. "My hands are bruised and bleeding, but the bolts stir not."

"Distraction!" cried Catesby, gnashing his teeth with rage. "Let me try."

And he was about to hasten to the priest's assistance, when the door below was burst open with a loud crash, and the assailants rushed up the steps. The passage was so narrow that they were compelled to mount singly, and Catesby's was scarcely a vain boast when he said he could maintain his ground against the whole host. Shouting to Garnet to renew his efforts, he prepared for the assault. Reserving his petronels to the last, he trusted solely to his rapier, and leaning against the newel, or circular column round which the stairs twined, he was in a great measure defended from the weapons of his adversaries, while they were completely exposed to his attack. The darkness, moreover, in which he was enveloped offered an additional protection, whereas the torches they carried made his mark certain.

As soon as the foremost of the band came within reach, Catesby plunged his sword into his breast, and pushed him back with all his force upon his comrades. The man fell heavily backwards, dislodging the next in advance, who in his turn upset his successor, and so on, till the whole band was thrown into confusion. A discharge of fire-arms followed; but, sheltered by the newel, Catesby sustained no injury. At this moment, he was cheered by a cry from Garnet that he had succeeded in forcing back the bolts, terror having supplied him with a strength not his own ; and, making another sally upon his assailants, amid the disorder that ensued, Catesby retreated, and rapidly tracking the steps, reached the door, through which the priest had already passed. When within a short distance of the outlet, Catesby felt, from the current of fresh air that saluted him, that it opened upon the roof of the church. Nor was he deceived. A few steps placed him upon the leads, where he found Garnet.

"It is you, my son," cried the latter, on beholding him; "I thought from the shouts you had fallen into the hands of the enemy."

"No, Heaven be praised! I am as yet safe, and trust to deliver you out of their hands. Come with me to the battlements."

"The battlements!" exclaimed Garnet. "A leap from such a height as that were certain destruction."

"It were so," replied Catesby, dragging him along. "But trust to me, and you shall yet reach the ground uninjured."

Arrived at the battlements, Catesby leaned over them, and endeavoured to ascertain what was beneath. It was still so dark that he could scarcely discern any objects but those close to him, but as far as he could trust his vision, he thought he perceived a projecting building some twelve or fourteen feet below; and calling to mind the form of the church, which he had frequently seen and admired, he remembered its chantries, and had no doubt but it was the roof of one of them that he beheld. If he could reach it, the descent from thence would be easy, and he immediately communicated the idea to Garnet, who shrank aghast from it. Little time, however, was allowed for consideration. Their pursuers had already scaled the stairs, and were springing one after another upon the leads, uttering the most terrible threats against the destroyer of their comrade. Hastily divesting himself of his cloak, Catesby clambered over the battlements, and impelled by fear, Garnet threw off his robe, and followed his example. Clinging to the grotesque stone waterspouts which projected below the battlements, and placing the points of his feet upon the arches of the clerestory windows, and thence upon the mullions and transom bars, Catesby descended in safety, and then turned to assist his companion, who was quickly by his side.

The most difficult and dangerous part of the descent had yet to be accomplished. They were now nearly thirty feet from the ground, and the same irregularities in the walls which had favoured them in the upper structure did not exist in the lower. But their present position, exposed as it was to their pursuers, who, having reached the point immediately overhead, were preparing to fire upon them, was too dangerous to allow of its occupation for a moment, and Garnet required no urging to make him clamber over the low embattled parapet. Descending a flying buttress that defended an angle of the building, Catesby, who was possessed of great strength and activity, was almost instantly upon the ground. Garnet was not so fortunate. Missing his footing, he fell from a considerable height, and his groans proclaimed that he had received some serious injury. Catesby instantly flew to him, and demanded, in a tone of the greatest anxiety, whether he was much hurt.

"My right arm is broken," gasped the sufferer, raising himself with difficulty. "What other injuries I have sustained I know not; but every joint seems dislocated, and my face is covered with blood. Heaven have pity on me!"

L

As he spoke, a shout of exultation arose from the hostile party, who, having heard Garnet's fall, and the groans that succeeded it, at once divined the cause, and made sure of a capture. A deep silence followed, proving that they had quitted the roof, and were hastening to secure their prey.

Aware that it would take them some little time to descend the winding staircase and traverse the long aisle of the church, Catesby felt certain of distancing them. But he could not abandon Garnet, who had become insensible from the agony of his fractured limb, and, lifting him carefully in his arms, he placed him upon his shoulder, and started at a swift pace towards the further extremity of the churchyard.

At the period of this history, the western boundary of the Collegiate Church was formed by a precipitous sandstone rock of great height, the base of which was washed by the waters of the Irwell, while its summit was guarded by a low stone wall. In after years, a range of small habitations was built upon this spot, but they have been recently removed, and the rock having been lowered, a road now occupies their site. Nerved by desperation, Catesby, who was sufficiently well acquainted with the locality to know whither he was shaping his course, determined to hazard a descent, which, under calmer circumstances, he would have deemed wholly impracticable. His pursuers, who issued from the church porch a few seconds after he had passed it, saw him hurry towards the low wall edging the precipice, and, encumbered as he was with the priest, vault over it. Not deeming it possible he would dare to spring from such a height, they darted after him. But they were deceived, and could scarcely credit their senses when they found him gone. By the light of their torches they perceived him shooting down the almost perpendicular side of the rock, and the next moment a hollow plunge told that he had reached the water. They stared at each other in mute astonishment.

"Will you follow him, Dick Haughton?" observed one, as soon as he had recovered his speech.

"Not I," replied the fellow addressed. "I have no fancy for a broken neck. Follow him thyself if thou hast a mind to try the soundness of thy pate; I warrant that rock will put it to the proof."

"Yet the feat has just been done, and by one burthened with a wounded comrade into the bargain," remarked the first speaker.

"He must be the devil, that's certain," rejoined Haughton; "and Doctor Dee himself is no match for him."

"He has the devil's luck, that's certain," cried a third soldier. "But, hark! he is swimming across the river. We may yet catch him on the opposite bank. Come along, comrades."

With this, they rushed out of the churchyard; made the best of their way to the bridge; and crossing it, flew to the bank of the river, where they dispersed in every direction, in search for the fugitive. But they could not discover a trace of him or his wounded companion.

XVII.

THE RENCOUNTER.

CATESBY himself could scarcely tell how he accomplished his hairbreadth escape. Reckless almost of the result, he slided down the rock, catching at occasional irregularities as he descended. The river was of great depth at this point, and broke the force of his fall. On rising, he struck out a few yards, and suffered himself to be carried down the stream. He had never for one moment relinquished his hold of Garnet, and being an admirable swimmer, found little difficulty in sustaining him with one arm, while with the other he guided his course in the water. In this way he reached the shore in safety, about a hundred yards below the bridge, by which means he avoided his pursuers, who, as has just been stated, searched for him above it.

After debating with himself for a short time as to what course he sould pursue, he decided upon conveying Garnet to the Hall, where he could procure restoratives and assistance; and though he was fully sensible of the danger of this plan, not doubting the mansion would be visited and searched by his pursuers before morning, yet the necessity of warning Guy Fawkes outweighed every other consideration. Accordingly, again shouldering the priest, who, though he had regained his sensibility, was utterly unable to move, he commenced his toilsome march; and being frequently obliged to pause and rest himself, more than an hour elapsed before he reached his destination.

It was just growing light as he crossed the drawbridge, and seeing a horse tied to a tree, and the gate open, he began to fear the enemy had preceded him. Full of misgiving, he laid Garnet upon a heap of straw in an outbuilding, and entered the house. He found no one below, though he glanced into each room. He then noiselessly ascended the stairs, with the intention of proceeding to Guy Fawkes's chamber.

As he traversed the gallery, he heard voices in one of the chambers, the door of which was ajar, and pausing to listen, distinguished the tones of Viviana. Filled with astonishment, he was about to enter the room to inquire by what means she had reached the Hall, when he was arrested by the voice of her companion. It was that of Humphrey Chetham. Maddened by jealousy, Catesby's first impulse was to rush into the room and stab his rival in the presence of his mistress. But he restrained his passion by a powerful effort.

After listening for a few minutes intently to their conversation, he found that Chetham was taking leave, and creeping softly down-stairs, stationed himself in the hall, through which he knew his rival must necessarily pass. Chetham presently appeared. His manner was dejected; his looks downcast; and he would have passed Catesby without observing him, if the latter had not laid his hand upon his shoulder.

"Mr. Catesby!" exclaimed the young merchant, starting as he beheld the stern glance fixed upon him. "I thought——"

"You thought I was a prisoner, no doubt," interrupted Catesby, bitterly. "But you are mistaken. I am here to confound you and your juggling and treacherous associate."

"I do not understand you," replied Chetham.

"I will soon make myself intelligible," retorted Catesby. "Follow me to the garden."

"I perceive your purpose, Mr. Catesby," replied Chetham, calmly; "but it is no part of my principles to expose my life to ruffianly violence. If you choose to lay aside this insolent demeanour, which is more befitting an Alsatian bully than a gentleman, I will readily give you such explanation of my conduct as will fully content you, and satisfy you that any suspicions you may entertain of me are unfounded."

"Coward!" exclaimed Catesby, striking him. "I want no explanation. Defend yourself, or I will treat you with still greater indignity."

"Lead on, then," cried Chetham; "I would have avoided the quarrel if I could. But this outrage shall not pass unpunished."

Guy Fawkes protecting Humphrey Chetham from Catesby.

As they quitted the Hall, Viviana entered it; and, though she was greatly surprised by the appearance of Catesby, his furious gestures left her in no doubt as to his purpose. She called to him to stop. But no attention was paid by either party to her cries.

On gaining a retired spot beneath the trees, Catesby, without giving his antagonist time to divest himself of the heavy horseman's cloak with which he was encumbered, and scarcely to draw his sword, assaulted him. The combat was furious on both sides, but it was evident that the young merchant was no match for his adversary. He maintained his ground, however, for some time with great resolution; but, being hotly pressed, in retreating to avoid a thrust, his foot caught in the long grass, and he fell. Catesby would have passed his sword through his body, if it had not been turned aside by another weapon. It was that of Guy Fawkes, who, followed by Martin Heydocke, had staggered towards the scene of strife, reaching it just in time to save the life of Humphrey Chetham.

"Heaven be praised! I am not too late!" he exclaimed. "Put up your blade, Catesby; or, turn it against me."

XVIII

THE EXPLANATION.

UTTERING an exclamation of rage, Catesby turned fiercely upon Fawkes, and for a moment appeared disposed to accept his invitation to continue the combat with him. But as he regarded the other's haggard features, and perceived in them the traces of his recent struggle with death—as he saw he was scarcely able to wield the blade he opposed against him —his wrath changed to compassion, and he sheathed his sword. By this time Humphrey Chetham had sprung to his feet, and picking up his fallen weapon, stood on his defence. But finding that Catesby meditated no further hostilities, he returned it to the scabbard.

"I owe my life to you," he said to Guy Fawkes, in a tone of deep gratitude.

"You owe it to Viviana Radcliffe, not to me," returned Fawkes, feebly, and leaning upon his sword for support. "Had it not been for her cries, I should have known nothing of this quarrel. And I would now gladly learn what has occasioned it."

"So would I," added Chetham ; "for I am as ignorant as yourself how I have offended Mr. Catesby."

"I will tell you, then," returned Catesby, sternly. "You were a party to the snare set for us by Doctor Dee, from which I narrowly escaped with life, and Father Garnet at the expense of a broken limb."

"Is Garnet hurt ?" demanded Fawkes, anxiously.

"Grievously," replied Catesby ; "but he is out of the reach of his enemies, of whom," he added, pointing to Chetham, "one of the most malignant and treacherous now stands before you."

"I am quite in the dark as to what has happened," observed Fawkes, "having only a few minutes ago been roused from my slumbers by the shrieks of Viviana, who entreated me to come and separate you. But I cannot believe Humphrey Chetham so treacherous as you represent him."

"So far from having any enmity towards Father Garnet," observed Chetham, "my anxious desire was to preserve him ; and with that view I was repairing to Doctor Dee when I encountered Mr. Catesby in the Hall, and before I could offer any explanation, I was forced by his violence and insults into this combat."

"Is this the truth, Catesby ?" asked Fawkes.

"Something near it," rejoined the latter ; "but perhaps Mr. Chetham will likewise inform you by whose agency Viviana was transported hither from the Collegiate Church ?"

"That inquiry ought rather to be made of the lady herself, sir," rejoined Chetham, coldly. "But, as I am assured she would have no objection to my answering it, I shall not hesitate to do so. She was conveyed hither by Kelley and an assistant, who departed as soon as their task was completed."

"Indeed !" exclaimed Catesby between his ground teeth. "But how chanced it, sir, that you arrived here so opportunely ?"

"I might well refuse to answer a question thus insolently put," rejoined Chetham. "But to prevent further misunderstanding, I will tell you, that I came by Viviana's invitation at midnight ; and, ascertaining from my servant, Martin Heydocke, whom I found watching by the couch of Guy Fawkes, the melancholy business on which she was engaged, I determined to await her return, which occurred about an hour afterwards, in the manner I have just related."

"I was in the court-yard when Mistress Viviana was brought back," interposed Martin Heydocke, who was standing at a respectful distance from the group; "and, after Kelley had delivered her to my charge, I heard him observe in an undertone to his companion, 'Let us ride back as fast as we can, and see what they have done with the prisoners.'"

"They made sure of their prey before it was captured," observed Catesby, bitterly. "But we have disappointed them. Dee and his associate may yet have reason to repent their perfidy."

"You will do well not to put yourself again in their power," observed Humphrey Chetham. "If you will be counselled by me, you and Guy Fawkes will seek safety in instant flight."

"And leave you with Viviana?" rejoined Catesby, sarcastically.

"She is in no present danger," replied Chetham. "But, if it is thought fitting or desirable, I will remain with her."

"I do not doubt it," returned Catesby, with a sneer; "but it is neither fitting nor desirable. And, hark ye, young sir, if you have indulged any expectations with regard to Viviana Radcliffe, it is time you were undeceived. She will never wed one of your degree, nor of your faith."

"I have her own assurance she will never wed at all," replied Chetham, in an offended tone. "But had she not crushed my hopes by declaring she was vowed to a convent, no menaces of yours, who have neither right nor title thus to interfere, should induce me to desist from my suit."

"Either resign all pretensions to her hand, or prepare to renew the combat," cried Catesby, fiercely.

"No more of this," interposed Guy Fawkes. "Let us return to the house, and adjust our differences there."

"I have no further business here," observed Humphrey Chetham. "Having taken leave of Viviana," he added, with much emotion, "I do not desire to meet her again."

"It is well, sir," rejoined Catesby; "yet stay! you mean us no treachery?"

"If you suspect me, I will remain," replied Humphrey Chetham.

"On no account," interposed Guy Fawkes. "I will answer for him with my life."

"Perhaps, when I tell you I have procured the liberation of Father Oldcorne," returned Chetham, "and have placed him in security in Ordsall Cave, you will admit that you have done me wrong."

"I have been greatly mistaken in you, sir, I must own," observed Catesby, advancing towards him, and extending his hand. But Humphrey Chetham folded his arms upon his breast, and bowing coldly, withdrew. He was followed by Martin Heydocke, and presently afterwards the tramp of his horse's feet was heard crossing the drawbridge.

XIX.

THE DISCOVERY.

TENDERING his arm to Fawkes, who was almost too feeble to walk unsupported, Catesby led him slowly to the Hall. On reaching it, they met Viviana, in a state bordering upon distraction, but her distress was speedily relieved by their assurances that the young merchant had departed unhurt,— a statement immediately afterwards confirmed by the entrance of Martin Heydocke, charged with a message from his master to her. Without communicating his design to the others, and, indeed, almost shunning Viviana, Catesby proceeded to the outbuilding where he had deposited Garnet. He found him in great pain, and praying fervently to be released from his suffering.

"Do not despair, father," said Catesby, in as cheerful a tone as he could assume, "the worst is over. Viviana is in safety. Father Oldcorne has escaped, and is within a short distance of us, and Guy Fawkes is fully able to undertake a journey of any distance. You are our sole concern. But I am assured, if you will allow me to exercise the slight surgical skill I possess in your behalf, that you will be able to accompany us."

"Do with me what you please, my son," groaned Garnet. "But, if my case is as desperate as I believe it, I entreat you not to bestow any further care upon me, and above all, not to expose yourself to risk on my account. Our enemies are sure to pursue us,—and what matter if I am captured? They will wreak their vengeance on a worthless carcass,—for such I shall soon be. But it would double the anguish I now endure, if you and Fawkes were to fall into their hands. Go, then, and leave me here to perish. My dying moments will be cheered by the conviction that the great enterprise—for which alone I desire to live—will not be unaccomplished."

" There is no need to leave you, father," replied Catesby,
" nor shall any consideration induce me to do so, till I have
rendered you every aid that circumstances will permit."

" My son," replied Garnet, faintly, " the most efficacious
balm you can apply will be the certainty that you are in
safety. You say Viviana is here. Fly with Fawkes, and
leave me to her care."

" She must go with us," observed Catesby, uneasily.

" Not so, my son," returned Garnet; " her presence will
only endanger you. She must *not* go. And you must abandon all hopes of an union with her."

" I would as soon abandon the great design itself," returned
Catesby, moodily.

" If you persist in this, you will ruin it," rejoined Garnet.
" Think of her no more. Bend your thoughts exclusively on
the one grand object, and be what you are chosen to be, the
defender and deliverer of our holy Church."

" I would gladly act as you advise me, father," replied
Catesby; " but I am spell-bound by this maiden."

" This is idle from you, my son," replied Garnet, reproachfully. " Separate yourself from her, and you will soon regain
your former mastery over yourself."

" Well, well, father," rejoined Catesby, " the effort, at
least, shall be made. But her large possessions, which would
be so useful to our cause, and which, if I wedded her, would
be wholly devoted to it,—think of what we lose, father."

" I *have* thought of it, my son," replied Garnet; " but the
consideration does not alter my opinion; and if I possess any
authority over you, I strictly enjoin you not to proceed farther in the matter. Viviana never can be yours."

" She *shall* be, nevertheless," muttered Catesby, " and
before many hours have elapsed—if not by her own free will,
by force. I have ever shown myself obedient to your commands, father," he added aloud, " and I shall not transgress
them now."

" Heaven keep you in this disposition, my dear son!" exclaimed Garnet, with a look of distrust; " and let me recommend you to remove yourself as soon as possible out of the
way of temptation."

Catesby muttered an affirmative, and taking Garnet in his
arms, conveyed him carefully to his own chamber, and placing
him on a couch, examined his wounds, which were not so
serious as either he or the sufferer imagined, and with no
despicable skill—for the experiences of a soldiers's life had

given him some practice—bandaged his broken arm, and fomented his bruises.

This done, Garnet felt so much easier, that he entreated Catesby to send Viviana to him, and to make preparations for his own immediate departure. Feigning acquiescence, Catesby quitted the room, but with no intention of complying with the request. Not a moment he felt must be lost if he would execute his dark design, and, after revolving many wild expedients, an idea occurred to him. It was to lure Viviana to the cave where Father Oldcorne was concealed; and he knew enough of the pliant disposition of the latter to be certain he would assent to his scheme. No sooner did this plan occur to him than he hurried to the cell, and found the priest, as Chetham had stated. As he had foreseen, it required little persuasion to induce Oldcorne to lend his assistance to the forced marriage, and he only feared the decided opposition they should encounter from Viviana.

"Fear nothing, then, father," said Catesby; "in this solitary spot no one will hear her cries. Whatever resistance she may make, perform the ceremony, and leave the consequences to me."

"The plan is desperate, my son," returned Oldcorne, "but so are our fortunes. And, as Viviana will not hear reason, we have no alternative. You swear that if you are once wedded to her, all her possessions shall be devoted to the furtherance of the great cause."

"All, father—I swear it," rejoined Catesby, fervently.

"Enough," replied Oldcorne. "The sooner it is done, the better."

It was then agreed between them that the plan least likely to excite suspicion would be for Oldcorne to proceed to the Hall, and under some plea prevail upon Viviana to return with him to the cave. Acting upon this arrangement, they left the cell together, shaping their course under the trees to avoid observation; and while Oldcorne repaired to the Hall, Catesby proceeded to the stable, and saddling the only steed left, rode back to the cave, and concealing the animal behind the brushwood, entered the excavation. Some time elapsed before the others arrived, and as in his present feverish state of mind moments appeared ages, the suspense was almost intolerable. At length, he heard footsteps approaching, and, with a beating heart, distinguished the voice of Viviana. The place was buried in profound darkness; but Oldcorne struck a light, and set fire to a candle in a lantern. The feeble glimmer diffused by it was not sufficient to penetrate the recesses of the cavern; and Catesby, who stood at the farther extremity, was completely sheltered from observation.

"And now, father," observed Viviana, seating herself with her back towards Catesby, upon the stone bench once used by the unfortunate prophetess, "I would learn the communication you desire to make to me. It must be something of importance since you would not disclose it at the Hall."

"It is, daughter," replied Oldcorne, who could scarcely conceal his embarrassment. "I have brought you hither, where I am sure we shall be uninterrupted, to confer with you on a subject nearest my heart. Your lamented father being taken from us, I, as his spiritual adviser, aware of his secret wishes and intentions, conceive myself entitled to assume his place."

"I consider you in the light of a father, dear sir," replied Viviana, "and will follow your advice as implicitly as I would that of him I have lost."

"Since I find you so tractable, child," returned Oldcorne, reassured by her manner, "I will no longer hesitate to declare the motive I had in bringing you hither. You will recollect that I have of late strongly opposed your intention of retiring to a convent."

"I know it, father," interrupted Viviana; "but——"

"Hear me out," continued Oldcorne; "recent events have strengthened my disapproval of the step. You are now called upon to active duties, and must take your share in the business of life,—must struggle and suffer like others,—and not shrink from the burthen imposed upon you by Heaven."

"I do not shrink from it, father," replied Viviana; "and if I were equal to the active life you propose, I would not hesitate to embrace it; but I feel I should sink under it."

"Not if you had one near you who could afford you that support which feeble woman ever requires," returned Oldcorne.

"What mean you, father?" inquired Viviana, fixing her dark eyes full upon him.

"That you must marry, daughter," returned Oldcorne; "unite yourself to some worthy man, who will be to you what I have described."

"And was it to tell me this that you brought me here?" asked Viviana, in a slightly offended tone.

"It was, daughter," replied Oldcorne; "but I have not yet done. It is not only needful you should marry, but your choice must be such as I, who represent your father, and have your welfare thoroughly at heart, can approve."

"You can find me a husband, I doubt not?" remarked Viviana, coldly.

"I have already found one," returned Oldcorne: "a gentleman suitable to you in rank, religion, years—for *your* husband should be older than yourself, Viviana."

"I will not affect to misunderstand you, father," she replied; "you mean Mr. Catesby."

"You have guessed aright, dear daughter," rejoined Oldcorne.

"I thought I had made myself sufficiently intelligible on this point before, father," she returned.

"True," replied Oldcorne; "but you are no longer, as I have just laboured to convince you, in the same position you were when the subject was formerly discussed."

"To prevent further misunderstanding, father," rejoined Viviana, "I now tell you, that in whatever position I may be placed, I will never, under any circumstances, wed Mr. Catesby."

"What are your objections to him, daughter?" asked Oldcorne.

"They are numberless," replied Viviana; "but it is useless to particularise them. I must pray you to change the conversation, or you will compel me to quit you."

"Nay, daughter, if you thus obstinately shut your ears to reason, I must use very different language towards you. Armed with parental authority, I shall exact obedience to my commands."

"I cannot obey you, father," replied Viviana, bursting into tears—"indeed, indeed I cannot. My heart, I have already told you, is another's."

"He who has robbed you of it is a heretic," rejoined Oldcorne, sternly, "and therefore your union with him is out of the question. Promise me you will wed Mr. Catesby, or, in the name of your dead father, I will invoke a curse upon your head. Promise me, I say."

"Never," replied Viviana, rising. "My father would never have enforced my compliance, and I dread no curse thus impiously pronounced. You are overstepping the bounds of your priestly office, sir. Farewell."

As she moved to depart, a strong grasp was laid on her arm, and turning, she beheld Catesby.

"You here, sir?" she cried, in great alarm.

"Ay," replied Catesby. "At last you are in my power, Viviana."

"I would fain misunderstand you, sir," she rejoined, trembling; "but your looks terrify me. You mean no violence?"

"I mean that Father Oldcorne shall wed us—and that too without a moment's delay," replied Catesby, sternly.

"Monster!" shrieked Viviana, "you will not—dare not commit this foul offence. And if you dare, Father Oldcorne will not assist you. Ah! what means that sign? I cannot be mistaken in you, father? You cannot be acting in concert with this wicked man? Save me from him!—save me."

But the priest kept aloof, and taking a missal from his vest, hastily turned over the leaves. Viviana saw that her appeal to him was vain.

"Let me go!" she shrieked, struggling with Catesby. "You cannot force me to wed you whether I will or not; and I will die rather than consent. Let me go, I say! Help!—help!" And she made the cavern ring with her screams.

"Heed her not, father," shouted Catesby, who still held her fast, "but proceed with the ceremony."

Oldcorne, however, appeared irresolute, and Viviana perceiving it, redoubled her cries.

"This will be no marriage, father," she said, "even if you proceed with it. I will protest against it to all the world, and you will be deprived of your priestly office for your share in so infamous a transaction."

"You will think otherwise anon, daughter," replied Oldcorne, advancing towards them with the missal in his hand.

"If it be no marriage," observed Catesby, significantly, "the time will come when you may desire to have the ceremony repeated."

"Mr. Catesby," cried Viviana, altering her manner, as if she had taken a sudden resolution, "one word before you proceed with your atrocious purpose, which must end in misery to us all. There are reasons why you can never wed me."

"Ha!" exclaimed Catesby, starting.

"Is it so, my son?" asked Oldcorne, uneasily.

"Pshaw!" exclaimed Catesby. "She knows not what she says. Proceed, father."

"I have proofs that will confound you," cried Viviana, breaking from him. And darting towards the light, she took from her bosom the packet given her by Guy Fawkes, and tore it open. A letter was within it and a miniature.

Opening the letter, she cast her eye rapidly over its contents, and then looking up, exclaimed in accents of delirious joy, "Saved! saved! Father Oldcorne, this man is married already."

Catesby, who had watched her proceedings in silent astonishment, and was now advancing towards her, recoiled as if a thunderbolt had fallen at his feet.

"Can this be true?" cried the priest, in astonishment.

"Let your own eyes convince you," rejoined Viviana, handing him the letter.

"I am satisfied," returned Oldcorne, after he had glanced at it. "We have both been spared the commission of a great crime. Mr. Catesby, it appears from this letter that you have a wife living in Spain."

"It is useless to deny it," replied Catesby. "But, as you were ignorant of the matter, the offence (if any) would have lain wholly at my door; nor should I have repented of it, if it had enabled me to achieve the object I have in view."

"Thank Heaven, it has gone no further!" exclaimed Oldcorne. "Daughter, I humbly entreat your forgiveness."

"How came that packet in your possession?" demanded Catesby fiercely of Viviana.

"It was given me by Guy Fawkes," she replied.

"Guy Fawkes!" exclaimed Catesby. "Has he betrayed his friend?"

"He has proved himself your best friend, by preventing you from committing a crime which would have entailed wretchedness on yourself and me," returned Viviana.

"I have done with him, and with all of you," cried Catesby, with a fierce glance at Oldcorne. "Henceforth, pursue your projects alone. You shall have no further assistance from me. I will serve the Spaniard. Englishmen are not to be trusted."

So saying, he rushed out of the cavern, and seeking his horse, mounted him, and rode off at full speed.

"How shall I obtain your forgiveness for my conduct in this culpable affair, dear daughter?" said Oldcorne, with an imploring look at Viviana.

"By joining me in thanksgivings to the Virgin for my deliverance," replied Viviana, prostrating herself before the stone cross. Oldcorne knelt beside her, and they continued for some time in earnest prayer. They then arose, and quitting the cave, proceeded to the Hall.

XX.

THE DEPARTURE FROM THE HALL.

GUY FAWKES was as much surprised to hear of the sudden departure of Catesby as he was concerned at the cause; but he still thought it probable he would return. In this expectation, however, he was disappointed. The day wore on, and no one came. The uncertainty in which Fawkes was kept, added to his unwillingness to leave Garnet, still detained him, in spite of the risk he ran at the Hall; and it was only when urged by Viviana that he began seriously to reflect whither he should bend his steps. Towards evening, Garnet was so much better that he was able to sit up, and he passed some hours in conference with Oldcorne.

"If I do not suffer a relapse," he observed to the latter, "I will set out with Guy Fawkes to-morrow, and we will proceed by easy stages to London."

"I cannot but approve your resolution," returned Oldcorne; "for though so long a journey may be inconvenient, and retard your recovery, yet every hour you remain here is fraught with additional peril. I will accompany you. We shall both be safer in the capital; and perhaps Viviana, now she will be no longer exposed to the persecutions of Catesby, will form one of the party."

"I should not wonder," replied Garnet. "I shall be deeply concerned if Catesby has really abandoned the enterprise. But I cannot think it. I did all I could to dissuade him from prosecuting this union, knowing how hopeless it was, and little thinking he would be rash enough to seek to accomplish it by force, or that he would find an assistant in you."

"Say no more about it, father, I entreat you," rejoined Oldcorne. "The scheme failed, as it deserved to do; and I sincerely repent the share I was induced by Catesby's artful representations to take in it. If we have lost our leader we have still Guy Fawkes, who is a host in himself, and as true as the steel that hangs by his side."

"We cannot spare Catesby," replied Garnet. "With many

faults, he has one redeeming quality, courage. I am not sorry he has been thwarted in his present scheme, as if he returns to us, as I doubt not he will, he will fix his mind steadily on the one object, which should be ever before it. Give me your arm, father. I am glad to find I can walk, though feebly. "That is well," he added, as they emerged upon the gallery; "I shall be able to reach Viviana's chamber without further assistance. Do you descend and see that Martin Heydocke is on the watch."

In obedience to the injunctions of his superior, Oldcorne went in search of Martin Heydocke, who had been stationed in the court-yard to give timely notice of any hostile approach; but not finding him there, he proceeded towards the drawbridge. Garnet, meanwhile, had reached the door of Viviana's chamber, which was slightly ajar, and he was about to pass through it, when he perceived that she was on her knees before Guy Fawkes, whom she was addressing in the most passionate terms. The latter was seated at a table, with his head upon his hand, in a thoughtful posture. Surprised at the sight, and curious to hear what Viviana could be saying, Garnet drew back to listen.

"When you quit this house," were the first words that caught the listener's ear, "we shall never meet again; and oh! let me have the consolation of thinking that, in return for the devoted attachment you have shown me, and the dangers from which you have preserved me, I have preserved you from one equally imminent. Catesby, from whatever motive, has abandoned the conspiracy. Do you act likewise, and the whole dreadful scheme will fall to the ground."

"Catesby cannot abandon it," replied Fawkes. "He is bound by ties that no human power can sunder. And, however he may estrange himself from us now, when the time for action arrives, rest assured he will not be absent."

"It may be so," replied Viviana; "but I deny that the oath either he or you have taken is binding. The deed you have sworn to do is evil, and no vow, however solemnly pronounced, can compel you to commit crime. Avoid this sin— avoid further connexion with those who would work your undoing, and do not stain your soul with guilt from which it will never be cleansed."

"You seek in vain to move me," replied Guy Fawkes, firmly. "My purpose is unalterable. The tempest that clears away the pestilence destroys many innocent lives, but it is not the less wholesome on that account. Our unhappy land is choked with the pestilence of heresy, and must be freed from it, cost what it will, and suffer who may. The wrongs of the English Catholics imperatively demand redress; and, since it is denied us, we must take it. Oppression can go no farther; nor endurance hold out longer. If this blow be not struck we shall have no longer a religion. And how comes it, Viviana, that you, a zealous Catholic, whose father perished by these very oppressors, and who are yourself in danger from them, can seek to turn me from my purpose?"

"Because I know it is wrongful," she replied. "I have no desire to avenge the death of my slaughtered father, still less to see our religion furthered by the dreadful means you propose. In his own due season the Lord will redress our wrongs."

"The Lord has appointed me one of the ministers of his vengeance," cried Fawkes, in a tone of enthusiasm.

"Do not deceive yourself," returned Viviana; "it is not by Heaven, but by the powers of darkness, that you are incited to this deed. Do not persevere in this fatal course," she continued, clasping her hands together, and gazing imploringly in his face, "do not—do not!"

Guy Fawkes continued in the same attitude as before, with his gaze turned upwards, and apparently lost in thought.

"Have I no power to move you?" cried Viviana, her eyes streaming with tears.

"None whatever," replied Guy Fawkes, firmly.

"Then you are lost," she rejoined.

"If it is Heaven's will, I am," answered Fawkes: "but at least I believe I am acting rightly."

"And rest assured you are so, my son," cried Garnet, throwing open the door, and stepping into the room. "I have overheard your conversation, and I applaud your resolution."

"You need have no fears of me, father," replied Fawkes. "I do not lightly undertake a project; but once embarked in it, nothing can turn me aside."

"In this case your determination is wisely formed, my son," returned Garnet; "and if Viviana will ever give me an opportunity of fully discussing the matter, I am sure I can satisfy her you are in the right."

"I will discuss it with you whenever you think proper," she replied. "But no arguments will ever convince me that your project is approved by Heaven."

"Let it pass now, daughter," rejoined Garnet; "enough has been said on the subject. I came hither to tell Guy Fawkes that, if our enemies permit us to pass the night

M

without molestation (as Heaven grant they may!), I think I
shall be strong enough to set out with him to-morrow, when
I propose we should journey together to London."

"Agreed," replied Fawkes.

"Father Oldcorne will accompany us," pursued Garnet.

"And I, too, will go with you, if you will permit me," said
Viviana. "I cannot remain here; and I have no further fears
of Mr. Catesby. Doctor Dee told me my future fate was
strangely mixed up with that of Guy Fawkes. I know not
how it may be, but I will not abandon him while there is a
hope to cling to."

"Viviana Radcliffe," rejoined Guy Fawkes, coldly, "deeply
as I feel the interest you take in me, I think it right to tell
you that no efforts you can use will shake me from my purpose. If I live, I will execute my design."

"While I live, I will urge you to it," remarked Garnet.

"And while *I* live, I will dissuade you from it," added
Viviana. "We shall see who will obtain the victory."

"We shall," replied Garnet, smiling confidently.

"Hear me further," continued Viviana; "I do not doubt
that your zeal is disinterested; yet still, your mode of life,
and the difficulties in which you are placed, may not un-
naturally influence your conduct. That this may no longer
be the case, I here place part of my fortune at your disposal.
I require little or nothing myself. But I would, if possible,
save one to whom I owe so much, and whom I value so much,
from destruction."

"I fully appreciate your generosity—to give it its lightest
term—Viviana," returned Guy Fawkes, in a voice of deep
emotion. "Under any circumstances I should reject it—
under the present, I do so the more positively, because the
offer, kind as it is, seems to imply that my poverty leads me
to act contrary to my principles. Gold has no power over
me; I regard it as dross; and when I could easily have won
it, I neglected the opportunity. As no reward would ever
induce me to commit an action my conscience disapproved, so
none will deter me from a purpose which I regard as my
duty."

"Enough," replied Viviana, sadly. "I will no longer
question your motives, or oppose your plan, but will pray
Heaven to open your eyes to the truth."

"Your conduct is in all respects worthy of you, daughter,"
observed Garnet, kindly.

"You have rejected one offer," continued Viviana, looking

at Fawkes; "but I trust you will not decline that I am about to propose to you."

"What is it?" asked Fawkes, in some surprise.

"It is that I may be permitted to regard you as a father," replied Viviana, with some hesitation. "Having lost my own father, I feel I need some protector, and I would gladly make choice of you, if you will accept the office."

"I willingly accede to your request, and am much flattered by it, Viviana," replied Fawkes. "I am a homeless man, and a friendless, and the affection of such a being as yourself will fill up the only void in my heart. But I am wedded to the great cause. I can never be more to you than a father."

"Nay, I ask nothing more," she replied, blushing deeply.

"Having thus arranged the terms upon which we shall travel," observed Garnet, with a smile, "nothing is needed but to prepare for our journey. We start early to-morrow morning."

"I shall be ready at daybreak," replied Viviana.

"And I am ready now," added Guy Fawkes. "In my opinion, we run great risk in remaining here another night. But be it as you will."

At this moment they were interrupted by the entrance of Father Oldcorne, who, with a countenance of great alarm, informed them he could nowhere find Martin Heydocke.

"Do you suspect any treachery on his part?" asked Garnet of Viviana.

"I have always found him trustworthy," she answered; "and his father was *my* father's oldest servant. I cannot think he would betray us. At the same time, I must admit his disappearance at this juncture looks suspicious."

"If my strength were equal to it," returned Guy Fawkes, "I would keep watch throughout the night; but that might prevent me from accompanying you to-morrow. My advice, I repeat is—to set out at once."

This opinion, however, was overruled by Garnet and Viviana, who did not think the danger so urgent, and attributed the absence of Martin Heydocke to some unimportant cause. Guy Fawkes made no further remonstrance, and it was agreed they should start as originally proposed at daybreak.

The party then separated, and Viviana wandered alone over the old house, taking a farewell, which she felt would be her last, of every familiar object. Few things were as she had known them, but even in their present forlorn state they were dear to her; and the rooms she trod, though dismantled, were the same she had occupied in childhood.

There is no pang more acute to a sensitive nature than that occasioned by quitting an abode or spot endeared by early recollections and associations, to which we feel a strong presentiment we shall never return. Viviana experienced this feeling in its full force, and she lingered in each room as if she had not the power to leave it. Her emotions at length became so overpowering, that to relieve them she strolled forth into the garden. Here, new objects awakened her attention, and recalled happier times with painful distinctness. Twilight was fast deepening, and, viewed through this dim and softened medium, everything looked as of old, and produced a tightening and stifling sensation in her breast, that nothing but a flood of tears could remove.

The flowers yielded forth their richest scents, and the whole scene was such as she had often beheld it in times long ago, when sorrow was wholly unknown to her. Perfumes, it is well known, exercise a singular influence over the memory. A particular odour will frequently call up an event and a long train of circumstances connected with the time when it was first inhaled. Without being aware whence it arose, Viviana felt a tide of recollections pressing upon her, which she would have willingly repressed, but which it was out of her power to control. Her tears flowed abundantly, and at length, with a heart somewhat lightened of its load, she arose from the bench on which she had thrown herself, and proceeded along a walk to gather a few flowers as memorials of the place.

In this way she reached the further end of the garden, and was stooping to pluck a spray of some fragrant shrub, when she perceived the figure of a man behind a tree at a little distance from her. From his garb, which was that of a soldier, she instantly knew he was an enemy, and, though greatly alarmed, she had the courage not to scream, but, breaking off the branch, she uttered a careless exclamation, and slowly retraced her steps. She half expected to hear that the soldier was following her, and prepared to start off at full speed to the house; but, deceived by her manner, he did not stir. On reaching the end of the walk, she could not resist the inclination to look back, and glancing over her shoulder, perceived the man watching her. But as she moved, he instantly withdrew his head.

Her first step on reaching the house was to close and fasten the door; her next to hasten to Guy Fawkes's chamber where she found him, together with Garnet and Oldcorne. All three were astounded at the intelligence, agreeing that an attack was intended, and that a large force was, in all probability, concealed in the garden awaiting only the arrival of night to surprise and seize them. The disappearance of the younger Heydocke was no longer a mystery. He had been secured and carried off by the hostile party, to prevent him from giving the alarm. The emergency was a fearful one, and it excited consternation amongst all except Guy Fawkes, who preserved his calmness.

"I foresaw we should be attacked to-night," he said, " and I am therefore not wholly unprepared. Our only chance is to steal out unobserved; for resistance would be in vain, as their force is probably numerous, and I am as helpless as an infant, while Father Garnet's broken arm precludes any assistance from him. The subterranean passage leading from the oratory to the further side of the moat having been stopped up by the pursuivant and his band, it will be necessary to cross the drawbridge, and as soon as it grows sufficiently dark, we must make the attempt. We have no horses, and must trust to our own exertions for safety. Catesby would now be invaluable. It is not his custom to desert his friends at the season of their greatest need."

"Great as is my danger," observed Viviana, "I would rather, so far as I am concerned, that he were absent, than owe my preservation to him. I have no fears for myself."

" And my only fears are for you," rejoined Fawkes.

Half an hour of intense anxiety was now passed by the party. Garnet was restless and uneasy. Oldcorne betrayed his agitation by unavailing lamentations, by listening to every sound, and by constantly rushing to the windows to reconnoitre, until he was checked by Fawkes, who represented to him the folly of his conduct. Viviana, though ill at ease, did not allow her terror to appear, but endeavoured to imitate the immovable demeanour of Guy Fawkes, who always became more collected in proportion to the danger by which he was threatened.

At the expiration of the time above-mentioned it had become quite dark, and desiring his companions to follow him, Guy Fawkes drew his sword, and, grasping Viviana's hand, led the way down stairs. Before opening the door, he listened intently, and, hearing no sound, issued cautiously forth. The party had scarcely gained the centre of the court, when a caliver was discharged at them, which, though it did no damage, served as a signal to the rest of their foes. Guy Fawkes, who had never relinquished his hold of Viviana, now pressed forward as rapidly as his strength would permit, and the two priests followed. But loud shouts were raised on the drawbridge, and it was evident it was occupied by the enemy.

Uncertain what to do, Guy Fawkes halted, and was about to return to the house, when a shout from behind told him their retreat was intercepted. In this dilemma there was nothing for it but to attempt to force a passage across the drawbridge, or to surrender at discretion; and though Guy Fawkes would not at other seasons have hesitated to embrace the former alternative, he knew that his strength was not equal to it now.

While he was internally resolving not to yield himself with life, and supporting Viviana, who clung closely to him, the clatter of hoofs was heard rapidly approaching along the avenue, and presently afterwards two horsemen galloped at full speed toward the drawbridge. The noise had likewise attracted the attention of the enemy; who, apprehensive of a rescue, prepared to stop them. But the tremendous pace of the riders rendered this impossible. A few blows were exchanged, a few shots fired, and they had crossed the drawbridge.

"Who goes there?" shouted Guy Fawkes, as the horsemen approached him.

"It is the voice of Guy Fawkes," cried the foremost, whose tones proclaimed it was Catesby. "They are here," he cried, reining in his steed.

"Where is Viviana?" vociferated his companion, who was no other than Humphrey Chetham.

"Here—here," replied Guy Fawkes.

With the quickness of thought the young merchant was by her side, and in another moment she was placed on the saddle before him, and borne at a headlong pace across the drawbridge.

"Follow me," cried Catesby; "I will clear a passage for you. Once across the drawbridge, you are safe. A hundred yards down the avenue, on the right, you will find a couple of horses tied to a tree. Quick! quick!"

As he spoke, a shot whizzed past his head, and a tumultuous din in the rear told that their pursuers were close upon them. Striking spurs into his steed, Catesby dashed forward, and dealing blows right and left, cleared the drawbridge of

its occupants, many of whom leaped into the moat to escape
his fury. His companions were close at his heels, and got
over the bridge in safety.

"Fly!—fly!" cried Catesby—"to the horses—the horses!
I will check all pursuit."

So saying, and while the others flew towards the avenue,
he faced his opponents, and making a desperate charge upon
them, drove them backwards. In this conflict, though several
shots were fired, and blows aimed at him on all sides, he sustained no injury, but succeeded in defending the bridge sufficiently long to enable his friends to mount.

He then rode off at full speed, and found the party waiting for him at the end of the avenue. Father Oldcorne was
seated on the same steed as his superior. After riding with
them upwards of a mile, Humphrey Chetham dismounted,
and resigning his horse to Viviana, bade her farewell, and
disappeared.

"And now to London!" cried Catesby, striking into a road
on the right, and urging his steed to a rapid pace.

"Ay, to London!—to the Parliament House!" echoed
Fawkes, following him with the others.

END OF THE FIRST BOOK.

Book the Second.

THE DISCOVERY.

The next point to be considered is the means to compass and work these
designs. These means were most cruel and damnable;—by mining, and by
thirty-six barrels of powder, having crows of iron, stones, and wood, laid
upon the barrels, to have made the breach the greater. Lord! what a
wind, what a fire, what a motion and commotion of earth and air would
there have been!—*Sir Edward Coke's Speech on the Trial of the Conspirators in the Gunpowder Plot.*

I.

THE LANDING OF THE POWDER.

TOWARDS the close of the sixth day after their departure
from Ordsall Hall, the party approached the capital. The
sun was setting as they descended Highgate Hill, and the
view of the ancient, and then most picturesque city, was so
enchanting, that Viviana, who beheld it for the first time,

entreated her companions to pause for a few minutes to allow
her to contemplate it. From the spot where they halted, the
country was completely open to Clerkenwell, and only a few
scattered habitations lay between them and the old grey
ramparts of the city, with their gates and fortifications,
which were easily discernible even at that distance. Above
them rose the massive body and central tower of Saint
Paul's Cathedral—a structure far surpassing that which has
succeeded it—while amid the innumerable gables, pointed
roofs, and twisted chimneys of the houses sprang a multitude
of lesser towers and spires, lending additional beauty to the
scene. Viviana was enraptured, and, while gazing on the
prospect, almost forgot her sorrows. Guy Fawkes and
Catesby, who were a little in advance of the others, turned
their gaze westward, and the former observed to his companion:

"The sun is setting over the Parliament House. The sky
seems stained with blood. It looks portentous of what is to
follow."

"I would gladly behold the explosion from this hill, or
from yon heights," replied Catesby, pointing towards Hamp-
stead. "It will be a sight such as man has seldom seen."

"I shall never live to witness it !" exclaimed Guy Fawkes,
in a melancholy tone.

"What! still desponding?" returned Catesby, reproachfully. "I thought, since you had fully recovered from your
wound, you had shaken off your fears."

"You misunderstand me," replied Fawkes. "I mean that
I shall perish with our foes."

"Why so?" cried Catesby. "There will be plenty of time
to escape after you have fired the train."

"I shall not attempt it," rejoined Fawkes, in a sombre
voice. "I will abide the result in the vault. If I perish it
will be a glorious death."

"Better live to see the regeneration of our faith, and our
restoration to our rights," rejoined Catesby. "But we will
speak of this hereafter. Here comes Garnet."

"Where do you propose we should lodge to-night?" asked
the latter, riding up.

"At the house at Lambeth, where the powder is deposited,"
returned Catesby.

"Will it be safe?" asked Garnet, uneasily.

"We shall be safer there than elsewhere, father," replied
Catesby. "If it is dark enough to-night, Fawkes and I will

remove a portion of the powder. But we are losing time.
We must pass through the City before the gates are closed."

In this suggestion Garnet acquiesced, and calling to
Viviana to follow them—for, since his late atrocious attempt,
Catesby had not exchanged a word or look with her, but during the whole of the journey kept sedulously aloof—the
whole party set forward, and proceeding at a brisk pace, soon
reached-the walls of the City. Passing through Cripplegate,
they shaped their course towards London Bridge. Viviana
was filled with astonishment at all she saw : the multitude
and magnificence of the shops, compared with such as she
had previously seen ; the crowds in the streets—for even at
that hour they were thronged; the varied dresses of the
passengers—the sober garb of the merchant, contrasting with
the showy cloak, the preposterous ruff, swelling hose, plumed
cap, and swaggering gait of the gallant or the ruffler ; the
brawls that were constantly occurring; the number of signs
projecting from the dwellings; all she witnessed or heard
surprised and amused her, and she would willingly have proceeded at a slower pace to indulge her curiosity, had not her
companions urged her onward.

As they were crossing Eastcheap, in the direction of
Crooked-lane, a man suddenly quitted the footpath, and,
rushing towards Garnet, seized his bridle, and cried :

"I arrest you. You are a Romish priest."

"It is false, knave," returned Garnet. "I am as good
a Protestant as thyself, and am just arrived with my companions from a long journey."

"Your companions are all rank Papists," rejoined the
stranger. "You yourself are Father Garnet, superior of the
Jesuits, and, if I am not deceived, the person next you is
Father Oldcorne, also of that order. If I am wrong you can
easily refute the charge. Come with me to the Council. If
you refuse, I will call assistance from the passengers."

Garnet saw he was lost if he did not make an immediate
effort at self-preservation, and resolving to be beforehand
with his assailant, he shouted at the top of his voice:

"Help! help! my masters. This villain would rob me of
my purse !"

"He is a Romish priest," vociferated the stranger. "I call
upon you to assist me to arrest him."

While the passengers, scarcely knowing what to make of
these contradictory statements, flocked round them, Guy
Fawkes, who was a little in advance of Catesby, rode back,

and seeing how matters stood, instantly drew a petronel, and with the butt-end felled the stranger to the ground. Thus liberated, Garnet struck spurs into his steed, and the whole party dashed off at a rapid pace. Shouts were raised by the bystanders, a few of whom started in pursuit, but the speed at which the fugitives rode soon bore them out of danger.

By this time they had reached London Bridge, and Viviana, in some degree recovered from the fright caused by the recent occurrence, ventured to look around her. She could scarcely believe she was crossing a bridge, so completely did the tall houses give it the appearance of a street; and, if it had not been for occasional glimpses of the river caught between the openings of these lofty habitations, she would have thought her companions had mistaken the road. As they approached the ancient gateway (afterwards denominated Traitor's Tower), at the Southwark side of the bridge, she remarked with a shudder the dismal array of heads garnishing its spikes, and pointing them out to Fawkes, cried:

"Heaven grant yours may never be amongst the number!"

Fawkes made no answer, but dashed beneath the low and gloomy arch of the gate.

Striking into a street on the right, the party skirted the walls of Saint Saviour's Church, and presently drew near the Globe theatre, above which floated its banner. Adjoining it was the old Bear Garden—the savage inmates of which made themselves sufficiently audible. Garnet hastily pointed out the first-mentioned place of amusement to Viviana as they passed it, and her reading having made her well acquainted with the noble dramas produced at that unpretending establishment—little better than a barn in comparison with a modern playhouse, — she regarded it with deep interest. Another theatre—the Swan—speedily claimed her attention; and, leaving it behind, they came upon the open country.

It was now growing rapidly dark, and Catesby, turning off into a narrow lane on the right, shouted to his companions to keep near him. The tract of land they were traversing was flat and marshy. The air was damp and unwholesome— for the swamp had not been drained as in later times,—and the misty exhalations arising from it added to the obscurity. Catesby, however, did not relax his pace, and his companions imitated his example. Another turn on the right seemed to bring them still nearer the river, and involved them in a thicker fog.

All at once Catesby stopped, and cried:

"We should be near the house. And yet this fog perplexes me. Stay here while I search for it."

"If you leave us, we shall not readily meet again," rejoined Fawkes.

But the caution was unheeded, Catesby having already disappeared. A few moments afterwards, Fawkes heard the sound of a horse's hoofs approaching him; and, thinking it was Catesby, he hailed the rider.

The horseman made no answer, but continued to advance towards them.

Just then the voice of Catesby was heard at a little distance, shouting, "I was right. It is here."

The party then hastened in the direction of the cry, and perceived through the gloom a low building, before the door of which Catesby, who had dismounted, was standing.

"A stranger is amongst us," observed Fawkes, in an undertone, as he rode up.

"Where is he?" demanded Catesby, hastily.

"Here," replied a voice. "But, fear nothing. I am a friend."

"I must have stronger assurance than that," replied Catesby. "Who are you?"

"Robert Keyes," replied the other. "Do you not know my voice?"

"In good truth I did not," rejoined Catesby; "and you have spoken just in time. Your arrival is most opportune. But what brings you here to-night?"

"The same errand as yourself, I conclude, Catesby," replied Keyes. "I came here to see that all was in safety. But who have you with you?"

"Let us enter the house, and you shall learn," replied Catesby.

With this, he tapped thrice at the door in a peculiar manner, and presently a light was seen through the windows, and a voice from within demanded who knocked.

"Your master," replied Catesby.

Upon this, the door was instantly unbarred. After a hasty greeting between Catesby and his servant, whom he addressed as Thomas Bates, the former inquired whether aught had occurred during his absence, and was answered that, except an occasional visit from Mr. Percy, one of the conspirators, no one had been near the house; everything being in precisely the same state he had left it.

"That is well," replied Catesby. "Now, then, to dispose of the horses."

All the party having dismounted, their steeds were led to
a stable at the back of the premises by Catesby and Bates,
while the others entered the house. It was a small, mean-
looking habitation, standing at a short distance from the
river-side, on the skirts of Lambeth Marsh, and its secluded
situation and miserable appearance seldom induced any one
to visit it. On one side was a deep muddy sluice communicating with the river. Within, it possessed but slight accommodation, and only numbered four apartments. One of the
best of these was assigned to Viviana, and she retired to it as
soon as it could be prepared for her reception. Garnet, who
still carried his arm in a sling, but who was in other respects
almost recovered from his accident, tendered every assistance
in his power, and would have remained with her, but she
entreated to be left alone. On descending to the lower room,
he found Catesby, who, having left Bates in care of the horses,
produced such refreshments as they had brought with them.
These were scanty enough; but a few flasks of excellent wine
which they found within the house made some amends for
the meagre repast. Viviana was solicited by Guy Fawkes
to join them; but she declined, alleging that she was greatly
fatigued, and about to retire to rest.

Their meal ended, Catesby proposed that they should ascertain the condition of the powder, as he feared it might have
suffered from being so long in the vault. Before making this
examination, the door was carefully barred; the shutters of
the windows closed; and Guy Fawkes placed himself as
sentinel at the door. A flag beneath the grate, in which a
fire was never kindled, was then raised, and disclosed a flight
of steps leading to a vault beneath. Catesby having placed
a light in a lantern, descended with Keyes; but both Garnet
and Oldcorne refused to accompany them.

The vault was arched and lofty, and, strange to say, for its
situation, dry—a circumstance owing, in all probability, to
the great thickness of the walls. On either side were ranged
twenty barrels filled with powder; and at the further end
stood a pile of arms, consisting of pikes, rapiers, demi-lances,
petronels, calivers, corslets, and morions. Removing one of
the barrels from its station, Catesby forced open the lid, and
examined its contents, which he found perfectly dry and
uninjured.

"It is fit for use," he observed, with a significant smile, as
he exhibited a handful of the powder to Keyes, who stood at
a little distance with the lantern; "if it will keep as well in

the cellar beneath the Parliament House, our foes will soon be nearer heaven than they would ever be if left to themselves."

"When do you propose to transport it across the river?" asked Keyes.

"To-night," replied Catesby. "It is dark and foggy, and fitting for the purpose. Bates!" he shouted; and at the call his servant instantly descended. "Is the wherry at her moorings?"

"She is, your worship," replied Bates.

"You must cross the river instantly, then," rejoined Catesby, "and proceed to the dwelling adjoining the Parliament House, which we hired from Ferris. Here is the key. Examine the premises, — and bring word whether all is secure."

Bates was about to depart, when Keyes volunteering to accompany him, they left the house together. Having fastened down the lid of the cask, Catesby summoned Fawkes to his assistance, and by his help as many barrels as could be safely stowed in the boat were brought out of the vault. More than two hours elapsed before Bates returned. He was alone, and informed them that all was secure, but that Keyes had decided on remaining where he was,—it being so dark and foggy, that it was scarcely possible to cross the river.

"I had some difficulty in landing," he added, "and got considerably out of my course. I never was out on so dark a night before."

"It is the better for us," rejoined Catesby. "We shall be sure to escape observation."

In this opinion Guy Fawkes concurred, and they proceeded to transport the powder to the boat, which was brought up the sluice within a few yards of the door. This done, and the barrels covered with a piece of tarpaulin, they embarked, and Fawkes, seizing an oar, propelled the skiff along the narrow creek.

As Bates had stated, the fog was so dense that it was wholly impossible to steer correctly, and Fawkes was therefore obliged to trust to chance as to the course he took. However, having fully regained his strength, he rowed with great swiftness, and, as far as he could judge, had gained the mid-stream, when, before he could avoid it, he came in violent contact with another boat, over-setting it, and plunging its occupants in the stream.

Disregarding the hints and even menaces of Catesby, who

urged him to proceed, Fawkes immediately lay upon his oars, and, as the water was perfectly smooth, succeeded, without much difficulty, in extricating the two men from their perilous situation. Their boat having drifted down the stream, could not be recovered. The chief of these personages was profuse in his thanks to his deliverers, whom he supposed were watermen, and they took care not to undeceive him.

"You may rely upon my gratitude," he said; "and when I tell you I am the Earl of Salisbury, you will be satisfied I have the means of evincing it."

"The Earl of Salisbury!" exclaimed Catesby, who was seated by Fawkes, having taken one of the oars. "Is it possible?"

"I have been on secret State business," replied the Earl, "and did not choose to employ my own barge. I was returning to Whitehall, when your boat struck against mine."

"It is our bitterest enemy," observed Catesby, in an undertone, to Fawkes. "Fate has delivered him into our hands."

"What are you about to do?" demanded Fawkes, observing that his companion no longer pulled at the oar.

"Shoot him," replied Catesby. "Keep still while I disengage my petronel."

"It shall not be," returned Fawkes, laying a firm grasp upon his arm. "Let him perish with the others."

"If we suffer him to escape now, we may never have such a chance again," rejoined Catesby. "I will shoot him."

"I say you shall not," rejoined Fawkes. "His hour is not yet come."

"What are you talking about, my masters?" demanded the Earl, who was shivering in his wet garments.

"Nothing," replied Catesby, hastily. "I will throw him overboard," he whispered to Fawkes.

"Again I say, you shall not," replied the latter.

"I see what you are afraid of," cried the Earl. "You are smugglers. You have got some casks of distilled waters on board, and are afraid I may report you. Fear nothing. Land me near the palace, and count upon my gratitude."

"Our course lies in a different direction," replied Catesby, sternly. "If your lordship lands at all, it must be where we choose."

"But I have to see the King to-night. I have some important papers to deliver to him respecting the Papists," replied Salisbury.

"Indeed!" exclaimed Catesby. "We must, at least, have those papers," he observed, in a whisper, to Fawkes.

"That is a different affair," replied Fawkes. "They may prove serviceable to us."

"My lord," observed Catesby, "by a strange chance you have fallen into the hands of Catholics. You will be pleased to deliver these papers to us."

"Ah! villains, would you rob me?" cried the Earl. "You shall take my life sooner."

"We will take both, if you resist," replied Catesby, in a menacing tone.

"Nay, then," returned Salisbury, attempting to draw his sword, "we will see who will obtain the mastery. We are equally matched. Come on; I fear you not."

But the waterman who had rowed the Earl was not of equal courage with his employer, and refused to take part in the conflict.

"It will be useless to contend with us," cried Catesby, relinquishing the oar to Fawkes, and springing forward. "I must have those papers," he added, seizing the Earl by the throat, "or I will throw you overboard."

"I am mistaken in you," returned Salisbury; "you are no common mariner."

"It matters not who or what I am," rejoined Catesby, fiercely. "Your papers, or you die."

Finding it in vain to contend with his opponent, the Earl was fain to yield, and reluctantly produced a packet from his doublet, and delivered it to him.

"You will repent this outrage, villain," he said.

"Your lordship will do well to recollect you are still in my power," rejoined Catesby. "One thrust of my sword will wipe off some of the injuries you have inflicted on our suffering party."

"I have heard your voice before," cried Salisbury; "you shall not escape me."

"Your imprudence has destroyed you," retorted Catesby, clutching the Earl's throat more tightly, and shortening his sword, with the intent to plunge in into his breast.

"Hold!" exclaimed Fawkes, grasping his arm, and preventing the blow. "I have already said you shall not slay him. You are in possession of his papers. What more would you have?"

"His life," replied Catesby, struggling to liberate his arm.

"Let him swear not to betray us," rejoined Fawkes. "If he refuses, I will not stay your hand."

"You hear what my companion says, my lord," cried Catesby. "Will you swear to keep silence as to what has just occurred?"

After a moment's hesitation, Salisbury assented, and Catesby relinquished his grasp.

During this time, the boat had drifted considerably down the stream, and, in spite of the darkness, Catesby noticed with some uneasiness that they were approaching more than one vessel. The Earl of Salisbury also perceived this, and raised a cry for help, but was instantly checked by Catesby, who took a seat beside him, and placing the point of his rapier at his breast, swore he would stab him if he made any further clamour.

The threat, and the dangerous propinquity of his enemy, effectually silenced the Earl, and Catesby directed Fawkes to make for the shore as quickly as he could. His injunctions were obeyed, and Fawkes plied the oars with so much good-will, that in a few minutes the wherry struck against the steps, which projected far into the water, a little to the right of the Star Chamber, precisely on the spot where West-minster Bridge now stands.

Here the Earl and his companion were allowed to disembark, and they had no sooner set foot on land than Guy Fawkes pushed off the boat, and rowed as swiftly as he could towards the centre of the stream. He then demanded of Catesby whether he should make for the Parliament House, or return.

"I scarcely know what to advise," replied Catesby. "I do not think the Earl will attempt pursuit. And yet I know not. The papers we have obtained may be important. Cease rowing for a moment, and let us listen."

Guy Fawkes complied and they listened intently, but could only hear the rippling of the current against the sides of the skiff.

"We have nothing to fear," observed Catesby. "He will not pursue us, or he cannot find a boat."

As he spoke, the glimmer of torches was visible on the shore, and the plunge of oars into the water convinced him his opinion was erroneous.

"What course shall we take?" inquired Fawkes.

"I care not," replied Catesby, sullenly. "If I had had my own way, this would not have happened."

"Have no fears," replied Fawkes, rowing swiftly down the stream. "We shall easily escape."

"We will not be taken alive," returned Catesby, seating himself on one of the barrels, and hammering against the lid with the butt-end of his petronel. "I will sooner blow us all to perdition than he shall capture us."

"You are right," replied Fawkes. "By my patron, Saint James, he is taking the same course as ourselves."

"Well, let him board us," replied Catesby. "I am ready for him."

"Do as you think proper if the worst occurs," returned Fawkes. "But, if we make no noise, I am assured we shall not be perceived."

With this he ceased rowing, and suffered the boat to drop down the stream. As ill-luck would have it, it seemed as if the hostile bark had struck completely into their track, and aided by the current, and four sturdy rowers were swiftly approaching.

"The Earl will be upon us in a few minutes," replied Catesby. "If you have any prayers to offer, recite them quickly, for I swear I will be as good as my word."

"I am ever prepared for death," replied Fawkes. "Ha! we are saved!"

This last exclamation was occasioned by his remarking a large barge, towards which they were rapidly drifting.

"What are you about to do?" cried Catesby. "Leap on board, and abandon the skiff, together with its contents?"

"No," replied Fawkes; "sit still, and leave the rest to me."

By this time, they had approached the barge, which was lying at anchor, and Guy Fawkes, grasping at a boat-hook, fixed it in the vessel as they passed, and drew their own boat close to its side—so close, in fact, that it could not be distinguished from it.

The next moment, the chase came up, and they distinctly perceived the Earl of Salisbury seated in the stern of the boat, holding a torch. As he approached the barge, he held the light towards it; but the skiff being on the off-side, entirely escaped notice. When the chase had got to a sufficient distance to be out of hearing, the fugitives rowed swiftly in the contrary direction.

Not judging it prudent to land, they continued to ply the oars, until fatigue compelled them to desist, and they had placed some miles between them and their pursuers.

N

"Long before this, the Earl must have given up the chase," observed Catesby. "We must return before day-break, and either land our powder near the Parliament House, or take it back to the vault at Lambeth."

"We shall run equal risk either way," replied Fawkes, "and, having ventured thus far, we may as well go through with it. I am for landing at Westminster."

"And I," rejoined Catesby. "I do not like giving up a project when I have once undertaken it."

"You speak my sentiments exactly," returned Fawkes. "Westminster be it."

After remaining stationary for about an hour, they rowed back again, and, aided by the stream, in a short time reached their destination. The fog had in a great degree cleared off, and day began to break as they approached the stairs lead-ing to Parliament House. Though this was not what they desired, inasmuch as the light added to the risk they would have run in landing the powder, it enabled them to ascertain that no one was on the watch.

Running swiftly in towards a sort of wharf, protected by a roofed building, Catesby leapt ashore, and tied the skiff to a ring in the steps. He then desired Fawkes to hand out the powder as quickly as he could. The order was promptly obeyed, and in a few minutes several barrels were on the strand.

"Had you not better fetch Keyes to help us, while I get out the rest?" observed Fawkes.

Catesby assented, and hurrying to the house, found Keyes, who was in great alarm about them. He instantly accom-panied the other to the wharf, and by their united efforts the powder was expeditiously and safely removed.

II.

THE TRAITOR.

THE habitation to which the powder was conveyed, ad-joined, as has already been stated, the Parliament House, and stood at the south-west corner of that structure. It was a small building, two stories high, with a little garden attached to it, surrounded by lofty walls, and belonged to Whin-neard, the keeper of the royal wardrobe, by whom it was let

to a person named Ferris. From the latter it was hired by
Thomas Percy, one of the conspirators, and a relative of the
Earl of Northumberland,—of whom it will be necessary to
speak more fully hereafter,—for the purpose to which it was
now put.

Having bestowed the barrels of powder carefully in the
cellar, and fastened the door of the house and the garden-
gate after them, the trio returned to the boat, and rowed
back to Lambeth, where they arrived without being noticed.
They then threw themselves upon the floor, and sought some
repose after their fatigue.

It was late in the day before they awoke. Garnet and
Oldcorne had been long astir; but Viviana had not quitted
her chamber. Catesby's first object was to examine the
packet he had obtained from the Earl of Salisbury, and withdrawing to a corner, he read over the papers one by one carefully.

Guy Fawkes watched his countenance as he perused them,
but he asked no questions. Many of the documents appeared
to have little interest, for Catesby tossed them aside with an
exclamation of disappointment. At length, however, a small
note dropped from the bundle. Catesby picked it up, opened
it, and his whole expression changed. His brow grew con-
tracted; and, springing to his feet, he uttered an ejaculation
of rage, crying, "It is as I suspected. We have traitors
among us."

"Whom do you suspect?" cried Fawkes.

"Tresham!" cried Catesby, in a voice of thunder,—"the
fawning, wily, lying Tresham. Fool that I was to league
him with us."

"He is your own kinsman," observed Garnet.

"He is," replied Catesby; "but were he my own brother
he should die. Here is a letter from him to Lord Mounteagle, which has found its way to the Earl of Salisbury, hinting
that a plot is hatching against the State, and offering to give
him full information of it."

"Traitor! false, perjured traitor!" cried Fawkes. "He
must die."

"He shall fall by my hand," rejoined Catesby. "Stay! a
plan occurs to me. He cannot be aware that this letter is in
my possession. I will send Bates to bid him come hither.
We will then charge him with his criminality, and put him
to death."

"He deserves severe punishment, no doubt," replied

N 2

Garnet: "but I am unwilling you should proceed to the last extremities with him."

"There is no alternative, father," replied Catesby. "Our safety demands his destruction."

Garnet returned no answer, but bowed his head sorrowfully upon his breast. Bates was then despatched to Tresham; and preparations were made by the three lay conspirators for executing their fell design.

It was agreed that, on his arrival, Tresham should be seized and disarmed, and after being interrogated by Catesby touching the extent of his treachery, should be stabbed by Guy Fawkes. This being resolved upon, it became a question how they should act in the interim. It was possible that, after the loss of his papers, some communication might take place between the Earl of Salisbury and Lord Mounteagle, and through the latter with Tresham. Thus prepared, on the arrival of Bates, Tresham, seeing through their design, instead of accompanying him, might give information of their retreat to the officers. The contingency was by no means improbable; and it was urged so strongly by Garnet, that Catesby began to regret his precipitancy in sending the message. Still, his choler was so greatly roused against Tresham, that he resolved to gratify his vengeance at any risk.

"If he betrays us, and brings the officers here, we shall know how to act," he remarked to Fawkes. "There is that below which will avenge us on them all."

"True," replied Fawkes. "But I trust we shall not be obliged to resort to it."

Soon after this, Bates returned with a message from Tresham, stating that he would be at the rendezvous at nightfall, and that he had important disclosures to make to them. He desired them, moreover, to observe the utmost caution, and not to stir abroad.

"He may, perhaps, be able to offer an explanation of his conduct," observed Keyes.

"Impossible," returned Catesby. "But he shall not die without a hearing."

"That is all I desire," returned Keyes.

While the others were debating upon the interrogations they should put to Tresham, and further examining the Earl of Salisbury's papers, Garnet repaired to Viviana's chamber, and informed her what was about to take place. She was filled with consternation, and entreated to be allowed to see

Guy Fawkes for a few moments alone. Moved by her supplications, Garnet complied, and presently afterwards Fawkes
entered the room.

"You have sent for me, Viviana," he said. "What would
you?"

"I have just heard you are about to put one of your companions to death," she replied. "It must not be."

"Viviana Radcliffe," returned Fawkes, "by your own
desire you have mixed yourself up with my fortunes. I will
not now discuss the prudence of the step you have taken.
But I deem it necessary to tell you, once for all, that any
attempts to turn me from the line of conduct I have marked
out to myself will fail. Tresham has betrayed us, and he
must pay the penalty of his treason."

"But not with his life," replied Viviana. "Do you not
now perceive into what enormities this fatal enterprise will
lead you? It is not one crime alone that you are about to
commit, but many. You constitute yourselves judges of
your companion, and without allowing him to defend himself,
take his life. Disguise it as you may, it is assassination—
cold-blooded assassination."

"His life is justly forfeited," replied Guy Fawkes, sternly.
"When he took the oath of secrecy and fidelity to our league,
he well knew what the consequences would be if he violated
it. He has done so. He has compromised our safety. Nay,
he has sold us to our enemies, and nothing shall save
him."

"If this is so," replied Viviana, "how much better would
it be to employ the time now left in providing for your safety
than in contriving means of vengeance upon one who will be
sufficiently punished for his baseness by his own conscience!
Even if you destroy him, you will not add to your own
security, while you will commit a foul and needless crime,
equal, if not exceeding in atrocity that you seek to punish."

"Viviana," replied Fawkes, in an angry tone, "in an evil
hour I consented to your accompanying me. I now repent
my acquiescence. But, having passed my word, I cannot
retract. You waste time, and exhaust my patience and your
own by these unavailing supplications. When I embarked in
this enterprise I embraced all its dangers, all its crimes if you
will, and I shall not shrink from them. The extent of Tresham's treachery is not yet known to us. There may be—and
God grant it!—extenuating circumstances in his conduct that
may save his life. But, as the case stands at present, his

offence appears of that dye that nothing can wash it out but his blood."

And he turned to depart.

"When do you expect this wretched man?" asked Viviana, arresting him.

"At nightfall," replied Fawkes.

"Oh! that there were any means of warning him of his danger!" she cried.

"There are none," rejoined Fawkes, fiercely—"none that you can adopt. And I must lay my injunctions upon you not to quit your chamber."

So saying, he retired.

Left alone, Viviana became a prey to the most agonizing reflections. Despite the strong, and almost unaccountable interest she felt in Guy Fawkes, she began to repent the step she had taken in joining him, as calculated to make her a party to his criminal conduct. But this feeling was transient, and was succeeded by a firmer determination to pursue the good work she had undertaken.

"Though slight success has hitherto attended my efforts," she thought, "that is no reason why I should relax them. The time is arrived when I may exert a beneficial influence over him; and it may be, that what occurs to-night will prove the first step towards complete triumph. In any case, nothing shall be wanting to prevent the commission of the meditated atrocity."

With this she knelt down and prayed long and fervently, and arose confirmed and strengthened in her resolution.

Meanwhile no alteration had taken place in the purposes of the conspirators. Night came, but with it came not Tresham. Catesby, who up to this time had managed to restrain his impatience, now arose, and signified his intention of going in search of him, and was with difficulty prevented from carrying his threat into execution by Guy Fawkes, who represented the folly and risk of such a course.

"If he comes not before midnight, we shall know what to think, and how to act," he observed; "but till then let us remain tranquil."

Keyes and the others adding their persuasions to those of Fawkes, Catesby sat sullenly down, and a profound silence ensued. In this way some hours were passed, when just at the stroke of midnight Viviana descended from her room, and appeared amongst them. Her countenance was deathly pale, and she looked anxiously around the assemblage. All, however, with the exception of Fawkes, avoided her gaze.

"Is he come?" she exclaimed at length. "I have listened intently, but have heard nothing. You cannot have murdered him. And yet your looks alarm me. Father Garnet, answer me—is the deed done?"

"No, my daughter," replied Garnet, sternly.

"Then he has escaped!" she cried, joyfully. "You expected him at nightfall."

"It is not yet too late," replied Fawkes, in a sombre tone; "his death is only deferred."

"Oh! do not say so," she cried, in a voice of agony. "I hoped you had relented."

At this moment a peculiar knock was heard at the door. It was thrice repeated, and the strokes vibrated, though with different effect, through every bosom.

"He is here," cried Catesby, rising.

"Viviana, go to your chamber," commanded Guy Fawkes, grasping her hand, and leading her towards the stairs.

But she resisted his efforts, and fell on her knees.

"I will not go," she cried, in a supplicating tone, "unless you will spare this man's life."

"I have already told you my fixed determination," rejoined Fawkes, fiercely. "If you will not retire of your own free will, I must force you."

"If you attempt it, I will scream, and alarm your victim," she replied. "Mr. Catesby," she added, "have my prayers, my entreaties, no weight with you? Will you not grant me his life?"

"No!" replied Catesby, fiercely. "She must be silenced," he added, with a significant look at Fawkes.

"She shall," replied the latter, drawing his poniard. "Viviana!" he continued, in a voice and with a look that left no doubt as to his intentions, "do not compel me to be your destroyer."

As he spoke, the knocking was repeated, and Viviana uttered a prolonged and piercing cry. Guy Fawkes raised his weapon, and was about to strike, but his resolution failed him, and his arm dropped nerveless to his side.

"Your better angel has conquered!" she cried, clasping his knees.

While this was passing, the door was thrown open by Catesby and Tresham entered the room.

"What means this outcry?" he asked, looking round in

alarm. "Ah! what do I see? Viviana Radcliffe here! Did she utter the scream?"

"She did," replied Viviana, rising, "and she hoped to warn you by it. But you were led on by your fate."

"Warn me from what?" ejaculated Tresham, starting. "I am among friends."

"You are among those who have resolved upon your death," replied Viviana.

"Ah!" exclaimed Tresham, making an effort to gain the door, and draw his sword.

In both attempts, however, he was foiled, for Catesby intercepted him, while Fawkes and Keyes flung themselves upon him, and binding his arms together with a sword-belt, forced him into a chair.

"Of what am I accused?" he demanded, in a voice tremulous with rage and terror.

"You shall learn presently," replied Catesby. And he motioned to Fawkes to remove Viviana.

"Let me remain," she cried, fiercely. "My nature is changed, and is become as savage as your own. If blood must be spilt, I will tarry to look upon it."

"This is no place for you, dear daughter," interposed Garnet.

"Nor for you either, father," retorted Viviana, bitterly; "unless you will act as a minister of Christ, and prevent this violence."

"Let her remain," if she will," observed Catesby. "Her presence need not hinder our proceedings."

So saying, he seated himself opposite Tresham, while the two priests placed themselves on either side. Guy Fawkes took up a position on the left of the prisoner, with his drawn dagger in his hand, and Keyes stationed himself near the door. The unfortunate captive regarded them with terrified glances, and trembled in every limb.

"Thomas Tresham," commenced Catesby, in a stern voice, "you are a sworn brother in our plot. Before I proceed further I will ask you what should be his punishment who violates his oath, and betrays his confederates? We await your answer."

But Tresham remained obstinately silent.

"I will tell you, since you refuse to speak," continued Catesby. "It is death—death by the hands of his associates."

"It may be," replied Tresham; "but I have neither broken my oath, nor betrayed you."

"Your letter to Lord Mounteagle is in my possession,"
replied Catesby. "Behold it!"

"Perdition!" exclaimed Tresham. "But you will not slay
me? I have betrayed nothing. I have revealed nothing. On
my soul's salvation, I have not! Spare me! spare me! and
I will be a faithful friend in future. I have been indiscreet—
I own it—but nothing more. I have mentioned no names;
and Lord Mounteagle, as you well know, is as zealous a Catholic
as any now present."

"Your letter has been sent to the Earl of Salisbury,"
pursued Catesby, coldly. "It was from him I obtained it."

"Then Lord Mounteagle has betrayed me," returned
Tresham, becoming as pale as death.

"Have you nothing further to allege'" demanded Catesby.
As Tresham made no answer, he turned to the others, and
said, "Is it your judgment he should die?"

All, except Viviana, answered in the affirmative.

"Tresham," continued Catesby, solemnly, "prepare to meet
your fate like a man. And do you, father," he added to Garnet,
"proceed to shrive him."

"Hold!" cried Viviana, stepping into the midst of them—
"hold!" she exclaimed in a voice so authoritative, and with
a look so commanding, that the whole assemblage were awe-
stricken. "If you think to commit this crime with impunity,
you are mistaken. I swear by everything sacred, if you take
this man's life, I will go forth instantly, and denounce you all
to the Council. You may stare, sirs, and threaten me, but
you shall find I will keep my word."

"We must put her to death too," observed Catesby, in an
undertone to Fawkes, "or we shall have a worse enemy left
than Tresham."

"I cannot consent to it," replied Fawkes.

"If you mistrust this person, why not place him in restraint?" pursued Viviana. "You will not mend matters by
killing him."

"She says well," observed Garnet; "let us put him in some
place of security."

"I am agreed," replied Fawkes.

"And I," added Keyes.

"My judgment, then, is overruled," rejoined Catesby.
"But I will not oppose you. We will imprison him in the
vault beneath this chamber."

"He must be without light," said Garnet.

"And without arms," added Keyes.

"And without food," muttered Catesby. "He has only exchanged one death for another."

The flag was then raised, and Tresham thrust into the vault, after which it was restored to its former position.

"I have saved you from the lesser crime," cried Viviana to Guy Fawkes; "and with Heaven's grace, I trust to preserve you from the greater!"

III.

THE ESCAPE PREVENTED.

VIVIANA having retired to her chamber, apparently to rest, a long and anxious consultation was held by the conspirators as to the next steps to be pursued. Garnet was of opinion that, as the Earl of Salisbury was aware of a conspiracy against the State being on foot among the Catholics, their project ought to be deferred, if not altogether abandoned.

"We are sure to be discovered," he said. "Arrests without end will take place. And such rigorous measures will be adopted by the Earl, such inquiries instituted, that all will infallibly be brought to light. Besides, we know not what Tresham may have revealed. He denies having betrayed our secret, but no credit can be attached to his assertions."

"Shall we examine him again, father?" cried Catesby, "and wring the truth from him by threats or torture?"

"No, my son," replied Garnet, "let him remain where he is till morning. A night of solitary confinement, added to the stings of his own guilty conscience, is likely to produce a stronger effect upon him than any torments we could inflict. He shall be interrogated strictly to-morrow, and I will answer for it, will make a full confession. But even if he has revealed nothing material, there exists another and equally serious ground of alarm. I allude to your meeting with the Earl on the river. I should be the last to counsel bloodshed. But if ever it could be justified, it might have been so in this case."

"I would have slain him if I had had my own way," returned Catesby, with a fierce and reproachful look at Fawkes.

"If I have done wrong, I will speedily repair my error," observed the latter. "Do you desire his death, father? and will you absolve me from the deed?" he added, turning to Garnet.

"It is better as it is," replied Garnet, making a gesture in the negative. "I would not have our high and holy purpose stained by common slaughter. The power that delivered him into your hands, and stayed them, no doubt preserved him for the general sacrifice. My first fear was lest, having noticed the barrels of powder within the boat, he might have suspected your design. But I am satisfied his eyes were blinded, and his reason benighted, so that he could discern nothing."

"Such was my opinion, father," replied Fawkes. "Let us observe the utmost caution, but proceed at all hazards with the enterprise. If we delay, we fail."

"Right," returned Catesby; "and for that counsel I forgive you for standing between me and our enemy."

Upon this, it was agreed that if nothing occurred in the interim, more powder should be transported to the habitation in Westminster on the following night—that Fawkes and Catesby, who might be recognised by Salisbury's description, should keep close house during the day—and that the rest of the conspirators should be summoned to assist in digging the mine. Prayers were then offered by the two priests for their preservation from peril, and for success in their enterprise; after which they threw themselves on benches or seats, and courted slumber. All slept soundly except Fawkes, who, not being able to close his eyes, from an undefinable apprehension of danger, arose, and cautiously opening the door, kept watch outside.

Shortly afterwards, Viviana, who had waited till all was quiet, softly descended the stairs, and, shading her light, gazed timorously round. Satisfied she was not observed, she glided swiftly and noiselessly to the fireplace, and endeavoured to raise the flag. But it resisted all her efforts, and she was about to abandon the attempt in despair, when she perceived a bolt on one side, that had escaped her notice. Hastily withdrawing it, she experienced no further difficulty. The stone revolved on hinges like a trap-door, and lifting it she hurried down the steps.

Alarmed by her approach, Tresham had retreated to the further end of the vault, and snatching up a halberd from the pile of weapons, cried, in a voice of desperation:

"Stand off! I am armed, and have severed my bonds.
Off, I say! You shall not take me with life."

"Hush!" cried Viviana, putting her finger to her lips, "I
am come to set you free."

"Do I behold an inhabitant of this world?" cried Tresham,
crossing himself, and dropping the halberd, "or some blessed
saint? Ah!" he exclaimed, as she advanced towards him,
"it is Viviana Radcliffe—my preserver. Pardon, sweet lady.
My eyes were dazzled by the light, and your sudden appearance and speech—and I might almost say looks—made me
think you were some supernatural being come to deliver me
from these bloody-minded men. Where are they?"

"In the room above," she replied in a whisper—"asleep—
and if you speak so loud you will arouse them."

"Let us fly without a moment's delay," returned Tresham,
in the same tone, and hastily picking up a rapier and a
dagger.

"Stay!" cried Viviana, arresting him. "Before you go,
you must tell me what you are about to do."

"We will talk of that when we are out of this accursed
place," he replied.

"You shall not stir a footstep," she rejoined, placing herself resolutely between him and the outlet, "till you have
sworn neither to betray your confederates, nor to do them
injury."

"May Heaven requite me, if I forgive them!" cried Tresham
between his ground teeth.

"Remember!—you are yet in their power," she rejoined.
"One word from me, and they are at your side. Swear!—and
swear solemnly, or you do not quit this spot."

Tresham gazed at her fiercely, and griped his dagger, as if
determined to free himself at any cost.

"Ah!" she ejaculated, noticing the movement, "you are
indeed a traitor. You have neither sense of honour nor gratitude, and I leave you to your fate. Attempt to follow me,
and I give the alarm."

"Forgive me, Viviana," he cried, abjectly prostrating himself at her feet, and clinging to the hem of her dress. "I
meant only to terrify you; I would not injure you for worlds.
Do not leave me with these ruthless cut-throats. They will
assuredly murder me. Do not remain with them yourself,
or you will come to some dreadful end. Fly with me, and I
will place you beyond their reach—will watch over your safety.
Or, if you are resolved to brave their fury, let me go, and

I will take any oath you propose. As I hope for salvation I will not betray them."

"Peace!" cried Viviana, contemptuously. "If I set you free, it is not to save you, but them."

"What mean you?" asked Tresham, hesitating.

"Question me not, but follow," she rejoined, "and tread softly, as you value your life."

Tresham needed no caution on this head, and as they emerged from the trap-door in breathless silence, and he beheld the figures of his sleeping foes, he could scarcely muster sufficient courage to pass through them. Motioning him to proceed quickly, Viviana moved towards the door, and to her surprise found it unfastened. Without pausing to consider whence this neglect could arise, she opened it, and Tresham, who trembled in every limb, and walked upon the points of his feet, stepped forth. As he crossed the threshold, however, a powerful grasp was laid upon his shoulder, and a drawn sword presented to his breast, while the voice of Fawkes thundered in his ear, "Who goes there? Speak, or I strike."

While the fugitive, not daring to answer, lest his accents should betray him, endeavoured vainly to break away, Viviana hearing the struggle, threw open the door and exclaimed, "It is Tresham. I set him free."

"You!" cried Fawkes, in astonishment. "Wherefore?"

"In the hope that his escape would induce you to abandon your design, and seek safety in flight," she rejoined. "But you have thwarted my purpose."

Fawkes made no reply, but thrust Tresham forcibly into the house, and called to Catesby, who by this time had been roused with the others, to close and bar the door. The command was instantly obeyed, and as Catesby turned, a strange and fearful group met his view. In the midst stood Tresham, his haggard features and palsied frame bespeaking the extremity of his terror. His sword having been beaten from his grasp by Fawkes, and his dagger wrested from him by Keyes, he was utterly defenceless. Viviana had placed herself between him and his assailants, and screening him from their attack, cried:

"Despatch me. The fault is mine—mine only—and I am ready to pay the penalty. Had I not released him, he would not have attempted to escape. I am the rightful victim."

"She speaks the truth," gasped Tresham. "If she had not offered to liberate me, I should never have thought of

flying. Would to Heaven I had never yielded to her solicitations !"

"Peace, craven hound !" exclaimed Fawkes, furiously ; "you
deserve to die for your meanness and ingratitude, if not for
your treachery. And it is for this miserable wretch, Viviana,"
he added, turning to her, "that you would have placed your
friends in such fearful jeopardy—it is for him, who would
sacrifice you without scruple to save himself, that you now
offer your own life ?"

"I deserve your reproaches," she rejoined, in confusion.

"Had I not fortunately intercepted him," pursued Fawkes,
"an hour would not have elapsed ere he would have returned
with the officers ; and we should have changed this dwelling
for a dungeon in the Tower—these benches for the rack."

"In pity stab me !" cried Viviana, falling at his feet. "But
oh ! do not wound me with your words. I have committed a
grievous wrong ; but I was ignorant of the consequences ;
and, as I hope for mercy hereafter, my sole motive, beyond
compassion for this wretched man, was to terrify you into
relinquishing your dreadful project."

"You have acted wrongfully—very wrongfully, Viviana,"
interposed Garnet : "but since you are fully convinced of
your error, no more need be said. There are seasons when
the heart must be closed against compassion, and when mercy
becomes injustice. Go to your chamber, and leave us to deal
with this unhappy man."

"To-morrow you must quit us," observed Fawkes, as she
passed him.

"Quit you !" she exclaimed. "I will never offend again."

"I will not trust you," replied Fawkes, "unless—but it is
useless to impose restrictions upon you, which you will not—
perhaps, cannot observe."

"Impose any restrictions you please," replied Viviana,
"But do not bid me leave you."

"The time is come when we *must* separate," rejoined
Fawkes. "See you not that the course we are taking is
slippery with blood, and beset with perils which the firmest
of your sex could not encounter ?"

"I will encounter them, nevertheless," replied Viviana.
"Be merciful," she added, pointing to Tresham, "and mercy
shall be shown you in your hour of need." And she slowly
withdrew.

While this was passing, Catesby addressed a few words
aside to Keyes and Oldcorne, and now stepping forward and

fixing his eye steadily upon the prisoner, to note the effect of his speech upon him, said:

" I have devised a plan by which the full extent of Tresham's treachery can be ascertained."

" You do not mean to torture him, I trust ?" exclaimed Garnet, uneasily.

" No, father," replied Catesby. " If torture is inflicted at all, it will be upon the mind, not the body."

" Then it will be no torture," observed Garnet. " State your plan, my son."

" It is this," returned Catesby. " He shall write a letter to Lord Mounteagle, stating that he has important revela. tions to make to him, and entreating him to come hither unattended."

" Here !" exclaimed Fawkes.

" Here," repeated Catesby ; " and alone. We will conceal ourselves in such manner that we may overhear what passes between them, and if attempt is made by the villain to betray our presence, he shall be immediately shot. By this means we cannot fail to elicit the truth."

" I approve your plan, my son," replied Garnet ; " but who will convey the letter to Lord Mounteagle ?"

" I will," replied Fawkes. " Let it be prepared at once, and the case will be thought the more urgent. I will watch him, and see that he comes unattended, or give you timely warning."

" Enough," rejoined Garnet. " Let writing materials be procured, and I will dictate the letter."

Tresham, meanwhile, exhibited no misgiving ; but, on the contrary, his countenance brightened up as the plan was approved.

" My life will be spared if you find I have not deceived you, will it not ?" he asked, in a supplicating voice.

" Assuredly," replied Garnet.

" Give me pen and ink, then," he cried, " and I will write whatever you desire."

" Our secret is safe," whispered Catesby to Garnet. " It is useless to test him further."

" I think so," replied Garnet. " Would we had made this experiment sooner !"

" Do not delay, I entreat you," implored Tresham. "I am eager to prove my innocence."

" We are satisfied with the proof we have already obtained," returned Garnet.

Tresham dropped on his knees in speechless gratitude.

"We are spared the necessity of being your executioners, my son," pursued Garnet, "and I rejoice at it. But I cannot acquit you of the design to betray us; and till you have unburthened your whole soul to me, and proved by severe and self-inflicted penance that you are really penitent, you must remain a captive within these walls."

"I will disguise nothing from you, father," replied Tresham, "and will strive to expiate my offence by the severest penance you choose to inflict."

"Do this, my son," rejoined Garnet; "leave no doubt of your sincerity, and you may be yet restored to the place you have forfeited and become a sharer in our great enterprise."

"I will never trust him more," observed Fawkes.

"Nor I," added Keyes.

"*I* will," rejoined Catesby: "not that I have more faith in him than either of you; but I will so watch him that he shall not dare to betray us. Nay more," he added, in an undertone to Garnet, "I will turn his treachery to account. He will be a useful spy upon our enemies."

"If he can be relied on," observed Garnet.

"After this, you need have no fears," rejoined Catesby, with a significant smile.

"The first part of your penance, my son," said Garnet, addressing Tresham, "shall be to pass the night in solitary vigil and prayer within the vault. Number your transgressions, and reflect upon their enormity. Consider not only the injury your conduct might have done us, but the holy Church of which you are so sinful a member. Weigh over all this, and to-morrow I will hear your confession; when, if I find you in a state of grace, absolution shall not be refused."

Tresham humbly bowed his head in token of acquiescence. He was then led to the vault, and the flag closed over him, as before. This done, after a brief conversation, the others again stretched themselves on the floor, and sought repose.

IV.

THE MINE.

Some days elapsed before the conspirators ventured forth from their present abode. They had intended to remove the rest of the powder without loss of time, but were induced to defer their purpose on the representations of Tresham, who stated to Garnet that, in his opinion, they would run a great and needless risk. Before the expiration of a week, Tresham's apparent remorse for his perfidy, added to his seeming zeal, had so far reinstated him in the confidence of his associates, that he was fully absolved of his offence by Garnet; and, after taking fresh oaths of even greater solemnity than the former, was again admitted to the league. Catesby, however, who placed little faith in his protestations, never lost sight of him for an instant, and, even if he meditated an escape, he had no opportunity of effecting it.

A coldness, stronger on his side than hers, seemed to have arisen between Viviana and Guy Fawkes. Whenever she descended to the lower room, he withdrew on some excuse; and though he never urged her departure by words, his looks plainly bespoke that he desired it. Upon one occasion she found him alone—the others being at the time within the vault. He was whetting the point of his dagger, and did not hear her approach, until she stood beside him. He was slightly confused, and a deep ruddy stain flushed his swarthy cheeks and brow; but he averted his gaze, and continued his occupation in silence.

"Why do you shun me?" asked Viviana, laying her hand gently upon his shoulder. And, as he did not answer, she repeated the question in a broken voice. Guy Fawkes then looked up, and perceived that her eyes were filled with tears.

"I shun you, Viviana, for two reasons," he replied gravely, but kindly; "first, because I would have no ties of sympathy to make me cling to the world, or care for it; and I feel that if I suffer myself to be interested about you, this will not long be the case: secondly, and chiefly, because you are constantly striving to turn me from my fixed purpose; and, though your efforts have been, and will be unavailing, yet I would not be exposed to them further."

"You fear me, because you think I shall shake your resolution," she rejoined, with a forced smile. "But I will trouble you no more. Nay, if you wish it, I will go."

"It were better," replied Fawkes, in accents of deep emotion, and taking her hand. "Painful as will be the parting with you, I shall feel more easy when it is over. It grieves me to the soul to see you—the daughter of the proud, the wealthy Sir William Radcliffe—an inmate of this wretched abode, surrounded by desperate men, whose actions you dis-

approve, and whose danger you are compelled to share.
Think how it would add to my suffering if our plot—which
Heaven avert—should be discovered, and you be involved
in it."

"Do not think of it," replied Viviana.

"I cannot banish it from my thoughts," continued Fawkes.
"I cannot reconcile it to my feelings that one so young, so
beautiful, should be thus treated. Dwelling on this idea
unmans me—unfits me for sterner duties. The great crisis
is at hand, and I must live only for it."

"Live for it, then," rejoined Viviana; "but, oh! let me
remain with you till the blow is struck. Something tells me I
may yet be useful to you—may save you."

"No more of this, if you would indeed remain," rejoined
Guy Fawkes, sternly. "Regard me as a sword in the hand
of fate, which cannot be turned aside—as a bolt launched from
the cloud, and shattering all in its course, which may not be
stopped—as something terrible, exterminating, immovable.
Regard me as this, and say whether I am not to be shunned."

"No," replied Viviana; "I am as steadfast as yourself. I
will remain."

Guy Fawkes gazed at her in surprise mixed with admiration, and pressing her hand affectionately, said:

"I applaud your resolution. If I had a daughter, I should
wish her to be like you."

"You promised to be a father to me," she rejoined. "How
can you be so if I leave you?"

"How *can* I be so if you stay?" returned Fawkes, mournfully. "No, you must indulge no filial tenderness for one so
utterly unable to requite it as myself. Fix your thoughts
wholly on Heaven. Pray for the restoration of our holy religion—for the success of the great enterprise—and haply
your prayers may prevail."

"I cannot pray for that," she replied; "for I do not wish
it success. But I will pray—and fervently—that all danger
may be averted from your head."

At this moment Catesby and Keyes emerged from the vault,
and Viviana hurried to her chamber.

As soon as it grew dark, the remaining barrels of powder
were brought out of the cellar, and carefully placed in the
boat. Straw was then heaped upon them, and the whole
covered with a piece of tarpaulin, as upon the former occasion.
It being necessary to cross the river more than once, the conduct of the first and most hazardous passage was entrusted to

Fawkes, and accompanied by Keyes and Bates, both of whom were well armed, he set out a little before midnight. It was a clear starlight night; but as the moon had not yet risen, they were under no apprehension of discovery. The few craft they encountered, bent probably on some suspicious errand like themselves, paid no attention to them; and plying their oars swiftly, they shot under the low parapet edging the gardens of the Parliament House, just as the deep bell of the Abbey tolled forth the hour of twelve. Keeping in the shade, they silently approached the stairs. No one was there, not even a waterman to attend to the numerous wherries moored to the steps; and, without losing a moment, they sprang ashore, and concealing the barrels beneath their cloaks, glided like phantoms summoned by the witching hour along the passage formed by two high walls, leading to Old Palace Yard, and speedily reached the gate of the habitation. In this way, and with the utmost rapidity, the whole of the fearful cargo was safely deposited in the garden; and leaving the others to carry it into the house, Guy Fawkes returned to the boat. As he was about to push off, two persons rushed to the stair-head, and the foremost, evidently mistaking him for a waterman, called to him to take them across the river.

"I am no waterman, friend," replied Fawkes; "and am engaged on business of my own. Seek a wherry elsewhere."

"By Heaven!" exclaimed the new comer, in accents of surprise, "it is Guy Fawkes. Do you not know me?"

"Can it be Humphrey Chetham?" cried Fawkes, equally astonished.

"It is," replied the other. "This meeting is most fortunate. I was in search of you, having somewhat of importance to communicate to Viviana,"

"State it quickly, then," returned Fawkes; "I cannot tarry here much longer."

"I will go with you," rejoined Chetham, springing into the boat, and followed by his companion. "You must take me to her."

"Impossible," cried Fawkes, rising angrily; "neither can I permit you to accompany me. I am busied about my own concerns, and will not be interrupted."

"At least, tell me where I can find Viviana," persisted Chetham.

"Not now—not now," rejoined Fawkes, impatiently. "Meet me to morrow night, at this hour, in the Great Sanctuary, at the farther side of the Abbey, and you shall learn all you desire to know."

"Why not now?" rejoined Chetham, earnestly. "You need not fear me. I am no spy, and will reveal nothing."

"But your companion?" hesitated Fawkes.

"It is only Martin Heydocke," answered Chetham. "He can keep a close tongue as well as his master."

"Well, sit down, then," returned Fawkes, sullenly. "There will be less risk in taking them to Lambeth," he muttered, "than in loitering here." And rowing with great swiftness, he soon gained the centre of the stream.

"And so," he observed, resting for a moment on his oars, "you still cherish your attachment to Viviana, I see. Nay, never start, man. I am no enemy to your suit, though others may be. And if she would place herself at my disposal, I would give her to you—certain that it would be to one upon whom her affections are fixed."

"Do you think any change likely to take place in her sentiments towards me?" faltered Chetham. "May I indulge a hope?"

"I would not have you despair," replied Fawkes. "Because, as far as I have noticed, women are not apt to adhere to their resolutions in matters of the heart; and because, as I have just said, she loves you, and I see no reasonable bar to your union."

"You give me new life," cried Chetham, transported with joy. "Oh, that you, who have so much influence with her, would speak in my behalf."

"Nay, you must plead your own cause," replied Fawkes. "I cannot hold out much hope at present; for recent events have cast a deep gloom over her spirit, and she appears to be a prey to melancholy. Let this wear off—and with one so young and so firm-minded it is sure to do so—and then your suit may be renewed. Urge it when you may, you have my best wishes for success, and shall have my warmest efforts to second you."

Humphrey Chetham murmured his thanks in accents almost unintelligible from emotion, and Guy Fawkes continued;

"It would be dangerous for you to disembark with me; but when I put you ashore, I will point out the dwelling at present occupied by Viviana. You can visit it as early as you please to-morrow. You will find no one with her but Father Oldcorne, and I need scarcely add that it will gladden me to

the heart to find on my return that she has yielded to your
entreaties."

"I cannot thank you," cried Chetham, warmly grasping
his hand; "but I hope to find some means of evincing my
gratitude."

"Prove it by maintaining the strictest secrecy as to all you
may see or hear—or even suspect—within the dwelling you
are about to visit," returned Guy Fawkes. "Knowing that
I am dealing with a man of honour, I require no stronger
obligation than your word."

"You have it," replied Chetham, solemnly.

"Your worship shall have my oath, if you desire it," remarked Martin Heydocke.

"No," rejoined Fawkes; "your master will answer for
your fidelity."

Shortly after this, Guy Fawkes pulled ashore, and his companions landed. After pointing out the solitary habitation,
which possessed greater interest in Humphrey Chetham's
eyes than the proud structures he had just quitted, and ex-
tracting a promise that the young merchant would not approach it till the morrow, he rowed off, and while the others
proceeded to Lambeth in search of lodging for the night,
made the best of his way to the little creek, and entered the
house.

He found the other conspirators anxiously awaiting his
arrival, and the certainty afforded by his presence that the
powder had been landed in safety gave general satisfaction.
Preparations were immediately made for another voyage. A
large supply of provisions, consisting of baked meat of various
kinds, hard-boiled eggs, pasties, bread, and other viands,
calculated to serve for a week's consumption, without the
necessity of having recourse to any culinary process, and which
had been previously procured with that view, together with a
few flasks of wine, occupied the place in the boat lately assigned to the powder. At the risk of overloading the vessel,
they likewise increased its burthen by a quantity of mining
implements—spades, pickaxes, augers, and wrenching irons.
To these were added as many swords, calivers, pikes, and
petronels, as the space left would accommodate. Garnet
and Catesby then embarked—the former having taken an
affectionate farewell of Viviana, whom he committed, with
the strictest injunction to watch over her, to the care of
Father Oldcorne. Guy Fawkes lingered for a moment, doubting whether he should mention his rencounter with Hum-

phrey Chetham. He was the more undecided from the deep
affliction in which she was plunged. At last he determined
upon slightly hinting at the subject, and to be guided as to
what he said further by the manner in which the allusion was
received.

"And you decide upon remaining here till we return,
Viviana," he said.

She made a sign in the affirmative.

"And you will see no one?"

"No one," she answered.

"But should any old friend find his way hither—Humphrey
Chetham, for instance—will you not receive him?"

"Why do you single out *him?*" demanded Viviana, inquiringly. "Is he in London? Have you seen him?"

"I have," replied Guy Fawkes; "I accidentally met him
to-night, and have shown him this dwelling. He will come
hither to-morrow."

"I wanted only this to make me thoroughly wretched,"
cried Viviana, clasping her hands with anguish. "Oh! what
unhappy chance threw him across your path? Why did you
tell him I was here? Why give him a hope that I would see
him? But I will *not* see him. I will quit this house rather
than be exposed to the meeting."

"What means this sudden excitement, Viviana?" cried
Guy Fawkes, greatly surprised by her agitation. "Why should
a visit from Humphrey Chetham occasion you uneasiness?"

"I know not," she answered, blushing deeply; "but I will
not hazard it."

"I thought you superior to your sex," rejoined Fawkes,
"and should never have suspected you of waywardness or
caprice."

"You charge me with failings that do not belong to me,"
she answered. "I am neither wayward nor capricious; but I
would be willingly spared the pain of an interview with one
whom I thought I loved."

"Thought you loved!" echoed Fawkes, in increased astonishment.

"Ay, *thought,*" repeated Viviana, "for I have since examined my heart, and find he has no place in it."

"You might be happy with him, Viviana," rejoined Fawkes,
reproachfully.

"I *might* have been," she replied, "had circumstances
favoured our union. But I should not be so now. Recent
events have wrought an entire change in my feelings. Were

I to abandon my resolution of retiring to a cloister—were I to return to the world—and were such an event possible as that Humphrey Chetham should conform to the faith of Rome—still, I would not—could not wed him."

"I grieve to hear it," replied Fawkes.

"Would *you* have me wed him?" she cried, in a slightly mortified tone.

"In good sooth would I," replied Fawkes; "and I repeat my firm conviction you would be happier with him than with one more highly born, and of less real worth."

Viviana made no reply, and her head declined upon her bosom.

"You will see him," pursued Fawkes, taking her hand, "if only to tell him what you have just told me."

"Since you desire it, I will," she replied, fixing a look of melancholy tenderness upon him; "but it will cost me a bitter pang."

"I would not tax you with it, if I did not think it needful," returned Fawkes. "And now, farewell."

"Farewell—it may be for ever," replied Viviana, sadly.

"The boat is ready, and the tide ebbing," cried Catesby, impatiently, at the door. "We shall be aground if you tarry longer."

"I come," replied Fawkes. And, waving an adieu to Viviana, he departed.

"Strange!" he muttered to himself, as he took his way to the creek. "I could have sworn she was in love with Humphrey Chetham. Who can have superseded him in her regard? Not Catesby, of a surety. 'Tis a perplexing sex. The best are fickle. Heaven be praised! I have long been proof against their wiles."

Thus musing, he sprang into the skiff, and assisting Catesby to push it into deep water, seized an oar, and exerted himself stoutly to make up for lost time. The second voyage was as prosperous as the first. A thick veil of cloud had curtained the stars; the steps were deserted as before, and the provisions, arms, and implements were securely conveyed to their destination.

Thus far fortune seemed to favour their undertaking, and Garnet, falling on his knees, offered up the most fervent thanksgivings. Prayers over, they descended to the cellar, and their first care was to seek out a place as free from damp as possible, where the powder could be deposited till the excavation, which it was foreseen would be a work of time and great labour, was completed. A dry corner being found, the barrels were placed in it, and carefully concealed with billets of wood and coals, so as to avert suspicion in case of search. This, with other arrangements, occupied the greater part of the night, and the commencement of the important undertaking was deferred till the morrow, when an increase of their party was anticipated.

Throughout the whole of the day no one stirred forth. The windows were kept closed; the doors locked; and, as no fires were lighted, the house had the appearance of being un-inhabited. In the course of the morning they underwent considerable alarm. Some mischievous urchins having scaled the garden wall, one of them fell within it, and his cries so terrified his playmates that they dropped on the other side, and left him. The conspirators reconnoitred the unhappy urchin, who continued his vociferations in a loud key, through the holes in the shutters, uncertain what to do, and fearing that this trifling mischance might lead to serious conse-quences, when the subject of their uneasiness relieved them by scrambling up the wall near the door, and so effecting a retreat. With this exception, nothing material occurred till evening, when their expected associates arrived.

The utmost caution was observed in admitting them. The new comers were provided with a key of the garden-gate, but a signal was given and repeated before the house-door was opened by Bates, to whom the office of porter was entrusted. As soon as the latter had satisfied himself that all was right, by unmasking a dark lantern, and throwing its radiance upon the faces of the elder Wright, Rookwood, and Percy, he stamped his foot thrice, and the conspirators emerged from their hiding-places. A warm greeting passed between the confederates, and they adjourned to a lower chamber, adjoin-ing the vault, where the sound of their voices could not be overheard, and where, while partaking of a frugal meal—for they desired to eke out their store of provisions as long as possible—they discoursed upon their plans, and all that had occurred since their last meeting. Nothing was said of the treachery of Tresham—his recent conduct, as already ob-served, having been such as to restore him in a great degree to the confidence of his companions. Percy, whose office as a gentleman-pensioner gave him the best opportunities of hearing court-whispers and secrets, informed them it was rumoured that the Earl of Salisbury had obtained a clue to some Catholic plot, whether their own he could not say; but it would seem from all that could be gathered, that his endea-vours to trace it out had been frustrated.

"Where is Lord Mounteagle ?" demanded Catesby.

"At his mansion near Hoxton," replied Percy.

"Have you observed him much about the court of late, or with the Earl of Salisbury ?" pursued Catesby.

"No," replied Percy. "Yet now, I bethink me, I did observe them together, and in earnest conversation, about a week ago. But Lord Mounteagle knows nothing of *our* plot."

"Hum !" exclaimed Catesby, shrugging his shoulders, while significant looks were exchanged by the others, and Tresham hung his head. "Lord Mounteagle may not know that you or I, or Fawkes, or Rookwood, are conspiring against the State, but he knows that a plot is hatching amongst our party. It is from him that the Earl of Salisbury derived his information."

"Amazement !" exclaimed Percy.

"A good Catholic, and betray his fellows !" cried Rook-wood ; "this passes my comprehension. Are you sure of it ?"

"Unhappily, we are so, my son," replied Garnet, gravely.

"We will speak of this hereafter," interposed Catesby. "I have a plan to get his lordship into our power, and make him serve our purposes in spite of himself. We will outwit the crafty Salisbury. Can any one tell if Tresham's sudden disappearance has been noticed ?"

"His household report that he is on a visit to Sir Everard Digby, at Gothurst," replied Rookwood. "I called at his residence yesterday, and was informed that a letter had just been received from him dated from that place. His departure, they said, was sudden, but his letter fully accounted for it."

"The messenger who bore that letter had only to travel from Lambeth," observed Catesby, smiling.

"So I conclude," returned Rookwood.

"And, now that our meal is ended, let us to work," cried Fawkes, who had taken no part in the foregoing conversa-tion. "I will strike the first blow," he added, rising and seizing a mattock.

"Hold, my son !" exclaimed Garnet, arresting him. "The work upon which the redemption of our holy Church hangs must be commenced with due solemnity."

"You are right, father," replied Fawkes, humbly.

Headed by Garnet, bearing a crucifix, they then repaired

to the vault. A silver chalice, filled with holy water, was
carried by Fawkes, and two lighted tapers by Catesby.
Kneeling down before that part of the wall against which
operations were about to be directed, and holding the crucifix
towards it, Garnet commenced praying in a low but earnest
tone, gradually raising his voice, and increasing in fervour as
he proceeded. The others knelt around him, and the whole
formed a strange and deeply-interesting group. The vault
itself harmonised with its occupants. It was of great anti-
quity; and its solid stone masonry had acquired a time-worn
hoary tint. In width it was about nine feet, and of corre-
sponding height, supported by a semicircular arch, and its
length was more than twenty feet.

The countenances of the conspirators showed that they
were powerfully moved by what was passing; but next to
Garnet, Guy Fawkes exhibited the greatest enthusiasm. His
ecstatic looks and gestures evinced the strong effect produced
upon his superstitious character by the scene. Garnet concluded his prayer as follows:

"Thus far, O Lord, we have toiled in darkness and in difficulty; but we have now arrived at a point where all thy
support is needed. Do not desert us, we beseech thee, but
let thy light guide us through these gloomy paths. Nerve
our arms,—sharpen our weapons,—and crumble these hard
and flinty stones, so that they may yield to our efforts. Aid
our enterprise, if thou approvest it, and it be really, as in
our ignorance we believe it to be, for the welfare of thy holy
Church, and the confusion of its enemies. Bear witness, O
Lord, that we devote ourselves wholly and entirely to this
one end,—and that we implore success only for thy glory and
honour."

With this he arose, and the following strains were chanted
by the whole assemblage:

HYMN OF THE CONSPIRATORS.

The heretic and heathen, Lord,
Consume with fire, cut down with sword;
The spoilers from thy temples thrust,
Their altars trample in the dust.

False princes and false priests lay low,
Their habitations fill with woe.
Scatter them, Lord, with sword and flame,
And bring them utterly to shame.

Thy vengeful arm no longer stay,
Arise! exterminate, and slay.
So shall thy fallen worship be
Restored to its prosperity.

This hymn raised the enthusiasm of the conspirators to the highest pitch; and such was the effect produced by it, as it rolled in sullen echoes along the arched roof of the vault, that several of them drew their swords, and crossed the blades, with looks of the most determined devotion to their cause. When it was ended, Garnet recited other prayers, and sprinkled holy water upon the wall, and upon every implement about to be used, bestowing a separate benediction on each. As he delivered the pick-axe to Guy Fawkes, he cried in a solemn voice:

"Strike, my son, in the name of the Most High, and in behalf of our holy religion,—strike!"

Guy Fawkes raised the weapon, and, stimulated by excitement, threw the whole strength of his arm into the blow. A large piece of the granite was chipped off, but the mattock snapped in twain. Guy Fawkes looked deeply disconcerted, and Garnet, though he concealed his emotion, was filled with dismay.

"Let me take your place," cried Keyes, advancing, as Guy Fawkes retired.

Keyes was a powerful man, and exerting his energies, he buried the point of the pick-axe so deeply in the mortar, that he could not remove it unassisted. These untoward circumstances cast a slight damp upon their ardour; but Catesby, who perceived it, went more cautiously to work, and in a short time succeeded with great labour in getting out the large stone upon which the others had expended so much useless exertion. The sight restored their confidence, and as many as could work in the narrow space joined him. But they found that their task was much more arduous than they had anticipated. More than an hour elapsed before they could loosen another stone, and though they laboured with the utmost perseverance, relieving each other by turns, they had made but a small breach when morning arrived. The stones were as hard and unyielding as iron, and the mortar in some places harder than the stones.

After a few hours' rest they resumed their task. Still, they made but small progress; and it was not until the third day that they had excavated a hole sufficiently wide and deep to admit one man within it. They were now arrived at a compost of gravel and flint stones; and if they had found their previous task difficult, what they had now to encounter was infinitely more so. Their implements made little or no impression on this unyielding substance, and though they toiled incessantly, the work proceeded with disheartening slowness. The stones and rubbish were conveyed at dead of night in hampers into the garden, and buried.

One night, when they were labouring as usual, Guy Fawkes, who was foremost in the excavation, thought he heard the tolling of a bell within the wall. He instantly suspended his task, and being convinced that he was not deceived, crept out of the hole, and made a sign to the others to listen. Each had heard the awful sound before; but as it was partially drowned by the noise of the pick-axe, it had not produced much impression upon them, as they attributed it to some vibration in the wall, caused by the echo of the blows. But it was now distinctly audible—deep, clear, slow,—like a passing bell,—but so solemn, so unearthly, that its tones froze the blood in their veins.

They listened for a while in speechless astonishment, scarcely daring to look at each other, and expecting each moment that the building would fall upon them, and bury them alive. The light of a single lantern placed upon an upturned basket fell upon figures rigid as statues, and countenances charged with awe.

"My arm is paralysed," said Guy Fawkes, breaking silence; "I can work no more."

"Try holy water, father," cried Catesby. "If it proceeds from aught of evil, that will quell it."

The chalice containing the sacred lymph was brought, and pronouncing a solemn exorcism, Garnet sprinkled the wall.

The sound immediately ceased.

"It is as I thought, father," observed Catesby; "it is the delusion of an evil spirit."

As he spoke, the tolling of the mysterious bell was again heard, and more solemnly,—more slowly than before.

"Sprinkle the wall again, in Heaven's name, father," cried Fawkes, crossing himself devoutly. "Avoid thee, Sathanas!"

Garnet complied, and throwing holy water upon the stones, the same result followed.

V.

THE CAPTURE OF VIVIANA.

On the morning after his encounter with Guy Fawkes, Humphrey Chetham, accompanied by Martin Heydocke, took his way to Lambeth Marsh. With a throbbing heart he approached the miserable dwelling he knew to be inhabited by Viviana, and could scarcely summon courage to knock at the door. His first summons not being answered, he repeated it more loudly, and he then perceived the face of Father Oldcorne at the window, who, having satisfied himself that it was a friend, admitted him and his attendant.

"You were expected, my son," said the priest, after a friendly greeting. "Guy Fawkes has prepared Viviana for your coming."

"Will she not see me?" demanded the young merchant, uneasily.

"I believe so," replied Oldcorne. "But I will apprise her of your arrival. Be seated, my son."

He then carefully fastened the door, and repaired to Viviana's chamber, leaving Chetham in that state of tremor and anxiety which a lover, hoping to behold his mistress, only knows.

It was some time before Viviana appeared, and the young merchant, whose heart beat violently at the sound of her footstep, was startled by the alteration in her looks, and the extreme coldness of her manner. Oldcorne was with her, and motioning Martin Heydocke to follow him, the youthful pair were left alone.

"You desire to see me, I am given to understand, sir," observed Viviana, in a freezing tone.

"I have journeyed to London for that express purpose," replied Humphrey Chetham, tremulously.

"I am much beholden to you, sir," returned Viviana, in the same repelling tone as before; "but I regret you should have taken so much trouble on my account."

"To serve you is happiness, not trouble, Viviana," replied Humphrey Chetham, ardently; "and I am overjoyed at finding an opportunity of proving my devotion."

"I have yet to learn what service I must thank you for," she returned.

"I can scarcely say that I am warranted in thus intruding upon you," replied Chetham, greatly abashed; "but, having learnt from my servant, Martin Heydocke, that Doctor Dee had set out for London, with the view of seeking you out, and withdrawing you from your present associates, I was determined to be beforehand with him, and to acquaint you, if possible, with his intentions."

"What you say surprises me," replied Viviana. "Doctor Dee has no right to interfere with my actions. Nor should I obey him were he to counsel me, as is scarcely probable, to quit my companions."

"I know not what connexion there may be between you to justify the interposition of his authority," replied Chetham; "neither did I tarry to inquire. But presuming from what I heard that he *would* attempt to exercise some control over you, I set out at once, and, without guide to your retreat, or the slightest knowledge of it, was fortunate enough, on the very night of my arrival in London, to chance upon Guy Fawkes, who directed me to you."

"I am aware of it," was the chilling answer.

"I will not avouch," pursued Chetham, passionately, "that I have not been actuated as much by an irrepressible desire to see you again, as by anxiety to apprise you of Doctor Dee's coming. I wanted only a slight excuse to myself to induce me to yield to my inclinations. Your departure made me wretched. I thought I had more control over myself. But I find I cannot live without you."

"Alas! alas!" cried Viviana, in a troubled tone, and losing all her self-command. "I expected this. Why—why did you come?"

"I have told you my motive," replied Chetham; "but, oh! do not reproach me!"

"I do not desire to do so," returned Viviana, with a look of agony. "I bitterly reproach myself that I cannot meet you as of old. But I would rather—far rather have encountered Doctor Dee, had he come hither resolved to exert all his magical power to force me away, than have met you."

"Have I unwittingly offended you, Viviana?" asked Chetham, in astonishment.

"Oh! no—no—no!" she replied, "you have not offended me; but——"

"But what?" he cried, anxiously.

"I would rather have died than see you," she answered.

"I will not inquire wherefore," rejoined Chetham, "because I too well divine the cause. I am no longer what I was to you."

"Press this matter no further, I pray of you," returned Viviana, in much confusion, and blushing deeply. "I shall ever esteem you,—ever feel the warmest gratitude to you. And what matters it whether my heart is estranged from you or not, since I can never wed you?"

"What matters it?" repeated the young merchant, in accents of despair,—"it matters much. Drowning love will cling to straws. The thought that I was beloved by you, though I could never hope to possess your hand, reconciled me in some degree to my fate. But now," he added, covering his face with his hands,—"now, my heart is crushed."

"Nay, say not so," cried Viviana, in a voice of the deepest emotion. "I *do* love you,—as a sister."

"That is small comfort," rejoined Chetham, bitterly. "I echo your own wish. Would we had never met again! I might, at least, have deluded myself into the belief that you loved me."

"It would have been better so," she returned. "I would inflict pain on no one—far less on you, whom I regard so much, and to whom I owe so much."

"You owe me nothing, Viviana," rejoined Chetham. "All I desired was to serve you. In the midst of the dangers we have shared together, I felt no alarm except for your sake. I have done nothing—nothing. Would I had died for you!"

"Calm yourself, sir, I entreat you," she returned.

"You did love me *once?*" demanded Chetham, suddenly.

"I thought so," she answered.

The young merchant uttered an exclamation of anguish, and a mournful pause ensued, broken only by his groans.

"Answer me, Viviana," he said, turning abruptly upon her, —"answer me, and, in mercy, answer truly,—do you love another?"

"It is a question I cannot answer," she replied, becoming ashy pale.

"Your looks speak for you!" he vociferated, in a terrible tone. "You do! His name?—his name?—that I may wreak my vengeance upon him."

"Your violence terrifies me," returned Viviana, withdrawing the hand he had seized. "I must put an end to this interview."

"Pardon me, Viviana!" cried Chetham, falling on his knees before her—"in pity pardon me! I am not myself. I shall be calmer presently. But if you knew the anguish of the wound you have inflicted, you would not add to it."

"Heaven knows I would not!" she returned, motioning him to rise. "And, if it will lighten your suffering, know that the love I feel for another—if love, indeed, it be,—is as hopeless as your own. But it is not a love of which even *you* could be jealous. It is a higher and a holier passion. It is affection mixed with admiration, and purified from all its grossness. It is more, perhaps, than the love of a daughter

for her father—but it is nothing more. I shall never wed
him I love—could not if I would. Nay, I would shun him,
if I did not feel that the hour will soon come when the extent
of my affection must be proved."

"This is strange sophistry," returned Chetham; "and you
may deceive yourself by it, but you cannot deceive me. You
love as all ardent natures do love. But in what way do you
mean to prove your affection?"

"Perhaps by the sacrifice of my life," she answered.

"I can tell you who is the object of your affections!" said
Chetham. "It is Guy Fawkes."

"I will not deny it," replied Viviana; "he is."

"Hear me, then," exclaimed Chetham, who appeared inexpressibly relieved by the discovery he had made; "in my
passage across the river with him last night, our conversation
turned on the one subject ever nearest my heart, yourself,—
and Guy Fawkes not only bade me not despair, but promised
to aid my suit."

"And he kept his word," replied Viviana; "for, while
announcing your proposed visit, he urged me strongly in
your behalf."

"Then he knows not of your love for him?" demanded
Chetham.

"He not only knows it not, but never shall know it from
me,—nor must he know it from you, sir," rejoined Viviana,
energetically.

"Fear it not," said Chetham, sighing. "It is a secret I
shall carefully preserve."

"And now that you are in possession of it," she answered,
"I no longer feel your presence as a restraint. Let me still
regard you as a friend."

"Be it so," replied Humphrey Chetham, mournfully; "and
as a friend let me entreat you to quit this place, and abandon
your present associates. I will not seek to turn your heart
from Fawkes—nor will I try to regain the love I have lost.
But let me implore you to pause ere you irretrievably mix
yourself up with the fortunes of one so desperate. I am too
well aware that he is engaged in a fearful plot against the
State,—though I know not its precise nature."

"You will not betray him?" she cried.

"I will not, though he is my rival," returned Chetham.
"But others may—nay, perhaps have done so already."

"Whom do you suspect?" demanded Viviana, in the
greatest alarm.

"I fear Doctor Dee," replied the young merchant; "but I know nothing certainly. My servant, Martin Heydocke, who is in the Doctor's confidence, intimated as much to me, and I have reason to think that his journey to town, under the pretext of searching for you, is undertaken for the purpose of tracing out the conspirators, and delivering them to the Government."

"Is he arrived in London?" inquired Viviana, eagerly.

"I should think not," returned Chetham. "I passed him, four days ago, on this side Leicester, in company with Kelley and Topcliffe."

"If the wretch Topcliffe was with him, your conjectures are too well founded," she replied. "I must warn Guy Fawkes instantly of his danger."

"Command my services in any way," said Chetham.

"I know not what to do," cried Viviana, after a pause, during which she betrayed the greatest agitation. "I dare not seek him out;—and yet, if I do not, he may fall into the hands of the enemy. I must see him at all hazards."

"Suffer me to go with you," implored Chetham. "You may rely upon my secrecy. And now I have a double motive for desiring to preserve Fawkes."

"You are, indeed, truly noble-hearted and generous," replied Viviana; "and I would fully confide in you. But, if you were to be seen by the others, you would be certainly put to death. Not even Fawkes could save you."

"I will risk it, if you desire it, and it will save *him*," replied the young merchant, devotedly. "Nay, I will go alone."

"That were to insure your destruction," she answered. "No—no—it must not be. I will consult with Father Old-corne."

With this, she hurried out of the room, and returned in a short time with the priest.

"Father Oldcorne is of opinion that our friends must be apprised of their danger," she said. "And he thinks it needful we should both go to their retreat, that no hindrance may be offered to our flight, in case such a measure should be resolved upon."

"You cannot accompany us, my son," added Oldcorne; "for though I am as fully assured of your fidelity as Viviana, and would confide my life to you, there are those who will not so trust you, and who might rejoice in the opportunity of removing you."

P

"Viviana!" exclaimed Chetham, looking entreatingly at her.

"For my sake,—if not for your own,—do not urge this further," she returned. "There are already dangers and difficulties enow without adding to them. You would be safer amid a horde of robbers than amidst these men."

"And it is to such persons you commit yourself?" cried Chetham, reproachfully. "Oh! be warned by me ere it is too late! Abandon them!"

"It is too late already," replied Viviana. "The die is cast."

"Then I can only lament it," returned Chetham, sadly. "Suffer me, at least, to accompany you to some place near their retreat, that you may summon me in case of need."

"There can be no objection to that, Viviana," observed Oldcorne, "provided Humphrey Chetham will promise not to follow us."

"Readily," replied the young merchant.

"I am unwilling to expose him to further risk on my account," said Viviana. "But be it as you will."

It was then agreed that they should not set out till nightfall, but proceed, as soon as it grew dark, to Lambeth, where Humphrey Chetham undertook to procure a boat for their conveyance across the river.

The hour of departure at length arrived. Viviana, who had withdrawn to her own room, appeared in her travelling habit, and was about to set forth with her companions, when they were all startled by a sudden and loud knocking at the door.

"We are discovered," she cried. "Doctor Dee has found out our retreat."

"Fear nothing," rejoined Chetham, drawing his sword, while his example was imitated by Martin Heydocke; "they shall not capture you while I live."

As he spoke, the knocking was repeated, and the door shaken so violently as to threaten to burst its fastenings.

"Extinguish the light," whispered Chetham, "and let Father Oldcorne conceal himself. We have nothing to fear."

"Where shall I fly?" cried Oldcorne, despairingly. "It will be impossible to raise the flag, and seek refuge in the vault."

"Fly to my room," cried Viviana. And finding he stood irresolute, as if paralysed with terror, she took his arm, and dragged him away. The next moment the door was burst open with a loud crash, and several armed men, with their swords drawn, followed by Topcliffe, and another middle-aged man, of slight stature, and rather under-sized, but richly dressed, and bearing all the marks of exalted rank, rushed into the room.

" You are my prisoner !" cried Topcliffe, rushing up to Chetham, who had planted himself, with Martin Heydocke, at the foot of the stairs. " I arrest you in the King's name !"

" You are mistaken in your man, sir," cried Chetham, fiercely. " I have committed no offence. Lay a hand upon me at your peril !"

" How is this ?" cried Topcliffe. " Humphrey Chetham here !"

" Ay," returned the young merchant ; " you have fallen upon the wrong house."

" Not so, sir," replied Topcliffe. " I am satisfied from your presence that I am right. Where *you* are, Viviana Radcliffe is not far off. Throw down your arms. You can offer no resistance to my force, and your zeal will not benefit your friends, while it will place your own safety in jeopardy."

But Chetham fiercely refused compliance, and, after a few minutes' further parley, the soldiers were about to attack him, when Viviana opened a door above, and slowly descended the stairs. At her appearance the young merchant, seeing that further resistance would be useless, sheathed his sword, and she passed between him and Heydocke, and advanced towards the leaders of the band.

" What means this intrusion ?" she asked.

" We are come in search of two Jesuit priests, whom we have obtained information are hidden here," replied Topcliffe ;— " as well as of certain other Papists, disaffected against the State, for whose apprehension I hold a warrant."

" You are welcome to search the house," replied Viviana. But there is no one within it except those you see."

As she said this, Chetham, who gazed earnestly at her, caught her eye, and from a scarcely-perceptible glance, felt certain that the priest, through her agency, had effected his escape. But the soldiers had not waited for her permission to make the search. Rushing up-stairs they examined the different chambers,—there were two small rooms besides those occupied by Viviana,—and found several of the priests' habiliments ; but though they examined every corner with the minutest attention, sounded the walls, peered up the chimneys, underneath the bed, and into every place, likely and unlikely, they could find no other traces of those they sought, and were compelled to return to their leader with tidings of their ill success. Topcliffe, with another party, continued his scrutiny below, and discovering the movable flag in the hearth, descended into the vault, where he made certain of discovering his prey. But no one was there; and, the powder and arms having been removed, he gained nothing by his investigations.

Meanwhile, his companion,—and evidently from his garb, and the deference paid him, though he was addressed by no title which could lead to the absolute knowledge of his rank, his superior,—seated himself, and put many questions in a courteous but authoritative tone to Viviana respecting her residence in this solitary abode,—the names of her companions,—where they were,—and upon what scheme they were engaged. To none of these questions would she return an answer, and her interrogator, at last, losing patience, said:

" I hold it my duty to inform you that you will be carried before the Council, and if you continue thus obstinate, means will be taken—and those none of the gentlest—to extort the truth from you."

" You may apply the torture to me," replied Viviana, firmly; " but it will wrest nothing from me."

" That remains to be seen," replied the other; " I only trust you will not compel me to put my threat into execution."

At this moment Topcliffe emerged from the vault, and the soldiers returned from their unsuccessful search above.

" They have escaped us now," remarked Topcliffe to his superior. " But I will conceal a party of men on the premises, who will be certain to capture them on their return."

Viviana uttered an exclamation of irrepressible uneasiness, which did not escape her auditors.

" I am right, you see," observed Topcliffe, significantly, to his companion.

" You are so," replied the other.

As this was said, Viviana hazarded a look at Humphrey Chetham, the meaning of which he was not slow to comprehend. He saw that she wished him to make an effort to escape, that he might warn her companions; and regardless of the consequence, he prepared to obey her. While those around were engaged in a last fruitless search, he whispered his intentions to Martin Heydocke, and only awaited a favourable opportunity to put them in execution. It occurred sooner than he expected. Before quitting the premises, Topcliffe determined to visit the upper rooms himself, and he took several of the men with him.

Chetham would have made an attempt to liberate Viviana, but feeling certain it would be unsuccessful, he preferred obeying her wishes to his own inclinations. Topcliffe gone, he suddenly drew his sword,—for neither he nor Heydocke had been disarmed,—and rushing towards the door, struck down the man next it, and, followed by his servant, passed through it before he could be intercepted. They both then flew at a swift pace towards the marshy fields, and, owing to the darkness and unstable nature of the ground, speedily distanced their pursuers.

Hearing the disturbance below, and guessing its cause, Topcliffe immediately descended. But he was too late; and though he joined in the pursuit, he was baffled like his attendants. Half an hour afterwards he returned to the house, with an angry and disappointed look.

"He has given us the slip," he observed to his superior, who appeared exceedingly provoked by the young merchant's flight; "but we will soon have him again."

After giving directions to his men how to conceal themselves, Topcliffe informed his companion that he was ready to attend him. Viviana, who had remained motionless and silent during the foregoing scene, was taken out of the house, and conducted towards the creek, in which lay a large wherry manned by four rowers. She was placed within it, and as soon as his superior was seated, Topcliffe inquired:

"Where will your lordship go first?"

"To the Star-Chamber," was the answer.

At this reply, in spite of herself, Viviana could not repress a shudder.

"All is lost!" she mentally ejaculated.

VI.

THE CELLAR.

It was long before the conspirators gained sufficient courage to recommence digging the mine. Whenever holy water was thrown upon the stones, the mysterious bell ceased tolling, but it presently began anew, and such was the appalling effect of the sound that it completely paralysed the listeners. Prayers were said by Garnet; hymns sung by the others; but all was of no avail. It continued to toll on with increased solemnity, unless checked by the same potent application as before.

The effect became speedily manifest in the altered looks and demeanour of the conspirators, and it was evident that if something was not done to arouse them, the enterprise would be abandoned. Catesby, equally superstitious with his confederates, but having nerves more firmly strung, was the first to conquer his terror. Crossing himself, he muttered a secret prayer, and, snatching up a pick-axe, entered the cavity, and resumed his labour.

The noise of the heavy blows dealt by him against the wall drowned the tolling of the bell. The charm was broken. And stimulated by his conduct, the others followed his example, and though the awful tolling continued at intervals during the whole of their operations, it offered no further interruption to them.

Another and more serious cause of anxiety, however, arose. As the work advanced, without being aware of it, they approached the bank of the river, and the water began to ooze through the sides of the excavation,—at first, slightly, but by degrees to such an extent as to convince them that their labour would be entirely thrown away. Large portions of the clay, loosened by the damp, fell in upon them, nearly burying those nearest the tumbling mass; and the floor was now in some places more than a foot deep in water, clearly proving it would be utterly impossible to keep the powder fit for use in such a spot.

Catesby bore these untoward circumstances with ill-concealed mortification. For a time, he struggled against them; and though he felt that it was hopeless, worked on like a desperate military leader conducting a forlorn hope to certain destruction. At length, however, the water began to make such incursions that he could no longer disguise from himself or his companions that they were contending against insurmountable difficulties, and that to proceed further would be madness. He, therefore, with a heavy heart, desisted, and throwing down his pick-axe, said it was clear that Heaven did not approve their design, and that it must be relinquished.

"We ought to have been warned by that doleful bell," he

observed in conclusion. "I now perceive its meaning. And as I was the first to act in direct opposition to the declared will of the Supreme Being, so now I am the first to admit my error."

"I cannot account for that dread and mysterious sound, my son," replied Garnet, "and can only attribute it, as you do, to Divine interference. But whether it was intended as a warning or a guidance, I confess I am unable to say."

"Can you longer doubt, father," returned Catesby, bitterly, "when you look at yon excavation? It took us more than a week's incessant labour to get through the first wall; and our toil was no sooner lightened than these fatal consequences ensued. If we proceed we shall drown ourselves, instead of blowing up our foes. And even if we should escape, were the powder stowed for one day in that damp place, it would never explode. We have failed, and must take measures accordingly."

"I entirely concur with you, my son," replied Garnet; "we must abandon our present plan. But do not let us be disheartened. Perhaps at this very moment Heaven is preparing for us a victory by some unlooked-for means."

"It may be so," replied Catesby, with a look of incredulity.

As he spoke, an extraordinary noise, like a shower of falling stones, was heard overhead. And coupling the sound with their fears of the encroachment of the damp, the conspirators glanced at each other in dismay, thinking the building was falling in upon them.

"All blessed saints protect us!" cried Garnet, as the sound ceased. "What was that?"

But no one was able to account for it, and each regarded his neighbour with apprehension. After a short interval of silence, the sound was heard again. There was then another pause—and again the same rushing and inexplicable noise.

"What can it be?" cried Catesby. "I am so enfeebled by this underground life, that trifles alarm me. Are our enemies pulling down the structure over our heads?—or are they earthing us up like vermin?" he added to Fawkes. "What is it?"

"I will go and see," replied the other.

"Do not expose yourself, my son," cried Garnet. "Let us abide the result here."

"No, father," replied Fawkes. "Having failed in our

scheme, what befals me is of little consequence. I will go. If I return not, you will understand what has happened."

Pausing for a moment to receive Garnet's benediction, he then strode away.

Half an hour elapsed before Fawkes returned, and the interval appeared thrice its duration in the eyes of the conspirators. When he reappeared, a smile sat upon his countenance, and his looks instantly dispelled the alarm that had been previously felt.

"You bring us good news, my son ?" cried Garnet.

"Excellent, father," replied Fawkes : "and you were right in saying that at the very moment we were indulging in misgiving, Heaven was preparing for us a victory by unforeseen and mysterious means."

Garnet raised his hands gratefully and reverentially upwards. And the other conspirators crowded round Fawkes to listen to his relation.

"The noise we heard," he said, "arose from a very simple circumstance—and when you hear it, you will smile at your fears. But you will not smile at the result to which it has led. Exactly overhead, it appears, a cellar is situated, belonging to a person named Bright, and the sound was occasioned by the removal of his coals, which he had been selling off."

"Is that all ?" cried Catesby. "We are indeed grown childish, to be alarmed by such a cause."

"It appears slight now it is explained," observed Keyes, gravely ; "but how were we to know whence it arose ?"

"True," returned Fawkes ; "and I will now show you how the hand of Heaven has been manifested in the matter. The noise which led me to this investigation, and which I regard as a signal from on high, brought me to a cellar I had never seen before, and knew not existed. *That cellar lies immediately beneath the House of Lords.*"

"Ah ! I see !" exclaimed Catesby. "You think it would form a good depository for the powder."

"If it had been built for the express purpose, it could not be better," returned Fawkes. "It is commodious and dry, and in an out-of-the-way place, as you may judge, when we ourselves have never hitherto noticed it."

"But what is all this to us, if we cannot use it ?" returned Catesby.

"We *can* use it," replied Fawkes. "It is ours."

There was a general exclamation of surprise.

Guy Fawkes laying the train.

"Finding, on inquiry, that Bright was about to quit the neighbourhood," continued Fawkes, "and did not require the place longer, I instantly proposed to take it from him, and to create no suspicion, engaged it in Percy's name, stating that he wanted it for his own fuel."

"You have done admirably," cried Catesby, in a tone of exultation. "The success of the enterprise will now be entirely owing to you."

"Not to me, but to the Providence that directed me," replied Fawkes, solemnly.

"Right, my son," returned Garnet. "And let this teach us never to despair again."

The next day, Percy having taken possession of the cellar, it was carefully examined, and proved, as Fawkes had stated, admirably adapted to their purpose. Their fears were now at an end, and they looked on the success of their project as certain. The mysterious bell no longer tolled, and their sole remaining task was to fill up the excavation so far as to prevent any damage from the wet.

This was soon done, and their next step was to transport the powder during the night to the cellar. Concealing the barrels as before with faggots and coals, they gave the place the appearance of a mere receptacle for lumber, by filling it with old hampers, boxes without lids, broken bottles, stone jars, and other rubbish.

They now began to think of separating, and Fawkes expressed his intention of returning that night to the house at Lambeth. No intelligence had reached them of Viviana's captivity, and they supposed her still an inmate of the miserable dwelling with Father Oldcorne.

Fawkes had often thought of her, and with uneasiness, during his toilsome labours; but they had so much engrossed him that her image was banished almost as soon as it arose. Now that grand obstacle was surmounted, and nothing was wanting, however, except a favourable moment to strike the blow, he began to feel the greatest anxiety respecting her.

Still, he thought it prudent to postpone his return to a late hour, and it was not until near midnight that he and Catesby ventured to their boat. As he was about to descend the steps, he heard his name pronounced by some one at a little distance; and the next moment, a man, whom he immediately recognised as Humphrey Chetham, rushed up to him.

"You here again!" cried Fawkes, angrily, and not unsuspiciously. "Do you play the spy upon me?"

"I have watched for you for the last ten nights," replied Chetham, hastily. "I knew not where you were. But I found your boat here, and I hoped you would not cross the water in any other."

"Why all this care?" demanded Fawkes. "Has aught happened?—Is Viviana safe?—Speak, man! do not keep me longer in suspense!"

"Alas!" rejoined Chetham, "she is a prisoner."

"A prisoner!" ejaculated Fawkes, in a hollow voice. "Then my forebodings were not without cause."

"How has this happened?" cried Catesby, who had listened to what was said in silent wonder.

Chetham then hastily related all that had taken place.

"I know not what has become of her," he said, in conclusion; "but I have heard that she was taken to the Star-Chamber by the Earl of Salisbury—for he, it appears, was the companion of Topcliffe—and, refusing to answer the interrogations of the Council, was conveyed to the Tower, and, I fear, subjected to the torture."

"Tortured!" exclaimed Fawkes, horror-stricken; "Viviana tortured! And I have brought her to this! Oh, God! Oh, God!"

"It is indeed an agonizing reflection," replied Humphrey Chetham, in a sombre tone, "and enough to drive you to despair. Her last wishes, expressed only in looks, for she did not dare to give utterance to them, were that I should warn you not to approach the house at Lambeth, your enemies being concealed within it. I have now fulfilled them. Farewell!"

And he turned to depart.

"Stay!" cried Catesby, arresting him. "Where is Father Oldcorne?"

"I know not," replied Humphrey Chetham. "As I have told you, Viviana by some means contrived his escape. I have seen nothing of him."

And, hurrying away, he was lost beneath the shadow of the wall.

"Is this a troubled dream, or dread reality?" cried Fawkes to Catesby.

"I fear it is too true," returned the other, in a voice of much emotion. "Poor Viviana!"

"Something must be done to set her free," cried Fawkes. "I will purchase her liberty by delivering up myself."

"Your oath—remember your oath!" rejoined Catesby. "You may destroy yourself, but not your associates."

"True—true," replied Fawkes, distractedly—"I *do* remember it. I am sold to perdition."

"Anger not Heaven by these idle lamentations—and at a time, too, when all is so prosperous," rejoined Catesby.

"What!" cried Fawkes, fiercely, "would you have me calm when she who called me father, and was dear to me as a child, is taken from me by these remorseless butchers—subjected to their terrible examinations—plunged in a dismal dungeon —and stretched upon the rack—and all for me—for me! I shall go mad if I think upon it!"

"You must *not* think upon it," returned Catesby—"at least, not here. We shall be observed. Let us return to the house; and perhaps—though I scarcely dare indulge the hope—some plan may be devised for her liberation."

With this, he dragged Fawkes, who was almost frenzied with anguish, forcibly along, and they returned to the house.

Nothing more was said that night. Catesby judged it prudent to let the first violence of his friend's emotion expend itself before he attempted to soothe him; and when he communicated the sad event to Garnet, the latter strongly approved the plan. Garnet was greatly distressed at the intelligence, and his affliction was shared by the other conspirators. No fears were entertained by any of them that Viviana would reveal aught of the plot, but this circumstance only added to their regrets.

"I will stake my life for her constancy," said Catesby.

"And so will I," returned Garnet. "She will die a martyr for us."

He then proposed that they should pray for her deliverance. And all instantly assenting, they knelt down, while Garnet poured forth the most earnest supplications to the Virgin in her behalf.

The next morning, Guy Fawkes set forth, and ascertained that Humphrey Chetham's statement was correct, and that Viviana was indeed a prisoner in the Tower. He repaired thither, and tried to ascertain in what part of the fortress she was confined, in the hope of gaining admittance to her. But as he could obtain no information, and his inquiries excited suspicion, he was compelled to return without accomplishing his object.

Crossing Tower Hill on his way back, he turned to glance at the stern pile he had just quitted, and which was fraught with the most fearful interest to him, when he perceived Chetham issue from the Bulwark Gate. He would have made up to him; but the young merchant, who had evidently seen him, though he looked sedulously another way, set off in the direction of the river, and was quickly lost to view. Filled with the gloomiest thoughts, Guy Fawkes proceeded to Westminster, where he arrived without further adventure of any kind.

In the latter part of the same day, as the conspirators were conferring together, they were alarmed by a knocking at the outer gate; and sending Bates to reconnoitre, he instantly returned with the intelligence that it was Lord Mounteagle. At the mention of this name, Tresham, who was one of the party, turned pale as death, and trembled so violently that he could scarcely support himself. Having been allowed to go forth on that day, the visit of Lord Mounteagle at this juncture, coupled with the agitation it occasioned him, seemed to proclaim him guilty of treachery for the second time.

"You have betrayed us, villain!" cried Catesby, drawing his dagger; "but you shall not escape. I will poniard you on the spot."

"As you hope for mercy, do not strike!" cried Tresham. "On my soul, I have not seen Lord Mounteagle, and know not, any more than yourselves, what brings him hither. Put it to the proof. Let him come in. Conceal yourselves, and you will hear what passes between us."

"Let it be so," interposed Fawkes. "I will step within this closet, the door of which shall remain ajar. From it I can watch him without being observed, and if aught occurs to confirm our suspicions, he dies."

"Bates shall station himself in the passage, and stab him if he attempts to fly," added Catesby. "Your sword, sir."

"It is here," replied Tresham, delivering it to Catesby, who handed it to Bates. "Are you satisfied?"

"Is Lord Mounteagle alone?" inquired Catesby, without noticing the question.

"He appears to be so," replied Bates.

"Admit him, then," rejoined Catesby.

Entering the closet with Keyes, he was followed by Fawkes, who drew his dagger, and kept the door slightly ajar, while Garnet and the rest retired to other hiding-places. A few moments afterwards, Bates returned with Lord Mounteagle, and, having ushered him into the room, took his station in the passage, as directed by Catesby. The room was very dark, the shutters being closed, and light only finding its way through the chinks in them; and it appeared totally so to Lord Mounteagle, who, groping his way, stumbled forward, and exclaimed in accents of some alarm:

"Where am I? Where is Mr. Tresham?"

"I am here," replied Tresham, advancing towards him. "How did your lordship find me out?" he added, after the customary salutations were exchanged.

"My servant saw you enter this house," replied Mounteagle, "and, knowing I was anxious to see you, waited for some hours without, in the expectation of your coming forth. But as this did not occur, he mentioned the circumstance to me on his return, and I immediately came in quest of you. When I knocked at the gate, I scarcely knew what to think of the place, and began to fear you must have fallen into the hands of cut-throats; and, now that I have gained admittance, my wonder—and I may add my uneasiness—is not diminished. Why do you hide yourself in this wretched place?"

"Be seated," replied Tresham, placing a chair for Lord Mounteagle, with his back to the closet, while he took one opposite him, and near a table, on which some papers were laid. "Your lordship may remember," he continued, scarcely knowing what answer to make to the question, "that I wrote to you some time ago, to say that a conspiracy was hatching among certain of our party against the State."

"I have reason to remember it," replied Mounteagle. "The letter was laid before the Earl of Salisbury, and inquiries instituted in consequence. But, owing to your disappearance, nothing could be elicited. What plot had you discovered?"

At this moment, Tresham, who kept his eye fixed on the closet, perceived the door noiselessly open, and behind it the figure of Guy Fawkes, with a dagger in his hand.

"I was misinformed as to the nature of the plot," he stammered.

"Was it against the King's life?" demanded Mounteagle.

"No," rejoined Tresham; "as far as I could learn, it was an insurrection."

"Indeed!" exclaimed Mounteagle, sceptically. "My information, then, differed from yours. Who were the parties you suspected?"

"As I *wrongfully* suspected them," replied Tresham, evasively, "your lordship must excuse my naming them."

"Was Catesby—or Winter—or Wright—or Rookwood—or Sir Everard Digby concerned in it?" demanded Mounteagle.

"Not one of them," asseverated Tresham.

"They are the persons *I* suspect," replied Mounteagle;

"and they are suspected by the Earl of Salisbury. But you have not told me what you are doing in this strange habitation. Are you ferreting out a plot, or contriving one?"

"Both," replied Tresham.

"How?" cried Mounteagle.

"I am plotting for myself, and counterplotting the designs of others," replied Tresham, mysteriously.

"Is this place, then, the rendezvous of a band of conspirators?" asked Mounteagle, uneasily.

Tresham nodded in the affirmative.

"Who are they?" continued Mounteagle. "There is no need of concealment with me."

As this was said, Tresham raised his eyes, and saw that Guy Fawkes had stepped silently forward, and placed himself behind Mounteagle's chair. His hand grasped his dagger, and his gaze never moved from the object of his suspicion.

"Who are they?" repeated Mounteagle. "Is Guy Fawkes one of them?"

"Assuredly not," replied Tresham. "Why should you name him? I never mentioned him to your lordship."

"I think you did," replied Mounteagle. "But I am certain you spoke of Catesby."

And Tresham's regards involuntarily wandered to the closet, when he beheld the stern glance of the person alluded to fixed upon him.

"You have heard of Viviana Radcliffe's imprisonment, I suppose?" pursued Mounteagle, unconscious of what was passing.

"I have," replied Tresham.

"The Earl of Salisbury expected he would be able to wring all from her, but he has failed," observed Mounteagle.

"I am glad of it," observed Tresham.

"I thought you were disposed to serve him?" remarked Mounteagle.

"So I am," replied Tresham. "But, if secrets are to be revealed, I had rather be the bearer of them than any one else. I am sorry for Viviana."

"I could procure her liberation, if I chose," observed Mounteagle.

"Say you so?" cried Fawkes, slapping him on the shoulder; "then you stir not hence till you have procured it!"

VII.

THE STAR-CHAMBER.

VIVIANA, as has already been intimated, after her capture at the house at Lambeth, was conveyed to the Star-Chamber. Here she was detained until a late hour on the following day when she underwent a long and rigorous examination by certain members of the Privy Council, who were summoned for that purpose by the Earl of Salisbury. Throughout this arduous trial she maintained the utmost composure, and never for a single moment lost her firmness. On all occasions, her matchless beauty and dignity produced the strongest impression on the beholders; but on no occasion had they ever produced so strong an effect as the present. Her features were totally destitute of bloom, but their very paleness, contrasted as it was with her large dark eyes, which blazed with unwonted brilliancy, as well as with her jet-black hair so far from detracting from her loveliness, appeared to add to it.

As she was brought before the Council, who were seated round a table, and remained standing at a short distance from them, guarded by Topcliffe and two halberdiers, a murmur of admiration pervaded the group—nor was this feeling lessened as the examination proceeded. Once, when the Earl of Salisbury adverted to the unworthy position in which she, the daughter of the proud and loyal Sir William Radcliffe, had placed herself, a shade passed over her brow, and a slight convulsion agitated her frame. But the next moment she recovered herself, and said:

"However circumstances may appear against me, and whatever opinion your lordships may entertain of my conduct, the King has not a more loyal subject than myself, nor have any of you made greater efforts to avert the danger by which he is threatened."

"Then you admit that his Majesty is in danger?" cried the Earl of Salisbury, eagerly.

"I admit nothing," replied Viviana. "But I affirm that I am his true and loyal subject."

"You cannot expect us to believe your assertion," replied the Earl, "unless you approve it by declaring all you know touching this conspiracy."

"I have already told you, my lord," she returned, "that my lips are sealed on that subject."

"You disclaim, then, all knowledge of the plot against the King's life, and against his government ?" pursued Salisbury.

Viviana shook her head.

"You refuse to give up the names of your companions, or to reveal their intentions ?" continued the Earl.

"I do," she answered, firmly.

"Your obstinacy will not save them," rejoined the Earl, in a severe tone, and after a brief pause. "Their names and their atrocious designs are known to us."

"If such be the case," replied Viviana, "why interrogate me on the subject ?"

"Because—but it is needless to give a reason for the course which justice requires me to pursue," returned the Earl. "You are implicated in this plot, and nothing can save you from condign punishment but a frank and full confession."

"Nothing *can* save me then, my lord," replied Viviana ; "but Heaven knows I shall perish unjustly."

A consultation was then held by the lords of the Council, who whispered together for a few minutes. Viviana regarded them anxiously, but suffered no expression of uneasiness to escape her. As they again turned towards her, she saw from their looks, some of which exhibited great commiseration for her, that they had come to a decision (she could not doubt what) respecting her fate. Her heart stopped beating, and she could scarcely support herself. Such, however, was the control she exercised over herself that though filled with terror, her demeanour remained unaltered. She was not long kept in suspense. Fixing his searching gaze upon her, the Earl of Salisbury observed, in a severe tone :

"Viviana Radcliffe, I ask you for the last time whether you will avow the truth ?"

No answer was returned.

"I will not disguise from you," continued the Earl, "that your youth, your beauty, your constancy, and, above all, your apparent innocence, have deeply interested me, as well as the other noble persons here assembled to interrogate you, and who would willingly save you from the sufferings you will necessarily undergo, from a mistaken fidelity to the heinous traitors with whom you are so unhappily leagued. I would give you time to reflect did I think the delay would answer any good purpose. I would remind you that no oath of secrecy, however solemn, can be binding in an unrighteous cause. I would tell you that your first duty is to your prince and governor ; and that it is as great a crime, as unpardonable in the eyes of God as of man, to withhold the revelation of a conspiracy against the State, should it come to your knowledge, as to conspire against it yourself. I would lay all this before you. I would show you the magnitude of your offence, the danger in which you stand, and the utter impossibility of screening your companions, who, ere long, will be confronted with you—did I think it would avail. But, as you continue obstinate, justice must take its course."

"I am prepared for the worst, my lord," replied Viviana, humbly. "I thank your lordship for your consideration: but I take you all to witness that I profess the utmost loyalty and devotion for my sovereign, and that, whatever may be my fate, those feelings will remain unchanged to the last."

"Your manner and your words are so sincere, that, were not your conduct at variance with them, they might convince us," returned the Earl. "As it is, even if we could credit your innocence, we are bound to act as if you were guilty. You will be committed to the Tower till his Majesty's pleasure is known. And I grieve to add, if you still continue obstinate, the severest measures will be resorted to, to extract the truth from you."

As he concluded, he attached his signature to a warrant which was lying on the table before him, and traced a few lines to Sir William Waad, lieutenant of the Tower.

This done, he handed the papers to Topcliffe, and waving his hand, Viviana was removed to the chamber in which she had been previously confined, and where she was detained under a strict guard, until Topcliffe, who had left her, returned to say that all was in readiness, and bidding her follow him, led the way to the river side, where a wherry, manned by six rowers, was waiting for them.

The night was profoundly dark, and, as none of the guard carried torches, their course was steered in perfect obscurity. But the rowers were too familiar with the river to require the guidance of light. Shooting the bridge in safety, and pausing only for a moment to give the signal of their approach to the sentinels on the ramparts, they passed swiftly under the low-browed arch of Traitor's Gate.

VIII.

THE JAILER'S DAUGHTER.

As Viviana set foot on those fatal stairs, which so many have trod, and none without feeling that they took their first step towards the scaffold, she involuntarily shrank backward. But it was now too late to retreat; and she surrendered her hand to Topcliffe, who assisted her up the steps. Half-a-dozen men-at-arms, with a like number of warders bearing torches, were present; and as it was necessary that Topcliffe should deliver his warrant into Sir William Waad's own hands, he committed his prisoner to the warders, with instructions to them to take her to the guard-room near the By-ward Tower, while he proceeded to the lieutenant's lodgings.

It was the first time Viviana had beheld the terrible pile in which she was immured, though she was well acquainted with its history, and with the persecutions which many of the professors of her faith had endured within it during the recent reign of Elizabeth; and as the light of the torches flashed upon the grey walls of the Bloody Tower, and upon the adjoining ramparts, all the dreadful tales she had heard rushed to her recollection. But having recovered the first shock, the succeeding impressions were powerless in comparison, and she accompanied the warders to the guard-room without expressing any outward emotion. Here a seat was offered her, and, as the men considerately withdrew, she was able to pursue her reflections unmolested. They were sad enough, and it required all her firmness to support her.

When considering what was likely to befall her in consequence of her adherence to the fortunes of Fawkes and his companions, she had often pictured some dreadful situation like the present, but the reality far exceeded her worst anticipations. She had deemed herself equal to any emergency, but as she thought upon the dark menaces of the Earl of Salisbury, she felt it would require greater fortitude than she had hitherto displayed to bear her through her trial. Nor were her meditations entirely confined to herself. While trembling for the perilous situation of Guy Fawkes, she reproached herself that she could not requite even in thought the passionate devotion of Humphrey Chetham.

"What matters it now," she thought, "that I cannot love him? I shall soon be nothing to him or to any one. And yet I feel I have done him wrong, and that I should be happier if I *could* requite his attachment. But the die is cast. It is too late to repent or to retreat. My heart acquits me of having been influenced by any unworthy motive, and I will strive to endure the keenest pang without a murmur."

Shortly after this, Topcliffe returned with Sir William Waad. On their entrance, Viviana arose, and the lieutenant eyed her with some curiosity. He was a middle-aged man, tall, stoutly-built, and having harsh features, stamped with an expression of mingled cunning and ferocity. His eyes had a fierce and bloodthirsty look, and were overshadowed by thick and scowling brows. Saluting the captive with affected courtesy, he observed:

"So you refuse to answer the interrogations of the Privy Council, madam, I understand. I am not sorry for it, because I would have the merit of wringing the truth from you. Those who have been most stubborn outside these walls have been the most yielding within them."

"That will not be my case," replied Viviana, coldly.

"We shall see," returned the lieutenant, with a significant glance at Topcliffe.

Ordering her to follow him, he then proceeded along the ward in the direction of the Bloody Tower, and passing beneath its arched gateway, ascended the steps on the left, and led her to his lodgings. Entering the habitation, he mounted to the upper story, and tracking a long gallery, brought her to a small circular chamber in the Bell Tower. Its sole furniture were a chair, a table, and a couch.

"Here you will remain for the present," observed the lieutenant, smiling grimly, and placing a lamp on the table. "It will depend upon yourself whether your accommodations are better hereafter."

With this, he quitted the cell with his attendants, and barred the door outside.

Left alone, Viviana, who had hitherto restrained her anguish, suffered it to find vent in tears. Never had she felt so utterly forlorn and desolate. All before her was threatening and terrible, full of dangers, real and imaginary; nor could she look back upon her past career without something like remorse.

"Oh, that Heaven would take me to itself!" she murmured, clasping her hands in an agony of distress, "for I feel unequal to my trials. Oh, that I had perished with my dear father! For what dreadful fate am I reserved?—Torture—

Q 2

I will bear it, if I *can*. But death by the hands of the public executioner—it is too horrible to think of! Is there no way to escape *that?*"

As this hideous thought occurred to her, she uttered a loud and prolonged scream, and fell senseless on the floor. When she recovered it was daylight; and, weak and exhausted, she crept to the couch, and throwing herself upon it, endeavoured to forget her misery in sleep. But, as is usually the case with the afflicted, it fled her eyelids, and she passed several hours in the severest mental torture, unrelieved by a single cheering thought.

About the middle of the day, the door of the cell was opened by an old woman with a morose and forbidding countenance, attended by a younger female, who resembled her in all but the expression of her features (her look was gentle and compassionate), and who appeared to be her daughter.

Without paying any attention to Viviana, the old woman took a small loaf of bread and other provisions from a basket she had brought with her, and placed them on the table. This done, she was about to depart, when her daughter, who had glanced uneasily at the couch, observed in a kindly tone:

"Shall we not inquire whether we can be of service to the poor young lady, mother?"

"Why should we concern ourselves about her, Ruth?" returned the old woman, sharply. "If she wants anything, she has a tongue, and can speak. If she desires further comforts," she added, in a significant tone, "they must be *paid* for."

"I desire nothing but death," groaned Viviana.

"The poor soul is dying, I believe," cried Ruth, rushing to the couch. "Have you no cordial-water about you, mother?"

"Truly have I," returned the old woman; "and I have other things besides. But I must be paid for them."

As she spoke she drew from her pocket a small, square, Dutch-shaped bottle.

"Give it me," cried Ruth, snatching it from her. "I am sure the young lady will pay for it."

"You are very kind," said Viviana, faintly. "But I have no means of doing so."

"I knew it," cried the old woman, fiercely. "I knew it. Give me back the flask, Ruth. She shall not taste a drop. Do you not hear she has no money, wench? Give it me, I say."

"Nay, mother, for pity's sake," implored Ruth.

"Pity, forsooth !" exclaimed the old woman, derisively.
"If I and thy father, Jasper Ipgreve, had any such feeling,
it would be high time for him to give up his post of jailer in
the Tower of London. Pity for a *poor* prisoner! Thou a
jailer's daughter, and talk so! I am ashamed of thee, wench.
But I thought this was a rich Catholic heiress, and had powerful and wealthy friends."

"So she is," replied Ruth; "and though she may have no
money with her now, she can command any amount she
pleases. I heard Master Topcliffe tell young Nicholas
Hardesty, the warder, so. She is the daughter of the late
Sir William Radcliffe, of Ordsall Hall, in Lancashire, and
sole heiress of his vast estates."

"Is this so, sweet lady?" inquired the old woman, stepping towards the couch. "Are you truly Sir William Radcliffe's daughter?"

"I am," replied Viviana. "But I have said I require
nothing from you. Leave me."

"No—no, dear young lady," rejoined Dame Ipgreve, in a
whining tone, which was infinitely more disagreeable to Viviana
than her previous harshness. "I cannot leave you in this
state. Raise her head, Ruth, while I pour a few drops of the
cordial down her throat."

"I will not taste it," replied Viviana, putting the flask
aside.

"You would find it a sovereign restorative," replied Dame
Ipgreve, with a mortified look; "but as you please. I will not
urge you against your inclination. The provisions I have
been obliged to bring you are too coarse for a daintily-nur-
tured maiden like you—but you shall have others presently."

"It is needless," rejoined Viviana. "Pray leave me."

"Well, well, I am going," rejoined Dame Ipgreve, hesitating. "Do you want to write to any one? I can find
means of conveying a letter secretly out of the Tower."

"Ah!" exclaimed Viviana, raising herself. "And yet no
—no—I dare not trust you."

"You may," replied the avaricious old woman—"provided
you pay me well."

"I will think of it," returned Viviana. "But I have not
strength to write now."

"You must not give way thus—indeed you must not, dear
lady," said Ruth, in a voice of great kindness. "It will not
be safe to leave you. Suffer me to remain with you."

"Willingly," replied Viviana; "most willingly."

"Stay with her, then, child," said Dame Ipgreve. "I will go and prepare a nourishing broth for her. Take heed and make a shrewd bargain with her for thy attendance," she added in a hasty whisper, as she retired.

Greatly relieved by the old woman's departure, Viviana turned to Ruth, and thanked her in the warmest terms for her kindness. A few minutes sufficed to convert the sympathy which these two young persons evidently felt towards each other into affectionate regard, and the jailer's daughter assured Viviana that, so long as she should be detained, she would devote herself to her.

By this time the old woman had returned with a mess of hot broth, which she carried with an air of great mystery beneath her cloak. Viviana was prevailed upon by the solicitations of Ruth to taste it, and found herself much revived in consequence. Her slight meal ended, Dame Ipgreve departed, with a promise to return in the evening with such viands as she could manage to introduce unobserved, and with a flask of wine.

"You will need it, sweet lady, I fear," she said; "for my husband tells me you are in peril of the torture. Oh! it is a sad thing, that such as you should be so cruelly dealt with! But we will take all the care of you we can. You will not forget to requite us. You must give me an order on your steward, or on some rich Catholic friend. I am half a Papist myself—that is, I like one religion as well as the other—and I like those best, whatever their creed may be, who pay best. That is my maxim: and it is the same with my husband. We do all we can to scrape together a penny for our child."

"No more of this, good mother," interrupted Ruth. "It distresses the lady. I will take care she wants nothing."

"Right, child, right," returned Dame Ipgreve; "do not forget what I told you," she added in a whisper.

And she quitted the cell.

Ruth remained with Viviana during the rest of the day, and it was a great consolation to the latter to find that her companion was of the same faith as herself—having been converted by Father Poole, a Romish priest who was confined in the Tower during the latter part of Elizabeth's reign, and whose sufferings and constancy for his religion had made a powerful impression on the jailer's daughter. As soon as Viviana ascertained this, she made Ruth, so far as she thought prudent, a confidante in her misfortunes, and after beguiling some hours in conversation, they both knelt down and offered up fervent prayers to the Virgin. Ruth then departed, promising to return in the evening with her mother.

Soon after it became dark, Dame Ipgreve and her daughter reappeared, the former carrying a lamp, and the latter a basket of provisions. Ruth's countenance was so troubled, that Viviana was certain that some fresh calamity was at hand.

"What is the matter?" she hastily demanded.

"Make your meal first, dear young lady," replied Dame Ipgreve. "Our news might take away your appetite, and you will have to pay for your supper, whether you eat it or not."

"You alarm me greatly," replied Viviana, anxiously. "What ill news do you bring?"

"I will not keep you longer in suspense, madam," said Ruth. "You are to be examined to-night by the lieutenant and certain members of the Privy Council, and if you refuse to answer their questions, I lament to say you will be put to the torture."

"Heaven give me strength to endure it!" ejaculated Viviana, in a despairing tone.

"Eat, madam, eat," replied Dame Ipgreve, pressing the viands upon her. "You will never be able to go through with the examination, if you starve yourself in this way."

"Are you sure," inquired Viviana, appealing to Ruth, "that it will take place so soon?"

"Quite sure," replied Ruth. "My father has orders to attend the lieutenant at midnight."

"Let me advise you to conceal nothing," insinuated the old woman. "They are determined to wring the truth from you —and they *will* do so."

"You are mistaken, good woman," replied Viviana, firmly. "I will die before I utter a word."

"You think so now," returned Dame Ipgreve, maliciously. "But the sight of the rack and the thumbscrews will alter your tone." At all events support nature."

"No," replied Viviana; "as I do not desire to live, I will use no effort to sustain myself. They may kill me if they please."

"Misfortune has turned her brain," muttered the old woman. "I must take care and secure my dues. Well, madam, if you will not eat the supper I have provided, it cannot be helped. I must find some one who will. You must pay for it all the same. My husband, Jasper Ipgreve,

will be present at your interrogation, and I am sure, for my
sake, he will use you as lightly as he can. Come, Ruth, you
must not remain here longer."

"Oh, let her stay with me," implored Viviana. "I will
make it well worth your while to grant me the indulgence."

"What will you give?" cried the old woman, eagerly.
"But no—no—I dare not leave her. The lieutenant may
visit you, and find her, and then I should lose my place.
Come along, Ruth. She shall attend you after the interrogation, madam. I shall be there myself."

"Farewell, madam," sobbed Ruth, who was almost drowned
in tears. "Heaven grant you constancy to endure your
trial."

"Be ruled by me," said the old woman. "Speak out, and
secure your own safety."

She would have continued in the same strain, but Ruth
dragged her away. And casting a commiserating glance at
Viviana, she closed the door.

The dreadful interval between their departure and midnight was passed by Viviana in fervent prayer. As she heard
through the barred embrasure of her dungeon the deep
strokes of the clock toll out the hour of twelve, the door
opened, and a tall, gaunt personage, habited in a suit of
rusty black, and with a large bunch of keys at his girdle,
entered the cell.

"You are Jasper Ipgreve?" said Viviana, rising.

"Right," replied the jailer. "I am come to take you before
the lieutenant and the Council. Are you ready?"

Viviana replied in the affirmative, and Ipgreve quitting the
cell, outside which two other officials in sable habiliments
were stationed, led the way down a short spiral staircase,
which brought them to a narrow vaulted passage. Pursuing
it for some time, the jailer halted before a strong door, cased
with iron, and opening it, admitted the captive into a square
chamber, the roof of which was supported by a heavy stone
pillar, while its walls were garnished with implements of
torture. At a table on the left sat the lieutenant and three
other grave-looking personages. Across the lower end of
the chamber a thick black curtain was stretched hiding a
deep recess; and behind it, as was evident from the glimmer
that escaped from its folds, there was a light. Certain indistinct but ominous sounds, issuing from the recess proved
that there were persons within it, and Viviana's quaking heart
told her what was the nature of their proceedings.

She had ample time to survey this dismal apartment and its occupants, for several minutes elapsed before a word was addressed to her by her interrogators, who continued to confer together in an undertone, as if unconscious of her presence. During this pause, broken only by the ominous sounds before mentioned, Viviana scanned the countenances of the group at the table, in the hope of discerning in them some glimpses of compassion; but they were inscrutable and inexorable, and scarcely less dreadful to look upon than the hideous implements on the walls.

Viviana wished the earth would open and swallow her, that she might escape from them. Anything was better than to be left at the mercy of such men. At certain times, and not unfrequently at the most awful moments, a double current of thought will flow through the brain, and at this frightful juncture it was so with Viviana. While shuddering at all she saw around her, nay, dwelling upon it, another and distinct train of thought led her back to former scenes of happiness, when she was undisturbed by any but remote apprehensions of danger. She thought of her tranquil residence at Ordsall —of the flowers she had tended in the garden—of her father, and of his affection for her—of Humphrey Chetham, and of her early and scarce-acknowledged attachment to him—and of his generosity and devotion, and how she had requited it. And then, like a sullen cloud darkening the fair prospect, arose the figure of Guy Fawkes—the sombre enthusiast—who had unwittingly exercised such a baneful influence upon her fortunes.

"Had he not crossed my path," she mentally ejaculated, "I might have been happy—might have loved Humphrey Chetham—might, perhaps, have wedded him!"

These reflections were suddenly dispersed by the lieutenant, who, in a stern tone, commenced his interrogations.

As upon her previous examination, Viviana observed the utmost caution, and either refused to speak, or answered such questions only as affected herself. At first, in spite of all her efforts, she trembled violently, and her tongue clove to the roof of her mouth. But after a while she recovered her courage, and regarded the lieutenant with a look as determined as his own.

"It is useless to urge me farther," she concluded; "I have said all I will say."

"Is it your pleasure, my lords," observed Sir William Waad to the others, "to prolong the examination?"

His companions replied in the negative, and the one nearest him remarked: "Is she aware what will follow?"

"I am," replied Viviana, resolutely, "and I am not to be intimidated."

"Sir William Waad then made a sign to Ipgreve, who immediately stepped forward, and seized her arm. "You will be taken to that recess," said the lieutenant, "where the question will be put to you. But, as we shall remain here, you have only to utter a cry if you are willing to avow the truth, and the torture shall be stayed. And it is our merciful hope that this may be the case."

Summoning up all her resolution, and walking with a firm footstep, Viviana passed with Ipgreve behind the curtain. She there beheld two men and a woman—the latter was the jailer's wife, who instantly advanced to her and besought her to confess.

"There is no help for it, if you refuse," she urged; "not all your wealth can save you."

"Mind your own business, dame," interposed Ipgreve, angrily, "and assist her to unrobe."

Saying this, he stepped aside with the two men, one of whom was the chirurgeon, and the other the tormentor, while Dame Ipgreve helped to take off Viviana's gown. She then tied a scarf over her shoulders, and informed her husband she was ready.

The recess was about twelve feet high, and ten wide. It was crossed near the roof, which was arched and vaulted, by a heavy beam with pulleys and ropes at either extremity. But what chiefly attracted the unfortunate captive's attention was a couple of iron gauntlets attached to it, about a yard apart. Upon the ground, under the beam, and immediately beneath that part of it where the gauntlets were fixed, were laid three pieces of wood, of a few inches in thickness, and piled one upon another.

"What must I do?" inquired Viviana, in a hollow voice, but with unaltered resolution, of the old woman.

"Step upon those pieces of wood," replied Dame Ipgreve, leading her towards them.

Viviana obeyed, and as soon as she had set foot upon the pile, the tormentor placed a joint-stool beside her, and mounting it, desired her to place her right hand in one of the gauntlets. She did so, and the tormentor then turned a screw, which compressed the iron glove so tightly as to give her excruciating pain. He then got down, and Ipgreve demanded if he should proceed.

A short pause ensued; but notwithstanding her agony, Viviana made no answer. The tormentor then placed the stool on the left side, and fastened the hand which was still at liberty within the other gauntlet. The torture was dreadful —and the fingers appeared crushed by the pressure. Still Viviana uttered no cry. After another short pause, Ipgreve said:

"You had better let us stop here. This is mere child's play compared with what is to come."

No answer being returned, the tormentor took a mallet, and struck one of the pieces of wood from under Viviana's feet. The shock was dreadful, and seemed to dislocate her wrists, while the pressure on the hands was increased in a ten-fold degree. The poor sufferer, who was resting on the points of her feet, felt that the removal of the next piece of wood would occasion almost intolerable torture. Her constancy, however, did not desert her, and, after the question had been repeated by Ipgreve, the second block was struck away. She was now suspended by her hands, and the pain was so exquisite, that nature gave way, and uttering a piercing scream, she fainted.

On recovering, she found herself stretched upon a miserable pallet, with Ruth watching beside her. A glance round the chamber, which was of solid stone masonry, with a deep embrasure on one side, convinced her that she had been removed to some other prison.

"Where am I?" she asked in a faint voice.

"In the Well Tower, madam," replied Ruth; "one of the fortifications near the moat, and now used as a prison-lodging. My father dwells within it, and you are under his custody."

"Your father," cried Viviana, shuddering as she recalled the sufferings she had recently undergone. "Will he torture me again?"

"Not if I can prevent it, dear lady," replied Ruth. "But hush; here comes my mother. Not a word before her."

As Ruth spoke, Dame Ipgreve, who had been lingering at the door, entered the room. She affected the greatest solicitude for Viviana—felt her pulse—looked at the bandages fastened round her swollen and crippled fingers, and concluded by counselling her not to persist in refusing to speak.

"I dare not tell you what tortures are in store for you," she said, "if you continue thus obstinate. But they will be a thousand times worse than what you endured last night."

"When will my next interrogation take place?" inquired Viviana.

"A week hence, it may be—or it may be sooner," returned the old woman. "It depends upon the state you are in—and somewhat upon the fees you give my husband, for he has a voice with the lieutenant."

"I would give him all I possess, if he could save me from further torture," cried Viviana.

"Alas! alas!" replied Dame Ipgreve, "you ask more than can be done. He would save you if he could. But you will not let him. However, we will do all we can to mitigate your sufferings—all we can—provided you pay us. Stay with her, child," she added with a significant gesture to her daughter, as she quitted the room, "stay with her."

"My heart bleeds for you, madam," said Ruth, in accents of the deepest commiseration, as soon as they were alone. "You may depend upon my fidelity. If I can contrive your escape, I will—at any risk to myself."

"On no account," replied Viviana. "Do not concern yourself about me more. My earthly sufferings, I feel, will have terminated before further cruelty can be practised upon me."

"Oh! say not so, madam," returned Ruth. "I hope— nay, I am sure you will live long and happily."

Viviana shook her head, and Ruth, finding her very feeble, thought it better not to continue the conversation. She accordingly applied such restoratives as were at hand, and observing that the eyes of the sufferer closed as if in slumber, glided noiselessly out of the chamber, and left her.

In this way a week passed. At the expiration of that time, the chirurgeon pronounced her in so precarious a state, that if the torture were repeated he would not answer for her life. The interrogation, therefore, was postponed for a few days, during which the chirurgeon constantly visited her, and by his care, and the restoratives she was compelled to take, she rapidly regained her strength.

One day, after the chirurgeon had departed, Ruth cautiously closed the door, and observed to her:

"You are now so far recovered, madam, as to be able to make an attempt to escape. I have devised a plan, which I will communicate to you to-morrow. It must not be delayed, or you will have to encounter a second and more dreadful examination."

"I will not attempt it if you are exposed to risk," replied Viviana,

"Heed me not," returned Ruth. "One of your friends has found out your place of confinement, and has spoken to me about you."

"What friend!" exclaimed Viviana, starting. "Guy Fawkes—I mean——" And she hesitated, while her pale cheeks were suffused with blushes.

"He is named Humphrey Chetham," returned Ruth. "Like myself, he would risk his life to preserve you."

"Tell him he must not do so," cried Viviana, eagerly. "He has done enough—too much for me already. I will not expose him to further hazard. Tell him so, and entreat him to abandon the attempt."

"But I shall not see him, dear lady," replied Ruth. "Besides, if I read him rightly, he is not likely to be turned aside by any selfish consideration."

"You are right, he is not," groaned Viviana. "But this only adds to my affliction. Oh! if you *should* see him, dear Ruth, try to dissuade him from his purpose."

"I will obey you, madam," replied the jailer's daughter. "But I am well assured it will be of no avail."

After some further conversation, Ruth retired, and Viviana was left alone for the night. Except the slumber procured by soporific potions, she had known no repose since she had been confined within the tower; and this night she felt more than usually restless. After ineffectually endeavouring to compose herself, she arose, and hastily robing herself—a task she performed with no little difficulty, her fingers being almost useless—continued to pace her narrow chamber.

It has been mentioned that on one side of the cell there was a deep embrasure. It was terminated by a narrow and strongly-grated loophole, looking upon the moat. Pausing before it, Viviana gazed forth. The night was pitchy dark, and not even a solitary star could be discerned; but as she had no light in her chamber, the gloom outside was less profound than that within.

While standing thus, buried in thought, and longing for daybreak, Viviana fancied she heard a slight sound as of some one swimming across the moat. Thinking she might be deceived, she listened more intently, and as the sound continued, she felt sure she was right in her conjecture. All at once the thought of Humphrey Chetham flashed upon her, and she had no doubt it must be him. Nor was she wrong. The next moment a noise was heard as of some one clambering up the wall; a hand grasped the bars of the loophole, which was only two or three feet above the level of the water; and a low voice, which she instantly recognised, pronounced her name.

"Is it Humphrey Chetham?" she asked, advancing as near as she could to the loophole.

"It is," was the reply. "Do not despair. I will accomplish your liberation. I have passed three days within the Tower, and only ascertained your place of confinement a few hours ago. I have contrived a plan for your escape, with the jailer's daughter, which she will make known to you to-morrow."

"I cannot thank you sufficiently for your devotion," replied Viviana, in accents of the deepest gratitude. "But I implore you to leave me to my fate. I am wretched enough now, Heaven knows; but if aught should happen to you, I shall be infinitely more so. If I possess any power over you, and that I do so, I well know—I entreat, nay, I command you to desist from this attempt."

"I have never yet disobeyed you, Viviana," replied the young merchant, passionately—"nor will I do so now. But if you bid me abandon you, I will plunge into this moat, never to rise again."

His manner, notwithstanding the low tone in which he spoke, was so determined, that Viviana felt certain he would carry his threat into execution; she therefore rejoined, in a mournful tone:

"Well, be it as you will. It is in vain to resist our fate. I am destined to bring misfortune to you."

"Not so," replied Chetham. "If I *can* save you, I would rather die than live. The jailer's daughter will explain her plan to you to-morrow. Promise me to accede to it."

Viviana reluctantly assented.

"I shall quit the Tower at daybreak," pursued Chetham; "and when you are once out of it, hasten to the stairs beyond the wharf at Petty Wales. I will be there with a boat. Farewell!"

As he spoke, he let himself drop into the water; but his foot slipping, the plunge was louder than he intended, and attracted the attention of a sentinel on the ramparts, who immediately called out to know what was the matter, and not receiving any answer, discharged his caliver in the direction of the sound.

Viviana, who heard the challenge and the shot, uttered a loud scream, and the next moment Ipgreve and his wife appeared. The jailer glanced suspiciously round the room; but after satisfying himself that all was right, and putting some questions to the captive, which she refused to answer, he departed with his wife, and carefully barred the door.

It is impossible to imagine greater misery than Viviana endured the whole of the night. The uncertainty in which she was kept as to Chetham's fate was almost insupportable, and the bodily pain she had recently endured appeared light when compared with her present mental torture. Day at length dawned; but it brought with it no Ruth. Instead of this faithful friend, Dame Ipgreve entered the chamber with the morning meal, and her looks were so morose and distrustful, that Viviana feared she must have discovered her daughter's design. She did not, however, venture to make a remark, but suffered the old woman to depart in silence.

Giving up all for lost, and concluding that Humphrey Chetham had either perished, or was, like herself a prisoner, Viviana bitterly bewailed his fate, and reproached herself with being unintentionally the cause of it. Later in the day, Ruth entered the cell. To Viviana's eager inquiries she replied, that Humphrey Chetham had escaped. Owing to the darkness, the sentinel had missed his aim, and although the most rigorous search was instituted throughout the fortress, he had contrived to elude observation.

"Our attempt," pursued Ruth, "must be made this evening. The lieutenant has informed my father that you are to be interrogated at midnight, the chirurgeon having declared that you are sufficiently recovered to undergo the torture (if needful) a second time. Now listen to me. The occurrence of last night has made my mother suspicious, and she watches my proceedings with a jealous eye. She is at this moment with a female prisoner in the Beauchamp Tower, or I should not be able to visit you. She has consented, however, to let me bring in your supper. You must then change dresses with me. Being about my height, you may easily pass for me, and I will take care there is no light below, so that your features will not be distinguished."

Viviana would have checked her, but the other would not be interrupted.

"As soon as you are ready," she continued, "you must lock the door upon me. You must then descend the short flight of steps before you, and pass as quickly as you can through the room where you will see my father and mother. As soon as you are out of the door, turn to the left, and go straight forward to the By-ward Tower. Show this pass to the warders. It is made out in my name, and they will suffer you to go forth. Do the same with the warders at the

next gate—the Middle Tower—and again at the Bulwark
Gate. That passed, you are free."

"And what will become of you?" asked Viviana, with a
bewildered look.

"Never mind me," rejoined Ruth : "I shall be sufficiently
rewarded if I save you. And now, farewell. Be ready at
the time appointed."

"I cannot consent," returned Viviana.

"You have no choice," replied Ruth, breaking from her,
and hurrying out of the room.

Time, as it ever does, when expectation is on the rack,
appeared to pass with unusual slowness. But as the hour at
length drew near, Viviana wished it farther off. It was with
the utmost trepidation that she heard the key turn in the
lock, and beheld Ruth enter the cell with the evening meal.

Closing the door, and setting down the provisions, the
jailer's daughter hastily divested herself of her dress, which
was of brown serge, as well as of her coif and kerchief, while
Viviana imitated her example. Without pausing to attire
herself in the other's garments, Ruth then assisted Viviana
to put on the dress she had just laid aside, and arranged her
hair and the head-gear so skilfully, that the disguise was
complete.

Hastily whispering some further instructions to her, and
explaining certain peculiarities in her gait and deportment,
she then pressed her to her bosom, and led her to the door.
Viviana would have remonstrated, but Ruth pushed her
through it and closed it.

There was now no help, so Viviana, though with great pain
to herself, contrived to turn the key in the lock. Descending
the steps, she found herself in a small circular chamber, in
which Ipgreve and his wife were seated at a table, discussing
their evening meal. The sole light was afforded by a few
dying embers on the hearth.

"What! has she done already?" demanded the old woman,
as Viviana appeared. "Why hast thou not brought the jelly
with thee, if she has not eaten it all, and those cates, which
Master Pilchard, the chirurgeon, ordered her? Go and fetch
them directly. They will finish our repast daintily; and
there are other matters too, which I dare say she has not
touched. She will pay for them, and that will make them
the sweeter. Go back, I say. What dost thou stand there
for, as if thou wert thunderstruck? Dost hear me, or not?"

"Let the wench alone, dame," growled Ipgreve. "You
frighten her."

"So I mean to do," replied the old woman; "she deserves to be frightened. Hark thee, girl, we must get an order from her on some wealthy Catholic family without delay—for I don't think she will stand the trial to-night."

"Nor I," added Ipgreve, "especially as she is to be placed on the rack."

"She has a chain of gold round her throat, I have observed," said the old woman; "we must get that."

"I have it," said Viviana, in a low tone, and imitating as well as she could the accents of Ruth. "Here it is."

"Did she give it thee?" cried the old woman, getting up, and grasping Viviana's lacerated fingers with such force, that she had difficulty in repressing a scream. "Did she give it thee, I say?"

"She gave it me for you," gasped Viviana. "Take it."

While the old woman held the chain to the fire, and called to her husband to light a lamp, that she might feast her greedy eyes upon it, Viviana flew to the door.

Just as she reached it, the shrill voice of Dame Ipgreve arrested her.

"Come back!" cried the dame. "Whither art thou going at this time of night? I will not have thee stir forth. Come back, I say."

"Pshaw! let her go," interposed Ipgreve. "I dare say she hath an appointment on the Green with young Nicholas Hardesty, the warder. Go, wench. Be careful of thyself, and return within the hour."

"If she does not, she will rue it," added the dame. "Go, then, and I will see to the prisoner."

Viviana required no further permission. Starting off as she had been directed on the left, she ran as fast as her feet could carry her; and passing between two arched gateways, soon reached the By-ward Tower. Showing the pass to the warder, he chucked her under the chin, and, drawing an immense bolt, opened the wicket, and gallantly helped her to pass through it. The like good success attended her at the Middle Tower, and at the Bulwark Gate. Scarcely able to credit her senses, and doubting whether she was indeed free, she hurried on till she came to the opening leading to the stairs at Petty Wales. As she hesitated, uncertain what to do, a man advanced towards and addressed her by name. It was Humphrey Chetham. Overcome by emotion, Viviana sank into his arms, and in another moment she was placed in a wherry, which was ordered to be rowed towards Westminster.

IX.

THE COUNTERPLOT.

STARTLED, but not dismayed—for he was a man of great courage—by the sudden address and appearance of Guy Fawkes, Lord Mounteagle instantly sprang to his feet, and drawing his sword, put himself into a posture of defence.

"You have betrayed me," he cried, seizing Tresham with his left hand; "but if I fall, you shall fall with me."

"You have betrayed yourself, my lord," rejoined Guy Fawkes; "or rather, Heaven has placed you in our hands as an instrument for the liberation of Viviana Radcliffe. You must take an oath of secrecy—a binding oath—such as, being a good Catholic, you cannot break—not to divulge what has come to your knowledge. Nay, you must join me and my confederates, or you quit not this spot with life."

"I refuse your terms," replied Mounteagle, resolutely; "I will never conspire against the monarch to whom I have sworn allegiance. I will not join you. I will not aid you in procuring Viviana Radcliffe's release. Nor will I take the oath you propose. On the contrary, I arrest you as a traitor, and I command you, Tresham, in the King's name, to assist me in his capture."

But suddenly extricating himself from the grasp imposed upon him, and placing Guy Fawkes between him and the Earl, Tresham rejoined:

"It is time to throw off the mask, my good lord and brother. I can render you no assistance. I am sworn to this league, and must support it. Unless you assent to the conditions proposed—and which for your own sake I would counsel you to do—I must, despite our near relationship, take part against you—even," he added, significantly, "if your destruction should be resolved upon."

"I will sell my life dearly, as you shall find," replied Mounteagle. "And but for the sake of my dear lady, your sister, I would stab you where you stand."

"Your lordship will find resistance in vain," replied Guy Fawkes, keeping his eye steadily fixed upon him. "We seek not your life, but your co-operation. You are a prisoner."

"A prisoner!" echoed Mounteagle, derisively. "You have not secured me yet."

And as he spoke, he rushed towards the door, but his departure was checked by Bates, who presented himself at the entrance of the passage with a drawn sword in his hand. At the same moment, Catesby and Keyes issued from the closet, while Garnet and the other conspirators likewise emerged from their hiding-places. Hearing the noise behind him, Lord Mounteagle turned, and beholding the group, uttered an exclamation of surprise and rage.

"I am fairly entrapped," he said, sheathing his sword, and advancing towards them. "Fool that I was to venture hither !"

"These regrets are too late, my lord," replied Catesby. "You came hither of your own accord. But being here, nothing, except compliance with our demands, can insure your departure."

"Yes, one thing else," thought Mounteagle—"cunning. It shall go hard if I cannot outwit you. Tresham will act with me. I know his treacherous nature too well to doubt which way he will incline. Interest, as well as relationship, binds him to me. He will acquaint me with their plans. I need not, therefore, compromise myself by joining them. If I take the oath of secrecy, it will suffice—and I will find means of eluding the obligation. I may thus make my own bargain with Salisbury. But I must proceed cautiously. Too sudden a compliance might awaken their suspicions."

"My lord," said Catesby, who had watched his countenance narrowly, and distrusted its expression, "we must have no double-dealing. Any attempt to play us false will prove fatal to you."

"I have not yet consented to your terms, Mr. Catesby," replied Mounteagle, "and I demand a few moments' reflection before I do so."

"What say you, gentlemen?" said Catesby. "Do you agree to his lordship's request?"

There was a general answer in the affirmative.

"I would also confer for a moment alone with my brother Tresham," said Mounteagle.

"That cannot be, my lord," rejoined Garnet, peremptorily. "And take heed you meditate no treachery towards us, or you will destroy yourself here and hereafter."

"I have no desire to speak with him, father," observed Tresham. "Let him declare what he has to say before you all."

Mounteagle looked hard at him, but he made no remark.

"In my opinion, we ought not to trust him," observed

Keyes. " It is plain he is decidedly opposed to us. And if
the oath is proposed to him, he may take it with some mental
reservation."

" *I* will guard against that," replied Garnet.

" If I take the oath, I will keep it, father," rejoined Mounteagle. " But I have not yet decided."

" You must do so, then, quickly, my lord," returned
Catesby. " You shall have five minutes for reflection. But
first, you must deliver up your sword."

The Earl started.

" We mean *you* no treachery, my lord," observed Keyes,
" and expect to be dealt with with equal fairness."

Surrendering his sword to Catesby, Mounteagle then
walked to the farther end of the room, and leaning against
the wall, with his back to the conspirators, appeared buried
in thought.

" Take Tresham aside," whispered Catesby to Wright. " I
do not wish him to overhear our conference. Watch him
narrowly, and see that no signal passes between him and
Lord Mounteagle."

Wright obeyed; and the others gathering closely together,
began to converse in a low tone."

" It will not do to put him to death," observed Garnet.
" From what he stated to Tresham, it appears that his
servant was aware of his coming hither. If he disappears,
therefore, search will be immediately made, and all will be
discovered. We must either instantly secure ourselves by
flight, and give up the enterprise, or trust him."

" You are right, father," replied Rookwood. " The danger
is imminent."

" We are safe at present," observed Percy, " and may
escape to France or Flanders before information can be given
against us. Nay, we may carry off Mounteagle with us, for
that matter. But I am loth to trust him."

" So am I," rejoined Catesby. " I do not like his looks."

" There is no help," said Fawkes. " We *must* trust him,
or give up the enterprise. He may materially aid us, and
has himself asserted that he can procure Viviana's liberation
from the Tower."

" Pshaw !" exclaimed Catesby, impatiently. " What has
that to do with the all-important question we are now considering ?"

" Much," returned Fawkes. " And I will not move further
in the matter unless that point is insisted on."

"You have become strangely interested in Viviana of late," observed Catesby, sarcastically. "Could I suspect you of so light a passion, I should say you loved her."

A deep flush dyed Fawkes's swarthy cheeks, but he answered in a voice of constrained calmness:

"I *do* love her,—as a daughter."

"Humph!" exclaimed the other, drily.

"Catesby," rejoined Fawkes, sternly, "you know me well —too well, to suppose I would resort to any paltry subterfuge. I am willing to let what you have said pass. But I counsel you not to jest thus in future."

"Jest!" exclaimed Catesby. "I was never more serious in my life."

"Then you do me wrong," retorted Fawkes, fiercely; "and you will repeat the insinuation at your peril."

"My sons—my sons," interposed Garnet, "what means this sudden—this needless quarrel, at a moment when we require the utmost calmness to meet the danger that assails us? Guy Fawkes is right. Viviana *must* be saved. If we desert her, our cause will never prosper. But let us proceed step by step, and first decide upon what is to be done with Lord Mounteagle."

"I am filled with perplexity," replied Catesby.

"Then I will decide for you," replied Percy. "Our project must be abandoned."

"Never!" replied Fawkes, energetically. "Fly, and secure your own safety. I will stay and accomplish it alone."

"A brave resolution!" exclaimed Catesby, tendering him his hand, which the other cordially grasped. "I will stand by you to the last. No—we have advanced too far to retreat."

"Additional caution will be needful," observed Keyes. "Can we not make it a condition with Lord Mounteagle to retire, till the blow is struck, to his mansion at Hoxton?"

"That would be of no avail," replied Garnet. "We must trust him wholly, or not at all."

"There I agree with you, father," said Percy. "Let us propose the oath of secrecy to him, and detain him here until we have found some secure retreat, utterly unknown to him or to Tresham, whence we can correspond with our friends. A few days will show whether he has betrayed us or not. We need not visit this place again till the moment for action arrives."

"You need not visit it again at all," rejoined Fawkes. "Everything is prepared, and I will undertake to fire the

train. Prepare for what is to follow the explosion, and leave
the management of that to me."

"I cannot consent to such a course, my son," said Garnet.
"The whole risk will thus be yours."

"The whole glory will be mine also, father," rejoined
Fawkes, enthusiastically. "I pray you, let me have my own
way."

"Well, be it as you will, my son," returned Garnet, with
affected reluctance. "I will not oppose the hand of Heaven,
which clearly points you out as the chief agent in this mighty
enterprise. In reference to what Percy has said about a
retreat till Lord Mounteagle's trustworthiness can be ascertained," he added to Catesby, "I have just bethought me of
a large retired house on the borders of Enfield Chase, called
White Webbs. It has been recently taken by Mrs. Brooksby,
and her sister, Anne Vaux, and will afford us a safe asylum."

"An excellent plan, father," cried Catesby. "Since Guy
Fawkes is willing to undertake the risk, we will leave Lord
Mounteagle in his charge, and go there at once."

"What must be done with Tresham?" asked Percy. "We
cannot take him with us, nor must he know of our retreat."

"Leave him with me," said Fawkes.

"You will be at a disadvantage," observed Catesby,
"should he take part, as there is reason to fear he may
do, with Lord Mounteagle."

"They are both unarmed," returned Fawkes; "but were it
otherwise, I would answer with my head for their detention."

"All good saints guard you, my son!" exclaimed Garnet.
"Henceforth we resign the custody of the powder to you."

"It will be in safe keeping," replied Fawkes.

The party then advanced towards Lord Mounteagle, who,
hearing their approach, instantly faced them.

"Your decision, my lord?" demanded Catesby.

"You shall have it in a word, sir," replied Mounteagle,
firmly. "I will *not* join you, but I will take the required
oath of secrecy."

"Is this your final resolve, my lord?" rejoined Catesby.

"It is," replied the Earl.

"It must content us," observed Garnet; "though we
hoped you would have lent your active services to further
a cause having for its sole object the restoration of the
Church to which you belong."

"I know not the means whereby you propose to restore it,
father," replied Mounteagle, "and I do not desire to know

them. But I guess that they are dark and bloody, and as such I can take no part in them."

"And you refuse to give us any counsel or assistance?" pursued Garnet.

"I will not betray you," replied Mounteagle. "I can say nothing further."

"I would rather be promised too little than too much," whispered Catesby to Garnet. "I begin to think him sincere."

"I am of the same opinion, my son," returned Garnet.

"One thing you *shall* do, before *I* consent to set you free, on any terms, my lord," observed Guy Fawkes. "You shall engage to procure the liberation of Viviana Radcliffe from the Tower. You told Tresham you could easily accomplish it."

"I scarcely know what I said," replied Mounteagle, with a look of embarrassment.

"You spoke confidently, my lord," rejoined Fawkes.

"Because I had no idea I should be compelled to make good my words," returned the Earl. "But as a Catholic, and related by marriage to Tresham, who is a suspected person, any active exertions in her behalf on my part might place me in jeopardy."

"This excuse shall not avail you, my lord," replied Fawkes. "You must weigh your own safety against hers. You stir not hence till you have sworn to free her."

"I must perforce assent, since you will have no refusal," replied Mounteagle. "But I almost despair of success. If I *can* effect her deliverance, I swear to do so."

"Enough," replied Fawkes.

"And now, gentlemen," said Catesby, appealing to the others, "are you willing to let Lord Mounteagle depart upon the proposed terms?"

"We are," they replied.

"I will administer the oath at once," said Garnet; "and you will bear in mind, my son," he added, in a stern tone to the Earl, "that it will be one which cannot be violated without perdition to your soul."

"I am willing to take it," replied Mounteagle.

Producing a primer, and motioning the Earl to kneel before him, Garnet then proposed an oath of the most solemn and binding description. The other repeated it after him, and at its conclusion placed the book to his lips.

"Are you satisfied?" he asked, rising.

"I am," replied Garnet.

"And so am I," thought Tresham, who stood in the rear,
—"that he will perjure himself."

"Am I now at liberty to depart?" inquired the Earl.

"Not yet, my lord," replied Catesby. "You must remain
here till midnight."

Lord Mounteagle looked uneasy, but seeing remonstrance
would be useless, he preserved a sullen silence.

"You need have no fear, my lord," said Catesby. "But
we must take such precautions as will insure our safety, in
case you intend us any treachery."

"You cannot doubt me, sir, after the oath I have taken,"
replied Mounteagle, haughtily. "But since you constitute
yourself my jailer, I must abide your pleasure."

"If I *am* your jailer, my lord," rejoined Catesby, "I will
prove to you that I am not neglectful of my office. Will it
please you to follow me?"

The Earl bowed in acquiescence; and Catesby, marching
before him to a small room, the windows of which were carefully barred, pointed to a chair, and instantly retiring, locked
the door upon him. He then returned to the others, and
taking Guy Fawkes aside, observed in a low tone:

"We shall set out instantly for White Webbs. You will
remain on guard with Tresham, whom you will, of course,
keep in ignorance of our proceedings. After you have set
the Earl at liberty, you can follow us if you choose. But
take heed you are not observed."

"Fear nothing," replied Fawkes.

Soon after this, Catesby, and the rest of the conspirators,
with the exception of Guy Fawkes and Tresham, quitted the
room, and the former concluded they were about to leave
the house. He made no remark, however, to his companion,
but getting between him and the door, folded his arms upon
his breast, and continued to pace backwards and forwards
before it.

"Am I a prisoner, as well as Lord Mounteagle?" asked
Tresham, after a pause.

"You must remain with me here till midnight," replied
Fawkes. "We shall not be disturbed."

"What! are the others gone?" cried Tresham.

"They are," was the reply.

Tresham's countenance fell, and he appeared to be meditating some project, which he could not muster courage to
execute.

"Be warned by the past, Tresham," said Fawkes, who had

regarded him fixedly for some minutes. " If I find reason to doubt you, I will put it out of your power to betray us a second time."

" You have no reason to doubt me," replied Tresham, with apparent candour. " I only wondered that our friends should leave me without any intimation of their purpose. It is for me, not you, to apprehend some ill design. Am I not to act with you further ?"

" That depends upon yourself, and on the proofs you give of your sincerity," replied Fawkes. " Answer me frankly. Do you think Lord Mounteagle will keep his oath ?"

" I will stake my life upon it, replied Tresham.

The conversation then dropped, and no attempt was made on either side to renew it. In this way several hours passed, when at length the silence was broken by Tresham, who requested permission to go in search of some refreshment ; and Guy Fawkes assenting, they descended to the lower, room, and partook of a slight repast.

Nothing further worthy of note occurred. On the arrival of the appointed hour, Guy Fawkes signified to his companion that he might liberate Lord Mounteagle; and immediately availing himself of the permission, Tresham repaired to the chamber, and threw open the door. The Earl immediately came forth, and they returned together to the room in which Guy Fawkes remained on guard.

" You are now at liberty to depart, my lord," said the latter ; " and Tresham can accompany you if he thinks proper. Remember that you have sworn to procure Viviana's liberation."

" I do," replied the Earl.

And he then quitted the house with Tresham.

" You have had a narrow escape, my lord," remarked the latter, as they approached Whitehall, and paused for a moment under the postern of the great western gate.

" True," replied the Earl; " but I do not regret the risk I have run. They are now wholly in my power."

" You forget your oath, my lord" said Tresham.

" If I do," replied the Earl, " I but follow your example. You have broken one equally solemn, equally binding, and would break a thousand more were they imposed upon you. But I will overthrow this conspiracy, and yet not violate mine."

" I see not how that can be, my lord," replied Tresham.

" You shall learn in due season," replied the Earl. " I have had plenty of leisure for reflection in that dark hole, and have hit upon a plan which, I think, cannot fail."

"I hope I am no party to it, my lord," rejoined Tresham. "I dare not hazard myself among them further."

"I cannot do without you," replied Mounteagle; "but I will insure you against all danger. It will be necessary for you, however, to act with the utmost discretion, and keep a constant guard upon every look and movement, as well as upon your words. You must fully regain the confidence of these men, and lull them into security."

"I see your lordship's drift," replied Tresham. "You wish them to proceed to the last point, to enhance the value of the discovery."

"Right," replied the Earl. "The plot must not be discovered till just before its outbreak, when its magnitude and danger will be the more apparent. The reward will then be proportionate. Now, you understand me, Tresham?"

"Fully," replied the other.

"Return to your own house," rejoined Mounteagle. "We need hold no further communication together till the time for action arrives."

"And that will not be before the meeting of Parliament," replied Tresham: "for they intend to whelm the King and all his nobles in one common destruction."

"By Heaven! a brave design!" cried Mounteagle. "It is a pity to mar it. I knew it was a desperate and daring project, but should never have conceived aught like this. Its discovery will indeed occasion universal consternation."

"It may benefit you and me to divulge it, my lord," said Tresham; "but the disclosure will deeply and lastingly injure the Church of Rome."

"It would injure it more deeply if the plot succeeded," replied Mounteagle, "because all loyal Catholics must disapprove so horrible and sanguinary a design. But we will not discuss the question further, though what you have said confirms my purpose, and removes any misgiving I might have felt as to the betrayal. Farewell, Tresham. Keep a watchful eye upon the conspirators, and communicate with me should any change take place in their plans. We may not meet for some time. Parliament, though summoned for the third of October, will, in all probability, be prorogued till November."

"In that case," replied Tresham, "you will postpone your disclosure likewise till November?"

"Assuredly," replied Mounteagle. "The King must be convinced of his danger. If it were found out now, he would think lightly of it. But if he has actually set foot upon the mine which a single spark might kindle to his destruction, he will duly appreciate the service rendered him. Farewell! and do not neglect my counsel."

X.

WHITE WEBBS.

TARRYING for a short time within the house after the departure of the others, Guy Fawkes lighted a lantern, and concealing it beneath his cloak, proceeded to the cellar, to ascertain that the magazine of powder was safe. Satisfied of this, he made all secure, and was about to return to the house, when he perceived a figure approaching him. Standing aside, but keeping on his guard for fear of a surprise, he would have allowed the person to pass, but the other halted, and after a moment's scrutiny addressed him by name in the tones of Humphrey Chetham.

"You seem to haunt this spot, young sir," said Fawkes, in answer to the address. "This is the third time we have met hereabouts."

"On the last occasion," replied Chetham, "I told you Viviana was a prisoner in the Tower. I have now better news for you. She is free."

"Free!" exclaimed Guy Fawkes, joyfully. "By Lord Mounteagle's instrumentality?—But I forget. He has only just left me."

"She has been freed by *my* instrumentality," replied the young merchant. "She escaped from the Tower a few hours ago."

"Where is she?" demanded Guy Fawkes, eagerly.

"In a boat at the stairs near the Parliament House," replied Chetham.

"Heaven and Our Lady be praised!" exclaimed Fawkes. "This is more than I hoped for. Your news is so good, young sir, that I can scarce credit it."

"Come with me to the boat, and you shall soon be satisfied of the truth of my statement," rejoined Chetham.

And followed by Guy Fawkes, he hurried to the river-side, where a wherry was moored. Within it sat Viviana, covered by the tilt

Assisting her to land, and finding she was too much exhausted to walk, Guy Fawkes took her in his arms, and carried her to the house he had just quitted.

Humphrey Chetham followed as soon as he had dismissed the waterman. Placing his lovely burthen in a seat, Guy Fawkes instantly went in search of such restoratives as the place afforded. Viviana was extremely faint, but after she had swallowed a glass of wine, she revived, and, looking around her, inquired where she was.

"Do not ask," replied Fawkes; "let it suffice you are in safety. And now," he added, "perhaps Humphrey Chetham will inform me in what manner he contrived your escape. I am impatient to know."

The young merchant then gave the required information, and Viviana added such particulars as were necessary to the full understanding of the story. Guy Fawkes could scarcely control himself when she related the tortures she had endured, nor was Chetham less indignant.

"You rescued me just in time," said Viviana. "I should have sunk under the next application."

"Thank Heaven! you have escaped it," exclaimed Fawkes. "You owe much to Humphrey Chetham, Viviana."

"I do, indeed," she replied.

"And can you not requite it?" he returned. "Can you not make him happy?—Can you not make *me* happy?"

Viviana's pale cheek was instantly suffused with blushes, but she made no answer.

"Oh, Viviana!" cried Humphrey Chetham, "you hear what is said. If you could doubt my love before, you must be convinced of it now. A hope will make me happy. Have I that?"

"Alas! no," she answered. "It would be the height of cruelty, after your kindness to deceive you. You have not."

The young merchant turned aside to hide his emotion.

"Not even a hope!" exclaimed Guy Fawkes, "after what he has done. Viviana, I cannot understand you. Does gratitude form no part of your nature?"

"I hope so," she replied,—nay, I am sure so,—for I feel the deepest gratitude towards Humphrey Chetham. But gratitude is not love, and must not be mistaken for it."

"I understand the distinction too well," returned the young merchant, sadly.

"It is more than I do," rejoined Guy Fawkes; "and I will frankly confess that I think the important services Humphrey Chetham has rendered you entitle him to your hand. It is seldom—whatever poets may feign—that love is so strongly proved as his has been; and it ought to be adequately requited."

"Say no more about it, I entreat," interposed Chetham.

"But I will deliver my opinion," rejoined Guy Fawkes; "because I am sure what I advise is for Viviana's happiness. No one can love her better than you. No one is more worthy of her. Nor is there any one to whom I so much desire to see her united."

"Oh, Heaven!" exclaimed Viviana. "This is worse than the torture."

"What mean you?" exclaimed Fawkes, in astonishment.

"She means," interposed Chetham, "that this is not the fitting season to urge the subject—that she will never marry."

"True—true," replied Viviana. "If I ever did marry—I *ought* to select you."

"You ought," replied Fawkes. "And I know nothing of the female heart, if it can be insensible to youth, devotion, and manly appearance like that of Humphrey Chetham."

"You *do* know nothing of it," rejoined Chetham, bitterly. "Women's fancies are unaccountable."

"Such is the received opinion," replied Fawkes; "but as I am ignorant of the sex, I can only judge from report. You are the person I should imagine she would love—nay, to be frank, whom I thought she *did* love."

"No more," said Humphrey Chetham. "It is painful both to Viviana and to me."

"This is not a time for delicacy," rejoined Guy Fawkes. "Viviana has given me the privilege of a father with her. And where her happiness is so much concerned as in the present case, I should imperfectly discharge my duty if I did not speak out. It would sincerely rejoice me, and I am sure contribute materially to her own happiness, if she would unite herself to you."

"I cannot—I cannot," she rejoined. "I will never marry."

"You hear what she says," remarked Chetham. "Do not urge the matter further."

"I admire maiden delicacy and reserve," replied Fawkes; "but when a man has acted as you have done, he deserves to be treated with frankness. I am sure Viviana loves you. Let her tell you so."

"You are mistaken," replied Chetham; "and it is time you should be undeceived. She loves another."

"Is this so?" cried Fawkes, in astonishment.

She made no answer.

"Whom do you love?" he asked.

Still no answer.

"I will tell you whom she loves—and let her contradict me if I am wrong," said Chetham.

"Oh, no!—no!—in pity spare me!" cried Viviana.

"Speak!" thundered Fawkes. "Who is it?"

"Yourself," replied Chetham.

"What!" exclaimed Fawkes, recoiling,—"love *me!* I will not believe it. She loves me as a father—but nothing more —nothing more. But you were right. Let us change the subject. A more fitting season may arrive for its discussion."

After some further conversation, it was agreed that Viviana should be taken to White Webbs; and leaving her in charge of Humphrey Chetham, Guy Fawkes went in search of a conveyance to Enfield.

Traversing the Strand,—every hostel in which was closed, —he turned up Wych-street, immediately on the right of which there was a large inn (still in existence), and entering the yard, discovered a knot of carriers moving about with lanterns in their hands. To his inquiries respecting a conveyance to Enfield, one of them answered, that he was about to return thither with his waggon at four o'clock,—it was then two,—and should be glad to take him and his friends. Overjoyed at the intelligence, and at once agreeing to the man's terms, Guy Fawkes hurried back to his companions, and, with the assistance of Humphrey Chetham, contrived to carry Viviana (for she was utterly unable to support herself) to the inn-yard, where she was immediately placed in the waggon, on a heap of fresh straw.

About an hour after this, but long before daybreak, the carrier attached his horses to the waggon, and set out. Guy Fawkes and Humphrey Chetham were seated near Viviana, but little was said during the journey, which occupied about three hours. By this time it was broad daylight; and as the carrier stopped at the door of a small inn, Guy Fawkes alighted, and inquired the distance to White Webbs.

"It is about a mile and a half off," replied the man. "If you pursue that lane, it will bring you to a small village about half a mile from this, where you are sure to find some one who will gladly guide you to the house, which is a little out of the road, on the borders of the forest."

He then assisted Viviana to alight, and Humphrey Chetham descending at the same time, the party took the road indicated—a winding country lane with high hedges, broken by beautiful timber—and proceeding at a slow pace, they arrived in about half an hour at a little cluster of cottages, which Guy Fawkes guessed to be the village alluded to by the carrier. As they approached it, a rustic leaped a hedge, and was about to cross to another field, when Guy Fawkes calling to him, inquired the way to White Webbs.

"I am going in that direction," replied the man. "If you desire it, I will show you the road."

"I shall feel much indebted to you, friend," returned Fawkes, "and will reward you for your trouble."

"I want no reward," returned the countryman, trudging forward.

Following their guide, after a few minutes' brisk walking they reached the borders of the forest, and took their way along a patch of greensward that skirted it. In some places their track was impeded by gigantic thorns and brushwood, while at others avenues opened upon them, affording them peeps into the heart of the wood. It was a beautiful sylvan scene. And as at length they arrived at the head of a long glade, at the farther end of which a herd of deer were seen, with their branching antlers mingling with the over-hanging boughs, Viviana could not help pausing to admire it.

"King James often hunts within the forest," observed the countryman. "Indeed, I heard one of the rangers say it was not unlikely he might be here to-day. He is at Theobald's Palace now."

"Indeed!" exclaimed Fawkes. "Let us proceed. We lose time. Are we far from the house?"

"Not above a quarter of a mile," was the answer. "You will see it at the next turn of the road."

As the countryman had intimated, they speedily perceived the roof and tall chimneys of an ancient house above the trees, and as it was now impossible to mistake the road, Guy Fawkes thanked their guide for his trouble, and would have rewarded him, but he refused the gratuity, and leaping a hedge, disappeared.

Pursuing the road, they shortly afterwards arrived at a gate leading to the house—a large building, erected probably at the beginning of Elizabeth's reign—and entering it, they passed under an avenue of trees. On approaching the mansion, they observed that many of the windows were closed, and the whole appearance of the place was melancholy and deserted. The garden was overgrown with weeds, and the door looked as if it were rarely opened.

Not discouraged by these appearances, but rather satisfied by them of the security of the asylum, Guy Fawkes proceeded to the back of the house, and entering a court, the flags and stones of which were covered with moss, while the interstices were filled with long grass, Guy Fawkes knocked against a small door, and, after repeating the summons, it was answered by an old woman-servant, who popped her head out of an upper window, and demanded his business.

Guy Fawkes was about to inquire for Mrs. Brooksby, when another head, which proved to be that of Catesby, appeared at the window. On seeing Fawkes and his companions, Catesby instantly descended and unfastened the door. The house proved far more comfortable within than its exterior promised; and the old female domestic having taken word to Anne Vaux that Viviana was below, the former lady, who had not yet risen, sent for her to her chamber, and provided everything for her comfort.

Guy Fawkes and Humphrey Chetham, neither of whom had rested during the night, were glad to obtain a few hours' repose on the floor of the first room into which they were shown, and they were not disturbed until the day had considerably advanced, when Catesby thought fit to rouse them from their slumbers.

Explanations were then given on both sides. Chetham detailed the manner of Viviana's escape from the Tower, and Catesby in his turn acquainted them that Father Oldcorne was in the house, having found his way thither after his escape from the dwelling at Lambeth. Guy Fawkes was greatly rejoiced at the intelligence, and shortly afterwards had the satisfaction of meeting with the priest. At noon, the whole party assembled, with the exception of Viviana, who, by the advice of Anne Vaux, kept her chamber, to recruit herself after the suffering she had undergone.

Humphrey Chetham, of whom no suspicions were now entertained, and of whom Catesby no longer felt any jealousy, was invited to stay in the house; and he was easily induced to pass his time near Viviana, although he might not be able to see her. Long and frequent consultations were held by the conspirators, and letters were despatched by Catesby to the elder Winter at his seat, Huddington, in Worcestershire, entreating him to make every preparation for the crisis, as well as to Sir Everard Digby, to desire him to assemble as many friends as he could muster against the meeting of Parliament, at Dunchurch, in Warwickshire, under the plea of a grand hunting party.

Arrangements were next made as to the steps to be taken by the different parties after the explosion. Catesby undertook, with a sufficient force, to seize the Princess Elizabeth the eldest daughter of James the First, who was then at the residence of the Earl of Harrington, near Coventry, and to proclaim her queen, in case the others should fail in securing the princes. It was supposed that Henry, Prince of Wales (who, it need scarcely be mentioned, died in his youth), would be present with the King, his father, in the Parliament House, and would perish with him; and in this case, as Charles, Duke of York (afterwards Charles the First), would become successor to the throne, it was resolved that he should be seized by Percy, and instantly proclaimed. Other resolutions were decided upon, and the whole time of the conspirators was spent in maturing their projects.

And thus weeks, and even months, stole on. Viviana had completely regained her strength, and passed a life of perfect seclusion, seldom, if ever, mixing with the others. She, however, took a kindly farewell of Humphrey Chetham before his departure for Manchester (for which place he set out about a fortnight after his arrival at White Webbs, having first sought out his servant, Martin Heydocke); but though strongly urged by Guy Fawkes, she would hold out no hopes of a change in her sentiments towards the young merchant. Meetings were occasionally held by the conspirators elsewhere, and Catesby and Fawkes had more than one interview with Tresham—but never except in places where they were secure from a surprise.

The latter end of September had now arrived, and the meeting of Parliament was still fixed for the third of October. On the last day of the month Guy Fawkes prepared to start for town; but before doing so he desired to see Viviana. They had not met for some weeks; nor, indeed, since Fawkes had discovered the secret of her heart (and perhaps of his own), had they ever met with the same freedom as heretofore. As she entered the room, in which he awaited her coming, a tremor agitated his frame, but he had nerved himself for the interview, and speedily subdued the feeling.

"I am starting for London, Viviana," he said, in a voice of forced calmness. "You may guess for what purpose. But as I may never behold you again, I would not part with you without a confession of my weakness. I will not deny that what Humphrey Chetham stated, and which you never contradicted—namely, that you loved me, for I must speak out—has produced a strong effect upon me. I have endeavoured to conquer it, but it will return. Till I knew you I never loved, Viviana."

s

"Indeed!" she exclaimed.

"Never," he replied. "The fairest had not power to move me. But I grieve to say—notwithstanding my struggles—I do not continue equally insensible."

"Ah!" she ejaculated, becoming as pale as death.

"Why should I hesitate to declare my feelings? Why should I not tell you that—though blinded to it so long—I have discovered that I do love you? Why should I hesitate to tell you that I regret this, and lament that we ever met?"

"What mean you?" cried Viviana, with a terrified look.

"I will tell you," replied Fawkes. "Till I saw you, my thoughts were removed from earth, and fixed on one object. Till I saw you, I asked not to live, but to die the death of a martyr."

"Die so still," rejoined Viviana. "Forget me—oh! forget me."

"I cannot," replied Fawkes. "I have striven against it. But your image is perpetually before me. Nay, at this very moment, when I am about to set out on the enterprise, you alone detain me."

"I am glad of it," exclaimed Viviana, fervently. "Oh, that I could prevent you—could save you!"

"Save me!" echoed Fawkes, bitterly. "You destroy me."

"How?" she asked.

"Because I am sworn to this project," he rejoined; "and if I were turned from it, I would perish by my own hand."

"Oh! say not so," replied Viviana, "but listen to me. Abandon it, and I will devote myself to you."

Guy Fawkes gazed at her for a moment passionately, and then, covering his face with his hands, appeared torn by conflicting emotions.

Viviana approached him, and pressing his arm, asked in an entreating voice, "Are you still determined to pursue your dreadful project?"

"I am," replied Fawkes, uncovering his face, and gazing at her; "but if I remain here a moment longer, I shall not be able to do so."

"I will detain you, then," she rejoined, "and exercise the power I possess over you for your benefit."

"No!" he replied, vehemently. "It must not be. Farewell, for ever!"

And breaking from her, he rushed out of the room.

As he gained the passage, he encountered Catesby, who looked abashed at seeing him.

"I have overheard what has passed," said the latter, "and applaud your resolution. Few men, similarly circumstanced, would have acted as you have done."

" *You* would not," said Fawkes, coldly.

"Perhaps not," rejoined Catesby. "But that does not lessen my admiration of your conduct."

"I am devoted to one object," replied Fawkes, "and nothing shall turn me from it."

"Remove yourself instantly from temptation, then," replied Catesby. "I will meet you at the cellar beneath the Parliament House to-morrow night."

With this, he accompanied Guy Fawkes to the door; and the latter, without hazarding a look behind him, set out for London, where he arrived at nightfall.

On the following night, Fawkes examined the cellar, and found it in all respects as he had left it; and, apprehensive lest some difficulty might arise, he resolved to make every preparation. He, accordingly, pierced the sides of several of the barrels piled against the walls with a gimlet, and inserted in the holes small pieces of slow-burning match. Not content with this, he staved in the tops of the uppermost tier, and scattered powder among them to secure their instantaneous ignition.

This done, he took a powder-horn, with which he was provided, and kneeling down, and holding his lantern so as to throw a light upon the floor, laid a train to one of the lower barrels, and brought it within a few inches of the door, intending to fire it from that point. His arrangements completed, he arose, and muttered:

"A vessel is provided for my escape in the river, and my companions advise me to use a slow match, which will allow me to get out of harm's way. But I will see the deed done, and if the train fails will hold a torch to the barrels myself."

At this juncture, a slight tap was heard without.

Guy Fawkes instantly masked his lantern, and cautiously opening the door, beheld Catesby.

"I am come to tell you that Parliament is prorogued," said the latter. "The House does not meet till the fifth of November. We have another month to wait."

"I am sorry for it," rejoined Fawkes. "I have just laid the train. The lucky moment will pass."

And, locking the door, he proceeded with Catesby to the adjoining house.

s 2

They had scarcely been gone more than a second, when two figures muffled in cloaks emerged from behind a wall.

"The train is laid," observed the foremost, "and they are gone to the house. You might seize them now without danger."

"That will not answer my purpose," replied the other. "I will give them another month."

"Another month!" replied the first speaker. "Who knows what may happen in that time? They may abandon their project."

"There is no fear of that," replied the other. "But you had better go and join them."

XI.

THE MARRIAGE IN THE FOREST.

TRESHAM, for it will have been conjectured that he was one of the speakers mentioned in the preceding chapter, on separating from Lord Mounteagle, took the same direction as the conspirators. He hesitated for some time before venturing to knock at the garden-gate; and when he had done so, felt half-disposed to take to his heels. But shame restrained him; and hearing footsteps approach, he gave the customary signal, and was instantly admitted by Guy Fawkes.

"What brings you here?" demanded the latter, as they entered the house, and made fast the door behind them.

"I have just heard that Parliament is prorogued to the fifth of November," replied Tresham, "and came to tell you so."

"I already know it," returned Fawkes, gloomily; "and for the first time feel some misgiving as to the issue of our enterprise."

"Why so!" inquired Tresham.

"November is unlucky to me," rejoined Fawkes, "and I cannot recollect a year in my life in which some ill has not befallen me during that month, especially on the fifth day. On the last fifth of November, I nearly died of a fever at Madrid. It is a strange and unfortunate coincidence that the meeting of the Parliament should be appointed for that particular day.

" Shall I tell you what I think it portends?" hesitated Tresham.

" Do so," replied Fawkes, " and speak boldly. I am no child to be frightened at shadows."

" You have more than once declared your intention of perishing with our foes," rejoined Tresham. " The design, though prosperous in itself, may be fatal to you."

" You are right," replied Fawkes. " I have little doubt I shall perish on that day. You are both aware of my superstitious nature, and are not ignorant that many mysterious occurrences have combined to strengthen the feeling—such as the dying words of the prophetess, Elizabeth Orton—her warning speech when she was raised from the dead by Doctor Dee—and lastly, the vision at Saint Winifred's Well. What if I tell you the saint has again appeared to me ?"

" In a dream?" inquired Catesby, in a slightly sceptical tone.

" Ay, in a dream," returned Fawkes. " But I saw her as plainly as if I had been awake. It was the same vapoury figure—the same transparent robes, the same benign countenance, only far more pitying than before—that I beheld at Holywell. I heard no sound issue from her lips, but I *felt* that she warned me to desist."

" Do you accept the warning?" asked Tresham, eagerly.

" It is needless to answer," replied Fawkes. " I have laid the train to-night."

" You have infected me with your misgivings," observed Tresham. " Would the enterprise had never been undertaken!"

" But being undertaken, it must be gone through with," rejoined Catesby, sternly. " Hark'e, Tresham. You promised us two thousand pounds in aid of the project, but have constantly deferred payment of the sum on some plea or other."

" Because I have not been able to raise it," replied Tresham, sullenly. " I have tried in vain to sell part of my estates at Rushton, in Northamptonshire. I cannot effect impossibilities."

" Tush!" cried Catesby, fiercely. " You well know I ask no impossibility. I will no longer be trifled with. The money must be forthcoming by the tenth of October, or you shall pay the penalty with your life."

" This is the language of a cut-throat, Mr. Catesby," replied Tresham.

" It is the only language I will hold towards you," rejoined

Catesby, contemptuously. "Look you disappoint me not, or take the consequences."

"I must leave for Northamptonshire at once, then," said Tresham.

"Do as you please," returned Catesby. "Play the cutthroat yourself, and ease some rich miser of his store, if you think fit. Bring us the money, and we will not ask how you came by it."

"Before we separate," said Tresham, disregarding these sneers, "I wish to be resolved on one point. Who are to be saved from destruction?"

"Why do you ask?" inquired Fawkes.

"Because I must stipulate for the lives of my brothers-in-law, the Lords Mounteagle and Stourton."

"If anything detains them from the meeting, well and good," replied Catesby. "But no warning must be given them. That would infallibly lead to a discovery of the plot."

"Some means might surely be adopted to put them on their guard without danger to ourselves?" urged Tresham.

"I know of none," replied Catesby.

"Nor I," added Fawkes. "If I did, I would warn Lord Montague and some others, whom I shall grieve to destroy."

"We are all similarly circumstanced," replied Catesby. "Keyes is anxious for the preservation of his patron and friend, Lord Mordaunt—Percy, for the Earl of Northumberland. I myself would gladly save the young Earl of Arundel. But we must sacrifice our private feeling for the general good."

"We must," acquiesced Fawkes.

"We shall not meet again till the night of the tenth of October," said Catesby, "when take care you are in readiness with the money."

Upon this, the conversation dropped, and soon afterwards Tresham departed.

When he found himself alone, he suffered his rage to find vent in words. "Perdition seize them!" he cried, "I shall now lose two thousand pounds, in addition to what I have already advanced; and, as Mounteagle will not have the disclosure made till the beginning of November, there is no way of avoiding payment. They would not fall into the snare I laid to throw the blame of the discovery, when it takes place, upon their own indiscretion. But I must devise some other plan. The warning shall proceed from an unknown quarter. A letter, written in a feigned hand, and giving some obscure intimation of danger, shall be delivered with an air of mystery to Mounteagle. This will serve as a plea for its divulgement to the Earl of Salisbury. Well, well, they shall have the money; but they shall pay me back in other coin."

Early on the following day, Catesby and Fawkes proceeded to White Webbs. Garnet was greatly surprised to see them, and could not conceal his disappointment at the cause of their return.

"This delay bodes no good," he observed. "Parliament has been so often prorogued, that I begin to think some suspicion is entertained of our design."

"Make your mind easy, then," replied Catesby. "I have made due inquiries, and find the meeting is postponed to suit the King's convenience, who wishes to prolong his stay at Royston. He may probably have some secret motive for the delay, but I am sure it in no way concerns us."

Everything being now fully arranged, the conspirators had only to wait patiently for the arrival of the expected fifth of November. Most of them decided upon passing the interval in the country. Ambrose Rookwood departed for Clopton, near Stratford-upon-Avon—a seat belonging to Lord Carew, where his family were staying; Keyes went to visit Lord Mordaunt at Turvey, in Bedfordshire; and Percy and the two Wrights set out for Gothurst, in Buckinghamshire, to desire Sir Everard Digby to postpone the grand hunting-party which he was to hold at Dunsmore Heath, as an excuse for mustering a strong party of Catholics, to the beginning of November. The two Winters repaired to their family mansion, Huddington, in Worcestershire; while Fawkes and Catesby, together with the two priests, remained at White Webbs. The three latter held daily conferences together, but were seldom joined by Fawkes, who passed his time in the adjoining forest, selecting its densest and most intricate parts for his rambles.

It was now the beginning of October, and, as is generally the case in the early part of this month, the weather was fine, and the air pure and bracing. The forest could scarcely have been seen to greater advantage. The leaves had assumed their gorgeous autumnal tints, and the masses of timber, variegated in colour, presented an inexpressibly beautiful appearance. Guy Fawkes spent hours in the depths of the wood. His sole companions were the lordly stag and the timid hare, that occasionally started across his path. Since his return he had sedulously avoided Viviana, and they had met

only twice, and then no speech had passed between them.
One day, when he had plunged even deeper than usual into
the forest, and had seated himself on the stump of a decayed
tree, with his eyes fixed on a small clear rivulet welling at his
feet, he saw the reflection of a female figure in the water;
and, filled with the idea of the vision of Saint Winifred, at
first imagined he was about to receive another warning. But
a voice that thrilled to his heart's core soon undeceived him,
and, turning, he beheld Viviana. She was habited in a riding-
dress, and appeared prepared to set out upon a journey.

"So you have tracked me to my solitude," he observed, in
a tone of forced coldness. "I thought I was secure from
interruption here."

"You will forgive me, I am sure, when you know my
errand," she replied. "It is to take an eternal farewell of
you."

"Indeed!" he exclaimed. "Are you about to quit White
Webbs?"

"I am," she mournfully rejoined. "I am about to set out
with Father Oldcorne for Gothurst, where I shall remain till
all is over."

"I entirely approve your determination," returned Fawkes,
after a short pause.

"I knew you would do so, or I should have consulted you
upon it," she rejoined. "And as you appear to avoid me, I
would fain have departed without taking leave of you, but
found it impossible to do so."

"You well know my motive for avoiding you, Viviana,"
rejoined Fawkes. "We are no longer what we were to each
other. A fearful struggle has taken place within me, though
I have preserved an unmoved exterior, between passion and
the sense of my high calling. I have told you I never loved
before, and fancied my heart immovable as adamant. But
I now find out my error. It is a prey to a raging and
constant flame. I have shunned you," he continued, with
increased excitement, "because the sight of you shakes my
firmness—because I feel it sinful to think of you in preference
to holier objects—and because, after I have quitted you, your
image alone engrosses my thoughts. Here in the depths of
this wood, by the side of this brook, I can commune with my
soul—can abstract myself from the world and the thoughts
of the world—from you—yes, you, who are all the world to
me now—and prepare to meet my end "

"Then you are resolved to die ?" she cried.

"I shall abide the explosion, and nothing but a miracle can save me," returned Fawkes.

"And think not it will be exerted in your behalf," she replied. "Heaven does not approve your design, and you will assuredly incur its vengeance by your criminal conduct."

"Viviana," replied Guy Fawkes, rising, "man cannot read my heart, but Heaven can; and the sincerity of my purpose will be recognised above. What I am about to do is for the regeneration of our holy religion; and if the welfare of that religion is dear to the Supreme Being, our cause must prosper. If the contrary, it deserves to fail, and will fail. I have ever told you that I care not what becomes of myself. I am now more than ever indifferent to life—or rather," he added, in a sombre tone, "I am anxious to die."

"Your dreadful wish, I fear, will be accomplished," replied Viviana, sadly. "I have been constantly haunted by frightful apprehensions respecting you, and my dead father has appeared to me in my dreams. His spirit, if such it were, seemed to gaze upon me with a mournful look, and, as I thought, pronounced your name in piteous accents."

"These forebodings chime with my own," muttered Fawkes, repressing a shudder; "but nothing shall shake me. It will inflict a bitter pang upon me to part with you, Viviana—the bitterest I can ever feel—and I shall be glad when it is over."

"I echo your own wish," she returned, "and deeply lament that we ever met. But the fate that brought us together must for ever unite us."

"What mean you?" he inquired, gazing fixedly at her.

"There is one sad consolation, which you can afford me, and which you owe me for the deep and lasting misery I shall endure on your account," replied Viviana; "a consolation that will enable me to bear your loss with fortitude, and to devote myself wholly to Heaven."

"Whatever I can do, that will not interfere with my purpose, you may command," he rejoined.

"What I have to propose will not interfere with it," she answered. "Now, hear me, and put the sole construction I deserve on my conduct. Father Garnet is at a short distance from us, behind those trees, waiting my summons. I have informed him of my design, and he approves of it. It is to unite us in marriage—solemnly unite us—that though I may never live with you, as a wife, I may mourn you as a widow. Do you consent?"

Guy Fawkes returned an affirmative, in a voice broken by emotion.

"The moment the ceremony is over," pursued Viviana, "I shall start with Father Oldcorne for Gothurst. We shall never meet again in this world."

"Unless I succeed," said Fawkes.

"You will *not* succeed," replied Viviana. "If I thought so, I should not take this step. I look upon it as an espousal with the dead."

So saying, she hurried away, and disappearing beneath the covert, returned in a few seconds with Garnet.

"I have a strange duty to perform for you, my son," said Garnet to Fawkes, who remained motionless and stupefied; "but I am right willing to perform it, because I think it will lead to your future happiness with the fair creature who has bestowed her affections on you."

"Do not speculate on the future, father," cried Viviana. "You know *why* I asked you to perform this ceremony. You know, also, that I have made preparations for instant departure; and that I indulge no hope of seeing Guy Fawkes again."

"All this I know, dear daughter," returned Garnet; "but, in spite of your anticipations of ill, I still hope that your union may prove auspicious."

"I take you to witness, father," said Viviana, "that in bestowing my hand upon Guy Fawkes, I bestow at the same time all my possessions upon him. He is free to use them as he thinks proper—even in the furtherance of his design against the State, which, though I cannot approve it, seems good to him."

"This must not be," cried Fawkes.

"It *shall be*," rejoined Viviana. "Proceed with the ceremony, father."

"Let her have her own way, my son," observed Garnet, in a low tone. "Under any circumstances, her estates must now be necessarily yours."

He then took a breviary from his vest, and placing them near each other, began to read aloud the marriage-service appointed by the Romish Church. And there, in that secluded spot, and under such extraordinary circumstances, with no other witnesses than the ancient trees around them, and the brook rippling at their feet, were Guy Fawkes and Viviana united. The ceremony over, Guy Fawkes pressed his bride to his breast, and imprinted a kiss upon her lips.

"I have broken my faith to Heaven, to which I was first espoused," he cried.

"No," she returned; "you will now return to your first and holiest choice. Think of me only as I shall think of you —as of the dead."

With this, the party slowly and silently returned to the house, where they found a couple of steeds, with luggage strapped to the saddles, at the door.

Father Oldcorne was already mounted, and in a few minutes Viviana was by his side. Before her departure, she bade Guy Fawkes a tender farewell; and at this trying juncture her firmness nearly deserted her. But rousing herself, she sprang upon her horse, and urging the animal into a quick pace, and followed by Oldcorne, she speedily disappeared from view. Guy Fawkes watched her out of sight, and shunning the regards of Catesby, who formed one of the group, struck into the forest, and was not seen again till the following day.

The tenth of October having arrived, Guy Fawkes and Catesby repaired to the place of rendezvous. But the night passed, and Tresham did not appear. Catesby was angry and disappointed, and could not conceal his apprehensions of treachery. Fawkes took a different view of the matter, and thought it not improbable that their confederate's absence might be occasioned by the difficulty he found in complying with their demands; and this opinion was confirmed the next morning by the arrival of a letter from Tresham, stating that he had been utterly unable to effect the sales he contemplated, and could not, therefore, procure the money till the end of the month.

"I will immediately go down to Rushton," said Catesby, "and if I find him disposed to palter with us, I will call him to instant account. But Garnet informs me that Viviana has bestowed all her wealth upon you. Are you willing to devote it to the good cause?"

"No!" replied Fawkes, in a tone so decisive that his companion felt it would be useless to urge the matter further. "I give my life to the cause—that must suffice."

The subject was never renewed. At night, Catesby, having procured a powerful steed, set out upon his journey to Northamptonshire, while Fawkes returned to White Webbs.

About a fortnight passed unmarked by any event of importance. Despatches were received from Catesby, stating that he had received the money from Tresham, and had expended it in procuring horses and arms. He also added that he had raised numerous recruits on various pretences. This letter was dated from Ashby Saint Leger's, the seat of his mother, Lady Catesby, but he expressed his intention of proceeding to Coughton Hall, near Alcester, in Warwickshire, the residence of Mr. Thomas Throckmorton (a wealthy Catholic gentleman), whither Sir Everard Digby had removed with his family, to be in readiness for the grand hunting party to be held on the fifth of November on Dunsmore Heath. Here he expected to be joined by the two Wrights, the Winters, Rookwood, Keyes, and the rest of the conspirators, and undertook to bring them all up to White Webbs on Saturday, the twenty-sixth of October.

By this time Guy Fawkes had in a great degree recovered his equanimity, and left alone with Garnet, held long and frequent religious conferences with him; it being evidently his desire to prepare himself for his expected fate. He spent the greater part of the nights in solitary vigils—fasted even more rigorously than he was enjoined to do—and prayed with such fervour and frequency, that, fearing an ill effect upon his health, and almost upon his mind, which had become exalted to the highest pitch of enthusiasm, Garnet thought it necessary to check him. The priest did not fail to note that Viviana's name never passed his lips, and that in all their walks in the forest he carefully shunned the scene of his espousals.

And thus time flew by. On the evening of the twenty-sixth of October, in accordance with Catesby's intimation, the conspirators arrived. They were assembled at supper, and were relating the different arrangements which had been made in anticipation of the important event, when Garnet observed with a look of sudden uneasiness to Catesby, "You said in one of your letters that you would bring Tresham with you, my son. Why do I not see him?"

"He sent a message to Coughton to state that, having been attacked by a sudden illness, he was unable to join us," replied Catesby, "but as soon as he could leave his bed, he would hasten to London. This may be a subterfuge, but I shall speedily ascertain the truth, for I have sent my servant Bates to Rushton, to investigate the matter. I ought to tell you," he added, "that he has given substantial proof of his devotion to the cause by sending another thousand pounds, to be expended in the purchase of arms and horses."

"I hope it is not dust thrown into our eyes," returned

Garnet. " I have always feared Tresham would deceive us at
the last."

"This sudden illness looks suspicious, I must own," said
Catesby. " Has aught been heard of Lord Mounteagle?"

" Guy Fawkes heard that he was at his residence at Southwark yesterday," returned Garnet.

" So far, good," replied Catesby. " Did you visit the
cellar where the powder is deposited?" he added, turning to
Fawkes.

" I did," replied the other, ["and found all secure. The
powder is in excellent preservation. Before quitting the
spot, I placed certain private marks against the door, by
which I can tell whether it is opened during our absence."

" A wise precaution," returned Catesby. " And now, gentlemen," he added, filling a goblet with wine, "success to our
enterprise! Everything is prepared," he continued, as the
pledge was enthusiastically drunk; "I have got together
a company of above two hundred men, all well armed and
appointed, who will follow me wherever I choose to lead
them. They will be stationed near Dunsmore Heath on the
fifth of next month, and as soon as the event of the explosion is known, I shall ride thither as fast as I can, and,
hurrying with my troops to Coventry, seize the Princess
Elizabeth. Percy and Keyes will secure the person of the
Duke of York, and proclaim him King; while upon the rest
will devolve the arduous duty of rousing our Catholic
brethren in London to rise to arms."

" Trust to us to rouse them," shouted several voices.

" Let each man swear not to swerve from the fulfilment of
his task," cried Catesby; "swear it upon this cup of wine,
in which we will all mix our blood."

And as he spoke, he pricked his arm with the point of his
sword, and suffered a few drops of blood to fall into the
goblet, while the others, roused to a state of frenzied enthusiasm, imitated his example, and afterwards raised the horrible mixture to their lips, pronouncing at the same time the
oath.

Guy Fawkes was the last to take the pledge, and crying in
a loud voice, "I swear not to quit my post till the explosion
is over," he drained the cup.

After this, they adjourned to a room in another wing of
the house, fitted up as a chapel, where mass was performed
by Garnet, and the sacrament administered to the whole
assemblage. They were about to retire for the night, when

a sudden knocking was heard at the door. Reconnoitring the intruder through an upper window, overlooking the court, Catesby perceived it was Bates, who was holding a smoking and mud-bespattered steed by the bridle.

"Well, what news do you bring?" cried Catesby, as he admitted him. "Have you seen Tresham?"

"No," replied Bates. "His illness was a mere pretence. He has left Rushton secretly for London."

"I knew it," cried Garnet. "He has again betrayed us."

"He shall die," said Catesby.

And the determination was echoed by all the other conspirators.

Instead of retiring to rest, they passed the night in anxious deliberation, and it was at last proposed that Guy Fawkes should proceed without loss of time to Southwark, to keep watch near the house of Lord Mounteagle, and if possible ascertain whether Tresham had visited it.

To this he readily agreed. But before setting out, he took Catesby aside for a moment, and asked, "Did you see Viviana at Coughton?"

"Only for a moment, and that just before I left the place," was the answer. "She desired to be remembered to you, and said you were never absent from her thoughts or prayers."

Guy Fawkes turned away to hide his emotion, and mounting one of the horses brought by the conspirators, rode off towards London.

XII.

THE FIFTH OF NOVEMBER.

On the same day as the occurrences last related, Lord Mounteagle, who was then staying at Southwark, suddenly intimated his intention of passing the night at his country mansion at Hoxton; a change of place which, trivial as it seemed at the moment, afterwards assumed an importance, from the circumstances that arose out of it. At the latter part of the day, he accordingly proceeded to Hoxton, accompanied by his customary attendants, and all appeared to pass on as usual, until, just as supper was over, one of his pages arrived from town, and desired to see his lordship immediately.

Affecting to treat the matter with indifference, Lord Mounteagle carelessly ordered the youth to be ushered into his presence; and when he appeared, he demanded his business. The page replied, that he brought a letter for his lordship, which had been delivered under circumstances of great mystery.

"I had left the house just as it grew dusk," he said, "on an errand of little importance, when a man, muffled in a cloak, suddenly issued from behind a corner, and demanded whether I was one of your lordship's servants? On my replying in the affirmative, he produced this letter, and enjoined me, as I valued my life, and your lordship's safety, to deliver it into your own hands without delay."

So saying, he delivered the letter to his lord, who, gazing at its address, which was, "To the Right Honourable the Lord Mounteagle," observed, "There is nothing very formidable in its appearance. What can it mean?"

Without even breaking the seal, which was secured with a silken thread, he gave it to one of his gentlemen, named Ward, who was standing near him.

"Read it aloud, sir," said the Earl, with a slight smile. "I have no doubt it is some vapouring effusion, which will afford us occasion for laughter. Before I hear what the writer has to say, I can promise him he shall not intimidate me."

Thus exhorted, Ward broke open the letter, and read as follows:

"My lord, out of the love I bear to some of your friends, I have a care of your preservation. Therefore I would advise you, as you tender your life, to devise some excuse to shift from your attendance at this Parliament, for God and man have concurred to punish the wickedness of this time. Think not slightingly of this advice, but retire into the country, where you may expect the event in safety; for though there be no appearance of any stir, yet I say they shall receive a terrible blow this Parliament, and yet they shall not know who hurts them. This counsel is not to be contemned. It may do you good, and can do you no harm, for the danger is past as soon as you have burnt the letter. God, I hope, will give you grace to make good use of it, to whose holy protection I commend you."

"A singular letter!" exclaimed Mounteagle, as soon as Ward had finished. "What is your opinion of it?"

"I think it hints at some dangerous plot, my lord," replied

Ward, who had received his instructions; "some treason against the State. With submission, I would advise your lordship instantly to take it to the Earl of Salisbury."

"I see nothing in it," replied the Earl. "What is your opinion, Mervyn?" he added, turning to another of his gentlemen, to whom he had likewise given his lesson.

"I am of the same mind as Ward," replied the attendant. "Your lordship will hardly hold yourself excused, if you neglect to give due warning, should aught occur hereafter."

"Say you so, sirs?" cried Lord Mounteagle. "Let me hear it once more."

The letter was accordingly read again by Ward, and the Earl feigned to weigh over each passage.

"I am advised not to attend the Parliament," he said, "'for God and man have concurred to punish the wickedness of this time.' That is too vague to be regarded. Then I am urged to retire into the country. The recommendation must proceed from some discontented Catholic, who does not wish me to be present at the opening of the House. This is not the first time I have been so adjured. 'They shall receive a terrible blow this Parliament, and yet shall not know who hurts them.' That is mysterious enough, but it may mean nothing—any more than what follows, namely, 'the danger is past as soon as you have burnt the letter.'"

"I do not think so, my lord," replied Ward; "and though I cannot explain the riddle, I am sure it means mischief."

"Well," said Lord Mounteagle, "since you are of this mind, I must lose no time in communicating the letter to the Secretary of State. It is better to err on the safe side."

Accordingly, after some further consultation, he set out at that late hour for Whitehall, where he roused the Earl of Salisbury, and showed him the letter. It is almost needless to state that the whole was a preconcerted scheme between these two crafty statesmen; but as the interview took place in the presence of their attendants, the utmost caution was observed.

Salisbury pretended to be greatly alarmed at the communication, and coupling it, he said, with previous intelligence which he had received, he could not help fearing, to adopt the words of the writer of the mysterious letter, that the Parliament was indeed threatened with some "terrible blow." Acting, apparently, upon this supposition, he caused such of the lords of the Privy Council as lodged at Whitehall to be summoned, and submitting the letter to them, they all concurred in the opinion that it referred to some dangerous plot, though none could give a guess at its precise nature.

"It is clearly some Popish project," said Salisbury, "or Lord Mounteagle would not have been the party warned. We must keep a look-out upon the disaffected of his faith."

"As I have been the means of revealing the plot to your lordship—if plot it be—I must pray you to deal gently with them," rejoined Mounteagle.

"I will be as lenient as I can," returned Salisbury; "but in a matter of this kind little favour can be shown. If your lordship will enable me to discover the principal actors in this affair, I will take care that no innocent party suffers."

"You ask an impossibility," replied Mounteagle. "I know nothing beyond what can be gathered from that letter. But I pray your lordship not to make it a means of exercising unnecessary severity towards the members of my religion."

"On that you may rely," returned the Earl. "His Majesty will not return from the hunting expedition on which he is engaged at Royston till Thursday next, the 30th. I think it scarcely worth while (considering his naturally timid nature, with which your lordships are well acquainted) to inform him of the threatened danger until his arrival at the palace. It will then be time enough to take any needful steps, as Parliament will not meet for four or five days afterwards."

In the policy of this course the Privy Councillors agreed, and it was arranged that the matter should be kept perfectly secret until the King's opinion had been taken upon the letter. The assemblage then broke up, it being previously arranged that, for fear of some attempt upon his life, Lord Mounteagle should remain within the palace till full inquiries had been instituted into the affair.

When the two confederate nobles were left alone, Salisbury observed, with a slight laugh, to his companion :

"Thus far we have proceeded well, and without suspicion, and, rely upon it, none shall fall on you. As soon as all is over, the most important post the King has to bestow shall be yours."

"But what of Tresham?" asked Mounteagle. "He was the deliverer of this letter, and I have little faith in him."

"Hum!" said Salisbury, after a moment's reflection, "if you think it desirable, we can remove him to the Tower, where he can be easily silenced."

"It will be better so," replied Mounteagle. "He may else

T

babble hereafter. I gave him a thousand pounds to send in his own name to the conspirators the other day to lure them into our nets."

"It shall be repaid you a hundred-fold," replied Salisbury. "But we are observed, and must therefore separate."

So saying, he withdrew to his own chamber, while Lord Mounteagle was ushered to the apartments allotted to him.

To return to Guy Fawkes. Arriving at Southwark, he stationed himself near Lord Mounteagle's residence. But he observed nothing to awaken his suspicions, until early in the morning he perceived a page approaching the mansion, whom, from his livery, he knew to be one of Lord Mounteagle's household (it was, in fact, the very youth who had delivered the mysterious letter), and from him he ascertained all that had occurred. Filled with alarm, and scarcely knowing what to do, he crossed the river, and proceeding to the cellar, examined the marks at the door, and finding all precisely as he had left it, felt certain that, whatever discovery had been made, the magazine had not been visited.

He next repaired to the house, of which he possessed the key, and was satisfied that no one had been there. Somewhat relieved by this, he yet determined to keep watch during the day, and concealing himself near the cellar, remained on the look-out till night. But no one came; nor did anything occur to excite his suspicions. He would not, however, quit his post till about six o'clock on the following evening, when, thinking further delay might be attended with danger, he set out to White Webbs, to give his companions intelligence of the letter.

His news was received by all with the greatest alarm, and not one, except Catesby, who strove to put a bold face upon the matter, though he was full of inward misgiving, but confessed that he thought all chance of success was at an end. While deliberating upon what should be done in this fearful emergency, they were greatly alarmed by a sudden knocking without. All the conspirators concealed themselves, except Guy Fawkes, who opening the door, found, to his infinite surprise, that the summons proceeded from Tresham. He said nothing till the other had entered the house, and then suddenly drawing his dagger, held it to his throat.

"Make your shrift quickly, traitor," he cried, in a furious tone, "for your last hour is arrived. What, ho!" he shouted to the others, who instantly issued from their hiding-places, "the fox has ventured into the lion's den."

"You distrust me wrongfully," rejoined Tresham, with more confidence than he usually exhibited in time of danger; "I am come to warn you, not betray you. Is this the return you make me for the service?"

"Villain!" cried Catesby, rushing up to him, and holding his drawn sword to his breast. "You have conveyed the letter to Lord Mounteagle."

"It is false," replied Tresham; "I have only just heard of it, and, in spite of the risk I knew I should run from your suspicions, I came to tell you what had happened."

"Why did you feign illness, and depart secretly for town, instead of joining us at Coughton?" demanded Catesby.

"I will instantly explain my motive, which, though it may not be satisfactory to you on one point, will be so on another," replied Tresham unhesitatingly, and with apparent frankness. "I was fearful you would make a further tool of me, and resolved not to join you again till a few days before the outbreak of the plot. To this determination I should have adhered, had I not learned to-night that a letter had been transmitted by some one to Lord Mounteagle, which he had conveyed to the Earl of Salisbury. It may not convey any notion of the plot, but it is certain to occasion alarm, and I thought it my duty, in spite of every personal consideration, to give you warning. If you design to escape, there is yet time. A vessel lies in the river, in which we can all embark for Flanders."

"Can he be innocent?" said Catesby in a whisper to Garnet.

"If I had betrayed you," continued Tresham, I should not have come hither. And I have no motive for such baseness, for I am in equal danger with yourselves. But though the alarm has been given, I do not think any discovery will be made. They are evidently on the wrong scent."

"I hope so," replied Catesby; "but I fear the contrary."

"Shall I put him to death?" demanded Fawkes of Garnet.

"Do not sully your hands with his blood, my son," returned Garnet. "If he has betrayed us, he will reap the traitor's reward here and hereafter. If he has not, it would be to take away a life unjustly. Let him depart. We shall feel more secure without him."

"Will it be safe to set him free, father?" cried Fawkes.

"I think so," replied Garnet. "We will not admit him to our further conferences; but let us act mercifully."

The major part of the conspirators concurring in this opinion, though Fawkes and Catesby were opposed to it,

Tresham was suffered to depart. As soon as he was gone, Garnet avowed that the further prosecution of the design appeared so hazardous, that it ought to be abandoned, and that, in his opinion, each of the conspirators had better consult his own safety by flight. He added, that at some future period the design might be resumed, or another planned, which might be more securely carried out.

After much discussion, all seemed disposed to acquiesce in the proposal, except Fawkes, who adhered doggedly to his purpose, and treated the danger so slightingly, that he gradually brought the others round to his views. At length it was resolved that Garnet should set out immediately for Coughton Hall, and place himself under the protection of Sir Everard Digby, and there await the result of the attempt, while the other conspirators decided upon remaining in town, in some secure places of concealment, until the event was known. Unmoved as ever, Guy Fawkes declared his intention of watching over the magazine of powder.

"If anything happens to me," he said, "you will take care of yourselves. You well know nothing will be wrung from me."

Catesby and the others, aware of his resolute nature, affected to remonstrate with him, but they willingly suffered him to take his own course. Attended by Bates, Garnet then set out for Warwickshire, and the rest of the conspirators proceeded to London, where they dispersed, after appointing Lincoln's Inn Walks as their place of midnight rendezvous. Each then made preparations for sudden flight, in case it should be necessary, and Rookwood provided relays of horses all the way to Dunchurch.

Guy Fawkes alone remained at his post. He took up his abode in the cellar, resolved to blow up himself together with his foes, in case of a surprise.

On Thursday, the 31st of October, the King returned to Whitehall, and the mysterious letter was laid before him in the presence of the Privy Council by the Earl of Salisbury. James perused it carefully, but could scarcely hide his perplexity.

"Your Majesty will not fail to remark the expressions, ' a terrible blow' to the Parliament, and that 'the danger will be past as soon as you have burnt the letter,' evidently referring to combustion," observed the Earl.

"You are right, Salisbury," said James, snatching at the suggestion. "I should not wonder if these mischievous Papists mean to blow us all up with gunpowder."

"Your Majesty has received a divine illumination," returned the Earl. "Such an idea never occurred to me; but it must be as you intimate."

"Undoubtedly—undoubtedly," replied the monarch, pleased with the compliment to his sagacity, though alarmed by the danger; "but what desperate traitors they must be to imagine such a deed! Blow us up! God's mercy, that were a dreadful death! And yet that must evidently be the meaning of the passage. How else can it be construed, except by reference to the suddenness of the act, which might be as quickly performed as that paper would take to be consumed in the fire?"

"Your Majesty's penetration has discovered the truth," replied Salisbury, "and by the help of your wisdom, I will fully develop this dark design. Where, think you, the powder may lie hidden?"

"Are there any vaults beneath the Parliament House?" demanded James, trembling. "Heaven save us! We have often walked there—perhaps, over a secret mine."

"There are," replied Salisbury; "and I am again indebted to your Majesty for a most important suggestion. Not a corner in the vaults shall be left unsearched. But, perhaps you will think with me, that in order to catch these traitors in their own trap, it will be well to defer the search till the very night before the meeting of Parliament."

"I was about to recommend such a course myself, Salisbury," replied James.

"I am sure you would think so," returned the Earl; "and now I must entreat you to dismiss the subject from your thoughts, and to sleep securely; for you may rely upon it (after your Majesty's discovery) that the plot shall be fully unravelled."

The significant tone in which the Earl uttered the latter part of this speech, convinced the King that he knew more of the matter than he cared to confess; and he contented himself with saying, "Well, let it be so. I trust all to you. But I at once divined their purpose—I at once divined it."

The Council then broke up, and James laughed and chuckled to himself at the discernment he had displayed. Nor was he less pleased with his minister for the credit given him in the affair. But he took care not to enter the Parliament House.

On the afternoon of Monday, the 4th of November, the Lord Chamberlain, accompanied by the Lords Salisbury and Mounteagle, visited the cellars and vaults beneath the Parliament House. For some time, they discovered nothing to excite suspicion. At length, probably at the suggestion of Lord Mounteagle, who, as will be recollected, was acquainted with the situation of the magazine, they proceeded to the cellar, where they found the store of powder; but not meeting with any of the conspirators, as they expected, they disturbed nothing, and went away, reporting the result of their search to the King.

By the recommendation of the Earl of Salisbury, James advised that a guard should be placed near the cellar during the whole of the night, consisting of Topcliffe and a certain number of attendants, and headed by Sir Thomas Knevet, a magistrate of Westminster, upon whose courage and discretion full reliance could be placed. Lord Mounteagle also requested permission to keep guard with them to witness the result of the affair. To this the King assented, and as soon as it grew dark, the party secretly took up their position at a point commanding the entrance of the magazine.

Fawkes, who chanced to be absent at the time the search was made, returned a few minutes afterwards, and remained within the cellar, seated upon a barrel of gunpowder, the head of which he had staved in, with a lantern in one hand, and petronel in the other, till past midnight.

The fifth of November was now at hand, and the clock of the adjoining abbey had scarcely ceased tolling the hour that proclaimed its arrival, when Fawkes, somewhat wearied with his solitary watching, determined to repair, for a short space, to the adjoining house. He accordingly quitted the cellar, leaving his lantern lighted within it in one corner.

Opening the door, he gazed cautiously around, but perceiving nothing, after waiting a few seconds, he proceeded to lock the door. While thus employed, he thought he heard a noise behind him, and turning suddenly, he beheld through the gloom several persons rushing towards him, evidently with hostile intent. His first impulse was to draw a petronel, and grasp his sword; but before he could effect his purpose, his arms were pinioned by a powerful grasp from behind, while the light of a lantern thrown full in his face revealed the barrel of a petronel levelled at his head, and an authoritative voice commanded him in the King's name to surrender.

XIII.

THE FLIGHT OF THE CONSPIRATORS.

On the same night, and at the same hour that Guy Fawkes was captured, the other conspirators held their rendezvous in Lincoln's Inn Walks. A presentiment of the fate awaiting them filled the breasts of all, and even Catesby shared in the general depression. Plan after plan was proposed, and, as soon as proposed, rejected; and they seemed influenced only by alarm and irresolution. Feeling at length that nothing could be done, and that they were only increasing their risk by remaining together longer, they agreed to separate, appointing to meet at the same place on the following night, if their project should not, in the interim, be discovered.

"Before daybreak," said Catesby, "I will proceed to the cellar under the Parliament House, and ascertain whether anything has happened to Guy Fawkes. My heart misgives me about him, and I reproach myself that I have allowed him to incur this peril alone."

"Guy Fawkes is arrested," said a voice near them, "and is at this moment under examination before the King."

"It is Tresham who speaks," cried Catesby; "secure him!"

The injunction was instantly obeyed. Tresham was seized, and several weapons pointed against his breast. He did not, however, appear to be dismayed, but, so far as could be discerned in the obscurity, seemed to maintain great boldness of demeanour.

"I have again ventured among you at the hazard of my life," he said, in a firm tone, "to give you this most important intelligence; and am requited, as I have ever been of late, with menaces and violence. Stab me, and see whether my death will avail you in this extremity. I am in equal danger with yourselves; and whether I perish by your hands, or by those of the executioner, is of little moment."

"Let me question him before we avenge ourselves upon him," said Catesby to Rookwood. "How do you know that Guy Fawkes is a prisoner?"

"I saw him taken," replied Tresham, "and esteem myself singularly fortunate that I escaped the same fate. Though excluded from further share in the project, I could not divest myself of a strong desire to know how matters were going on, and I resolved to visit the cellar secretly at midnight. As I stealthily approached it, I remarked several armed figures beneath a gateway, and conjecturing their purpose, instantly concealed myself behind a projection of the wall. I had not been in this situation many minutes, when the cellar door opened, and Guy Fawkes issued from it."

"Well!" cried Catesby, breathlessly.

"The party I had noticed immediately rushed forward, and secured him before he could offer any resistance," continued Tresham. "After a brief struggle, certain of their number dragged him into the cellar, while others kept watch without. I should now have flown, but my limbs refused their office, and I was therefore compelled, however reluctantly, to see the end of it. In a short time, Guy Fawkes was brought forth again, and I heard some one in authority give directions that he should be instantly taken to Whitehall, to be interrogated before the King and the Privy Council. He was then led away, and a guard placed at the door of the cellar. Feeling certain I should be discovered, I continued for some time in an agony of apprehension, not daring to stir. But, at length, summoning up sufficient resolution, I crept cautiously along the side of the wall, and got off unperceived. My first object was to warn you."

"How did you become acquainted with our place of rendezvous?" demanded the elder Wright.

"I overheard you, at our last interview at White Webbs, appoint a midnight meeting in this place," replied Tresham, "and I hurried hither in the hope of finding you, and have not been disappointed."

"When I give the word, plunge your swords into his breast," said Catesby, in a low tone.

"Hold!" cried Percy, taking him aside. "If we put him to death in this spot, his body will be found, and his slaughter may awaken suspicions against us. Guy Fawkes will reveal nothing."

"Of that I am well assured," said Catesby. "Shall we take the traitor with us to some secure retreat, where we can detain him till we learn what takes place at the palace, and if we find he has betrayed us, despatch him ?"

"That would answer no good purpose," returned Percy. "The sooner we are rid of him, the better. We can then deliberate as to what is best to be done."

"You are right," rejoined Catesby. "If he *has* betrayed us, life will be a burthen to him, and the greatest kindness we could render him would be to rid him of it. Let him go. Tresham," he added, in a loud voice, " you are free. But we meet no more."

" We have not parted yet," cried the traitor, springing backwards and uttering a loud cry. " I arrest you all in the King's name."

The signal was answered by a band of soldiers, who emerged from behind the trees where they had hitherto been concealed, and instantly surrounded the conspirators.

" It is now my turn to threaten," laughed Tresham.

Catesby replied by drawing a petronel, and firing it in the supposed direction of the speaker. But he missed his mark. The ball lodged in the brain of a soldier who was standing beside him, and the ill-fated wretch fell to the ground.

A desperate conflict now ensued. Topcliffe, who commanded the assailing party, ordered his followers to take the conspirators alive, and it was mainly owing to this injunction that the latter were indebted for their safety. Whispering his directions to his companions, Catesby gave the word, and making a simultaneous rush forward, they broke through the opposing ranks, and instantly dispersing, and favoured by the gloom, they baffled pursuit.

" We have failed in this part of our scheme," said Tresham, to Topcliffe, as they met half an hour afterwards. " What is to be done ?"

" We must take the Earl of Salisbury's advice upon it," returned Topcliffe. " I shall now hasten to Whitehall to see how Guy Fawkes's interrogation proceeds, and will communicate with his lordship."

Upon this they separated.

None of the conspirators met again that night. Each fled in a different direction, and, ignorant of what had happened to the rest, sought some secure retreat. Catesby ran towards Chancery-lane, and passing through a narrow alley, entered the large gardens which then lay between this thoroughfare and Fetter-lane. Listening to hear whether he was pursued, and finding nothing to alarm him, he threw himself on the sod beneath a tree, and was lost in painful reflection.

" All my fair schemes are marred by that traitor, Tresham," he muttered. " I could forgive myself for being duped by him, if I had slain him when he was in my power. But that he should escape to exult in our ruin, and reap the reward of his perfidy, afflicts me even more than failure."

Tortured by thoughts like these, and in vain endeavouring

to snatch such brief repose as would fit him for the fatigue he might have to endure on the morrow, he did not quit his position till late in the morning of a dull November day— it was, as will be recollected, the memorable Fifth—had arrived.

He then arose, and slouching his hat, and wrapping his cloak around him, shaped his course towards Fleet-street. From the knots of persons gathered together at different corners,—from their muttered discourse and mysterious looks, as well as from the general excitement that prevailed,—he felt sure that some rumour of the plot had gone abroad. Shunning observation as much as he could, he entered a small tavern near Fleet Bridge, and called for a flask of wine and some food. While discussing these, he was attracted by the discourse of the landlord, who was conversing with his guests about the conspiracy.

" I hear that all the Papists are to be hanged, drawn, and quartered," cried the host; "and if it be true, as I have heard, that this plot is their contrivance, they deserve it. I hope I have no believer in that faith—no recusant in my house."

" Don't insult us by any such suspicion," cried one of the guests. " We are all loyal men—all good Protestants."

" Do you know whether the conspirators have been discovered sir ?" asked the host of Catesby.

" I do not even know of the plot," replied the other. "What was its object ?"

" What was its object !" cried the host. " You will scarcely credit me when I tell you. I tremble to speak of it. Its object was to blow up the Parliament House, and the King and all the nobles and prelates of the land along with it."

" Horrible !" exclaimed the guests.

" But how do you know it is a scheme of the Papists ?" asked Catesby.

" Because I have been told so," rejoined the host. " But who else could devise such a monstrous plan ? It would never enter into the head or heart of a Protestant to conceive so detestable an action. We love our King too well for that, and would shed the last drop of our blood rather than a hair of his head should be injured. But these priest-ridden Papists think otherwise. They regard him as a usurper; and having received a dispensation from the Pope to that effect, fancy it would be a pious act to remove him. There will be no tranquillity in the kingdom while one of them is left alive; and I hope his Majesty will take advantage of the present ferment to order a general massacre of them, like that of the poor Protestants on Saint Bartholomew's day in Paris."

"Ay—massacre them," cried the guests; "that's the way. Burn their houses and cut their throats. Will it be lawful to do so without further authority, mine host? If so, we will set about it immediately."

"I cannot resolve you on that point," replied the landlord. "You had better wait a short time. I dare say their slaughter will be publicly commanded."

"Heaven grant it may be so!" cried one of the guests. "I will bear my part in the business."

Catesby arose, paid his reckoning, and strode out of the tavern.

"Do you know, mine host," said the guest who had last spoken, "I half suspect that tall fellow, who has just left us, is a Papist."

"Perhaps a conspirator," said another.

"Let us watch him," cried a third.

"Stay," cried the host, "he has paid me double my reckoning. I believe him to be an honest man and a good Protestant."

"What you say confirms my suspicions," rejoined the first speaker. "We will follow him."

On reaching Temple Bar, Catesby found the gates closed, and a guard stationed at them,—no one being allowed to pass through without examination. Not willing to expose himself to this scrutiny, Catesby turned away, and in doing so, perceived three of the persons he had just left in the tavern. The expression of their countenances satisfied him they were dogging him; but affecting not to perceive it, he retraced his steps, gradually quickening his pace until he reached a narrow street leading into Whitefriars, down which he darted. The moment his pursuers saw this, they hurried after him, shouting, "A Papist—a Papist!—a conspirator!"

But Catesby was now safe. Claiming the protection of certain Alsatians who were lounging at the door of a tavern, and offering to reward them, they instantly drew their swords, and drove the others away, while Catesby, tossing a few pieces of money to his preservers, passed through a small doorway into the Temple, and making the best of his way to the stairs, leapt into a boat, and ordered the waterman to row to Westminster. The man obeyed, and plying his oars, soon gained the middle of the stream. Little way, however, had been made, when Catesby descried a large wherry, manned by several rowers, swiftly approaching them, and instinctively comprehending whom it contained, ordered the man to rest on his oars till it had passed.

In a few moments the wherry approached them. It was filled with sergeants of the guard and halberdiers, in the midst of whom sat Guy Fawkes. Catesby could not resist the impulse that prompted him to rise, and the movement attracted the attention of the prisoner. The momentary glance they exchanged convinced Catesby that Fawkes perceived him, though his motionless features gave no token of recognition, and he immediately afterwards fixed his eyes towards heaven, as if to intimate—at least Catesby so construed the gesture—that his earthly career was well-nigh ended. Heaving a deep sigh, Catesby watched the wherry sweep on towards the Tower—its fatal destination—until it was lost to view.

"All is over, I fear, with the bravest of our band," he thought, as he tracked its course; "but some effort must be made to save him. At all events, we will die sword in hand, and like soldiers, and not as common malefactors."

Abandoning his intention of proceeding to Westminster, he desired the man to pull ashore, and, landing at Arundel Stairs, hastened to the Strand. Here he found large crowds collected, the shops closed, and business completely at a stand. Nothing was talked of but the conspiracy, and the most exaggerated and extraordinary accounts of it were circulated and believed. Some would have it that the Parliament House was already blown up, and that the city of London itself had been set fire to in several places by the Papists. It was also stated that numerous arrests had taken place, and it was certain that the houses of several Catholic nobles and wealthy gentlemen had been searched. To such a height was the popular indignation raised, that it required the utmost efforts of the soldiery to prevent the mob from breaking into these houses, and using violence towards their inmates.

Every gate and avenue to the palace was strictly guarded, and troops of horse were continually scouring the streets. Sentinels were placed before suspected houses, and no one was suffered to enter them or to go forth without special permission. Detachments of soldiery were also stationed at the end of all the main thoroughfares. Bars were thrown across the smaller streets and outlets, and proclamation was made that no one was to quit the city, however urgent his business, for three days.

On hearing this announcement, Catesby saw at once that if he did not effect his escape immediately, it would be impracticable. Accordingly, he hurried towards Charing Cross, and turning up Saint Martin's-lane, at the back of the King's Mews, contrived to elude the vigilance of the guard, and speeded along the lane—for it was then literally so, and surrounded on either side by high hedges—until he came to Saint Giles's,—at this time nothing more than a few scattered houses, intermixed with trees. Here he encountered a man mounted on a powerful steed, and seeing this person look hard at him, would have drawn out of the way, if the other had not addressed him by name. He then regarded the equestrian more narrowly, and found it was Martin Heydocke.

"I have heard what has happened, Mr. Catesby," said Martin, "and can imagine the desperate strait in which you must be placed. Take my horse,—it may aid your flight. I was sent to London by my master, Mr. Humphrey Chetham, to bring him intelligence of the result of your attempt, and I am sure I am acting in accordance with his wishes in rendering you such a service. At all events, I will risk it. Mount, sir,—mount, and make the best of your way hence."

Catesby needed no further exhortation, but, springing into the saddle, hastily murmured his thanks, and striking into a lane on the right, rode off at a swift pace towards Highgate.

On reaching the brow of this beautiful hill, he drew in the bridle for a moment, and gazed towards the city he had just quitted. Dark and bitter were his thoughts as he fixed his eye upon Westminster Abbey, and fancied he could discern the neighbouring pile, whose destruction he had meditated. Remembering that from this very spot, when he had last approached the capital, in company with Guy Fawkes and Viviana Radcliffe, he had looked in the same direction, he could not help contrasting his present sensations with those he had then experienced. At that time he was full of ardour, and confident of success. Now all was lost to him, and he was anxious for little more than self-preservation. Involuntarily his eye wandered along the great city, until passing over the mighty fabric of Saint Paul's, it settled upon the Tower,—upon the place of Guy Fawkes's captivity.

"And can nothing be done for his deliverance?" sighed
Catesby, as he turned away, his eyes filling with moisture:
"must that brave soldier die the death of a felon—must he
be subjected to the torture? Horror! If he had died
defending himself, I should scarcely have pitied him. And
if he had destroyed himself, together with his foes, as he
resolved to do, I should have envied him. But the idea
of what he will have to suffer in that dreadful place—nay,
what he is now, perhaps, suffering—makes the life-blood
curdle in my veins. I will never fall alive into their hands."

With this resolve, he struck spurs into his steed, and,
urging him to a swift pace, dashed rapidly forward. He had
ridden more than a mile, when, hearing shouts behind him,
he perceived two troopers galloping after him as fast as their
horses could carry them. They shouted to him to stay, and
as they were better mounted than he was, it was evident
they would soon come up with him. Determined, however,
to adhere to the resolution he had just formed, and not to
yield himself with life, he prepared for a conflict, and suddenly halting, he concealed a petronel beneath his cloak, and
waited till his foes drew near.

"I command you, in the King's name, to surrender," said
the foremost trooper, riding up. "You are a rebel and a
traitor."

"Be this my answer," replied Catesby, aiming at the man,
and firing with such certainty, that he fell from his horse
mortally wounded. Unsheathing his sword, he then prepared to attack the other trooper. But, terrified at the
fate of his comrade, the man turned his horse's head, and
rode off.

Without bestowing a thought on the dying man, who lay
groaning in the mire, Catesby caught hold of the bridle of
his horse, and satisfied that the animal was better than his
own, mounted him, and proceeded at the same headlong pace
as before.

In a short time he reached Finchley, where several persons
rushed from their dwellings to inquire whether he brought
any intelligence of the plot, rumours of which had already
reached them. Without stopping, Catesby replied that most
important discoveries had been made, and that he was carrying despatches from the King to Northampton. No opposition was therefore offered him, and he soon left all traces
of habitation behind him. Urging his horse to its utmost,
he arrived, in less than a quarter of an hour, at Chipping

Barnet. Here the same inquiries were made as at Finchley, and returning the same answer—for he never relaxed his speed for a moment—he pursued his course.

In less than three quarters of an hour after this, he arrived at Saint Alban's, and proceeding direct to the post-house, asked for a horse. But instead of complying with the request, the landlord of the Rose and Crown—such was the name of the hostel—instantly withdrew, and returned the next moment with an officer, who desired to speak with Catesby before he proceeded further. The latter, however, took no notice of the demand, but rode off.

The clatter of horses' hoofs behind him soon convinced him he was again pursued, and he was just beginning to consider in what way he should make a second defence, when he observed two horsemen cross a lane on the left, and make for the main road. His situation now appeared highly perilous, especially as his pursuers, who had noticed the other horsemen at the same time as himself, shouted to them. But he was speedily relieved. These persons instead of stopping, accelerated their pace, and appeared as anxious as he was to avoid those behind him.

They were now within a short distance of Dunstable, and were ascending the lovely downs which lie on the London side of this ancient town, when one of the horsemen in front chancing to turn round, Catesby perceived it was Rookwood. Overjoyed at the discovery, he shouted to him at the top of his voice, and the other, who it presently appeared was accompanied by Keyes, instantly stopped. In a few seconds Catesby was by their side, and a rapid explanation taking place, they all three drew up in order of battle.

By this time their pursuers had arrived within a hundred yards of them, and seeing how matters stood, and not willing to hazard an engagement, after a brief consultation, retired. The three friends then pursued their route, passed through Dunstable, and without pausing a moment on the road, soon neared Fenny Stratford. Just before they arrived at this place, Catesby's horse fell from exhaustion. Instantly extricating himself from the fallen animal, he ran by the side of his companions till they got to the town, where Rookwood, who had placed relays on the road, changed his horse, and the others were fortunate enough to procure fresh steeds.

Proceeding with unabated impetuosity, they soon cleared a few more miles, and had just left Stony Stratford behind them, when they overtook a solitary horseman, who proved to be John Wright, and a little further on they came up with Percy, and Christopher Wright.

Though their numbers were thus increased, they did not consider themselves secure, but, flinging their cloaks away to enable them to proceed with greater expedition, hurried on to Towcester. Here Keyes quitted his companions, and shaped his course into Warwickshire, where he was afterwards taken, while the others, having procured fresh horses, made the best of their way to Ashby Saint Leger's.

About six o'clock, Catesby and his companions arrived at his old family seat, which he had expected to approach in triumph, but which he now approached with feelings of the deepest mortification and disappointment. They found the house filled with guests—among whom was Robert Winter—who were just sitting down to supper. Catesby rushed into the room in which these persons were assembled, covered with mud and dirt, his haggard looks and dejected appearance proclaiming that his project had failed. His friends followed, and their appearance confirmed the impression that he had produced. Lady Catesby hastened to her son, and strove to comfort him; but he rudely repulsed her.

"What is the matter?" she anxiously inquired.

"What is the matter!" cried Catesby, in a furious tone, and stamping his foot to the ground. "All is lost! our scheme is discovered; Guy Fawkes is a prisoner, and ere long we shall all be led to the block. Yes, all!" he repeated, gazing sternly around.

"I will never be led thither with life," said Robert Winter.

"Nor I," added a young Catholic gentleman, named Acton of Ribbesford, who had lately joined the conspiracy. "Though the great design has failed, we are yet free, and have swords to draw, and arms to wield them."

"Ay," exclaimed Robert Winter, "all our friends are assembled at Dunchurch. Let us join them instantly, and we may yet stir up a rebellion which may accomplish all we can desire. I, myself, accompanied Humphrey Littleton to Dunchurch, this morning, and know we shall find everything in readiness."

"Do not despair," cried Lady Catesby; "all will yet be well. Every member of our faith will join you, and you will soon muster a formidable army."

"We must not yield without a blow," cried Percy, pouring out a bumper of wine, and swallowing it at a draught.

"You are right," said Rookwood, imitating his example. "We will sell our lives dearly."

"If you will adhere to this resolution, gentlemen," rejoined Catesby, "we may yet retrieve our loss. With five hundred stanch followers, who will stand by me to the last, I will engage to raise such a rebellion in England as shall not be checked, except by the acknowledgment of our rights or the dethronement of the King."

"We will all stand by you," cried the others.

"Swear it," cried Catesby, raising the glass to his lips.

"We do," was the reply.

"Wearied as we are," cried Catesby, "we must at once proceed to Dunchurch, and urge our friends to rise in arms with us."

"Agreed," cried the others.

Summoning all his household, and arming them, Catesby then set out with the rest for Dunchurch, which lay about five miles from Ashby Saint Leger's. They arrived there in about three quarters of an hour, and found the mansion crowded with Catholic gentlemen and their servants. Entering the banquet-hall, they found Sir Everard Digby at the head of the board, with Garnet on his right hand. Upwards of sixty persons were seated at the table. Their arrival was greeted with loud shouts, and several of the guests drew their swords and flourished them over their heads.

"What news?" cried Sir Everard Digby. "Is the blow struck?"

"No," replied Catesby; "we have been betrayed."

A deep silence prevailed. A change came over the countenances of the guests. Significant glances were exchanged, and it was evident that general uneasiness prevailed.

"What is to be done?" cried Sir Everard Digby, after a pause.

"Our course is clear," returned Catesby. "We must stand by each other. In that case, we have nothing to fear, and shall accomplish our purpose, though not in the way originally intended."

"I will have nothing further to do with the matter," said Sir Robert Digby of Coleshill, Sir Everard's uncle. And rising, he quitted the room with several of his followers, while his example was imitated by Humphrey Littleton and others.

"All chance for the restoration of our faith in England is over," observed Garnet, in a tone of despondency.

"Not so, father," replied Catesby, "if we are true to each other. My friends," he cried, stopping those who were about

to depart, "in the name of our holy religion I beseech you to
pause. Much is against us now. But let us hold together,
and all will speedily be righted. Every Catholic in this
county, in Cheshire, in Lancashire, and Wales, must flock to
our standard when it is once displayed—do not desert us—do
not desert yourselves—for our cause is your cause. I have a
large force at my command; so has Sir Everard Digby, and
together we can muster nearly five hundred adherents. With
these, we can offer such a stand as will enable us to make
conditions with our opponents, or even to engage with them
with a reasonable prospect of success. I am well assured,
moreover, if we lose no time, but proceed to the houses of
our friends, we shall have a large army with us. Do not fall
off, then. On you depends our success."

This address was followed by loud acclamations; and all
who heard it agreed to stand by the cause in which they had
embarked to the last.

As Catesby left the banqueting-hall with Sir Everard, to
make preparations for their departure, they met Viviana and
a female attendant.

"I hear the enterprise has failed," she cried, in a voice suffocated by emotion. "What has happened to my husband?
Is he safe? Is he with you?"

"Alas! no," replied Catesby; "he is a prisoner."

Viviana uttered a cry of anguish, and fell senseless into the
arms of the attendant.

XIV.

THE EXAMINATION.

DISARMED by Sir Thomas Knevet and his followers, who
found upon his person a packet of slow matches and touchwood, and bound hand and foot, Guy Fawkes was dragged
into the cellar by his captors, who instantly commenced their
search. In a corner behind the door they discovered a dark
lantern, with a light burning within it; and, moving with the
utmost caution—for they were afraid of bringing sudden
destruction upon themselves—they soon perceived the barrels
of gunpowder ranged against the wall. Carefully removing

the planks, billets, and iron bars with which they were covered, they remarked that two of the casks were staved in, while the hoops from a third were taken off, and the powder scattered around it. They also noticed that several trains were laid along the floor—everything, in short, betokening that the preparations for the desperate deed were fully completed.

While they were making this investigation, Guy Fawkes, who, seeing that further resistance was useless, had remained perfectly motionless up to this moment, suddenly made a struggle to free himself ; and so desperate was the effort that he burst the leathern thong that bound his hands, and seizing the soldier nearest to him, bore him to the ground. He then grasped the lower limbs of another, who held a lantern, and strove to overthrow him, and wrest the lantern from his grasp, evidently intending to apply the light to the powder. And he would unquestionably have executed his terrible design, if three of the most powerful of the soldiers had not thrown themselves upon him, and overpowered him. All this was the work of a moment; but it was so startling, that Sir Thomas Knevet and Topcliffe, though both courageous men, and used to scenes of danger—especially the latter—rushed towards the door, expecting some dreadful catastrophe would take place.

"Do him no harm," cried Knevet, as he returned to the soldiers, who were still struggling with Fawkes—"do him no harm. It is not here he must die."

"A moment more, and I had blown you all to perdition," cried Fawkes. "But Heaven ordained it otherwise."

"Heaven will never assist such damnable designs as yours," rejoined Knevet. "Thrust him into that corner," he added to his men, who instantly obeyed his injunctions, and held down the prisoner so firmly that he could not move a limb. "Keep him there. I will question him presently."

"You *may* question me," replied Fawkes, sternly ; "but you will obtain no answer."

"We shall see," returned Knevet.

Pursuing the search with Topcliffe, he counted thirty-six hogsheads and casks of various sizes, all of which were afterwards found to be filled with powder. Though prepared for this discovery, Knevet could not repress his horror at it, and gave vent to execrations against the prisoner, to which the other replied by a disdainful laugh. They then looked about in the hope of finding some document or fragment of a letter, which might serve as a clue to the other parties con-

nected with the fell design, but without success. Nothing
was found except a pile of arms; but though they examined
them, no name or cipher could be traced on any of the
weapons.

"We will now examine the prisoner more narrowly," said
Knevet.

This was accordingly done. On removing Guy Fawkes's
doublet, a horse-hair shirt appeared, and underneath it, next
his heart, suspended by a silken cord from his neck, was a
small silver cross. When this was taken from him, Guy
Fawkes could not repress a deep sigh.

"There is some secret attached to that cross," whispered
Topcliffe, plucking Knevet's sleeve.

Upon this, the other held it to the light, while Topcliffe
kept his eye fixed upon the prisoner, and observed that, in
spite of all his efforts to preserve an unmoved demeanour, he
was slightly agitated.

"Do you perceive anything?" he asked.

"Yes," replied Knevet, "there is a name. But the character is so small I cannot decipher it."

"Let me look at it," said Topcliffe. "This is most important," he added, after gazing at it for a moment: "the words
inscribed on it are, ' *Viviana Radcliffe, Ordsall Hall.*' You
may remember that this young lady was examined a short
time ago, on suspicion of being connected with some Popish
plot against the State, and committed to the Tower, whence
she escaped in a very extraordinary manner. This cross,
found upon the prisoner, proves her connexion with the present plot. Every effort must be used to discover her
retreat."

Another deep sigh involuntarily broke from the breast of
Guy Fawkes.

"You hear how deeply interested he is in the matter," observed Topcliffe, in a low tone. "This trinket will be of
infinite service to us in future examinations, and may do more
for us with this stubborn subject even than the rack itself."

"You are right," returned Knevet. "I will now convey
him to Whitehall, and acquaint the Earl of Salisbury with
his capture."

"Do so," replied Topcliffe. "I have a further duty to
perform. Before morning I hope to net the whole of this
wolfish pack."

"Indeed!" exclaimed Knevet. "Have you any knowledge
of the others?"

Topcliffe smiled significantly.

"Time will show," he said. "But if you do not require me further, I will leave you."

With this he quitted the cellar, and joined the Earl of Mounteagle and Tresham, who were waiting for him outside at a little distance from the cellar. After a brief conference it was arranged, in compliance with the Earl of Salisbury's wishes, that if they failed in entrapping the conspirators, nothing should be said about the matter. He then departed with Tresham. Their subsequent proceedings have already been related.

By Sir Thomas Knevet's directions, Guy Fawkes was now raised by two of the soldiers, and led out of the cellar. As he passed through the door he uttered a deep groan.

"You groan for what you have done, villain," said one of the soldiers.

"On the contrary," rejoined Fawkes, sternly, "I groan for what I have not done."

He was then hurried along by his conductors, and conveyed through the great western gate into the palace of Whitehall, where he was placed in a small room, the windows of which were strongly grated.

Before quitting him, Sir Thomas Knevet put several questions to him, but he maintained a stern and obstinate silence. Committing him to the custody of an officer of the guard, whom he enjoined to keep strict guard over him, as he valued his life, Knevet then went in search of the Earl of Salisbury.

The secretary, who had not retired to rest, and was anxiously awaiting his arrival, was delighted with the success of the scheme. They were presently joined by Lord Mounteagle; and after a brief conference it was resolved to summon the Privy Council immediately, to rouse the King and acquaint him with what had occurred, and to interrogate the prisoner in his presence.

"Nothing will be obtained from him, I fear," said Knevet. "He is one of the most resolute and determined fellows I ever encountered."

And he then related the desperate attempt made by Fawkes in the vault to blow them all up.

"Whether he will speak or not, the King must see him," said Salisbury. As soon as Knevet was gone, the Earl observed to Mounteagle, "You had now better leave the palace. You must not appear further in the matter, except as we have arranged. Before morning I trust we shall have the whole of the conspirators in our power, with damning proofs of their guilt."

"By this time, my lord, they are in Tresham's hands," replied Mounteagle.

"If he fails, not a word must be said," observed Salisbury. "It must not be supposed we have moved in the matter. All great statesmen have contrived treasons, that they might afterwards discover them; and though I have not contrived this plot, I have known of its existence from the first, and could at any time have crushed it had I been so minded. But that would not have answered my purpose. And I shall now use it as a pretext to crush the whole Catholic party, except those on whom, like yourself, I can confidently rely."

"Your lordship must admit that I have well seconded your efforts," observed Mounteagle.

"I do so," replied Salisbury, "and you will not find me ungrateful. Farewell!" I hope soon to hear of our further success."

Mounteagle then took his departure, and Salisbury immediately caused all such members of the Privy Council as lodged in the palace to be aroused, desiring they might be informed that a terrible plot had been discovered, and a conspirator arrested. In a short time the Duke of Lennox, the Earl of Marr, Lord Hume, the Earl of Southampton, Lord Henry Howard, Lord Mountjoy, Sir George Hume, and others were assembled, and all eagerly inquired into the occasion of the sudden alarm.

Meanwhile the Earl of Salisbury had himself repaired to the King's bedchamber, and acquainted him with what had happened. James immediately roused himself, and desired the chamberlain, who accompanied the Earl, to quit the presence.

"Will it be safe to interrogate the prisoner here?" he asked.

"I will take care your Majesty shall receive no injury," replied Salisbury; "and it is absolutely necessary you should examine him before he is committed to the Tower."

"Let him be brought before me, then, directly," said the King. "I am impatient to behold a wretch who has conceived so atrocious—so infernal a design against me, and against my children. Hark'e, Salisbury, one caution I wish to observe. Let a captain of the guard, with his drawn sword in hand, place himself between me and the prisoner, and let two halberdiers stand beside him, and if the villain moves a step, bid them strike him dead. You understand ?"

" Perfectly," replied Salisbury, bowing.

" In that case, you may take off his bonds—that is, if you think it prudent to do so—not otherwise," continued James. " I would not have the knave suppose he can awe me."

" Your Majesty's commands shall be fulfilled to the letter," returned the Earl.

" Lose no time, Salisbury," cried James, springing out of bed, and beginning to dress himself without the assistance of his chamberlain.

The Earl hastily retired, and ordered the attendants to repair to their royal master. He next proceeded to the chamber where Guy Fawkes was detained, and ordered him to be unbound, and brought before the King. When the prisoner heard this mandate, a slight smile crossed his countenance, but he instantly resumed his former stern composure. The smile, however, did not escape the notice of Salisbury, and he commanded the halberdiers to keep near to the prisoner, and if he made the slightest movement in the King's presence, instantly to despatch him.

Giving some further directions, the Earl then led the way across a court, and entering another wing of the palace, ascended a flight of steps, and traversed a magnificent corridor. Guy Fawkes followed, attended by the guard. They had now reached the ante-chamber leading to the royal sleeping apartment, and Salisbury ascertained from the officers in attendance that all was in readiness. Motioning the guard to remain where they were, he entered the inner room alone, and found James seated on a chair of state near the bed, surrounded by his council ;—the Earl of Marr standing on his right hand, and the Duke of Lennox on his left, all anxiously awaiting his arrival. Behind the King were stationed half a dozen halberdiers.

" The prisoner is without," said Salisbury. " Is it your Majesty's pleasure that he be admitted ?"

" Ay, let him come in forthwith," replied James. " Stand by me, my lords. And do you, varlets, keep a wary eye upon him. There is no saying what he may attempt."

Salisbury then waved his hand. The door was thrown open, and an officer entered the room, followed by Guy Fawkes, who marched between two halberdiers. When within a couple of yards of the King, the officer halted, and withdrew a little on the right, so as to allow full view of the prisoner, while he extended his sword between him and the King. Nothing could be more undaunted than the looks and demeanour of Fawkes. He strode firmly into the room, and without making any reverence, folded his arms upon his breast, and looked sternly at James.

"A bold villain!" cried the King, as he regarded him with curiosity not unmixed with alarm. "Who, and what are you, traitor?"

"A conspirator," replied Fawkes.

"That I know," rejoined James, sharply. "But how are you called?"

"John Johnson," answered Fawkes. "I am servant to Mr. Thomas Percy."

"That is false," cried Salisbury. "Take heed that you speak the truth, traitor, or the rack shall force it from you."

"The rack will force nothing from me," replied Fawkes, sternly; "neither will I answer any question asked by your lordship."

"Leave him to me, Salisbury,—leave him to me," interposed James. "And it was your hellish design to blow us all up with gunpowder?" he demanded.

"It was," replied Fawkes.

"And how could you resolve to destroy so many persons, none of whom have injured you?" pursued James.

"Dangerous diseases require desperate remedies," replied Fawkes. "Milder means have been tried, but without effect. It was God's pleasure that this scheme, which was for the benefit of His holy religion, should not prosper, and therefore I do not repine at the result."

"And are you so blinded as to suppose that Heaven can approve the actions of him who raises his hand against the King—against the Lord's anointed?" cried James.

"He is no king who is excommunicated by the apostolic see," replied Fawkes.

"This to our face!" cried James, angrily. "Have you no remorse—no compunction for what you have done?"

"My sole regret is that I have failed," replied Fawkes.

"You will not speak thus confidently on the rack," said James.

"Try me," replied Fawkes.

"What purpose did you hope to accomplish by this atrocious design?" demanded the Earl of Marr.

Guy Fawkes interrogated by King James the First.

"My main purpose was to blow back the beggarly Scots to their native mountains," returned Fawkes.

"This audacity surpasses belief," said James. "Mutius Scævola, when in the presence of Porsenna, was not more resolute. Hark'e, villain, if I give you your life, will you disclose the names of your associates?"

"No," replied Fawkes.

"They shall be wrung from you," cried Salisbury.

Fawkes smiled contemptuously. "You know me not," he said.

"It is idle to interrogate him further," said James. "Let him be removed to the Tower."

"Be it so," returned Salisbury; "and when next your Majesty questions him, I trust it will be in the presence of his confederates."

"Despite the villain's horrible intent, I cannot help admiring his courage," observed James, in a low tone; "and were he as loyal as he is brave, he should always be near our person."

With this, he waved his hand, and Guy Fawkes was led forth. He was detained by the Earl of Salisbury's orders till the morning,—it being anticipated that before that time the other conspirators would be arrested. But as this was not the case, he was placed in a wherry, and conveyed, as before related, to the Tower.

END OF THE SECOND BOOK.

Book the Third.

THE CONSPIRATORS.

The conclusion shall be from the admirable clemency and moderation of
the king; in that, howsoever these traitors have exceeded all others in
mischief, yet neither will the king exceed the usual punishment of law,
nor invent any new torture or torment for them, but is graciously pleased
to afford them as well an ordinary course of trial as an ordinary punishment much inferior to their offence. And surely worthy of observation is
the punishment by law provided and appointed for high treason: for, first,
after a traitor hath had his just trial, and is convicted and attainted, he
shall have his judgment to be drawn to the place of execution from
his prison, as being not worthy any more to tread upon the face of the
earth whereof he was made; also, for that he hath been retrograde to
nature, therefore he is drawn backward at a horsetail. After, to have his
head cut off which had imagined the mischief. And, lastly, his body to
be quartered, and the quarters set up in some high and eminent place, to
the view and detestation of men, and to become a prey for the fowls of the
air. And this is a reward due to traitors, whose hearts be hardened; for
that it is a physic of state and government to let out corrupt blood from
the heart.—*Sir Edward Coke's Speech on the Gunpowder Treason.*

I.

HOW GUY FAWKES WAS PUT TO THE TORTURE.

INTIMATION of the arrest of Guy Fawkes having been sent
to the Tower, his arrival was anxiously expected by the
warders and soldiers composing the garrison, a crowd of
whom posted themselves at the entrance of Traitor's Gate to
obtain a sight of him. As the bark that conveyed the prisoner
shot through London Bridge, and neared the fortress, notice
of its approach was given to the lieutenant, who, scarcely less
impatient, had stationed himself in a small circular chamber
in one of the turrets of Saint Thomas's or Traitor's Tower,
overlooking the river. He hastily descended, and had scarcely
reached the place of disembarkation, when the boat passed
beneath the gloomy archway, the immense wooden wicket
closed behind it; and the officer in command springing
ashore, was followed more deliberately by Fawkes, who

mounted the slippery stairs with a firm footstep. As he gained the summit, the spectators pressed forward; but Sir William Waad, ordering them in an authoritative tone to stand back, fixed a stern and scrutinizing glance on the prisoner.

"Many vile traitors have ascended those steps," he said, "but none so false-hearted, none so bloodthirsty as you."

"None ever ascended them with less misgiving, or with less self-reproach," replied Fawkes.

"Miserable wretch! Do you glory in your villany?" cried the lieutenant. If anything could heighten my detestation of the pernicious creed you profess, it would be to witness its effects on such minds as yours. What a religion must that be, which can induce its followers to commit such monstrous actions, and delude them into the belief that they are pious and praiseworthy!"

"It is a religion, at least, that supports them at seasons when they most require it," rejoined Fawkes.

"Peace!" cried the lieutenant, fiercely, "or I will have your viperous tongue torn out by the roots."

Turning to the officer, he demanded his warrant, and glancing at it, gave some directions to one of the warders, and then resumed his scrutiny of Fawkes, who appeared wholly unmoved, and steadily returned his gaze.

Meanwhile several of the spectators, eager to prove their loyalty to the King and abhorrence of the plot, loaded the prisoner with execrations, and, finding these produced no effect, proceeded to personal outrage. Some spat upon his face and garments; some threw mud, gathered from the slimy steps, upon him; some pricked him with the points of their halberds; while others, if they had not been checked, would have resorted to greater violence. Only one by-stander expressed the slightest commiseration for him. It was Ruth Ipgreve, who, with her parents, formed part of the assemblage.

A few kindly words pronounced by this girl, moved the prisoner more than all the insults he had just experienced. He said nothing, but a slight and almost imperceptible quivering of the lip told what was passing within. The jailer was extremely indignant at his daughter's conduct, fearing it might prejudice him in the eyes of the lieutenant.

"Get hence, girl," he cried, "and stir not from thy room for the rest of the day. I am sorry I allowed thee to come forth."

"You must look to her, Jasper Ipgreve," said Sir William Waad, sternly. "No man shall hold an office in the Tower who is a favourer of Papacy. If you were a good Protestant, and a faithful servant of King James, your daughter could never have acted thus unbecomingly. Look to her, I say— and to yourself."

"I will, honourable sir," replied Jasper, in great confusion. "Take her home directly," he added, in an undertone to his wife. "Lock her up till I return, and scourge her if thou wilt. She will ruin us by her indiscretion."

In obedience to this injunction, Dame Ipgreve seized her daughter's hand, and dragged her away. Ruth turned for a moment to take a last look at the prisoner, and saw that his gaze followed her, and was fraught with an expression of the deepest gratitude. By way of showing his disapproval of his daughter's conduct, the jailer now joined the bitterest of Guy Fawkes's assailants; and ere long the assemblage became infuriated to such an ungovernable pitch, that the lieutenant, who had allowed matters to proceed thus far in the hope of shaking the prisoner's constancy, finding his design fruitless, ordered him to be taken away. Escorted by a dozen soldiers with calivers on their shoulders, Guy Fawkes was led through the archway of the Bloody Tower, and across the Green to the Beauchamp Tower. He was placed in the spacious chamber on the first floor of that fortification, now used as a mess-room by the Guards. Sir William Waad followed him, and seating himself at a table, referred to the warrant.

"You are here called John Johnson. Is that your name?" he demanded.

"If you find it thus written, you need make no further inquiry from me," replied Fawkes. "I am the person so described. That is sufficient for you."

"Not so," replied the lieutenant; "and if you persist in this stubborn demeanour, the severest measures will be adopted towards you. Your sole chance of avoiding the torture is in making a full confession."

"I do not desire to avoid the torture," replied Fawkes. "It will wrest nothing from me."

"So all think till they have experienced it," replied the lieutenant; "but greater fortitude than yours has given way before our engines."

Fawkes smiled disdainfully, but made no answer.

The lieutenant then gave directions that he should be placed

within a small cell adjoining the larger chamber, and that two
of the guard should remain constantly beside him, to prevent
him from doing himself any violence.

"You need have no fear," observed Fawkes. "I shall not
destroy my chance of martyrdom."

At this juncture a messenger arrived, bearing a despatch
from the Earl of Salisbury. The lieutenant broke the seal,
and after hurriedly perusing it, drew his sword, and desiring
the guard to station themselves outside the door, approached
Fawkes.

"Notwithstanding the enormity of your offence," he observed, "I find his Majesty will graciously spare your life,
provided you will reveal the names of all your associates, and
disclose every particular connected with the plot."

Guy Fawkes appeared lost in reflection, and the lieutenant,
conceiving he had made an impression upon him, repeated the
offer.

"How am I to be assured of this?" asked the prisoner.

"My promise must suffice," rejoined Waad.

"It will not suffice to me," returned Fawkes. "I must
have a pardon signed by the King."

"You shall have it on one condition," replied Waad.
"You are evidently troubled with few scruples. It is the
Earl of Salisbury's conviction that the heads of many important Catholic families are connected with this plot. If
they should prove to be so—or, to be plain, if you will accuse
certain persons, whom I will specify, you shall have the
pardon you require."

"Is this the purport of the Earl of Salisbury's despatch?"
asked Guy Fawkes.

The lieutenant nodded.

"Let me look at it, continued Fawkes. "You may be
practising upon me."

"You own perfidious nature makes you suspicious of
treachery in others," cried the lieutenant. "Will this satisfy
you?"

And he held the letter towards Guy Fawkes, who instantly
snatched it from his grasp.

"What ho!" he shouted in a loud voice; "what ho!" and
the guards instantly rushed into the room. "You shall
learn why you were sent away. Sir William Waad has
offered me my life, on the part of the Earl of Salisbury,
provided I will accuse certain innocent parties—innocent,

except that they are Catholics—of being leagued with me in
my design. Read this letter, and see whether I speak not
the truth,"

And he threw it among them. But no one stirred, except
a warder, who, picking it up, delivered it to the lieutenant.

"You will now understand whom you have to deal with,"
pursued Fawkes.

"I do," replied Waad. "But were you as unyielding as
the walls of this prison, I would shake your obduracy."

"I pray you not to delay the experiment," said Fawkes.

"Have a little patience," retorted Waad. "I will not
balk your humour, depend upon it."

With this he departed, and repairing to his lodgings wrote
a hasty despatch to the Earl, detailing all that had passed,
and requesting a warrant for the torture, as he was apprehensive, if the prisoner expired under the severe application
that would be necessary to force the truth from him, he
might be called to account. Two hours afterwards the messenger returned with the warrant. It was in the handwriting
of the King, and contained a list of interrogations to be put
to the prisoner, concluding by directing him "to use the
gentler torture first, *et sic per gradus ad ima tenditur*. And
so God speed you in your good work!"

Thus armed, and fearless of the consequences, the lieutenant
summoned Jasper Ipgreve.

"We have a very refractory prisoner to deal with," he said,
as the jailer appeared. "But I have just received the royal
authority to put him through all the degrees of torture if he
continues obstinate. How shall we begin?"

"With the Scavenger's Daughter, and the Little Ease, if it
please you, honourable sir," replied Ipgreve. "If these fail,
we can try the gauntlets and the rack; and, lastly, the dungeon among the rats, and the hot stone."

"A good progression," said the lieutenant, smiling. "I
will now repair to the torture-chamber. Let the prisoner
be brought there without delay. He is in the Beauchamp
Tower.

Ipgreve bowed and departed, while the lieutenant, calling
to an attendant to bring a torch, proceeded along a narrow
passage communicating with the Bell Tower. Opening a
secret door within it, he descended a flight of stone steps, and
traversing a number of intricate passages, at length stopped
before a strong door, which he pushed aside, and entered the
chamber he had mentioned to Ipgreve. This dismal apart-

Guy Fawkes subscribing his Examination after the torture.

ment has already been described. It was that in which
Viviana's constancy was so fearfully approved. Two officials
in the peculiar garb of the place—a sable livery—were occupied in polishing the various steel implements. Besides
these, there was the chirurgeon, who was seated at a side-
table reading by the light of a brazen lamp. He instantly
arose on seeing the lieutenant, and began, with the other
officials, to make preparations for the prisoner's arrival.
The two latter concealed their features by drawing a large
black capoch, or hood, attached to their gowns over them, and
this disguise added materially to their lugubrious appearance.
One of them then took down a broad iron hoop, opening in
the centre with a hinge, and held it in readiness. Their
preparations were scarcely completed when heavy footsteps
announced the approach of Fawkes and his attendants.
Jasper Ipgreve ushered them into the chamber, and fastened
the door behind them. All the subsequent proceedings were
conducted with the utmost deliberation, and were therefore
doubly impressive. No undue haste occurred, and the
officials, who might have been mistaken for phantoms or
evil spirits, spoke only in whispers. Guy Fawkes watched
their movements with unaltered composure. At length,
Jasper Ipgreve signified to the lieutenant that all was
ready.

"The opportunity you desired of having your courage
put to the test is now arrived," said the latter to the prisoner.

"What am I to do?" was the reply.

"Remove your doublet, and prostrate yourself," subjoined
Ipgreve.

Guy Fawkes obeyed, and when in this posture began
audibly to recite a prayer to the Virgin.

"Be silent," cried the lieutenant, " or a gag shall be thrust
into your mouth."

Kneeling upon the prisoner's shoulders, and passing the
hoop under his legs, Ipgreve then succeeded, with the help
of his assistants, who added their weight to his own, in
fastening the hoop with an iron button. This done, they
left the prisoner with his limbs and body so tightly compressed together that he was scarcely able to breathe. In
this state he was allowed to remain for an hour and a half.
The chirurgeon then found on examination that the blood
had burst profusely from his mouth and nostrils, and in a
slighter degree from the extremities of his hands and feet.

"He must be released," he observed in an undertone to the lieutenant. "Further continuance might be fatal."

Accordingly, the hoop was removed, and it was at this moment that the prisoner underwent the severest trial. Despite his efforts to control himself, a sharp convulsion passed across his frame, and the restoration of impeded circulation and respiration occasioned him the most acute agony.

The chirurgeon bathed his temples with vinegar, and his limbs being chafed by the officials, he was placed on a bench.

"My warrant directs me to begin with the 'gentler tortures,' and to proceed by degrees to extremities," observed the lieutenant, significantly. "You have now had a taste of the milder sort, and may form some conjecture what the worst are like. Do you still continue contumacious?"

"I am in the same mind as before," replied Fawkes, in a hoarse but firm voice.

"Take him to the Little Ease, and let him pass the night there," said the lieutenant. "To-morrow I will continue the investigation."

Fawkes was then led out by Ipgreve and the officials, and conveyed along a narrow passage, until arriving at a low door, in which there was an iron grating, it was opened, and disclosed a narrow cell about four feet high, one and a few inches wide, and two deep. Into this narrow receptacle, which seemed wholly inadequate to contain a tall and strongly-built man like himself, the prisoner was with some difficulty thrust, and the door locked upon him.

In this miserable plight, with his head bent upon his breast—the cell being so contrived that its wretched inmate could neither sit, nor recline at full length within it—Guy Fawkes prayed long and fervently; and, no longer troubled by the uneasy feelings which had for some time haunted him, he felt happier in his present forlorn condition than he had been when anticipating the full success of his project.

"At least," he thought, "I shall now win myself a crown of martyrdom; and whatever my present sufferings may be, they will be speedily effaced by the happiness I shall enjoy hereafter."

Overcome, at length, by weariness and exhaustion, he fell into a sort of doze—it could scarcely be called sleep—and while in this state, fancied he was visited by Saint Winifred, who, approaching the door of the cell, touched it, and it instantly opened. She then placed her hand upon his limbs, and the pain he had hitherto felt in them subsided.

"Your troubles will soon be over," murmured the saint, "and you will be at rest. Do not hesitate to confess. Your silence will neither serve your companions nor yourself." With these words the vision disappeared, and Guy Fawkes awoke. Whether it was the effect of imagination, or that his robust constitution had in reality shaken off the effects of the torture, it is impossible to say, but it is certain that he felt his strength restored to him, and attributing his recovery entirely to the marvellous interposition of the saint, he addressed a prayer of gratitude to her. While thus occupied, he heard—for it was so dark he could distinguish nothing—a sweet low voice at the grating of the cell, and imagining it was the same benign presence as before, paused and listened.

"Do you hear me?" asked the voice.

"I do," replied Fawkes. "Is it the blessed Winifred, who again vouchsafes to address me?"

"Alas, no!" replied the voice; "it is one of mortal mould. I am Ruth Ipgreve, the jailer's daughter. You may remember that I expressed some sympathy in your behalf at your landing at Traitor's Gate to-day, for which I incurred my father's displeasure. But you will be quite sure I am a friend, when I tell you I assisted Viviana Radcliffe to escape."

"Ha!" exclaimed Guy Fawkes, in a tone of great emotion.

"I was in some degree in her confidence," pursued Ruth; "and, if I am not mistaken, you are the object of her warmest regard."

The prisoner could not repress a groan.

"You are Guy Fawkes," pursued Ruth. "Nay, you need have no fear of me. I have risked my life for Viviana, and would risk it for you."

"I will disguise nothing from you," replied Fawkes. "I am he you have named. As the husband of Viviana—for such I am—I feel the deepest gratitude to you for the service you rendered her. She bitterly reproached herself with having placed you in so much danger. How did you escape?"

"I was screened by my parents," replied Ruth. "It was given out by them that Viviana escaped through the window of her prison, and I was thus preserved from punishment. Where is she now?"

x

"In safety, I trust," replied Fawkes. "Alas! I shall never behold her again."

"Do not despair," returned Ruth. "I will try to effect your liberation; and though I have but slender hope of accomplishing it, still there is a chance."

"I do not desire it," returned Fawkes. "I am content to perish. All I live for is at an end."

"This shall not deter me from trying to save you," replied Ruth; "and I still trust there is happiness in store for you with Viviana. Amid all your sufferings, rest certain there is one who will ever watch over you. I dare not remain here longer, for fear of a surprise. Farewell!"

She then departed, and it afforded Guy Fawkes some solace to ponder on the interview during the rest of the night.

On the following morning Jasper Ipgreve appeared, and placed before him a loaf of the coarsest bread and a jug of dirty water. His scanty meal ended, he left him, but returned in two hours afterwards with a party of halberdiers, and desiring him to follow him, led the way to the torture-chamber. Sir William Waad was there when he arrived, and demanding in a stern tone whether he still continued obstinate, and receiving no answer, ordered him to be placed in the gauntlets. Upon this, he was suspended from a beam by his hands, and endured five hours of the most excruciating agony—his fingers being so crushed and lacerated that he could not move them.

He was then taken down, and still refusing to confess, was conveyed to a horrible pit adjoining the river, called, from the loathsome animals infesting it, "the dungeon among the rats." It was about twenty feet wide and twelve deep, and at high tide was generally more than two feet deep in water.

Into this dreadful chasm was Guy Fawkes lowered by his attendants, who, warning him of the probable fate that awaited him, left him in total darkness. At this time the pit was free from water; but he had not been there more than an hour, when a bubbling and hissing sound proclaimed that the tide was rising, while frequent plashes convinced him that the rats were at hand. Stooping down, he felt that the water was alive with them—that they were all around him—and would not, probably, delay their attack. Prepared as he was for the worst, he could not repress a shudder at the prospect of the horrible death with which he was menaced.

At this juncture he was surprised by the appearance of a light, and perceived at the edge of the pit a female figure bearing a lantern. Not doubting it was his visitant of the former night, he called out to her, and was answered in the voice of Ruth Ipgreve.

"I dare not remain here many minutes," she said, "because my father suspects me. But I could not let you perish thus. I will let down this lantern to you, and the light will keep away the rats. When the tide retires you can extinguish it."

So saying, she tore her kerchief into shreds, and tying the slips together, lowered the lantern to the prisoner, and with-out waiting to receive his thanks, hurried away.

Thus aided, Guy Fawkes defended himself as well as he could against his loathsome assailants. The light showed that the water was swarming with them—that they were creeping by hundreds up the sides of the pit, and preparing to make a general attack upon him.

At one time Fawkes determined not to oppose them, but to let them work their will upon him; but the contact of the noxious animals made him change his resolution, and he instinctively drove them off. They were not, however, to be easily repulsed, and returned to the charge with greater fury than before. The desire of self-preservation now got the better of every other feeling, and the dread of being de-voured alive giving new vigour to his crippled limbs, he rushed to the other side of the pit. His persecutors, how-ever, followed him in myriads, springing upon him, and mak-ing their sharp teeth meet in his flesh in a thousand places.

In this way the contest continued for some time, Guy Fawkes speeding round the pit, and his assailants never for one moment relaxing in the pursuit, until he fell from ex-haustion, and his lantern being extinguished, the whole host darted upon him.

Thinking all over, he could not repress a loud cry, and it was scarcely uttered, when lights appeared, and several gloomy figures bearing torches were seen at the edge of the pit. Among these he distinguished Sir William Waad, who offered instantly to release him if he would confess.

"I will rather perish," replied Fawkes, "and I will make no further effort to defend myself. I shall soon be out of the reach of your malice."

"This must not be," observed the lieutenant to Jasper Ipgreve, who stood by. "The Earl of Salisbury will never forgive me if he perishes."

"Then not a moment must be lost, or those ravenous

brutes will assuredly devour him," replied Ipgreve. "They are so fierce, that I scarcely like to venture among them."

A ladder was then let down into the pit, and the jailer and the two officials descended. They were just in time. Fawkes had ceased to struggle, and the rats were attacking him with such fury that his words would have been speedily verified, but for Ipgreve's timely interposition.

On being taken out of the pit, he fainted from exhaustion and loss of blood; and when he came to himself, found he was stretched upon a couch in the torture-chamber, with the chirurgeon and Jasper Ipgreve in attendance. Strong broths and other restoratives were then administered; and his strength being sufficiently restored to enable him to converse, the lieutenant again visited him, and questioning him as before, received a similar answer.

In the course of that day and the next, he underwent at intervals various kinds of torture, each more excruciating than the preceding, all of which he bore with unabated fortitude. Among other applications, the rack was employed with such rigour, that his joints started from their sockets, and his frame seemed torn asunder.

On the fourth day he was removed to another and yet gloomier chamber, devoted to the same dreadful objects as the first. It had an arched stone ceiling, and at the further extremity yawned a deep recess. Within this there was a small furnace, in which fuel was placed, ready to be kindled; and over the furnace lay a large black flag, at either end of which were stout leathern straps. After being subjected to the customary interrogations of the lieutenant, Fawkes was stripped of his attire, and bound to the flag. The fire was then lighted, and the stone gradually heated. The writhing frame of the miserable man ere long showed the extremity of his suffering; but as he did not even utter a groan, his tormentors were compelled to release him.

On this occasion there were two personages present who had never attended any previous interrogation. They were wrapped in large cloaks, and stood aloof during the proceedings. Both were treated with the most ceremonious respect by Sir William Waad, who consulted them as to the extent to which he should continue the torture. When the prisoner was taken off the heated stone, one of those persons advanced towards him, and gazed curiously at him.

Fawkes, upon whose brow thick drops were standing, and

who was sinking into the oblivion brought on by overwrought endurance, exclaimed, "It is the King!" and fainted.

"The traitor knew your Majesty," said the lieutenant. "But you see it is in vain to attempt to extort anything from him."

"So it seems," replied James; "and I am greatly disappointed, for I was led to believe that I should hear a full confession of the conspiracy from his own lips. How say you, good Master Chirurgeon, will he endure further torture?"

"Not without danger of life, your Majesty, unless he has some days' repose," replied the chirurgeon, "even if he can endure it then."

"It will not be necessary to apply it further," replied Salisbury. "I am now in full possession of the names of all the principal conspirators; and when the prisoner finds further concealment useless, he will change his tone. To-morrow, the commissioners appointed by your Majesty for the examination of all those concerned in this dreadful project, will interrogate him in the lieutenant's lodgings, and I will answer with my life that the result will be satisfactory."

"Enough," said James. "It has been a painful spectacle which we have just witnessed, and yet we would not have missed it. The wretch possesses undaunted resolution, and we can never be sufficiently grateful to the beneficent Providence that prevented him from working his ruthless purpose upon us. The day on which we were preserved from this Gunpowder Treason shall ever hereafter be kept sacred in our Church, and thanks shall be returned to Heaven for our wonderful deliverance."

"Your Majesty will act wisely," replied Salisbury. "The Ordinance will impress the nation with a salutary horror of all Papists and traitors—for they are one and the same thing—and keep alive a proper feeling of enmity against them. Such a fearful example shall be made of these miscreants as shall, it is to be hoped, deter all others from following their cause. Not only shall they perish infamously, but their names shall for ever be held in execration."

"Be it so," rejoined James. "It is a good legal maxim—*Crescente malitiâ, crescere debuit et pœna.*"

Upon this he left the chamber, and, traversing a number of subterranean passages with his attendants, crossed the drawbridge near the Byward Tower to the wharf, where his barge was waiting for him, and returned in it to Whitehall.

At an early hour on the following day, the commissioners appointed to the examination of the prisoner met together in a large room on the second floor of the lieutenant's lodgings, afterwards denominated, from its use on this occasion, the Council Chamber. Affixed to the walls of this room may be seen at the present day a piece of marble sculpture, with an inscription commemorative of the event. The commissioners were nine in number, and included the Earls of Salisbury, Northampton, Nottingham, Suffolk, Worcester, Devon, Marr, and Dunbar, and Sir John Popham, Lord Chief Justice. With these were associated Sir Edward Coke, attorney-general, and Sir William Waad.

The apartment in which the examination took place is still a spacious one, but at the period in question it was much larger and loftier. The walls were panelled with dark lustrous oak, covered in some places with tapestry, and adorned in others with paintings. Over the chimneypiece hung a portrait of the late sovereign, Elizabeth. The commissioners were grouped round a large heavily carved oak table, and, after some deliberation together, it was agreed that the prisoner should be introduced.

Sir William Waad then motioned to Topcliffe, who was in attendance with half a dozen halberdiers, and a few moments afterwards a panel was pushed aside, and Guy Fawkes was brought through it. He was supported by Topcliffe and Ipgreve, and it was with the greatest difficulty he could drag himself along. So severe had been the sufferings to which he had been subjected, that they had done the work of time, and placed more than twenty years on his head. His features were thin and sharp, and of a ghastly whiteness, and his eyes hollow and bloodshot. A large cloak was thrown over him, which partially concealed his shattered frame and crippled limbs; but his bent shoulders, and the difficulty with which he moved, told how much he had undergone.

On seeing the presence in which he stood, a flush for a moment rose to his pallid cheek, his eye glowed with its wonted fire, and he tried to stand erect; but his limbs refused their office; and the effort was so painful, that he fell back into the arms of his attendants. He was thus borne forward by them, and supported during his examination. The Earl of Salisbury then addressed him, and enlarging on the magnitude and horrible nature of his treason, concluded by saying that the only reparation he could offer was to disclose not only all his own criminal intentions, but the names of his associates.

"I will hide nothing concerning myself," replied Fawkes; "but I shall be for ever silent respecting others."

The Earl then glanced at Sir Edward Coke, who proceeded to take down minutes of the examination.

"You have hitherto falsely represented yourself," said the Earl. "What is your real name?"

"Guy Fawkes," replied the prisoner.

"And do you confess your guilt?" pursued the Earl.

"I admit that it was my intention to blow up the King and the whole of the lords spiritual and temporal assembled in the Parliament House with gunpowder," replied Fawkes.

"And you placed the combustibles in the vault where they were discovered?" demanded Salisbury.

The prisoner answered in the affirmative.

"You are a Papist?" continued the Earl.

"I am a member of the Church of Rome," returned Fawkes.

"And you regard this monstrous design as righteous and laudable—as consistent with the religion you profess, and as likely to uphold it?" said the Earl.

"I did so," replied Fawkes. "But I am now convinced that Heaven did not approve it, and I lament that it was ever undertaken."

"Still, you refuse to make the only reparation in your power —you refuse to disclose your associates?" said Salisbury.

"I cannot betray them," replied Fawkes.

"Traitor! it is needless," cried the Earl; "they are known to us—nay, they have betrayed themselves. They have risen in open and armed rebellion against the King: but a sufficient power has been sent against them; and if they are not ere this defeated and captured, many days will not elapse before they will be lodged in the Tower."

"If this is the case, you require no information from me," rejoined Fawkes. "But I pray you name them to me."

"I will do so," replied Salisbury; "and if I have omitted any, you can supply the deficiency. I will begin with Robert Catesby, the chief contriver of this hell-engendered plot—I will next proceed to the superior of the Jesuits, Father Garnet—next, to another Jesuit priest, Father Oldcorne—next, to Sir Everard Digby—then, to Thomas Winter and Robert Winter—then, to John Wright and Christopher Wright—

then, to Ambrose Rookwood, Thomas Percy, and John Grant
—and, lastly, to Robert Keyes."

"Are these all?" demanded Fawkes.

"All we are acquainted with," said Salisbury.

"Then add to them the names of Francis Tresham, and of
his brother-in-law, Lord Mounteagle," rejoined Fawkes. "I
charge both with being privy to the plot."

"I have forgotten another name," said Salisbury, in some
confusion, "that of Viviana Radcliffe, of Ordsall Hall. I have
received certain information that she was wedded to you
while you were resident at White Webbs, near Epping Forest,
and was cognisant of the plot. If captured, she will share
your fate."

Fawkes could not repress a groan.

Salisbury pursued his interrogations, but it was evident,
from the increasing feebleness of the prisoner, that he would
sink under it if the examination was further protracted. He
was therefore ordered to attach his signature to the minutes
taken by Sir Edward Coke, and was placed in a chair for that
purpose. A pen was then given him, but for some time his
shattered fingers refused to grasp it. By a great effort, and
with acute pain, he succeeded in tracing his Christian name
thus:—

While endeavouring to write his surname, the pen fell from
his hand, and he became insensible.

II.

SHOWING THE TROUBLES OF VIVIANA.

ON coming to herself, Viviana inquired for Garnet; and
being told that he was in his chamber alone, she repaired
thither, and found him pacing to and fro in the greatest
perturbation.

"If you come to me for consolation, daughter," he said,

"you come to one who cannot offer it. I am completely pro-strated in spirit by the disastrous issue of our enterprise; and though I tried to prepare myself for what has taken place, I now find myself utterly unable to cope with it."

" If such is your condition, father" replied Viviana, " what must be that of my husband, upon whose devoted head all the weight of this dreadful calamity now falls? You are still at liberty—still able to save yourself—still able, at least, to resist unto the death, if you are so minded. But he is a captive in the Tower, exposed to every torment that human ingenuity can invent, and with nothing but the prospect of a lingering death before his eyes. What is your condition, compared with his?"

" Happy—most happy, daughter," replied Garnet; "and I have been selfish and unreasonable. I have given way to the weakness of humanity, and I thank you from the bottom of my heart for enabling me to shake it off."

" You have indulged false hopes, father," said Viviana, " whereas I have indulged none; or rather, all has come to pass as I desired. The dreadful crime with which I feared my husband's soul would have been loaded is now uncom-mitted, and I have firm hope of his salvation. If I might counsel you, I would advise you to surrender yourself to jus-tice, and by pouring out your blood on the scaffold, wash out your offence. Such will be my own course. I have been in-voluntarily led into connexion with this plot; and though I have ever disapproved of it, since I have not revealed it, I am as guilty as if I had been its contriver. I shall not shun my punishment. Fate has dealt hardly with me, and my path on earth has been strewn with thorns, and cast in grief and trouble. But I humbly trust that my portion hereafter will be with the blessed."

" I cannot doubt it, daughter," replied Garnet; "and though I do not view our design in the light that you do, but regard it as justifiable, if not necessary, yet, with your feelings, I cannot sufficiently admire your conduct. Your devotion and self-sacrifice is wholly without parallel. At the same time, I would try to dissuade you from surrendering yourself to our relentless enemies. Believe me, it will add the severest pang to your husband's torture to know that you are in their power. His nature is stern and unyielding, and, persuaded as he is of the justice of his cause, he will die happy in that conviction, certain that his name, though despised by our heretical persecutors, will be held in reverence by all true professors of our faith. No, daughter; fly and conceal your-self till pursuit is relinquished, and pass the rest of your life in prayer for the repose of your husband's soul."

"I will pass it in endeavouring to bring him to repentance," replied Viviana. "The sole boon I shall seek from my judges will be permission to attempt this."

"It will be refused, daughter," replied Garnet, "and you will only destroy yourself, not aid him. Rest satisfied that the Great Power who judges the hearts of men, and implants certain impulses within them, for his own wise but inscrutable purposes, well knows that Guy Fawkes, however culpable his conduct may appear in your eyes, acted according to the dic-tates of his conscience, and in the full confidence that the design would restore the true worship of God in this kingdom. The failure of the enterprise proves that he was mistaken —that we were all mistaken—and that Heaven was un-favourable to the means adopted—but it does not prove his insincerity."

"These arguments have no weight with me, father," re-plied Viviana; "I will leave nothing undone to save his soul, and whatever may be the result, I will surrender myself to justice."

"I shall not seek to move you from your purpose, daughter," replied Garnet, "and can only lament it. Before, however, you finally decide, let us pray together for directions from on high."

Thus exhorted, Viviana knelt down with the priest before a small silver image of the Virgin, which stood in a niche in the wall, and they both prayed long and earnestly. Garnet was the first to conclude his devotions; and as he gazed at the upturned countenance and streaming eyes of his com-panion, his heart was filled with admiration and pity.

At this juncture the door opened, and Catesby and Sir Everard Digby entered. On hearing them, Viviana imme-diately arose.

"The urgency of our business must plead an excuse for the interruption, if any is needed," said Catesby; "but do not retire, madam. We have no secrets from you now. Sir Everard and I have fully completed our preparations," he added to Garnet. "Our men are all armed and mounted in the court, and are in high spirits for the enterprise. As the service, however, will be one of the greatest danger and diffi-culty, you had bettter seek a safe asylum, father, till the first decisive blow is struck."

"I would go with you, my son," rejoined Garnet, "if I did not think my presence might be an hindrance. I can only aid you with my prayers, and those can be more efficaciously uttered in some secure retreat, than during a rapid march or dangerous encounter."

"You had better retire to Coughton with Lady Digby and Viviana," said Sir Everard. "I have provided a sufficient escort to guard you thither—and, as you are aware, there are many hiding-places in the house, where you can remain undiscovered in case of a search."

"I place myself at your disposal," replied Garnet. "But Viviana is resolved to surrender herself."

"This must not be," returned Catesby. "Such an act at this juncture would be madness, and would materially injure our cause. Whatever your inclinations may prompt, you must consent to remain in safety, madam."

"I have acquiesced in your proceedings thus far," replied Viviana, "because I could not oppose them without injury to those dear to me. But I will take no further share in them. My mind is made up as to the course I shall pursue."

"Since you are bent upon your own destruction—for it is nothing less—it is the duty of your friends to save you," rejoined Catesby. "You shall not do what you propose, and when you are yourself again, and have recovered from the shock your feelings have sustained, you will thank me for my interference."

"You are right, Catesby," observed Sir Everard; "it would be worse than insanity to allow her to destroy herself thus."

"I am glad you are of this opinion," said Garnet. "I tried to reason her out of her design, but without avail."

"Catesby," cried Viviana, throwing herself at his feet, "by the love you once professed for me—by the friendship you entertained for him who unhesitatingly offered himself for you and your cause, I implore you not to oppose me now!"

"I shall best serve you, and most act in accordance with the wishes of my friend, by doing so," replied Catesby. "Therefore, you plead in vain."

"Alas!" cried Viviana. "My purposes are ever thwarted. You will have to answer for my life."

"I should, indeed, have it to answer for, if I permitted you to act as you desire," rejoined Catesby. "I repeat you will thank me ere many days are passed."

"Sir Everard," exclaimed Viviana, appealing to the knight, "I entreat you to have pity upon me."

"I do sincerely sympathise with your distress," replied Digby, in a tone of the deepest commiseration; "but I am sure what Catesby advises is for the best. I could not reconcile it to my conscience to allow you to sacrifice yourself thus. Be governed by prudence."

"Oh, no—no!" cried Viviana, distractedly. "I will not be stayed. I command you not to detain me."

"Viviana," said Catesby, taking her arm, "this is no season for the display of silly weakness, either on our part or yours. If you cannot control yourself, you must be controlled. Father Garnet, I entrust her to your care. Two of my troop shall attend you, together with your own servant, Nicholas Owen. You shall have stout horses, able to accomplish the journey with the greatest expedition, and I should wish you to convey her to her own mansion, Ordsall Hall, and to remain there with her till you hear tidings of us."

"It shall be as you direct, my son," said Garnet. "I am prepared to set out at once."

"That is well," replied Catesby.

"You will not do me this violence, sir," cried Viviana. "I appeal against it to you, Sir Everard."

"I cannot help you, madam," replied the knight; "indeed I cannot."

"Then Heaven, I trust, will help me," cried Viviana, "for I am wholly abandoned of man."

"I beseech you, madam, put some constraint upon yourself," said Catesby. "If, after your arrival at Ordsall, you are still bent upon your rash and fatal design, Father Garnet shall not oppose its execution. But give yourself time for reflection."

"Since it may not be otherwise, I assent," replied Viviana. "If I must go, I will start at once."

"Wisely resolved," replied Sir Everard.

Viviana then retired, and soon afterwards appeared equipped for her journey. The two attendants and Nicholas Owen were in the court-yard, and Catesby assisted her into the saddle.

"Do not lose sight of her," he said to Garnet, as the latter mounted.

"Rest assured I will not," replied the other.

And taking the direction of Coventry, the party rode off at a brisk pace.

Catesby then joined the other conspirators, while Sir Everard sent off Lady Digby and his household, attended by a strong escort, to Coughton. This done, the whole party repaired to the court-yard, where they called over the muster-roll of their men, to ascertain that none were missing—examined their arms and ammunition—and finding all in order, sprang to their steeds, and putting themselves at the head of the band, rode towards Southam and Warwick.

III.

HUDDINGTON.

ABOUT six o'clock in the morning the conspirators reached Leamington Priors, at that time an inconsiderable village; and having ridden nearly twenty miles over heavy and miry roads—for a good deal of rain had fallen in the night—they stood in need of some refreshment. Accordingly, they entered the first farm-yard they came to, and proceeding to the cow-houses and sheepfolds, turned out the animals within them, and fastening up their own steed in their places, set before them whatever provender they could find. Those—and they were by far the greater number—who could not find better accommodation, fed their horses in the yard, which was strewn with trusses of hay and great heaps of corn. The whole scene formed a curious picture. Here was one. party driving away the sheep and cattle, which were bleating and lowing—there, another rifling a hen-roost, and slaughtering its cackling inmates. On this hand, by the direction of Catesby, two stout horses were being harnessed with ropes to a cart, which he intended to use as a baggage-wagon; on that, Sir Everard Digby was interposing his authority to prevent the destruction of a fine porker.

Their horses fed, the next care of the conspirators was to obtain something for themselves: and ordering the master of the house, who was terrified almost out of his senses, to open his doors, they entered the dwelling, and causing a fire to be lighted in the chief room, began to boil a large kettle of broth upon it, and to cook other provisions. Finding a good store of eatables in the larder, rations were served out to the band.

Two casks of strong ale were likewise broached, and their
contents distributed ; and a small keg of strong waters being
also discovered, it was disposed of in the same way.

This, however, was the extent of the mischief done All
the conspirators, but chiefly Catesby and Sir Everard Digby,
dispersed themselves amongst the band, and checked any disposition to plunder. The only articles taken away from the
house were a couple of old rusty swords and a caliver. Catesby
proposed to the farmer to join their expedition. But having
now regained his courage, the sturdy churl obstinately refused to stir a foot with them, and even ventured to utter a
wish that the enterprise might fail.

"I am a good Protestant, and a faithful subject of King
James, and will never abet Popery and treason," he said.

This bold sally would have been answered by a bullet from
one of the troopers, if Catesby had not interfered.

"You shall do as you please, friend," he said, in a concilia-
tory tone. "We will not compel any man to act against his
conscience, and we claim the same right ourselves. Will you
join us, good fellows ?" he added, to two farming men, who
were standing near their master.

"Must I confess to a priest ?" asked one of them.

"Certainly not," replied Catesby. "You shall have no
constraint whatever put upon you. All I require is obedience
to my commands in the field."

"Then I am with you," replied the fellow.

"Thou'rt a traitor and rebel, Sam Morrell," cried the other
hind, "and will come to a traitor's end. I will never fight
against King James. And if I must take up arms, it shall
be against his enemies, and in defence of our religion. No
priests—no Papistry for me."

"Well said, Hugh," cried his master ; "we'll die in that
cause, if need be."

Catesby turned angrily away, and giving the word to his
men to prepare to set forth, in a few minutes all were in the
saddle ; but on inquiring for the new recruit, Sam Morrell,
it was found he had disappeared. The cart was laden with
arms, ammunition, and a few sacks of corn ; and the line
being formed, they commenced their march.

The morning was dark and misty, and all looked dull and
dispiriting. The conspirators, however, were full of confidence, and their men, exhilarated and refreshed by their
meal, appeared anxious for an opportunity of distinguishing
themselves. Arrived within half a mile of Warwick, whence

the lofty spire of the church of Saint Nicholas, the tower of Saint Mary's, and the ancient gates of this beautiful old town could just be discerned through the mist, a short consultation was held by the rebel leaders as to the expediency of attacking the castle, and carrying off the horses with which they had learnt its stables were filled.

Deciding upon making the attempt, their resolution was communicated to their followers, and received with loud acclamations. Catesby then put himself at the head of the band, and they all rode forward at a brisk pace. Crossing the bridge over the Avon, whence the castle burst upon them in all its grandeur and beauty, Catesby dashed forward to an embattled gate commanding the approach to the structure, and knocking furiously against it, a wicket was opened by an old porter, who started back on beholding the intruders. He would have closed the wicket, but Catesby was too quick for him, and springing from his steed, dashed aside the feeble opposition of the old man, and unbarred the gate. Instantly mounting again, he galloped along a broad and winding path cut so deeply in the rock, that the mighty pile they were approaching was completely hidden from view. A few seconds, however, brought them to a point, from which its three towers reared themselves full before them. Another moment brought them to the edge of the moat, at this time crossed by a stone bridge, but then filled with water, and defended by a drawbridge.

As no attack like the present was apprehended, and as the owner of the castle, the celebrated Fulke Greville, afterwards Lord Brooke, to whom it had been recently granted by the reigning monarch, was then in the capital, the drawbridge was down, and though several retainers rushed forth on hearing the approach of so many horsemen, they were too late to raise it. Threatening these persons with destruction if any resistance was offered, Catesby passed through the great entrance, and rode into the court, where he drew up his band.

By this time, the whole of the inmates of the castle had collected on the ramparts, armed with calivers and partisans, and whatever weapons they could find, and though their force was utterly disproportioned to that of their opponents, they seemed disposed to give them battle. Paying no attention to them, Catesby proceeded to the stables where he found upwards of twenty horses, which he exchanged for the worst and most jaded of his own, and was about to enter the castle in search of arms, when he was startled by hearing the alarm-bell rung. This was succeeded by the discharge of a culverin on the summit of the tower, named after the redoubted Guy, Earl of Warwick; and though the bell was instantly silenced, Rookwood, who had dislodged the party from the ramparts, brought word that the inhabitants of Warwick were assembling, that drums were beating at the gates, and that an attack might be speedily expected. Not desiring to hazard an engagement at this juncture, Catesby gave up the idea of ransacking the castle, and ordered his men to their horses.

Some delay, however, occurred before they could all be got together, and, meanwhile, the ringing of bells and other alarming sounds continued. At one time, it occurred to Catesby to attempt to maintain possession of the castle; but this design was overruled by the other conspirators, who represented to him the impracticability of the design. At length, the whole troop being assembled, they crossed the drawbridge, and speeded along the rocky path. Before the outer gate they found a large body of men, some on horseback, and some on foot, drawn up. These persons, however, struck with terror at their appearance, retreated, and allowed them a free passage.

On turning to cross the bridge, they found it occupied by a strong and well-armed body of men, headed by the Sheriff of Warwickshire, who showed no disposition to give way. While the rebel party were preparing to force a passage, a trumpet was sounded, and the sheriff, riding towards them, commanded them in the King's name to yield themselves prisoners.

"We do not acknowledge the supremacy of James Stuart, whom you call king," rejoined Catesby, sternly. "We fight for our liberties, and for the restoration of the holy Catholic religion, which we profess. Do not oppose us, or you will have cause to rue your temerity."

"Hear me," cried the sheriff, turning from him to his men: "I promise you all a free pardon in the King's name, if you will throw down your arms, and deliver up your leaders. But if, after this warning, you continue in open rebellion against your sovereign, you will all suffer the vilest death."

"Rejoin your men, sir," said Catesby, in a significant tone, and drawing a petronel.

"A free pardon and a hundred pounds to him who will

bring me the head of Robert Catesby," said the sheriff, disregarding the menace.

"Your own is not worth half the sum," rejoined Catesby; and levelling the petronel, he shot him dead.

The sheriff's fall was the signal for a general engagement. Exasperated by the death of their leader, the royalist party assailed the rebels with the greatest fury, and as the latter were attacked at the same time in the rear, their situation began to appear perilous. But nothing could withstand the vigour and determination of Catesby. Cheering on his men, he soon cut a way across the bridge, and would have made good his retreat, if he had not perceived, to his infinite dismay, that Percy and Rookwood had been captured.

Regardless of any risk he might run, he shouted to those near to follow him, and made such a desperate charge upon the royalists that in a few minutes he was by the side of his friends, and had liberated them. In trying, however, to follow up his advantage, he got separated from his companions, and was so hotly pressed on all sides, that his destruction seemed inevitable. His petronels had both brought down their mark; and in striking a blow against a stalwart trooper, his sword had shivered close to the handle. In this defenceless state his enemies made sure of him, but they miscalculated his resources.

He was then close to the side of the bridge, and, before his purpose could be divined, struck spurs deeply into his horse, and cleared the parapet with a single bound. A shout of astonishment and admiration arose alike from friend and foe, and there was a general rush towards the side of the bridge. The noble animal that had borne him out of danger was seen swimming towards the bank, and, though several shots were fired at him, he reached it in safety. This gallant action so raised Catesby in the estimation of his followers, that they welcomed him with the utmost enthusiasm, and rallying round him, fought with such vigour, that they drove their opponents over the bridge and compelled them to flee towards the town.

Catesby now mustered his men, and finding his loss slighter than he expected, though several were so severely wounded that he was compelled to leave them behind, rode off at a quick pace. After proceeding for about four miles along the Stratford road, they turned off on the right into a narrow lane leading to Snitterfield, with the intention of visiting Norbrook, the family residence of John Grant. On arriving

Y

there, they put the house into a state of defence, and then
assembled in the hall, while their followers recruited themselves in the court-yard.

"So far, well," observed Catesby, flinging himself into a
chair; "the first battle has been won."

"True," replied Grant; "but it will not do to tarry here
long. This house cannot hold out against a prolonged
attack."

"We will not remain here more that a couple of hours,"
replied Catesby; "but where shall we go next? I am for
making some desperate attempt, which shall strike terror
into our foes."

"Are we strong enough to march to the Earl of Harrington's mansion near Coventry, and carry off the Princess
Elizabeth?" asked Percy.

"She were indeed a glorious prize," replied Catesby; "but
I have no doubt, on the first alarm of our rising, she has
been conveyed to a place of safety. And even if she were
there, we should have the whole armed force of Coventry to
contend with. No, no; it will not do to attempt that."

"Nothing venture, nothing have!" cried Sir Everard
Digby. "We ought, in my opinion, to run any risk to
secure her."

"You know me too well, Digby," rejoined Catesby, "to
doubt my readiness to undertake any project, however hazardous, which would offer the remotest chance of success. But
in this I see none, unless, indeed, it could be accomplished by
stratagem. Let us first ascertain what support we can obtain,
and then decide upon the measures to be adopted."

"I am content," returned Digby.

"Old Mr. Talbot of Grafton is a friend of yours, is he
not?" continued Catesby, addressing Thomas Winter. "Can
you induce him to join us?"

"I will try," replied Thomas Winter; "but I have some
misgivings."

"Be not faint-hearted," rejoined Catesby. "You and
Stephen Littleton shall go to him at once, and join us at
your own mansion of Huddington, whither we will proceed
as soon as our men are thoroughly recruited. Use every
argument you can devise with Talbot,—tell him that the
welfare of the Catholic cause depends on our success,—and
that neither his years nor infirmities can excuse his absence
at this juncture. If he will not or cannot come himself, cause
him to write letters to all his Catholic neighbours, urging

them to join us, and bid him send all his retainers and servants to us."

"I will not neglect a single plea," replied Thomas Winter,
"and I will further urge compliance by his long friendship
towards myself. But, as I have just said, I despair of success."

Soon after this, he and Stephen Littleton, with two of the
troopers well mounted and well armed, rode across the
country through lanes and by-roads, with which they were
well acquainted, to Grafton. At the same time, Catesby
repaired to the court-yard, and assembling his men, found
there were twenty-five missing. More than half of these it
was known had been killed or wounded at Warwick ; but the
rest, it was suspected, had deserted.

Whatever effect this scrutiny might secretly have upon
Catesby, he maintained a cheerful and confident demeanour,
and mounting a flight of steps, harangued the band in ener-
getic and exciting terms. Displaying a small image of the
Virgin to them, he assured them they were under the special
protection of Heaven, whose cause they were fighting—and
concluded by reciting a prayer, in which the whole assemblage
heartily joined. This done, they filled the baggage-cart with
provisions and further ammunition, and forming themselves
into good order, took the road to Alcester.

They had not gone far, when torrents of rain fell, and the
roads being in a shocking condition, and ploughed up with
ruts, they turned into the fields wherever it was practicable,
and continued their march very slowly, and under excessively
disheartening circumstances. On arriving at the ford across
the Avon, near Bishopston, they found the stream so swollen
that it was impossible to get across it. Sir Everard Digby,
who made the attempt, was nearly carried off by the current.
They were therefore compelled to proceed to Stratford, and
cross the bridge.

"My friends," said Catesby, commanding a halt at a short
distance of the town, " I know not what reception we may
meet with here. Probably much the same as at Warwick.
But I command you not to strike a blow, except in self-
defence."

Those injunctions given, attended by the other conspirators,
except Percy and Rookwood, who brought up the rear, he
rode slowly into Stratford, and proceeding to the market-
place, ordered a trumpet to be sounded. On the first appearance of the troop, most of the inhabitants fled to their houses,

and fastened the doors, but some few courageous persons followed them at a wary distance. These were harangued at some length by Catesby, who called upon them to join the expedition, and held out promises, which only excited the derision of the hearers.

Indeed, the dejected looks of most of the band, and the drenched and muddy state of their apparel, made them objects of pity and contempt, rather than of serious apprehension; and nothing but their numbers prevented an attack being made upon them. Catesby's address concluded amid groans of dissatisfaction; and finding he was wasting time, and injuring his own cause, he gave the word to march, and moved slowly through the main street, but not a single recruit joined them.

Another unpropitious circumstance occurred just as they were leaving Stratford. Two or three of his followers tried to slink away, when Catesby, riding after them, called to them to return, and no attention being paid to his orders, he shot the man nearest him, and compelled the others, by threats of the same punishment, to return to their ranks. This occurrence, while it occasioned much discontent and ill-will among the band, gave great uneasiness to their leaders. Catesby and Percy now brought up the rear, and kept a sharp look-out to check any further attempt at desertion.

Digby and Winter, being well acquainted with all the Catholic gentry in the neighbourhood, they proceeded to their different residences, and were uniformly coldly received, and in some cases dismissed with reproaches and menaces. In spite of all their efforts, too, repeated desertions took place; and long before they reached Alcester, their force was diminished by a dozen men. Not thinking it prudent to pass through the town, they struck into a lane on the right, and fording the Arrow near Ragley, skirted that extensive park, and crossing the hills near Weethly and Stoney Moreton, arrived in about an hour and a half, in a very jaded condition, at Huddington, the seat of Robert Winter. Affairs seemed to wear so unpromising an aspect, that Catesby, on entering the house, immediately called a council of his friends, and asked them what they proposed to do.

"For my own part," he said, "I am resolved to fight it out. I will continue my march as long as I can get a man to follow me, and when they are all gone, will proceed alone. But I will never yield."

"We will all die together, if need be," said Sir Everard

Digby. "Let us rest here to-night, and in the morning proceed to Lord Windsor's mansion, Hewel Grange, which I know to be well stocked with arms, and, after carrying off all we can, we will fortify Stephen Littleton's house at Holbeach, and maintain it for a few days against our enemies."

This proposal agreed to, they repaired to the court-yard, and busied themselves in seeing the wants of their followers attended to; and such a change was effected by good fare and a few hours' repose, that the spirits of the whole party revived, and confidence was once more restored. A slight damp, however, was again thrown upon the satisfaction of the leaders, by the return of Thomas Winter and Stephen Littleton from Grafton. Their mission had proved wholly unsuccessful. Mr. Talbot had not merely refused to join them, but had threatened to detain them.

"He says we deserve the worst of deaths," observed Thomas Winter, in conclusion, "and that we have irretrievably injured the Catholic cause."

"And I begin to fear he speaks the truth," rejoined Christopher Wright. "However, for us there is no retreat."

"None whatever," rejoined Catesby, in a sombre tone. "We must choose between death upon the battle-field or on the scaffold."

"The former be my fate," cried Percy.

"And mine," added Catesby.

An anxious and perturbed night was passed by the conspirators, and many a plan was proposed and abandoned. It had been arranged among them that they should each in succession make the rounds of the place, to see that the sentinels were at their posts—strict orders having been given to the latter to fire upon whomsoever might attempt to fly— but as Catesby, despite his great previous fatigue, was unable to rest, he took this duty chiefly upon himself.

Returning at midnight from an examination of the court-yard, he was about to enter the house, when he perceived before him a tall figure, with a cloak muffled about its face, standing in his path. It was perfectly motionless, and Catesby, who carried a lantern in his hand, threw the light upon it, but it neither moved forward, nor altered its position. Catesby would have challenged it, but an undefinable terror seized him, and his tongue clove to the roof of his mouth. An idea rose to his mind that it was the spirit of Guy Fawkes, and, by a powerful effort, he compelled himself to address it.

" Are you come to warn me ?" he demanded.

The figure moved in acquiescence, and withdrawing the cloak, revealed features of ghastly paleness, but resembling those of Fawkes.

" Have I long to live ?" demanded Catesby.

The figure shook its head.

" Shall I fall to-morrow ?" pursued Catesby.

The figure again made a gesture in the negative.

" The next day ?"

Solemnly inclining its head, the figure once more muffled its ghastly visage in its cloak, and melted from his view.

For some time Catesby remained in a state almost of stupefaction. He then summoned up all the resolution of his nature, and instead of returning to the house, continued to pace to and fro in the court, and at last walked forth into the garden. It was profoundly dark; and he had not advanced many steps when he suddenly encountered a man. Repressing the exclamation that rose to his lips, he drew a petronel from his belt, and waited till the person addressed him.

" Is it you, Sir John Foliot ?" asked a voice, which he instantly recognised as that of Topcliffe.

" Ay," replied Catesby, in a low tone.

" Did you manage to get into the house ?" pursued Topcliffe.

" I did," returned Catesby; " but speak lower. There is a sentinel within a few paces of us. Come this way."

And grasping the other's arm he drew him further down the walk.

" Do you think we may venture to surprise them ?" demanded Topcliffe.

" Hum !" exclaimed Catesby, hesitating, in the hope of inducing the other to betray his design.

" Or shall we wait the arrival of Sir Richard Walsh, the Sheriff of Worcestershire, and the *posse comitatûs* ?" pursued Topcliffe.

" How soon do you think the sheriff will arrive ?" asked Catesby, scarcely able to disguise his anxiety.

" He cannot be here before daybreak, if so soon," returned Topcliffe, " and then we shall have to besiege the house; and though I have no fear of the result, yet some of the conspirators may fall in the skirmish; and my orders from the Earl of Salisbury, as I have already apprised you, are, to take them alive."

"True," replied Catesby.

"I would not, for twice the reward I shall receive for the capture of the whole party, that that desperate traitor, Catesby, should be slain," continued Topcliffe. "The plot was contrived by him, and the extent of its ramifications can alone be ascertained through him."

"I think I can contrive their capture," observed Catesby; "but the utmost caution must be used. I will return to the house, and find out where the chief conspirators are lodged. I will then throw open the door, and will return to this place, where you can have our men assembled. If we can seize and secure the leaders, the rest will be easy."

"You will run great risk, Sir John," said Topcliffe, with affected concern.

"Heed not that," replied Catesby. "You may expect me in a few minutes. Get together your men as noiselessly as you can."

With this he hastily withdrew.

On returning to the house, he instantly roused his companions, and acquainted them with what had occurred.

"My object," he said, "is to make Topcliffe a prisoner. We may obtain much useful information from him. As to the others, if they offer resistance, we will put them to death."

"What force have they?" asked Sir Everard Digby, with some uneasiness.

"It is impossible to say precisely," replied Catesby; "but not more than a handful of men, I should imagine, as they are waiting for Sir Richard Walsh."

"I know not what may be the issue of this matter," observed Robert Winter, whose looks were unusually haggard; "but I have had a strange and ominous dream, which fills me with apprehension."

"Indeed!" exclaimed Catesby, upon whose mind the recollection of the apparition he had beheld rushed."

"Catesby," pursued Robert Winter, taking him aside, "if you have any sin unrepented of, I counsel you to make your peace with Heaven, for I fear you are not long for this world."

"It may be so," rejoined Catesby, firmly; "and I have many dark and damning sins upon my soul, but I will die as I have lived, firm and unshaken to the last. And now, let us prepare for our foes."

So saying, he proceeded to call up the trustiest of his men, and enjoining profound silence upon them, disposed them in various places, that they might instantly appear at his signal. After giving them other directions, he returned to the garden, and coughed slightly. He was answered by a quickly-approaching footstep, and a voice demanded:

"Are you there, Sir John?"

Catesby answered in a low tone in the affirmative.

"Come forward, then," rejoined Topcliffe.

As he spoke there was a rush of persons towards the spot, and seizing Catesby, he cried, in a triumphant tone, while he unmasked a lantern, and threw its light full upon his face:

"You are caught in your own trap, Mr. Catesby. You are my prisoner."

"Not so, villain," cried Catesby, disengaging himself by a powerful effort.

Springing backwards, he drew his sword, and making the blade describe a circle round his body, effected his retreat in safety, though a dozen shots were fired at him. Leaping the garden wall, he was instantly surrounded by the other conspirators, and the greater part of the band, who, hearing the reports of the fire-arms, had hurried to the spot. Instantly putting himself at their head, Catesby returned to the garden; but Topcliffe and his party had taken the alarm and fled. Torches were brought, and, by Catesby's directions, a large heap of dry stubble was set on fire. But, though the flames revealed every object for a considerable distance around them, no traces of the hostile party could be discerned.

After continuing their ineffectual search for some time, the conspirators returned to the house, and abandoning all idea of retiring to rest, kept strict watch during the remainder of the night. Little conversation took place. All were deeply depressed; and Catesby paced backwards and forwards within a passage leading from the hall to the dining-chamber. His thoughts were gloomy enough, and he retraced the whole of his wild and turbulent career, pondering upon its close, which he could not disguise from himself was at hand.

"It matters not," he mentally ejaculated; "I shall not die ignominiously; and I would rather perish in the vigour of manhood than linger out a miserable old age. I have striven hard to achieve a great enterprise, and having failed, have little else to live for. This band cannot hold together two days longer. Our men will desert us, or turn upon us to obtain the price set upon our heads. And, were they true, I have little reliance upon my companions. They have no longer the confidence that can alone insure success, and I expect each moment some one will propose a surrender. Surrender! I will never do so with life. Something must be done—something worthy of me—and then let me perish. I have ever prayed to die a soldier's death."

As he uttered these words unconsciously aloud, he became aware of the presence of Robert Winter, who stood at the end of the passage, watching him.

"Your prayer will not be granted, Catesby," said the latter. "Some dreadful doom, I fear, is reserved for you and all of us."

"What mean you?" demanded the other, uneasily.

"Listen to me," replied Robert Winter. "I told you I had a strange and appalling dream to-night, and I will now relate it. I thought I was in a boat upon the river Thames, when all at once the day, which had been bright and smiling, became dark and overcast—not dark like the shades of night, but gloomy and ominous, as when the sun is shrouded by an eclipse. I looked around, and every object was altered. The tower of Saint Paul's stood awry, and seemed ready to topple down,—so did the spires and towers of all the surrounding fanes. The houses on London Bridge leaned frightfully over the river, and the habitations lining its banks on either side seemed shaken to their foundations. I fancied some terrible earthquake must have occurred, or that the end of the world was at hand."

"Go on," said Catesby, who had listened with profound attention to the relation.

"The stream, too, changed its colour," continued Robert Winter, "and became red as blood, and the man who rowed my boat was gone, and his place occupied by a figure masked and habited like an executioner. I commanded him to row me ashore, and in an instant the bark shot to land, and I sprang out, glad to be liberated from my mysterious conductor. My steps involuntarily led me towards the cathedral, and on entering it I found its pillars, shrines, monuments, and roof hung with black. The throng that ever haunt Paul's Walk had disappeared, and a few dismal figures alone traversed the aisles. On approaching them, I recognised in their swollen, death-like, and blackened lineaments, some resemblance to you and our friends. I was about to interrogate them, when I was awakened by yourself."

"A strange dream, truly," observed Catesby, musingly,

"and coupled with what I myself have seen to-night, would seem to bode evil."

And he then proceeded to describe the supernatural appearance he had beheld to his companion.

"All is over with us," rejoined Robert Winter. "We must prepare to meet our fate."

"We must meet it like men—like brave men, Robert," replied Catesby. "We must not disgrace ourselves and our cause."

"You are right," rejoined Robert Winter; "but these visions are more terrible than the contemplation of death itself."

"If you require further rest, take it," returned Catesby. "In an hour I shall call up our men, and march to Hewel Grange."

"I am wearied enough," replied Robert Winter, "but I dare not close my eyes again."

"Then recommend your soul to Heaven," said Catesby. "I would be alone. Melancholy thoughts press upon me, and I desire to unburthen my heart to God."

Robert Winter then left him, and he withdrew into a closet where there was an image of the Virgin, and kneeling before it, prayed long and fervently. Arising in a calmer frame of mind, he returned to the hall, and summoning his companions and followers, their horses were brought forth, and they commenced their march.

It was about four o'clock when they started, and so dark that they had some difficulty in finding the road. They proceeded at a slow pace, and with the utmost caution; but notwithstanding this, and though the two Winters and Grant, who were well acquainted with the country, led the way, many trifling delays and disasters occurred. Their baggage-cart frequently stuck fast in the deep ruts, while the men, missing their way, got into the trenches skirting the lane, and were not unfrequently thrown from their horses. More than once, too, the alarm was given that they were pursued, and a sudden halt ordered; but these apprehensions proved groundless, and after a most fatiguing ride, they found themselves at Stoke Prior, and within two miles of Hewel Grange.

Originally built in the early part of the reign of Henry the Eighth, and granted by that monarch to an ancestor of its present possessor, Lord Windsor, this ancient mansion was quadrangular in form, and surrounded by a broad, deep fosse.

Situated in the heart of an extensive park, at the foot of a gentle hill, it was now approached from the brow of the latter beautiful eminence by the rebel party. But at this season, and at this hour, both park and mansion had a forlorn look. The weather still continued foggy, with drizzling showers; and though the trees were not yet entirely stripped of their foliage, their glories had altogether departed. The turf was damp and plashy, and in some places partook so much of the character of a swamp that the horsemen were obliged to alter their course.

But all obstacles were eventually overcome, and in ten minutes after their entrance into the park they were within gunshot of the mansion. There were no symptoms of defence apparent; but the drawbridge being raised, it was Catesby's opinion, notwithstanding appearances, that their arrival was expected. He was further confirmed in this idea when, sounding a trumpet, and calling to the porter to let down the drawbridge, no answer was returned.

The entrance to the mansion was through a lofty and machiolated gateway, strengthened at each side by an embattled turret. Perceiving a man at one of the loopholes, Catesby discharged his petronel at him, and it was evident from the cry that followed that the person was wounded. An instant afterwards calivers were thrust through the other loopholes, and several shots fired upon the rebels, while some dozen armed men appeared upon the summit of the tower, and likewise commenced firing.

Perceiving Topcliffe among the latter, and enraged at the sight, Catesby discharged another petronel at him, but without effect. He then called to some of his men to break down the door of an adjoining barn, and to place it in the moat. The order was instantly obeyed, and the door afloat in the fosse, and springing upon it, he impelled himself with a pike towards the opposite bank. Several shots were fired at him, and though more than one struck the door, he crossed the moat uninjured. So suddenly was this daring passage effected that before any of the defenders of the mansion could prevent him, Catesby had severed the links of the chain fastening the drawbridge, and it fell clattering down.

With a loud shout, his companions then crossed it. But they had still a difficulty to encounter. The gates, which were of great strength, and covered with plates of iron, were barred. But a ladder having been found in the barn, it was brought forward, and Catesby mounting it sword in hand, drove back all who opposed him, and got upon the wall. He was followed by Sir Everard Digby, Percy, and several others, and driving the royalists before them, they made their way down a flight of stone steps, and proceeding to the gateway, threw it open, and admitted the others. All this was the work of a few minutes.

Committing the ransacking of the mansion to Digby and Percy, and commanding a dozen men to follow him, Catesby entered a small arched doorway, and ascended a winding stone staircase in search of Topcliffe. His progress was opposed by the soldiers, but beating aside all opposition, he gained the roof. Topcliffe, however, was gone. Anticipating the result of the attack, he had let himself drop from the summit of the tower to the walls, and descending by the ladder, had made good his retreat.

Disarming the soldiers, Catesby then descended to the court-yard, where in a short time a large store of arms, consisting of corslets, demi-lances, pikes, calivers, and two falconets, were brought forth. These, together with a cask of powder, were placed in the baggage-waggon. Meanwhile, the larder and cellar had been explored, and provisions of all kinds, together with a barrel of mead, and another of strong ale, being found, they were distributed among the men.

While this took place, Catesby searched the mansion, and, partly by threats, partly by persuasion, induced about twenty persons to join them. This unlooked-for success so encouraged the conspirators, that their drooping spirits began to revive. Catesby appeared as much elated as the others, but at heart he was full of misgiving.

Soon afterwards the rebel party quitted Hewel Grange, taking with them every weapon they could find. The forced recruits were placed in the midst of the band, so that escape was impracticable.

IV.

HOLBEACH.

AVOIDING the high road, and traversing an unfrequented part of the country, the conspirators shaped their course towards Stourbridge. As they reached Forfield Green, they perceived a large party descending the hilly ground near Bromsgrove, and evidently in pursuit of them. An immediate halt was ordered, and, taking possession of a farm-house, they prepared for defence.

Seeing these preparations, their pursuers, who proved to be Sir Richard Walsh, the Sheriff of Worcestershire, Sir John Foliot, three gentlemen named Ketelbye, Salwaye, and Conyers, attended by a large posse of men, all tolerably well armed, drew up at some distance from the farm, and appeared to be consulting as to the prudence of making an attack. Topcliffe was with them; and Catesby, who reconnoitred their proceedings from a window of the dwelling, inferred from his gestures that he was against the assault. And so it proved. The royalist party remained where they were, and as one or two of their number occasionally disappeared, Catesby, judged, and correctly, that they were dispatched for a reinforcement.

Not willing to wait for this, he determined to continue his march, and, accordingly, formed his men into a close line, and bringing up the rear himself, they again set forward. Sir Richard Walsh and his party followed them, and whenever they were in a difficult part of the road, harassed them with sudden attack. In this way, several stragglers were cut off, and a few prisoners made. So exasperated did Catesby become by these annoyances, that, though desirous to push forward as fast as possible, he halted at the entrance of a common, and prepared for an engagement. But his purpose was defeated, for the royalist party took another course, nor did he see anything more of them for some time.

In about an hour the rebels arrived at the banks of the river Stour, not far from the little village of Churchill, and here, just as they were preparing to ford the stream, the sheriff and his followers again made their appearance. By this time, also, the forces of their opponents were considerably augmented, and as more than a third of their own party were engaged in crossing the stream, which was greatly swollen by the recent rains, and extremely dangerous, their position was one of no slight peril.

Nothing daunted, Catesby instantly drew up his men on the bank, and, after a short skirmish, drove away the enemy, and afterwards contrived to cross the river without much loss. He found, however, that the baggage-cart had got immersed in the stream, and it was feared that the powder would be damaged. They remained on the opposite bank for some time; but as their enemies did not attempt to follow them, they took the way to Holbeach, a large and strongly-built mansion, belonging, as has been already stated, to Stephen Littleton. Here they arrived without further molestation, and their first business was to put it into a complete state of defence.

After a long and anxious consultation, Sir Everard Digby quitted them, undertaking to return on the following day with succours. Stephen Littleton also disappeared on the same evening. His flight produced a strong impression on Catesby, and he besought the others not to abandon the good cause, but to stand by it, as he himself meant to do, to the last. They all earnestly assured him that they would do so except Robert Winter, who sat apart and took no share in their discourse.

Catesby then examined the powder that had been plunged in the water in crossing the Stour, and found it so much wetted as to be nearly useless. A sufficient stock of powder being of the utmost consequence to them, he caused all the contents of the barrel, not dissolved by the immersion, to be poured into a large platter, and proceeded to dry it before a fire which had been kindled in the hall. A bag of powder, which had likewise been slightly wetted, was also placed at what was considered a safe distance from the fire.

"Heaven grant this may prove more destructive to our enemies than the combustibles we placed in the mine beneath the Parliament House!" observed Percy.

"Heaven grant so, indeed!" rejoined Catesby with a moody smile. "They would call it retribution, were we to perish by the same means which we designed for others."

"Jest not on so serious a matter, Catesby," observed Robert Winter. "For my own part, I dread the sight of powder, and shall walk forth till you have dried this, and put it away."

"You are not going to leave us, like Stephen Littleton?" rejoined Catesby, suspiciously.

"I will go with him," said Christopher Wright; "so you need be under no apprehension."

Accordingly, he quitted the hall with Robert Winter, and they proceeded to the court-yard and were conversing together on the dismal prospects of the party, when a tremendous explosion took place. The roof of the building seemed rent in twain, and amidst a shower of tiles, plaster, bricks, and broken wood falling around, the bag of powder dropped untouched at their feet.

"Mother of mercy!" exclaimed Christopher Wright, picking it up. "Here is a providential occurrence. Had this exploded, we must all have been destroyed."

"Let us see what has happened," cried Robert Winter.

And, followed by Christopher Wright, he rushed towards the hall, and bursting open the door, beheld Catesby enveloped in a cloud of smoke, and pressing his hand to his face, which was scorched and blackened by the explosion. Rookwood was stretched on the floor in a state of insensibility, and it at first appeared that life was extinct. Percy was extinguishing the flames, which had caught his dress, and John Grant was similarly occupied.

"Those are the very faces I beheld in my dream," cried Robert Winter, gazing at them with affright. "It was a true warning."

Rushing up to Catesby, Christopher Wright clasped him in his arms, and extinguishing his flaming apparel, cried, "Wretch that I am! that I should live to see this day!"

"Be not alarmed!" gasped Catesby. "It is nothing—it was a mere accident."

"It is no accident, Catesby," replied Robert Winter. "Heaven is against us and our design."

And he quitted the room, and left the house. Nor did he return to it.

"I will pray for forgiveness!" cried John Grant, whose vision was so much injured by the explosion that he could as yet see nothing. And dragging himself before an image of the Virgin, he prayed aloud, acknowledging that the act he had designed was so bloody that it called for the vengeance of Heaven, and expressing his sincere repentance.

"No more of this," cried Catesby, staggering up to him, and snatching the image from him. "It was a mere accident, I tell you. We are all alive, and shall yet succeed."

On inquiry, Christopher Wright learnt that a blazing coal had shot out of the fire, and falling into the platter containing the powder, had occasioned the disastrous accident above described.

V.

THE CLOSE OF THE REBELLION.

UNABLE longer to endure the agony occasioned by his scorched visage, Catesby called for a bucket of water, and plunged his head into it. Somewhat relieved by the immersion, he turned to inquire after his fellow-sufferers. Rookwood having been carried into the open air, had by this time regained his consciousness; Percy was shockingly injured, his hair and eyebrows burnt, his skin blackened and swollen with unseemly blisters, and the sight of one eye entirely destroyed; while John Grant, though a degree less hurt than his companions, presented a grim and ghastly appearance. In fact, the four sufferers looked as if they had just escaped from some unearthly place of torment, and were doomed henceforth to bear the brand of Divine wrath on their countenances. Seeing the effect produced on the others, Catesby rallied all his force, and treating the accident as a matter of no moment, and which ought not to disturb the equanimity of brave men, called for wine, and quaffed a full goblet. Injured as he was, and smarting with pain, Percy followed his example, but both John Grant and Rookwood refused the cup.

"Hark'e, gentlemen," cried Catesby, fiercely, "you may drink or not, as you see fit; but I will not have you assume a deportment calculated to depress our followers. Stephen Littleton and Robert Winter have basely deserted us. If you have any intention of following them, go at once. We are better without you than with you."

"I have no thought of deserting you, Catesby," rejoined Rookwood, mournfully; "and when the time arrives for action, you will find I shall not be idle. But I am now assured that we have sold ourselves to perdition."

"Pshaw!" cried Catesby, with a laugh that communicated an almost fiendish expression to his grim features; "because a little powder has accidentally exploded and blackened our faces, are we to see in the occurrence the retributive justice of Heaven? Are we to be cast down by such a trifle? Be a man, and rouse yourself. Recollect that the eyes of all England are upon us; and if we must fall, let us perish in a manner that becomes us. No real mischief has been done. My hand is as able to wield a blade, and my sight to direct a shot, as heretofore. If Heaven had meant to destroy us, the bag of powder which has been taken up in the yard, and which was sufficient not only to annihilate us, but to lay this house in ruins, would have been suffered to explode."

"Would it *had* exploded!" exclaimed John Wright. "All would then have been over."

"Are you, too, fainthearted, John?" cried Catesby. "Well, well, leave me, one and all of you. I will fight it out alone."

"You wrong me by the suspicion, Catesby," returned John Wright. "I am as true to the cause as yourself. But I perceive that our last hour is at hand, and I would it were past."

"The indulgence of such a wish at such a moment is a weakness," rejoined Catesby. "I care not when death comes, provided it comes gloriously; and such should be your feeling. On the manner in which we meet our fate will depend the effect which our insurrection will produce throughout the country. We must set a brave example to our brethren. Heaven be praised, we shall not perish on the scaffold!"

"Be not too sure of that," said Grant, gloomily. "It may yet be our fate."

"It shall never be mine," cried Catesby.

"Nor mine," added Percy. "I am so far from regarding the recent disaster as a punishment, though I am the severest sufferer by it, that I think we ought to return thanks to Heaven for our preservation."

"In whatever light the accident is viewed," observed John Wright, "we cannot too soon address ourselves to Heaven. We know not how long it may be in our power to do so."

"Again desponding," cried Catesby. "But no matter. You will recover your spirits anon."

John Wright shook his head, and Catesby, pulling his hat over his brows to hide his features, walked forth into the court-yard. He found, as he expected, that general consternation prevailed amongst the band. The men were gathered together in little knots, and, though they became silent as he approached, he perceived they were discussing the necessity of a surrender. Nothing daunted by these unfavourable appearances, Catesby harangued them in such bold terms that he soon inspired them with some of his own confidence, and completely resteadied their wavering feelings.

Elated with his success, he caused a cup of strong ale to be given to each man, and proposed as a pledge, "The restoration of the Romish Church." He then returned to the house;

z

and summoning the other conspirators to attend him in a chamber on the ground-floor, they all prayed long and fervently, and concluded by administering the sacrament to each other.

It was now thought necessary to have the damage done by the explosion repaired, and a few hours were employed in the operation. Evening was fast approaching, and Catesby, who was anxiously expecting the return of Sir Everard Digby, stationed himself on the turreted walls of the mansion to look out for him. But he came not; and, fearing some mischance must have befallen him, Catesby descended. Desirous of concealing his misgivings from his companions, he put on a cheerful manner as he joined them.

"I am surprised ere this that we have not been attacked," remarked Percy. "Our enemies may be waiting for the darkness, to take us by surprise. But they will be disappointed."

"I can only account for the delay by supposing they have encountered Sir Everard Digby, and the force he is bringing to us," remarked Christopher Wright.

"It may be so," returned Catesby, "and if so, we shall soon learn the result."

In spite of all Catesby's efforts, he failed to engage his companions in conversation; and feeling it would best suit his present frame of mind, and contribute most to their safety, to keep in constant motion, he proceeded to the courtyard, saw that all the defences were secure, that the drawbridge was raised, the sentinels at their posts, and everything prepared for the anticipated attack. Every half hour he thus made his rounds, and when towards midnight he was going forth, Percy said to him:

"Do you not mean to take any rest, Catesby?"

"Not till I am in my grave," was the moody reply.

Catesby's untiring energy was in fact a marvel to all his followers. His iron frame seemed wholly unsusceptible of fatigue; and even when he returned to the house, he continued to pace to and fro in the passage in preference to lying down.

"Rest tranquilly," he said to Christopher Wright, who offered to take his place. "I will rouse you on the slightest approach of danger." But though he preserved this stoical exterior, Catesby's breast was torn by the keenest pangs. He could not hide from himself that, to serve his own ambitious purposes, he had involved many loyal and worthy (till he had deluded them) persons in a treasonable project, which must now terminate in their destruction; and their blood, he feared, would rest upon his head. But what weighed heaviest of all upon his soul was the probable fate of Viviana.

"If I were assured she would escape," he thought, "I should care little for all the rest, even for Fawkes. They say it is never too late to repent; but my repentance shall lie between my Maker and myself. Man shall never know it."

The night was dark, and the gloom was rendered more profound by a dense fog. Fearing an attack might now be attempted, Catesby renewed his vigilance. Marching round the edge of the moat, he listened to every sound that might betray the approach of a foe. For some time nothing occurred to excite his suspicions, until about an hour after midnight, as he was standing at the back of the house, he fancied he detected a stealthy tread on the other side of the fosse, and soon became convinced that a party of men were there. Determined to ascertain their movements before giving the alarm, he held his breath, and drawing a petronel, remained perfectly motionless. Presently, though he could discern no object, he distinctly heard a plank pushed across the moat, and could distinguish in the whispered accents of one of the party the voice of Topcliffe. A thrill of savage joy agitated his bosom, and he internally congratulated himself that revenge was in his power.

A footstep, though so noiseless as to be inaudible to any ear less acute than his own, was now heard crossing the plank, and feeling certain it was Topcliffe, Catesby allowed him to land, and then suddenly advancing, kicked the plank, on which were two other persons, into the water, and unmasking a dark lantern, threw its light upon the face of a man near him, who proved, as he suspected, to be Topcliffe.

Aware of the advantage of making a prisoner of importance, Catesby controlled the impulse that prompted him to sacrifice Topcliffe to his vengeance, and firing his petronel in the air as a signal, he drew his sword, and sprang upon him. Topcliffe attempted to defend himself, but he was no match for the skill and impetuosity of Catesby, and was instantly overpowered and thrown to the ground. By this time Percy and several of the band had come up, and delivering Topcliffe to the charge of two of the stoutest of them, Catesby turned his attention to the other assailants. One of them got across the moat; but the other, encumbered by

his arms, was floundering about, when Catesby pointing a
petronel at his head, he was fain to surrender, and was
dragged out.

A volley of musketry was now fired by the rebels in the
supposed direction of their opponents, but it could not be
ascertained what execution was done. After waiting for
some time in expectation of a further attack, Catesby placed
a guard upon the spot, and proceeded to examine Topcliffe.
He had been thrown into a cellar beneath the kitchen, and
the two men were on guard over him. He refused to answer
any of Catesby's questions, though enforced by threats of
instant death. On searching him some letters were found
upon him, and thrusting them into his doublet, Catesby left
him, with the strictest injunctions to the men as to his safe
custody.

He then proceeded to examine the other captive, and found
him somewhat more tractable. This man informed him that
Topcliffe had intended to steal into the house with the design
of capturing the conspirators, or, failing in that, of setting
fire to the premises. He also ascertained that Topcliffe's
force consisted only of a dozen men, so that no further
attack need be apprehended.

Notwithstanding this information, Catesby determined to
be on the safe side, and doubling the sentinels, he stationed
one of the conspirators, all of whom had sprung to arms at
his signal, at each of the exposed points. He then withdrew to the mansion, and examined Topcliffe's papers. The
first despatch he opened was from the Earl of Salisbury,
bearing date about the early part of Fawkes's confinement
in the Tower, in which the Earl expressed his determination
of wringing a full confession from the prisoner. A bitter
smile curled Catesby's lip as he read this, but his brow
darkened as he proceeded, and found that a magnificent
reward was offered for his own arrest.

"I must have Catesby captured," ran the missive,—"so
see you spare no pains to take him. I would rather all
escaped than he did. His confession is of the last importance
in the matter, and I rely upon your bringing him to me
alive."

"I will at least balk him of that satisfaction," muttered
Catesby. "But what is this of Viviana?"

Reading further, he found that the Earl had issued the
same orders respecting Viviana, and that she would be
rigorously dealt with if captured,

"Alas !" groaned Catesby ; " I hope she will escape these in-
human butchers."

The next despatch he opened was from Tresham, and with
a savage satisfaction he found that the traitor was apprehensive of double-dealing on the part of Salisbury and Mounteagle. He stated that he had been put under arrest, and
was detained a prisoner in his own house ; and fearing he
should be sent to the Tower, besought Topcliffe to use his
influence with the Earl of Salisbury not to deal unfairly with
him.

" He is rightly served !" cried Catesby, with a bitter smile ;
"Heaven grant they may deal with him as he dealt with us !"

The consideration of these letters furnished Catesby with
food for much bitter reflection. Pacing the room to and fro
with uncertain footsteps, he remained more than an hour by
himself, and at last yielding to the promptings of vengeance,
repaired to the cellar in which he had placed Topcliffe, with
the intention of putting him to death. What was his rage
and mortification to find both the guard and the prisoner
gone ! A door was open, and it was evident that the fugitives had stolen to the moat, and, swimming noiselessly
across it in the darkness, had securely effected their retreat.

Fearful of exciting the alarm of his followers, Catesby controlled his indignation, and said nothing of the escape of the
prisoner to any but his confederates, who entirely approved
of the policy of silence. They continued on the alert during
the remainder of the night, and no one thought of seeking
repose till it was fully light, and all danger of a surprise at
an end.

Day dawned late and dismally. The fog that had hung
round the mansion changed just before daybreak into
drizzling rain, and this increased ere long to heavy and
drenching showers. Everything looked gloomy and depress-
ing, and the conspirators were so disheartened, that they
avoided each other's regards.

Catesby mounted the walls of the mansion to reconnoitre.

The prospect was forlorn and melancholy to the last
degree. The neighbouring woods were obscured by mist ;
the court-yard and garden flooded with rain ; and the waters
of the moat spotted by the heavy shower. Not an object
was in view, except a hind driving cattle to a neighbouring
farm. Catesby shouted to him, and the fellow with evident
reluctance approaching the brink of the moat, was asked

whether he had seen any troops in the neighbourhood. The man answered in the negative, but said he had heard that an engagement had taken place in the night, about five miles from thence, near Hales Owen, between Sir Everard Digby and Sir Richard Walsh, and that Sir Everard's party had been utterly routed, and himself taken prisoner.

This intelligence was a severe blow to Catesby, as it destroyed the last faint hope he had clung to. For some time he contined wrapt in thought, and then descended to the lower part of the house. A large fire had been kept up during the night in the hall, and the greater part of the band were now gathered round it, drying their wet clothes and conversing together. A plentiful breakfast had been served out to them, so that they were in tolerably good spirits, and many of them talked loudly of the feats they meant to perform in case of an attack.

Catesby heard these boasts, but they fell upon an idle ear. He felt that all was over; that his last chance was gone; and that the struggle could not be much longer protracted. Entering the inner room, he sat down at table with his companions, but he ate nothing, and continued silent and abstracted.

"It is now my turn to reproach you," observed Grant. "You look deeply depressed."

"Sir Everard Digby is a prisoner," replied Catesby, sternly. "His capture grieves me sorely. He should have died with us."

All echoed the wish.

Catesby arose and closed the door.

"The attack will not be many hours delayed," he said; "and unless there should be some miraculous interposition in our behalf, it must end in our defeat. Do not let us survive it," he continued earnestly. "Let us swear to stand by each other as long as we can, and to die together."

"Agreed!" cried the others.

"And now," continued Catesby, "I must compel myself to take some nourishment, for I have much to do."

Having swallowed a few mouthfuls of bread and drained a goblet of wine, he again visited every part of the habitation, examined the arms of the men, encouraged them by his looks and words, and became satisfied, unless some unlooked-for circumstance occurred to damp their ardour, they would offer a determined and vigorous resistance.

"If I could only come off victorious in this last conflict, I should die content," thought Catesby. "And I do not despair of it."

The rain continued till eleven o'clock, when it ceased, and the mist that had attended it partially cleared off. About noon, Catesby, who was on the look-out from the walls of the mansion, descried a large troop of horsemen issuing from the wood. He immediately gave the alarm. The bell was rung, and all sprang to arms.

By this time the troop had advanced to within a hundred yards of the house, and Catesby, who had rushed into the court-yard, mounted a turret near the gate to watch their movements and issue his commands. The royalists were headed by Sir Richard Walsh, who was attended on the right by Sir John Foliot, and on the left by Topcliffe. Immediately behind them were Ketelbye, Salwaye, Conyers, and others who had accompanied the *posse comitatûs* the day before. A trumpet was then sounded, and a proclamation made in a loud voice by a trooper, commanding the rebels in the King's name to surrender, and to deliver up their leaders. The man had scarcely concluded his speech when he was for ever silenced by a shot from Catesby.

A loud and vindictive shout was raised by the royalists, and the assault instantly commenced. Sir Richard Walsh directed the attack against the point opposite the drawbridge, while Sir John Foliot, Topcliffe, and the others dispersed themselves, and completely surrounded the mansion. Several planks were thrust across the moat, and in spite of the efforts of the rebels many of the assailants effected a passage.

Catesby drove back the party under Sir Richard Walsh, and with his own hand hewed asunder their plank. In doing this he so much exposed himself that, but for the injunctions of the sheriff, who commanded his followers not to fire upon him, he must have been slain.

The other rebel-leaders displayed equal courage and equal indifference to danger, and though, as has just been stated, a considerable number of the royalists had got across the moat and entered the garden, they had obtained no material advantage. Sir John Foliot and Topcliffe commanded this party, and encouraged them to press on. But such a continued and well-directed firing was kept up upon them from the walls and windows of the mansion, that they soon began to show symptoms of wavering.

At this juncture, and while Topcliffe was trying to keep

his men together, a concealed door in the wall was opened, and Catesby issued from it at the head of a dozen men. He instantly attacked Topcliffe and his band, put several to the sword, and drove those who resisted into the moat. Foliot and Topcliffe with difficulty escaped across the plank, which was seized and pulled over to his own side by Catesby.

But the hope which this success inspired was instantly crushed. Loud shouts were raised from the opposite wing of the mansion, and Catesby to his great dismay perceived from the volumes of smoke ascending from it that it was on fire. Uttering an exclamation of rage and despair, he commanded those with him not to quit their present position, and set off in the direction of the fire.

He found that an outbuilding had been set in flames by a lighted brand thrown across the moat by a trooper. The author of the action was named John Streete, and was afterwards rendered notorious by another feat to be presently related. Efforts were made to extinguish the conflagration, but such was the confusion prevailing that it was found wholly impossible to do so, and it was feared that the destruction of the whole mansion would ensue.

Disaster after disaster followed. Another party had crossed the moat, and burst into the court-yard. In the desperate conflict that ensued, Rookwood was shot through the arm, and severely wounded by a pike, and was borne into the house by one of his followers, whom he entreated to kill him outright, but his request was refused.

Meantime, the drawbridge was lowered, and with loud and exulting shouts the great body of the royalists crossed it. Catesby now perceived that the day was irretrievably lost. Calling to Christopher Wright, who was standing near him, to follow him, and rushing towards the court-yard, he reached it just as the royalists gained an entrance.

In numbers both parties were pretty well matched; but the rebels were now thoroughly disheartened, and seeing how matters must end, many of them threw down their arms, and begged for mercy. A destructive fire, however, was still kept up on the royalists by a few of the rebels stationed on the walls of the mansion, under the command of John Wright.

Putting himself at the head of a few faithful followers, Catesby fought with all the fury of despair. Christopher Wright was shot by his side. Grant instantly sprang forward, but was cut down by a trooper. Catesby was too busily occupied to attend to the fate of his companions, but seeing Thomas Winter near him, called to him to come on.

"I can fight no longer," said Thomas Winter. "My right arm is disabled by a bolt from a cross-bow."

"Then die," cried Catesby.

"He *shall* die—on the scaffold," rejoined Topcliffe, who had heard the exclamation. And rushing up to Thomas Winter, he seized him, and conveyed him to the rear of his party.

Catesby continued to fight with such determined bravery that Sir Richard Walsh, seeing it would be vain to take him alive, withdrew his restrictions from his men, and ordered them to slay him.

By this time most of the rebels had thrown down their arms. Those on the walls had been dislodged, and John Wright, refusing to yield, was slaughtered. Catesby, however, having been joined by Percy and half a dozen men, made a last desperate charge upon his opponents.

In doing this, his sword shivered, and he would have fallen back, but found himself surrounded. Percy was close behind him, and keeping together, they fought back to back. Even in this disabled state, they made a long and desperate resistance.

"Remember your oath, Percy," cried Catesby. "You have sworn not to be taken to the scaffold."

"Fear nothing," replied Percy. "I will never quit this spot alive."

The words were scarcely out of his mouth when he fell to the ground mortally wounded, and the same shot that had pierced his breast had likewise stricken Catesby. It was fired by the trooper, John Streete, who has just been mentioned.

Collecting all his force, Catesby struck a few terrible blows at his opponents, and, dashing through them, made for the house. Just as he reached the door, which was standing open, his strength failed, and he fell to the ground. In this condition he dragged himself into the vestibule, where there was a large wooden statue of the Virgin, and clasping his arms around it, pressed his lips to the feet of the image. He was followed by Streete, with his drawn sword in one hand, and a petronel in the other, prepared to finish his work. But ere he could reach him, Catesby had expired.

"So," exclaimed Topcliffe, who came up the next moment, with Sir Richard Walsh, "we have been robbed of our prey. The Earl of Salisbury will never forgive me for this disappointment."

"I am glad I have done it, though," observed Streete. "To kill two such traitors with one shot is something to talk of."

"You will be well rewarded for it, no doubt," remarked Topcliffe, sarcastically.

"I care not whether I am or not," rejoined Streete. "I have done my duty, and besides I have avenged my comrade, Richard Trueman, who was shot by this traitor when he read the proclamation."

"I will take care that your brave action is duly represented to his Majesty," observed Sir Richard Walsh.

And he failed not to keep his promise. Streete received a pension of two shillings a day for the rest of his life—no inconsiderable sum in those days.

The conflict was now at an end, for though some few of the more desperate of the rebels continued to struggle after their leaders had fallen, they were soon disarmed. Sir Richard Walsh and Topcliffe went in search of the other conspirators, and finding Rookwood and Grant, who, though severely wounded, were not dead, lying in the hall, immediately secured them. Rookwood on their approach made an effort to plunge his dagger into his breast, but his hand was stayed by Sir Richard Walsh.

"We shall not go away quite empty-handed," cried Topcliffe. "But these are sorry substitutes for Catesby."

"Has Catesby escaped?" demanded Grant, faintly.

"Ay, to the other world," replied Topcliffe.

"He has kept his word," groaned Grant.

"He may have escaped some part of his punishment," said Topcliffe, bitterly; "but the worst remains. His quarters will be exposed on every gate in London, and his head on the bridge. As to you, traitors, you know your doom."

"And are prepared for it," rejoined Grant.

A guard being left over the prisoners, Sir Richard Walsh and Topcliffe then went to see that the other captives were properly secured. Some few having made their escape into the adjoining fields, they were pursued and recaptured.

The whole of the prisoners were then conveyed to Stourbridge, where they were lodged in the jail, after which Sir Richard Walsh despatched a messenger to the Earl of Salisbury and the Lords of the Council acquainting them with what he had done.

VI.

HAGLEY.

ROBERT WINTER, it may be remembered, immediately after the explosion, quitted Holbeach, and did not return to it. He proceeded to the neighbouring thicket, and while wandering about in a state bordering on distraction encountered Stephen Littleton, who had likewise deserted his companions on the same day. Acquainting him with the disastrous occurrence that had taken place, and stating his impression that both God and man were against them, and that it would be vain as well as impious to struggle longer, he proposed to him to surrender. But Stephen Littleton so strongly combated this opinion, that he at last consented to make an effort to escape. This, however, was no easy matter, nor could they devise a plan that appeared feasible. Both were well provided with money; but under present circumstances it would be of little use to them. A large price being set on their heads, and the whole country alarmed, they scarcely knew where to seek shelter. After a long debate, they quitted the covert, and keeping clear of all habitations, took the direction of Stourbridge.

On approaching the Stour, at a point opposite Churchill, where they knew the river was fordable, they perceived Sir Richard Walsh's force approaching, and threw themselves into a ditch to avoid observation. It was quite dark when they again ventured forth, and at the peril of their lives they forded the Stour, which was swollen more than it had been in the morning by the long continued rain. Their design was to proceed to Hagley, the residence of Stephen Littleton's sister, Mrs. Littleton, and to claim her protection. This magnificent mansion lay about two miles on the other side of the river, in the heart of an extensive park, but they were obliged to take a circuitous route of nearly double the distance to reach it, and when at length they arrived there, and were about to steal into the court-yard, they found it occupied by a portion of Sir Richard Walsh's troop.

Overcome by anxiety and fatigue, and scarcely knowing whither to proceed, they recrossed the park, and sought out the cottage of a poor woman, whose two sons had joined their ill-fated expedition, and were at that moment under arms at Holbeach. She was a good Catholic, and they thought they might confide in her. Arriving at her cottage, they glanced in at the window, and perceiving her, as they concluded, alone, and cooking a small piece of meat at the fire, they raised the latch and entered the house. The woman turned at their approach, and uttering a cry of surprise and alarm, pointed towards a back room. They then saw that they had betrayed themselves; but the caution came too late, and a stalwart trooper, alarmed by the cry, issued from the back room. From the wretched appearance of the new-comers, he at once guessed that they were rebels, and felt satisfied, from the richness of their apparel, dirtied and stained as it was, that they were persons of consequence. Accordingly, he drew a brace of petronels, and holding them at their heads, commanded them to surrender.

They were too much taken by surprise, and too enfeebled to offer resistance, and the trooper calling to the old woman to bring a cord to bind them, at the same time unloosed his own girdle, with which he fastened Robert Winter's arms behind his back. In doing this he was compelled to lay down his petronels, and he had scarcely done so, when the woman snatched them up, and gave them to Stephen Littleton, who presented them at his head.

It was now the turn of the conspirators to triumph. In another instant, Robert Winter was released by the old woman, and the pair throwing themselves upon the trooper, forced him to the ground. They then dragged him to the back room, and stripped him of his habiliments, which Stephen Littleton put on instead of his own attire, and binding him hand and foot, returned to the old woman. At the request of Robert Winter, she furnished him with a suit of clothes belonging to one of her sons, and then set before them the best eatables she possessed. They were ravenously hungry, and soon disposed of the viands. Meanwhile, their hostess told them that the whole country was in arms against them; that Mrs. Littleton being suspected, though she had always been adverse to the design, her house had undergone a rigorous search; but that Mr. Humphrey Littleton, not having taken any part in the insurrection, had not as yet been arrested, though it was feared he would be proved to be connected with the plot. She concluded by strongly counselling them to use the utmost caution, and to expose themselves as little as possible. They assured her she need have no apprehension on that score, and expressed great anxiety as to what would befall her when they were gone.

"I do not desire to shed blood, if it can be helped," said

Stephen Littleton; but in a case of necessity like the present, where life must be weighed against life, I hold it lawful to shed it. Shall we put the trooper to death?"

"Not unless your own safety requires it, good sirs," she said. "I shall quit this cottage soon after you have left it, and obtain a safe asylum with one of my neighbours. It matters not what becomes of me. Having lost my two sons —for I consider them as already dead—I have nothing left to bind me to life."

Unable to make any reply, the conspirators remained for some time silent, when, by the poor woman's advice, they withdrew to an upper chamber, and stretching themselves on a bed, sought a few hours' repose. The old woman kept watch below, and they gave her one of the petronels, with strict injunctions to blow out the trooper's brains if he attempted to move. Nothing, however, occurred to alarm her, and at three o'clock she awakened them.

Offering the woman a handsome reward, which, however, she declined, they then set out; and shortly afterwards their hostess quitted her habitation, and withdrew to the cottage of a neighbour, where she remained concealed for some weeks, and then died of grief on learning that her sons had been slain during the assault of Holbeach by the royalists.

Recruited by the rest they had enjoyed, the conspirators pursued their course over the fields. The weather was the same as that which disheartened their confederates at Holbeach, and the rain fell so heavily that they had soon not a dry thread upon them. But being now disguised, they were not under so much apprehension of detection. Shaping their course towards Rowley Regis, in Staffordshire, which lay about five miles from Hagley, where a farmer named Pelborrow, a tenant of Humphrey Littleton, resided, and whom they thought would befriend them, they proceeded swiftly on their way; but, though well acquainted with the country, they were so bewildered and deceived by the fog, that they strayed materially out of their course, and when it grew light found themselves near Weoley Castle, and about four miles from Birmingham.

Confiding in their disguises, and in their power of sustaining the characters they assumed, they got into the high road, and approaching a farm-house, Stephen Littleton, who had tied his companion's arms behind him with his belt, represented himself as a trooper conveying a prisoner from Stourbridge to Birmingham, and in consequence of this obtained a breakfast from the farmer. After their meal was over, the host, who had eyed them suspiciously, observed to the supposed trooper:

"You will overtake some of your comrades before you reach Egbaston, and had better lose no time in joining them. You are known to me, my masters," he added, in a tone that could not be heard by the household; "but I will not betray you. Get you gone."

The conspirators did not fail to act upon the suggestion, and as soon as they got out of sight, struck across the country in the direction of Rowley Regis, and arrived at the farm-house, which was their destination, in about an hour.

Pelborrow chanced to be in a barn adjoining his house, and alone, and on seeing them readily offered to hide them. No one had noticed their approach, and carefully concealing them amid the hay in the loft, he proceeded about his business as if nothing had happened. He could not just then procure them provisions without exciting suspicion; but when night arrived brought them a sufficient supply for the next day.

In this way they passed nearly a week, never venturing to stir forth, for they had been traced to the neighbourhood, and constant search was going on after them. Pelborrow had great difficulty in keeping his men out of the barn, and the disappearance of the provisions excited the suspicions of his female domestics, who began to think all was not right. He therefore intimated to the conspirators that they must change their quarters, and, in the dead of the night, they removed to the house of another farmer named Perkes, residing on the borders of Hagley Park, to whom Pelborrow had confided the secret of their being in the neighbourhood, and who, on promise of a large reward, readily undertook to secrete them.

Perkes met them at a little distance from his house, and conducted them to a barley-mow, where he had contrived a hiding-place amid the straw for them. A woman-servant and a man were both let into the secret by Perkes, and a sum of money, given him for that purpose by the conspirators, bribed them to silence. Here they remained close prisoners, unable to stir forth, or even to change their habiliments for nearly six weeks, during which time they received constant intelligence from their protector of what was going forward, and learnt that the search for them had not relaxed. They were not without hope, however, that the worst was over, when an incident occurred that gave them serious uneasiness.

One night, Perkes, who was a stout, hale yeoman, and had formerly been warrener to Mrs. Littleton, went to catch conies, with a companion named Poynter, and returned laden with spoil. After drinking a cup or two of ale together, the pair separated, and Poynter feeling fatigued with his exertions, as well as drowsy with the liquor he had swallowed, determined to pass the night in his friend's barn, and entering it, clambered up to the loft, and laid himself in the straw. In doing this, he slipped into the hole made for the conspirators, who, aroused by his fall, instantly seized him. Terrified to death, and fancying he had fallen into the hands of gipsies or other plunderers, Poynter roared for mercy, which they were not at first disposed to show him ; but the poor wretch, finding into whose hands he had fallen, besought them in such piteous terms to spare his life, affirming with the strongest oaths that he would never betray them, that they consented to spare him, on condition of his remaining with them as long as they should occupy their place of concealment.

When Perkes appeared in the morning, he was not a little surprised at finding his comrade caught in such a trap, but entirely approved of the course taken by the conspirators. Poynter, as may be supposed, was no willing captive ; and being constantly pondering on the means of escape, and of obtaining the reward for the apprehension of the conspirators, at last hit upon the following expedient. While engaged in the poaching expedition with Perkes, he had received a slight wound in the leg, and the close confinement to which he was now subjected inflamed it to such a degree as to render it highly dangerous. This he represented to the conspirators, who, however, would not suffer him to depart ; but desired Perkes to bring him some ointment to dress his wound. The request was complied with, and feigning that it was necessary to approach the light to apply the salve, Poynter scrambled up the straw, apparently for that sole purpose. He did not attempt to fly for several days ; but at last, when they were grown less suspicious, he slided down the other side of the loft, and made good his retreat.

The conspirators saw the error they had committed when too late. Not daring to pursue him, they remained in fearful anticipation of an arrest throughout the day. But they were not disturbed until night, when Perkes made his appearance. They told him what had happened ; but he did not appear to be much alarmed.

"I do not think you need be afraid of him," he said. "Let me have some money, and I will go in quest of him at once, and bribe him to silence."

"Here are fifty marks," replied Stephen Littleton. "If that is not enough, take more."

"It will amply suffice," replied Perkes. "I will answer for his silence."

This assurance greatly relieved the conspirators, and they were made completely easy by the return of Perkes in less than an hour afterwards, who told them he had seen Poynter, and had given him the money, binding him by the most solemn oaths not to betray them.

"I have still better news for you, my masters," he added. "Mrs. Littleton has set out for London to-day; and I have received orders from Mr. Humphrey Littleton to bring you to the hall at midnight."

This last intelligence completed their satisfaction, and they awaited Perkes's return with impatience. Shortly before midnight, he came to summon them, and they set forth together. Perkes's house lay about a mile from the hall, and they soon entered the park. The night was clear and frosty, —it was now the middle of December,—and as the conspirators trod the crisp sod, and gazed at the noble but leafless trees around them, they silently returned thanks to Heaven for their restoration to freedom. Humphrey Littleton was waiting for them at the end of an avenue near the mansion, and tenderly embraced them.

Tears of joy were shed on both sides, and it seemed to Humphrey Littleton as if his brother had been restored from the grave. Dismissing Perkes with warm thanks, and promises of a further recompense, they then entered the house by a window, which had been left purposely open. Humphrey Littleton conducted them to his own chamber, where fresh apparel was provided for them; and to poor wretches who had not been able to put off their attire for so long a period, the luxury of the change was indescribably great.

The arrival of the fugitives was kept secret from all the household except the man-cook, John Ocklie, upon whose fidelity Humphrey Littleton thought he could rely. A good supper was prepared by this man, and brought up into his master's chamber, where the conspirators were now seated before a hearth heaped with blazing logs. The conspirators needed no solicitation to fall to, and they did ample justice to the good things before them. His spirits being raised by the good cheer, Robert Winter observed to the cook, who was in attendance upon them:

"Ah! Jack, thy mistress little thinks what guests are now in her house, who have neither seen fire nor tasted a hot morsel for well-nigh two months."

"Ay, it is a sad matter," returned the cook, shaking his head, "and I wish I could offer your worships a flask of wine, or a cup of stout ale at the least. But the butler is in bed, and if I were to rouse him at this hour it might excite his suspicion. If you are willing, sir," he added, to Humphrey Littleton, "I will hie to my mother's cottage in the park, and bring a jug of ale from her."

This was agreed to, and the cook left the house. His sole object, however, was to instruct his mother to give the alarm, so that the conspirators might be arrested before morning.

On reaching her cottage, he was surprised to see a light within it, and two men there, one of whom was Poynter, and the other Mrs. Littleton's steward, Robert Hazlewood. Poynter had acquainted Hazlewood with all he knew respecting the conspirators, supposing them still in the barley-mow, and they were discussing the best means of arresting them, when the cook entered the house.

"The birds are flown," he said, "as you will find, if you search the nest. But come to the hall with a sufficient force betimes to-morrow morning, and I will show you where to find them. I shall claim, however, my share of the reward, though I must not appear in the matter."

Having fully arranged their plan, he procured the ale from his mother, and returned to the hall. The conspirators soon disposed of the jug, threw themselves on a couch in the room, and instantly dropping asleep, enjoyed such repose as only falls to the lot of those who have similarly suffered. And it was well they did sleep soundly, for it was the last tranquil night they ever enjoyed!

Humphrey Littleton, who, as has been stated, reposed implicit confidence in the cook, had committed the key of the chamber to him, strictly enjoining him to call them in the morning; and the fellow, feeling secure of his prey, retired to rest.

About seven o'clock he burst suddenly into the room, and with a countenance of well-feigned alarm, which struck terror into the breasts of the conspirators, cried:

"Master Hazlewood and the officers are below, and say they must search the house. Poynter is with them."

"The villain has betrayed us!" cried Stephen Littleton. "Fools that we were to spare his life!"

"There is no use in lamenting your indiscretion now, sir," replied the cook; "leave it to me, and I will yet effect your escape."

"We place ourselves entirely in your hands," said Stephen Littleton.

"Go down-stairs, sir," said the cook to Humphrey Littleton, "and hold Master Hazlewood in conversation for a few minutes, and I will engage to get the gentlemen safely out of the house."

Humphrey Littleton obeyed, and descending to the steward, told him he was willing to conduct him to every room in the house.

"I am certain they are here, and shall not quit it till I find them," rejoined Hazlewood. "Ah!" he exclaimed, as if struck by a sudden thought, "you say they are not in the house. Perhaps they are in the garden—in the summer-house? We will go and see."

So saying, he took half a dozen of his men with him, leaving Poynter and the rest with Humphrey Littleton, who was perplexed and alarmed at his conduct.

Meanwhile, the cook led the two conspirators along the gallery, and from thence down a back staircase, which brought them to a small door communicating with the garden. A few seconds were lost in opening it, and when they issued forth they encountered Hazlewood and his men, who instantly arrested them. The unfortunate conspirators were conveyed under a strong guard to London, where they were committed to the Tower, to take their trial with their confederates.

VII.

VIVIANA'S LAST NIGHT AT ORDSALL HALL.

ON the evening of the third day after quitting Dunchurch, Viviana Radcliffe and her companions arrived at Ordsall Hall. They had encountered many dangers and difficulties on the journey, and were well-nigh overcome with fatigue and anxiety. Fearful of being detained, Garnet had avoided all the larger towns in the way, and had consequently been driven greatly out of the direct course. He had assumed the disguise which he usually wore when travelling, that of a lawyer, and, as he possessed great mimetic talent, he sustained the character admirably. Viviana passed for his daughter, and his servant, Nicholas Owen, who was almost as clever an actor as his master, represented his clerk, while the two attendants performed the parts of clients. At Abbots'-Bromley, where they halted for refreshment on the second day, having spent the night at a small village near Lichfield, they were detained by the landlord, who entertained some suspicions of them; but Garnet succeeded in frightening the man into allowing them to depart. They underwent another alarm of the same kind at Leek, and were for two hours locked up. But on the arrival of a magistrate, who had been sent for by the host, Garnet gave so plausible an account of himself that the party were instantly set at liberty, and arrived without further molestation at their journey's end.

Viviana's last visit to the Hall had been sad enough, but it was not so sad as the present. It was a dull November evening, and the wind moaned dismally through the trees, scattering the yellow leaves on the ground. The house looked forlorn and desolate. No smoke issued from the chimneys, nor was there any external indication that it was inhabited. The drawbridge was down, and as they passed over it, the hollow trampling of their steeds upon the planks vibrated painfully upon Viviana's heart. Before dismounting, she cast a wistful look around, and surveyed the grass-grown and neglected court, where, in years gone by, she had sported; the moat on whose brink she had lingered; and the surrounding woods, which she had never looked upon, even on a dreary day like the present, and when they were robbed in some measure of their beauty, without delight. Scanning the deserted mansion from roof to foundation, she traced all its gables, angles, windows, doors, and walls, and claimed every piece of carved work, every stone, as a familiar object, and as associated with other and happier hours.

"It is but the wreck of what it was," she thought. "The spirit that animated it is fled. Grass grows in its courts— no cheerful voices echo in its chambers—no hospitality is maintained in its hall—but neglect, gloom, and despair claim it as their own. The habitation and its mistress are well matched."

Guessing from the melancholy expression of her countenance what was passing within, and thinking it advisable to turn the current of her thoughts, Garnet assisted her to alight, and, committing the care of the steeds to Owen and the others, proceeded with her to the principal entrance. Everything appeared in nearly the same state as when they had last seen it, and the only change that had taken place was for the worse. The ceilings were mapped and mildewed with damps; the once gorgeously stained glass was shivered in the windows; the costly arras hung in tattered fragments from the walls; while the floors, which were still strewn with plaster and broken furniture, were flooded with the moisture that had found its way through the holes in the roof.

"Bear up, dear daughter," said Garnet, observing that Viviana was greatly distressed by the sight, "and let the contemplation of this scene of havoc, instead of casting you down, inspire you with just indignation against enemies from whom it is vain to expect justice or mercy. How many Catholic mansions have been thus laid waste! How many high-born and honourable men, whose sole fault was their adherence to the religion of their fathers, and their refusal to subscribe to doctrines against which their consciences revolted, have been put to death like your father; nay, have endured a worse fate, for they have languished out their lives in prison, while their families and retainers have undergone every species of outrage! How many a descendant of a proud line, distinguished for worth, for loyalty, and for devotion, has stood as you now stand, upon his desolate hearth—has seen misery and ruin usurp the place of comfort and happiness—and has heard the very stones beneath his feet cry out for vengeance! Accursed be our oppressors!" he added, lifting up his hands, and elevating his voice. "May their churches be thrown down—their faith crushed—their rights invaded—their children delivered to bondage—their hearths laid waste, as ours have been. May this, and worse come to pass, till the whole stock of heresy is uprooted!"

"Hold, father!" exclaimed Viviana; "even here, beholding this miserable sight, and with feelings keenly excited, I cannot join in your terrible denunciation. What I hope for—what I pray for, is toleration, not vengeance. The sufferings of our brethren will not have been in vain, if they enable our successors to worship God in their own way, and according to the dictates of their consciences. The ruthless conduct of our persecutors must be held in as much abhorrence by all good Protestants as our persecution of that sect, when we were in the ascendant, is regarded by all worthy members of our own Church. I cannot believe that by persecution we can work out the charitable precepts inculcated by our

Saviour; and I am sure such a course is as adverse to the spirit of religion as it is to that of humanity. Let us bear our sorrows with patience—let us utter no repinings, but turn the other cheek to the smiter, and we shall find, in due time, that the hearts of our oppressors will relent, and that all the believers in the True God will be enabled to worship him in peace, though at different altars."

"Such a season will never arrive, daughter," replied Garnet, severely, "till heresy is extirpated, and the false doctrines now prevailing utterly abolished. Then, indeed, when the Church of Rome is re-established, and the old and true religion restored, universal peace will prevail. And let me correct the grievous and sinful error into which you have fallen. Our Church is always at war with heresy; and if it cannot uproot it by gentle means, authorizes, nay enjoins, the employment of force."

"I will not attempt to dispute with you upon points of faith, father," returned Viviana; "I am content to think and act according to my own feelings and convictions. But I will not give up the hope that in some milder and wiser age, persecution on either side will cease, and the sufferings of its victims be remembered only to soften the hearts of fanatics, of whatever creed, towards each other. Were a lesson wanting to ourselves, surely it might be found in the result that has attended your dark and criminal enterprise, and in which the disapproval of Heaven has been signally manifested."

"Not so, daughter," replied Garnet. "An action is not to be judged or justified by the event attending it, but by its own intrinsic merits. To aver the contrary were to throw a doubt upon the Holy Scriptures themselves, where we read in the Book of Judges that the eleven tribes of Israel were commanded to make war upon the tribe of Benjamin, and yet were twice defeated. We have failed. But this proves nothing against our project, which I maintain to be righteous and praiseworthy, undertaken to overthrow an heretical and excommunicated monarch, and to re-establish the true faith of the Most High throughout this land."

"I lament to find that you still persist in error, father," replied Viviana; "but you cannot by any sophistry induce me to coincide with you in opinion. I hold the attempt an offence alike against God and man, and while I rejoice at the issue that has attended it, I deplore the irreparable harm it will do to the whole body of Catholics, all of whom will be connected by the bigotted and unthinking of the hostile

party, with the atrocious design. Not only have you done
our cause an injury, but you have in a measure justified
our opponents' severity, and given them a plea for further
persecution."

"No more of this," daughter," rejoined Garnet, impatiently,
" or I shall deem it necessary to reprove you. Let us search
the house, and try to find some habitable chamber in which
you can pass the night."

After a long search they discovered a room in comparatively
good order, and leaving Viviana within it, Garnet descended
to the lower part of the house, where he found Nicholas Owen,
and the two other attendants.

" We have chanced upon a scanty supply of provender for
our steeds," remarked Owen, with a doleful look; " but we
are not likely to obtain a meal ourselves, unless we can feed
upon rats and mice, which appear to be the sole tenants of
this miserable dwelling."

" You must go to Manchester instantly, and procure provisions," returned Garnet. " But take heed you observe the
utmost caution."

" Fear nothing," replied Owen. " If I am taken, your
reverence will lose your supper—that is all."

He then set out upon his errand, and Garnet proceeded to
the kitchen, where, to his great surprise, he found the hearth-
stone still warm, and a few lighted embers upon it, while
crumbs of bread, and little fragments of meat scattered about,
proved that some one had taken a meal there. Startled by
this discovery, he continued his search, but as fruitlessly as
before; and though he called to any one who might be hidden
to come forth, the summons was unanswered. One of the
attendants had placed a few sticks upon the smouldering
ashes, and on returning to the kitchen, it was found that
they had kindled. A fire being thus obtained, some of the
broken furniture was used to replenish it, and by Garnet's
commands another fire was speedily lighted in Viviana's
chamber. Night had now come on, and Owen not returning,
Garnet became extremely uneasy, and had almost given him
up, when the absentee made his appearance, with a large
basket of provisions under his arm.

" I have had some difficulty in obtaining them," he said;
" and fancying I observed two persons following me, was
obliged to take a circuitous route to get back. The whole
town is in commotion about the plot, and it is said that the
most rigorous measures are to be adopted towards all the
Catholic families in the neighbourhood."

Sighing at the latter piece of intelligence, Garnet selected such provisions as he thought would be acceptable to Viviana, and took them up-stairs to her. She ate a little bread and drank a cup of water, but refused to taste anything else, and finding it in vain to press her, Garnet returned to the kitchen, where, being much exhausted, he recruited himself with a hearty meal and a cup of wine.

Left alone, Viviana knelt down, and clasping a small crucifix to her breast, prayed long and fervently. While she was thus engaged, she heard the door open gently behind her, and turning her head, beheld an old man clothed in a tattered garb, with long white hair flowing over his shoulders, and a beard of the same snowy hue descending upon his breast. As he advanced slowly towards her, she started to her feet, and a brighter flame arising at the moment from the fire, it illumined the intruder's wo-begone features.

"Is it possible!" she exclaimed—"can it be my father's old steward, Jerome Heydocke?"

"It is, indeed, my dear young mistress," replied the old man, falling on his knee before her. "Heaven be praised!" he continued, seizing her hand, and bedewing it with tears; "I have seen you once again, and shall die content."

"I never expected to behold you more, good Heydocke," returned Viviana, raising him. "I heard you had died in prison."

"It was so given out by the jailers, to account for my escape," replied the old steward; "and I took care never to contradict the report by making my appearance. I will not distress you by the recital of all I have endured, but will simply state that I was confined in the prison upon Hunt's Bank, whence I escaped in the night by dropping upon the rocks, and from them into the river, where it was supposed I was drowned. Making my way into the country, I concealed myself for a time in barns and outbuildings, until, at length, I ventured back to the old house, and have dwelt in it unmolested ever since. I should have perished of want long ago, but for the kindness of Mr. Humphrey Chetham. He used to send my son regularly to me with provisions; and, now that Martin is gone to London, on business, as I understood, relating to you, he brings them to me himself. He will be here to-morrow."

"Indeed!" exclaimed Viviana. "I must see him."

"As you please," returned the old man. "I suppose those are your companions below. I was in my hiding-place, and hearing voices and footsteps, did not dare to venture forth till all was still. On approaching this room, which I have been in the habit of occupying lately, and peeping through the door, which was standing ajar, I perceived a female figure, and thinking it must be you, though I scarcely dared to trust the evidence of my senses, I ventured in. Oh! my dear, dear young mistress, what a joy it is to see you again! I fear you must have suffered much, for you are greatly altered."

At this moment Garnet entered the room. He started on seeing the old steward. But an explanation was instantly given him.

"You, then, are the person by whom the fire was recently lighted in the kitchen?" he asked.

Heydocke replied in the affirmative.

"I came to bid you farewell for the night, dear daughter," said Garnet, "and to assure you that you may rest without fear, for we have contrived to make fast the doors. Come with me, my son," he added to the steward, "and you shall have a comfortable meal below."

Making a profound reverence to Viviana, the old man followed him down stairs.

Viviana continued to pace to and fro within her chamber for some time, and then, overcome with fatigue, flung herself upon the bedstead, on which a cloak had been thrown. Sleep soon closed her eyes, but it was disturbed by frightful and distressing dreams, from which she was suddenly aroused by a touch upon the arm. Starting up, she perceived the old steward by the side of her couch, with a light in his hand.

"What brings you here, Heydocke?" she demanded, with surprise and alarm.

"You have slept soundly, my dear young mistress, or you would not require to be informed," replied the steward. "There! do you not hear it?" he added, as a loud knocking resounded from below.

Viviana listened for a moment, and then, as if struck by a sudden idea, hurried down stairs. She found Garnet and the others assembled in the hall, but wholly unnerved by fright. "Hide yourselves," she said, "and no ill shall befall you. Quick!—not a moment is to be lost!"

Having allowed them sufficient time for concealment, she demanded in a loud voice who was without?

"Friends," was the reply.

"It is the voice of Doctor Dee," replied Heydocke.

"Indeed!" exclaimed Viviana. "Admit him instantly."

Heydocke obeyed, and throwing open the door, gave entrance to the Doctor, who was wrapped in his long fur gown, and carried a lantern. He was accompanied by Kelley and Humphrey Chetham.

"Your visit is singularly timed, Mr. Chetham," said Viviana, after she had saluted the party; "but you are not the less welcome on that account. I much desire to see you, and indeed should have sent for you to-morrow. But how did you know I was here?"

"The only explanation I can offer you is this," replied Chetham. "I was hastily summoned from my residence at Crumpsall by Kelley, who told me you were at Ordsall Hall, and that Doctor Dee was about to visit you, and desired my company. Thus summoned, I came at once."

"A strange explanation, indeed!" replied Viviana.

"Close and fasten the door," said Dee, in an authoritative tone to Kelley; and as soon as his commands were obeyed, he took Viviana's hand, and led her to the farther end of the hall.

"My art informed me of your arrival, Viviana," he said. "I am come to save you. You are in imminent danger."

"I well know it," she replied; "but I have no wish to fly from justice. I am weary of my life, and would gladly resign it."

"I would call to your recollection, Viviana," pursued Dee, "that I foretold the disastrous result of this plot, in which you have become unhappily involved, to Guy Fawkes, and warned him not to proceed in it. But he would not be advised, and is now a prisoner in the Tower."

"All I wish is to go thither and die with him," rejoined Viviana.

"If you go thither, you will die before him," said Dee.

"I would do so," she replied.

"Viviana Radcliffe," returned Dee, in a compassionate tone, "I truly grieve for you. Your attachment to this heinous traitor completely blinds you. The friendship I entertained for your mother makes me anxious to serve you—to see you happy. It is now in your power to be so. But if you take another false step, your fate is decided, and you will die an early death. I will answer for your safety—nay, what is more, I will undertake that ere long you shall again be mistress of this mansion, and have your estates restored to you."

"You promise fairly, sir," she replied, with a mournful smile.

"I have not yet done," pursued Dee. "All I require for the service is, that when freed by the death of Guy Fawkes from the chain that now binds you—for I am aware of your ill-starred union with him—you shall bestow your hand upon Humphrey Chetham."

"It may not be," replied Viviana, firmly. "And if you could in truth read the secrets of the heart, you would know that mine would instantly reject the proposal."

"Think not it originates with me, Viviana," said Humphrey Chetham, who had approached them unobserved. "My previous experience of your character would alone have prevented me from becoming a party to any such proposal, had I known it would be made. Do not, I beseech you, sir," he added to Dee, "clog your offer with conditions which will effectually prevent its accomplishment."

"You are true to yourself, Mr. Chetham," rejoined Viviana, "and will not, therefore, wonder that I continue so. Were I to assent to Doctor Dee's proposal, I should be further from happiness than I am now, even if he could make good his words, and restore me to the station I have forfeited. I have received a shock from which I shall never recover, and the only haven of repose to which I look forward is the grave."

"Alas!" exclaimed Chetham, in a pitying tone.

"You will think I trespass too much upon your kindness," she pursued; "but you can render me a great service, and it will be the last I shall ever require from you."

"Name it!" cried Chetham, eagerly.

"I would beg you to escort me to London," she rejoined; "and to deliver me to the Lords of the Council. I would willingly escape the indignities to which I shall be exposed if I am conveyed thither as a prisoner. Will you do this?"

"I will," replied Chetham.

"Lest you should think I have offered more than I can perform, Viviana," said Dee, who had listened attentively to the foregoing conversation, "I will now tell you on what grounds I build my expectation of procuring your pardon. The conspiracy was first revealed by me to the Earl of Salisbury, though for his own purposes he kept it secret to the last. He owes me a heavy debt, and shall pay it in the way I propose, if you desire it."

"I will abide by what I have done," replied Viviana.

"You know, then, what fate awaits you?" said Dee.

"I shall not shrink from it," she rejoined.

"It is well," he replied. "Before I leave, I will give you another caution. Father Garnet is here. Nay, attempt not to deny it. You cannot deceive me. Besides, I desire to serve, not harm him. If he remains here till to-morrow he will be captured. A proclamation has been issued for his arrest, as well as for that of Father Oldcorne. Deliver him this warning. And now, farewell!"

With this he took up his lantern, and, followed by Kelley, quitted the Hall.

Humphrey Chetham only tarried a few moments to inform Viviana that he would return soon after daybreak with a couple of steeds for the journey. As soon as he was gone, Viviana communicated Dee's warning to Garnet, who was so alarmed by it that he resolved not to delay his own departure a moment. Taking an affectionate leave of Viviana, and confiding her to the care of the old steward, he set out with his three attendants.

Faithful to his promise, Humphrey Chetham appeared at the appointed time. Viviana bade an eternal farewell to the old steward, who was overwhelmed with grief, and looked as if his sorrows would soon be ended, and mounting one of the steeds brought by the young merchant, they took the direction of London.

VIII.

HENDLIP.

GARNET proceeded at a rapid pace for some miles before he acquainted his companions whither he was going. He then informed Nicholas Owen, who rode by his side, that he should make the best of his way to Hendlip House, the seat of Mr. Thomas Abingdon, near Droitwich, in Worcestershire, where he knew that Father Oldcorne and Anne Vaux had retired, and where he was certain to meet with a friendly reception and protection. Owen, who was completely in his master's confidence, agreed that no safer asylum could be found, and they pursued their journey with so much ardour, that early on the following night they arrived within a short distance of the mansion. Owen was sent forward to reconnoitre, and returned in about half an hour with Mr. Abingdon, who embraced Garnet, and told him he was truly happy in being able to offer him a retreat.

"And I think it will prove a secure one," he added. "There are so many hiding-places in the old house, that if it is beset for a year you will scarcely be discovered. Have you heard of the fate of your confederates?"

"Alas! no, my son," replied Garnet; "and I tremble to ask it."

"It had better be told at once," rejoined Abingdon. "Catesby, Percy, and the two Wrights, have been slain in the defence of Holbeach; while Rookwood, Grant, and Thomas Winter, all of whom were severely wounded in the siege, have been made prisoners, and are now on their way to the Tower."

"A fearful catalogue of ills!" exclaimed Garnet.

"It is not yet complete," pursued Abingdon. "Sir Everard Digby has been defeated and made prisoner in an attempt to bring additional force to his friends, and Keyes has been arrested in Warwickshire."

"These are woful tidings truly, my son," returned Garnet. "But Heaven's will be done!"

He then dismissed his two attendants, to whom he gave a sum of money, together with the steeds, and, attended by Nicholas Owen, repaired to the house with Mr. Abingdon, who admitted them through a secret door.

Hendlip House, which, unfortunately for the lovers of picturesque and storied habitations, was pulled down a few years ago, having been latterly used as a ladies' boarding-school, was a large and irregular structure, with walls of immense thickness, tall stacks of chimneys, turrets, oriel windows, and numberless projections, contrived to mask the labyrinths and secret chambers within. Erected by John Abingdon, father of the proprietor at the period of this history, and cofferer to Queen Elizabeth in the early part of the reign of that princess, it was filled with secret staircases, masked entrances, trap-doors, vaults, subterranean passages, secret recesses, and every other description of hiding-place. An immense gallery surrounded three sides of the entrance-hall, containing on each side a large chimney-piece, surmounted by a shield displaying the arms of the family—*argent, a bend, gules, three eaglets displayed, or.* Behind each of these chimney-pieces was a small cell, or "priest's-hole," as it was termed, contrived in the thickness of the wall. Throughout the mansion, the chambers were so sombre, and the passages so numerous and intricate, that in the words of one who described it from personal observation, the whole place presented "a picture of gloom, insecurity, and suspicion." Standing on an elevated situation, it commanded the country on all sides, and could not be approached during the day-time without alarm being given to its inmates.

Thomas Abingdon, the owner of the mansion at the period

in question, and the eldest son of its founder, was born at
Thorpe, near Chertsey, in Surrey, in 1560. He was educated
at Oxford, and finished his studies at the Universities of
Paris and Rheims. A man of considerable taste and learning, but of a plotting disposition, he became a willing tool
of the Jesuits, and immediately on his return to England,
connected himself with the different conspiracies set on foot
for the liberation of the imprisoned Queen of Scots. For
these offences he was imprisoned in the Tower for the term
of six years, and only escaped death from the fact of his
being the Queen's godson, coupled with the estimation in
which she had held his father. On his liberation, he remained
perfectly tranquil till the accession of James, when he became
a secret plotter against that monarch. His concealment of
the two priests, about to be related, occasioned his being
again sent to the Tower; and if it had not been for the intercession of Lord Mounteagle, whose sister he had espoused,
he would have been executed. He was pardoned on condition
of never stirring beyond the precincts of Worcestershire, and
he employed his retirement in compiling an account of the
antiquities of that county, which he left behind him in manu-
script, and of which Doctor Nash, its more recent historian,
has largely availed himself.

With a habitation so contrived, Mr. Abingdon might fairly
promise his guests a safe asylum. Conducting them along a
secret passage to a chamber of which he alone possessed the
key, he left Garnet within it, and taking Owen with him to
another place of concealment, returned shortly afterwards
with Anne Vaux and Father Oldcorne. The two priests tenderly embraced each other, and Oldcorne poured forth his
tears on his superior's shoulder. Garnet next turned to Anne
Vaux, between whom and himself, as has before been mentioned, an affectionate intimacy subsisted, and found her
quite overcome by her feelings. Supper was now served to
Garnet by a confidential servant, and after a few hours spent
in conversation with his friends, during which they discussed
the disastrous issue of the affair, and the probable fate of the
conspirators, they quitted him, and he retired to rest—but
not before he had returned thanks to Heaven for enabling
him once more to lay down his head in safety.

On the following morning he was visited by Mrs. Abingdon,
a lady of considerable personal attractions, and Anne Vaux;
and when he had recovered from the fatigue of his journey,
and the anxieties he had recently undergone, he experienced
great delight in their society. The chamber he occupied was

lighted by a small loop-hole, which enabled him to breathe the fresh air, and gaze upon the surrounding country.

In this way nearly two months passed on, during which, though rigorous inquiries were made throughout the country, no clue was found by the searchers to lead them to Hendlip; and the concealed parties began to indulge hopes that they should escape detection altogether. Being in constant correspondence with her brother, Lord Mounteagle, though she did not trust him with the important secret of the concealment of the priests, Mrs. Abingdon ascertained all that was done in reference to the conspirators, whose trials were now approaching, and communicated the intelligence to Garnet.

On the morning of the 20th of January, and when long quietude had bred complete fancied security in Garnet, Anne Vaux and Mrs. Abingdon suddenly entered his chamber, and with countenances of the utmost alarm, informed him that Mr. Abingdon's confidential servant had just returned from Worcester, where his master then was, and had brought word that Topcliffe, armed with a search-warrant from the Earl of Salisbury, had just passed through that city on his way to Holt Castle, the residence of Sir Henry Bromley.

"It appears," said Mrs. Abingdon, "that Humphrey Littleton, who has been apprehended and condemned to death at Worcester for harbouring his brother and Robert Winter, has sought to procure a remission of his sentence by betraying your retreat. In consequence of this, Topcliffe has been sent down from London, with a warrant addressed to Sir Henry Bromley, to aid him in searching Hendlip. My husband has given particular orders that you are to be removed to the most secure hiding-place without delay; and he deeply regrets that he himself cannot return till evening, for fear of exciting suspicion."

"Take me where you please, daughter," replied Garnet, who was thrown into great perturbation by the intelligence, "I thought myself prepared for any emergency. But I was wofully deceived."

"Be not alarmed, father," said Anne Vaux, in an encouraging tone. "Let them search as long as they will, they will never discover your retreat."

"I have a strong presentiment to the contrary," replied Garnet.

At this moment Oldcorne made his appearance, and on learning the alarming news, was as much dismayed as his superior.

After a short consultation, and while the priests were putting aside every article necessary to be removed, Mrs. Abingdon proceeded to the gallery, and contrived on some plausible pretext to send away the whole of the domestics from this part of the house. This done, she hastily returned, and conducted the two priests to one of the large fireplaces.

A raised stone about two feet high occupied the inside of the chimney, and upon it stood an immense pair of iron dogs. Obeying Mrs. Abingdon's directions, Garnet got upon the stone, and setting his foot on the large iron knob on the left, found a few projections in the masonry on the side, up which he mounted, and opening a small door, made of planks of wood, covered with bricks, and coloured black, so as not to be distinguishable from the walls of the chimney, crept into a recess contrived in the thickness of the wall. This cell was about two feet wide, and four high, and was connected with another chimney at the back, by means of three or four small holes. Around its sides ran a narrow stone shelf, just wide enough to afford an uncomfortable seat. Garnet was followed by Oldcorne, who brought with him a quantity of books, vestments, and sacred vessels used in the performance of the rites of the Church of Rome. These articles, which afterwards occasioned them much inconvenience, they did not dare to leave behind.

Having seen them safely bestowed, Mrs. Abingdon and her companion went in search of provisions, and brought them a piece of cold meat and a pasty, together with some bread, dried fruit, conserves, and a flask of wine. They did not dare to bring more, for fear of exciting the suspicion of the household. Their next care was to conduct Owen, and Oldcorne's servant, Chambers, to a similar retreat in one of the other chimneys, and to provide them with a scanty supply of provisions and a flask of wine. All this was accomplished without being noticed by any of the domestics.

As may be imagined, a most anxious day was passed by all parties. Towards evening, Sir Henry Bromley, the sheriff of the county, accompanied by Topcliffe, and attended by a troop of soldiers, appeared at the gates of the mansion, and demanded admittance. Just at this moment, Mr. Abingdon rode up, and affecting to know nothing of the matter, saluted Sir Henry Bromley, with whom he was on terms of intimacy, and inquired his business.

"You are charged with harbouring two Jesuit priests, Fathers Garnet and Oldcorne, supposed to be connected with the late atrocious conspiracy against the King, Mr. Abingdon," interposed Topcliffe; "and I brought a warrant from the

Earl of Salisbury, which I have delivered to Sir Henry Bromley, commanding him to search your house for them."

"I was loth to accept the office, Mr. Abingdon," said Sir
Henry Bromley, who was a handsome, middle-aged man;
"but my duty to my sovereign allows me no alternative. I
trust, though a Catholic, that you share my own detestation
of this diabolical plot, and would not shelter any of its contrivers or abettors."

"You judge me rightly, Sir Henry," replied Abingdon,
who, meanwhile, had received a private signal from his confidential servant that all was safe. "I would not. I am just
returned from Worcester, where I have been for the last two
days. Enter my house, I pray you, and search every corner
of it; and if you find a Jesuit priest concealed within it, you
shall hang me at my own gate."

"You must be misinformed, sir," observed Sir Henry, who
was completely imposed upon by Abingdon's unconcerned
demeanour; "they cannot be here."

"Trust me, they are," returned the other, "and I should
like to take him at his word."

Giving directions to the band to environ the house, and
guard all its approaches, so as to prevent any one from
escaping from it, Topcliffe took half a dozen men with him,
and instructed them how to act. They first repaired to the
great dining-chamber, where, in accordance with the instructions received from the Earl of Salisbury, Topcliffe proceeded
to the further end of the room, and directed his men to break
down the wainscot. With some difficulty the order was
obeyed, and the entrance to a vault discovered, into which
Topcliffe descended, but he found nothing to repay his
trouble.

Returning to the dining-chamber, he questioned Mr.
Abingdon, who secretly enjoyed his disappointment, as to
the use of the vault, but the latter professed entire ignorance
of its existence. The searchers next proceeded to the cellar,
and bored the floors with a broach to a considerable depth,
to try whether there were any vaults beneath them, but they
made no discovery. Meanwhile Topcliffe hurried up-stairs,
and examined the size of the rooms, to see whether they corresponded with those below, and wherever any difference was
observable, he caused the panels to be pulled down, and holes
broken in the walls. In this way several secret passages were
discovered, one of which led to the chamber lately occupied
by Garnet.

Encouraged by this discovery, the searchers continued their

operations to a late hour, when they desisted for the night. On the following day they resumed their task, and Sir Henry Bromley took a general survey of the house, both externally and internally, noting the appearances outside, and seeing that they corresponded with the rooms within. The three extraordinary chimneypieces in the gallery attracted Topcliffe's attention; but the contrivances within were so well managed, that they escaped his notice. He even got into the chimneys, and examined the walls on either side, but could detect nothing. And, lastly, he ordered large fires to be lighted within them, but the experiment proving fruitless, he turned his attention elsewhere.

Mr. Abingdon had attended him during this part of the search, and, though he preserved an unmoved exterior, he was full of apprehension, and was greatly relieved when it was abandoned. In the course of the same day, two other hiding-places were found in the thickness of the walls, but nothing was discovered within them. In order to prevent any communication with the concealed persons, Topcliffe stationed a sentinel at the door of Mr. Abingdon's chamber, and another at that of Anne Vaux.

On the third day the search was continued more rigorously than ever. Wainscots were taken down; walls broken open; the boards of the floor removed; and other secret passages, vaults, and hiding-places discovered. Some priests' vestments and articles used in the Romish service were found in one of these places, and shown to Mr. Abingdon. He at first denied all knowledge of them; but when Topcliffe brought forward the title-deeds of his property, which had been found in the same place, he was obliged to confess he had put them there himself. Still, though these discoveries had been made, the searchers were as far from their aim as ever; and Sir Henry Bromley, who began to despair of success, would have departed on the fifth day, if Topcliffe had not prevented him.

"I am certain they are here," said the latter, "and have hit upon a plan which cannot fail to bring them forth."

The prisoners meanwhile suffered grievously from their confinement, and hearing the searchers knocking against the walls, and even within the chimney, felt certain they should be discovered. Not being able to stand upright, or to stretch themselves within the cell, the sitting posture they were compelled to adopt became, after a time, intolerably irksome. Broths, milk, wine, and other nutritious fluids, were conveyed

2 B

to them by means of a reed from the adjoining chimney ; but
after the fifth day this supply was stopped, as Mrs. Abingdon
and Anne Vaux were compelled by Topcliffe to remove to a
different part of the house.

They now began to experience all the horrors of starvation,
and debated whether they should die where they were, or
yield themselves up to their enemies. Wretched as their
condition was, however, it was not so bad as that of their
domestics, Owen and Chambers, whose wants had not been
so carefully attended to, and who were now reduced to the
most deplorable state. Nor were their friends less uneasy.
Aware that the captives, whom there was no means of relieving, for the searchers were constantly on the watch, could not
hold out much longer, Mrs. Abingdon consulted with her
husband whether it would not be better to reveal their hiding-places ; but this he would not permit.

By this time every secret chamber, vault, and passage in
the place, except the actual retreats of the conspirators, had
been discovered by Topcliffe ; and though nothing material
was found, he felt assured, from the uneasiness displayed by
Mr. Abingdon and his wife, and above all by Anne Vaux,
that it could not be long before his perseverance was rewarded. Though he narrowly watched the two ladies from
the first, he could never detect them in the act of conveying
food to the captives ; but feeling convinced that they did so,
he determined to remove them to a different part of the
house, and their unwillingness to obey the order confirmed
his suspicions.

"We are sure of our prey now," he observed to Sir Henry
Bromley. "They must be half-starved by this time, and
will speedily surrender themselves."

"Pray Heaven they do so !" returned the other. "I am
wearied to death with my long stay here."

"Have a few hours' patience," rejoined Topcliffe, "and
you will find that your time has not been thrown away."

And he was right. Soon after midnight a trooper, who
was watching in the gallery, beheld two spectral-looking
figures approach him, and appalled by their ghastly appearance, uttered a loud cry. This brought Topcliffe, who was in
the hall below, to his aid, and instantly perceiving what was
the matter, he ran towards the supposed phantoms and seized
them. The poor wretches, who were no other than Owen
and Chambers, and were well-nigh famished, offered no resistance, but would neither confess where they had been

hidden, nor who they were. As the trooper had not seen them come forth, though he affirmed with a tremendous oath that they had issued from the floor, the walls were again sounded, but with no result.

Food being placed before the captives, they devoured it voraciously; but Topcliffe forebore to question them further that night, feeling confident that he could extract the truth from them on the morrow, either by promises or threats. He was, however, mistaken. They continued as obstinate as before, and when confronted with Mr. Abingdon, denied all knowledge of him; neither would they explain how they got into the house.

Sir Henry Bromley, however, now considered himself justified in placing Mr. Abingdon and his lady under arrest, and Topcliffe redoubled his exertions to discover the hiding-place of the two priests. He examined every part of the gallery most carefully—took down one of the chimney-pieces (singularly enough, it was the wrong one), but was still unable to discover their retreat.

Meanwhile the poor wretches inside found it impossible to endure their condition longer. Anything seemed preferable to the lingering and agonizing death they were now enduring, and they resolved to delay their surrender no longer. Had they been able to hold out a few hours more, they would have escaped; for Sir Henry Bromley was so fatigued with the search, and so satisfied that nothing further would come of it, that he resolved, notwithstanding Topcliffe's efforts to dissuade him, to depart on the morrow. Of this they were ignorant, and having come to the determination to surrender, Garnet opened the entrance to the chimney, and hearing voices below, and being too feeble to get out unassisted, he called to the speakers for aid. His voice was so hollow, and had such a sepulchral sound, that those who heard it stared at each other in astonishment and affright.

"Who calls?" cried one of the troopers, after a pause.

"One of those you seek," replied Garnet. "Come and help us forth."

Upon hearing this, and ascertaining whence the voice came from, one of the men ran to fetch Sir Henry Bromley and Topcliffe, both of whom joyfully obeyed the summons.

"Is it possible they can be in the chimney?" cried Topcliffe. "Why, I myself have examined it twice."

"We are here, nevertheless," replied Garnet, who heard the remark; "and if you would take us alive, lose no time."

The hint was not lost upon Topcliffe. Casting a triumphant look at Bromley, he seized a torch from one of his attendants, and getting into the chimney, soon perceived the entrance to the recess.

On beholding his prey, he uttered an exclamation of joy, and the two miserable captives, seeing the savage and exulting grin that lighted up his features, half repented the step they had taken. It was now, however, too late, and Garnet begged him to help them out.

"That I will readily do, father," replied Topcliffe. "You have given us a world of trouble. But you have made ample amends for it now."

"Had we been so minded, you would never have found us," rejoined Garnet. "This cell would have been our sepulchre."

"No doubt," retorted Topcliffe, with a bitter laugh. "But a death on the scaffold is preferable to the horrors of starvation."

Finding it impossible to remove Garnet, whose limbs were so cramped that they refused their office, he called to the troopers below to bring a ladder, which was placed in the chimney, and then with some exertion he succeeded in getting him down. This done, he supported him towards Sir Henry Bromley, who was standing near a small table in the gallery.

"I told you your time would not be thrown away, Sir Henry," he observed; "here is Father Garnet. It is well you yielded yourself to-night, father," he added, to Garnet, with his customary cynical chuckle; "for Sir Henry had resolved to depart to-morrow."

"Indeed!" groaned Garnet. "Help me to a chair."

While this was passing, Oldcorne was brought down by two of the troopers, and the unfortunate priests were conveyed to an adjoining chamber, where they were placed in a bed, their stiffened limbs chafed, and cordials administered to them. They were reduced, however, to such extremity of weakness, that it was not judged prudent to remove them till the third day, when they, together with their two servants, Owen and Chambers, who were as much enfeebled as themselves, were conveyed to Worcester.

IX.

WHITEHALL.

SUCH was the expedition used by Humphrey Chetham and Viviana, that they accomplished the journey to London in an extraordinarily short space of time. Proceeding direct to Whitehall, Viviana placed a letter in the hands of a halberdier, and desired that it might be given without delay to the Earl of Salisbury. After some demur, the man handed it to an usher, who promised to lay it before the Earl. Some time elapsed before the result of its reception was known, when an officer, accompanied by two sergeants of the guard, made his appearance, and commanded Viviana and her companion to follow him.

Crossing a wide hall, which was filled with the various retainers of the palace, who regarded them with a sort of listless curiosity, and ascending a flight of marble steps, they traversed a long corridor, and were at length ushered into the presence of the Earl of Salisbury. He was seated at a table, covered with a multitude of papers, and was busily employed in writing a despatch, but immediately stopped on their entrance. He was not alone. His companion was a middle-aged man, attired in a suit of black velvet, with a cloak of the same material; but as he sat with his back towards the door, it was impossible to discern his features.

"You may leave us," said Salisbury to the officer, "but remain without."

"And be ready to enter at a moment's notice," added his companion, without altering his position.

The officer bowed, and retired with his followers.

"Your surrender of yourself at this time, Viviana Radcliffe," said the Earl, "weighs much in your favour; and if you are disposed freely to declare all you know of the conspiracy, it is not impossible that the King may extend his mercy towards you."

"I do not desire it, my lord," she replied. "In surrendering myself, I have no other aim than to satisfy the laws I have outraged. I do not seek to defend myself, but I desire to offer an explanation to your lordship. Circumstances which it is needless to detail, drew me into connexion with the conspirators, and I became unwillingly the depositary of their dark design."

"You were guilty of misprision of treason in not revealing it," remarked the Earl.

"I am aware of it," she rejoined; "but this, I take Heaven to witness, is the extent of my criminality. I held the project in the utmost abhorrence, and used every argument I was mistress of to induce its contrivers to abandon it."

"If such were the case," demanded the Earl, "what withheld you from disclosing it?"

"I will now confess what torture could not wring from me before," she replied. "I was restrained from the disclosure by a fatal passion."

"I suspected as much," observed the Earl, with a sneer. "For whom?"

"For Guy Fawkes," returned Viviana.

"God's mercy! Guy Fawkes!" ejaculated the Earl's companion, starting to his feet. And turning as he spoke, and facing her, he disclosed heavy but not unintellectual features, now charged with an expression of the utmost astonishment. "Did you say Guy Fawkes, mistress?"

"It is the King," whispered Humphrey Chetham.

"Since I know in whose presence I stand, sire," replied Viviana, "I will answer the interrogation. Guy Fawkes was the cause of my concealing my acquaintance with the plot. And more, I will confess to your Majesty, that much as I abhor the design, if he had not been a conspirator, I should never have loved him. His sombre and enthusiastic character first gave him an interest in my eyes, which heightened by several important services which he rendered me, soon ripened into love. Linked to his fortunes, shrouded by the same gloomy cloud that enveloped him, and bound by a chain from which I could not extricate myself, I gave him my hand. But the moment of our union was the moment of our separation. We have not met since, and shall meet no more, unless to part for ever."

"A strange history!" exclaimed James, in a tone that showed he was not unmoved by the relation.

"I beseech your Majesty to grant me one boon," cried Viviana, falling at his feet. "It is to be allowed a single interview with my husband—not for the sad gratification of beholding him again—not for the indulgence of my private sorrows—but that I may endeavour to awaken a feeling of repentance in his breast, and be the means of saving his soul alive."

"My inclinations prompt me to grant the request, Salisbury," said the King, irresolutely. "There can be no risk in doing it—eh?"

"Not under certain restrictions, my liege," replied the Earl.

"You shall have your wish, then, mistress," said James, "and I trust your efforts may be crowned with success. Your husband is a hardy traitor—a second Jacques Clement —and we never think of him without the floor shaking beneath our feet, and a horrible smell of gunpowder assailing our nostrils. Blessed be God for our preservation! But whom have we here?" he added, turning to Humphrey Chetham. "Another conspirator come to surrender himself?"

"No, my liege," replied Chetham; "I am a loyal subject of your Majesty, and a stanch Protestant."

"If we may take your word for it, doubtless," replied the King, with an incredulous look. "But how come you in this lady's company?"

"I will hide nothing from your Majesty," replied Chetham. "Long before Viviana's unhappy acquaintance with Fawkes —for such I must ever consider it—my affections had been fixed upon her, and I fondly trusted she would not prove indifferent to my suit. Even now, sire, when all hope is dead within me, I have not been able to overcome my passion, but love her as devotedly as ever. When, therefore, she desired my escort to London to surrender herself, I could not refuse the request."

"It is the truth, my liege," added Viviana. "I owe Humphrey Chetham (for so this gentleman is named) an endless debt of gratitude; and not the least of my present distresses is the thought of the affliction I have occasioned him."

"Dismiss it from your mind, then, Viviana," rejoined Chetham. "It will not mitigate my sorrows to feel that I have added to yours."

"Your manner and looks seem to give a warranty for loyalty, young sir," said the King. "But I must have some assurance of the truth of your statement before you are set at large."

"I am your willing prisoner, my liege," returned Chetham. "But I have a letter for the Earl of Salisbury, which may vouch perhaps for me."

And as he spoke, he placed a letter in the Earl's hands, who broke open the seal, and hastily glanced at its contents."

"It is from Doctor Dee," he said, "from whom, as your

Majesty is aware, we have received much important information relative to this atrocious design. He answers for this young man's loyalty."

"I am glad to hear it," rejoined the King. "It would have been mortifying to be deceived by so honest a physiognomy."

"Your Majesty will be pleased to attach your signature to this warrant for Viviana Radcliffe's committal to the Tower," said Salisbury, placing a paper before him.

James complied, and the Earl summoned the guard.

"Have I your Majesty's permission to attend this unfortunate lady to the fortress?" cried Chetham, prostrating himself before the King.

James hesitated, but glancing at the Earl, and reading no objection in his looks, he assented.

Whispering some private instructions to the officer respecting Chetham, Salisbury delivered the warrant to him. Viviana and her companion were then removed to a small chamber adjoining the guard-room, where they remained for nearly an hour, at the expiration of which time the officer again appeared, and conducted them to the palace-stairs, where a large wherry awaited them, in which they embarked.

James did not remain long with his councillor, and as soon as he had retired, Salisbury summoned a confidential attendant, and told him to acquaint Lord Mounteagle, who was in an adjoining apartment, that he was now able to receive him. The attendant departed, and presently returned with the nobleman in question. As soon as they were alone, and Salisbury had satisfied himself they could not be overheard, he observed to the other:

"Since Tresham's committal to the Tower yesterday, I have received a letter from the lieutenant, stating that he breathes nothing but revenge against yourself and me, and threatens to betray us, if he is not released. It will not do to let him be examined by the Council; for though we can throw utter discredit on his statement, it may be prejudicial to my future designs."

"True, my lord," replied Mounteagle. "But how do you propose to silence him?"

"By poison," returned Salisbury. "There is a trusty fellow in the Tower, a jailer named Ipgreve, who will administer it to him. Here is the powder," he added, unlocking a coffer, and taking out a small packet; it was given me by its compounder, Doctor Dee. It is the same, I am assured, as the celebrated Italian poison prepared by Pope Alexander the Sixth; is without scent or taste; and destroys its victim without leaving a trace of its effects."

"I must take heed how I offend your lordship," observed Mounteagle.

"Nay," rejoined Salisbury, with a ghastly smile, "it is for traitors like Tresham, not true men like you to fear me."

"I understand the distinction, my lord," replied the other.

"I must intrust the entire management of this affair to you," pursued Salisbury.

"To me!" exclaimed Mounteagle. "Tresham is my brother-in-law. I can take no part in his murder."

"If he lives, you are ruined," rejoined Salisbury, coldly. "You must sacrifice him or yourself. But I see you are reasonable. Take this powder, and proceed to the Tower. See Ipgreve alone, and instruct him to drug Tresham's wine with it. A hundred marks shall be his reward when the deed is done."

"My soul revolts from the deed," said Mounteagle, as he took the packet. "Is there no other way of silencing him."

"None whatever," replied Salisbury, sternly. "His blood be upon his own head."

With this Mounteagle took his departure.

X.

THE PARTING OF VIVIANA AND HUMPHREY CHETHAM.

HUMPHREY CHETHAM was so oppressed by the idea of parting with Viviana, that he did not utter a single word during their transit to the Tower. Passing beneath the gloomy archway of Traitor's Gate, they mounted the fatal steps, and were conducted to the guard-room near the By-ward Tower. The officer then despatched one of the warders to inform the lieutenant of Viviana's arrival, and telling Humphrey Chetham he would allow him a few minutes to take leave of her, considerately withdrew, and left them alone together.

"Oh, Viviana!" exclaimed Chetham, unable to repress his grief, "my heart bleeds to see you here. If you repent the step you have taken, and desire freedom, say so, and I will use every effort to liberate you. I have been successful once, and may be so again."

"I thank you for your devotion," she replied, in a tone of profound gratitude; "but you have rendered me the last service I shall ever require of you. I deeply deplore the misery I have occasioned you, and regret my inability to requite your attachment as it deserves to be requited. My last prayers shall be for your happiness; and I trust you will meet with some being worthy of you, and who will make amends for my insensibility."

"Be not deceived, Viviana," replied Chetham, in a broken voice; "I shall never love again. Your image is too deeply imprinted upon my heart ever to be effaced."

"Time may work a change," she rejoined; "though I ought not to say so, for I feel it would work none in me. Suffer me to give you one piece of counsel. Devote yourself resolutely to the business of life, and you will speedily regain your peace of mind."

"I will follow your instructions implicitly," replied Chetham; "but have little hope of the result you promise me."

"Let the effort be made," she rejoined;—"and now promise me to quit London to-morrow. Return to your native town; employ yourself in your former occupations; and strive not to think of the past, except as a troubled dream from which you have fortunately awakened. Do not let us prolong our parting, or your resolution may waver. Farewell!"

So saying, she extended her hand towards him, and he pressed it passionately to his lips.

"Farewell, Viviana!" he cried with a look of unutterable anguish. "May Heaven support you in your trials!"

"One of them I am now enduring," she replied in a broken voice. "Farewell for ever, and may all good angels bless you!"

At this moment, the officer appeared, and announcing the approach of the lieutenant, told Chetham that his time had expired. Without hazarding another look at Viviana, the young merchant tore himself away, and followed the officer out of the Tower.

Obedient to Viviana's last request, he quitted London on the following day, and, acting upon her advice, devoted himself on his return to Manchester sedulously to his mercantile pursuits. His perseverance and integrity were crowned with entire success, and he became in due season the wealthiest merchant of the town. But the blighting of his early affections tinged his whole life, and gave a melancholy to his thoughts and an austerity to his manner originally foreign to them. True to his promise, he died unmarried. His long

and worthy career was marked by actions of the greatest
benevolence. In proportion as his means increased, his
charities were extended, and he truly became "a father to the
fatherless and the destitute." To him the town of Manchester is indebted for the noble library and hospital bearing
his name; and for these admirable institutions by which
they so largely benefit, his memory must ever be held in
veneration by its inhabitants.

XI.

THE SUBTERRANEAN DUNGEON.

REGARDING Viviana with a smile of savage satisfaction,
Sir William Waad commanded Jasper Ipgreve, who accompanied him, to convey her to one of the subterranean dungeons
below the Devereux Tower.

"She cannot escape thence without your connivance," he
said; "and you shall answer to me for her safe custody with
your life."

"If she escapes again, your worship shall hang me in her
stead," rejoined Ipgreve.

"My instructions from the Earl of Salisbury state that it
is the King's pleasure that she be allowed a short interview
with Guy Fawkes," said the lieutenant, in a low tone. "Let
her be taken to his cell to-morrow."

The jailer bowed, and motioning the guard to follow him
with Viviana, he led the way along the inner ward till he
arrived at a small strong door in the wall a little to the north
of the Beauchamp Tower, which he unlocked, and descended
into a low cavernous-looking vault. Striking a light, and
setting fire to a torch, he then led the way along a narrow
gloomy passage, which brought them to a circular chamber,
from which other passages diverged, and selecting one of
them, threaded it till he came to the door of a cell.

"Here is your dungeon," he said to Viviana, as he drew
back the heavy bolts, and disclosed a small chamber, about
four feet wide and six long, in which there was a pallet.
"My dame will attend you soon."

With this, he lighted a lamp, and departing with the guard,
barred the door outside. Viviana shuddered as she surveyed
the narrow dungeon in which she was placed. Roof, walls
and floor were of stone; and the aspect of the place was so
dismal and tomb-like, that she felt as if she were buried alive

Some hours elapsed before Dame Ipgreve made her appearance. She was accompanied by Ruth, who burst into tears on beholding Viviana. The jailer's wife had brought a few blankets and other necessaries with her, together with a loaf of bread and a jug of water. While disposing the blankets on the couch, she never ceased upbraiding Viviana for her former flight. Poor Ruth, who was compelled to assist her mother, endeavoured by her gestures and looks to convey to the unfortunate captive that she was as much devoted to her as ever. Their task completed, the old woman withdrew, and her daughter, casting a deep-commiserating look at Viviana, followed her, and the door was barred without.

Determined not to yield to despondency, Viviana knelt down, and addressed herself to Heaven; and, comforted by her prayers, threw herself on the bed, and sank into a peaceful slumber. She was awakened by hearing the bolts of her cell withdrawn, and the next moment Ruth stood before her.

"I fear you have exposed yourself to great risk in thus visiting me," said Viviana, tenderly embracing her.

"I would expose myself to any risk for you, sweet lady," replied Ruth. "But, oh! why do I see you here again? The chief support of Guy Fawkes during his sufferings has been the thought that you were at liberty."

"I surrendered myself in the hope of beholding him again," rejoined Viviana.

"You have given a fond, but fatal proof of your affection," returned Ruth. "The knowledge that you are a captive will afflict him more than all the torments he has endured."

"What torments has he endured, Ruth?" inquired Viviana, with a look of anguish.

"Do not ask me to repeat them," replied the jailer's daughter. "They are too dreadful to relate. When you behold his shattered frame and altered looks, you will comprehend what he has undergone."

"Alas!" exclaimed Viviana, bursting into tears, "I almost fear to behold him."

"You must prepare for a fearful shock," returned Ruth. "And now, madam, I must take my leave. I will endeavour to see you again to-morrow, but dare not promise to do so. I should not have been able to visit you now, but that my father is engaged with Lord Mounteagle."

"With Lord Mounteagle!" cried Viviana. "Upon what business?"

"Upon a foul business," rejoined Ruth. "No less than the destruction of Mr. Tresham. who is now a prisoner in the

Tower. Lord Mounteagle came to the Well Tower this evening, and I accidentally overheard him propose to my father to administer poison to the person I have named."

"I do not pity their victim," returned Viviana. "He is a double-dyed traitor, and will meet with the fate he deserves."

"Farewell, madam," said Ruth. "If I do not see you again, you will know that you have one friend in this fortress who deeply sympathizes with your afflictions."

So saying, she withdrew, and Viviana heard the bolts slipped gently into their sockets.

Vainly, after Ruth's visit, did she try to compose herself. Sleep fled her eyes, and she was haunted all night by the image of Fawkes, haggard and shattered by torture, as he had been described by the jailer's daughter. Day and night were the same to her, and she could only compute progress of the time by her own feelings, judging by which, she supposed it to be late in the day when she was again visited. The bolts of her cell being withdrawn, two men clad in long black gowns, and having hoods drawn over their faces, entered it. They were followed by Ipgreve; and Viviana, concluding she was about to be led to the torture, endeavoured to string herself to its endurance. Though he guessed what was passing in her breast, Jasper Ipgreve did not care to undeceive her, but motioning the hooded officials to follow him with her, quitted the cell. Seizing each a hand, the attendants led her after him along a number of intricate passages, until he stopped before the door of a cell, which he opened.

"Be brief in what you have to say," he cried, thrusting her forward. "I shall not allow you much time."

Viviana no sooner set foot in the cell than she felt in whose presence she stood. On a stool at the further end of the narrow chamber, with his head upon his breast, and a cloak wrapped around his limbs, sat Fawkes. A small iron lamp, suspended by a rusty chain from the ceiling, served to illumine his ghastly features. He lifted his eyes from the ground on her entrance, and recognising her, uttered a cry of anguish. Raising himself by a great effort, he opened his arms, and she rushed into them. For some moments, both continued silent. Grief took away their utterance; but at length Guy Fawkes spoke.

"My cup of bitterness was not sufficiently full," he said. "This alone was wanting to make it overflow."

"I fear you will blame me," she replied, "when you learn that I have voluntarily surrendered myself."

Guy Fawkes uttered a deep groan.

"I am the cause of your doing so," he said.

"You are so," she replied. "But you will forgive me when you know my motive. I came here to urge you to repentance. Oh! if you hope that we shall meet again hereafter—if you hope that we shall inherit joys which will requite us for all our troubles, you will employ the brief time left you on earth in imploring forgiveness for your evil intentions."

"Having had no evil intentions," replied Fawkes, coldly, "I have no pardon to ask."

"The Tempter who led you into the commission of sin under the semblance of righteousness, puts these thoughts into your heart," replied Viviana. "You have escaped the commission of an offence which must have deprived you of the joys of Heaven, and I am thankful for it. But if you remain impenitent, I shall tremble for your salvation."

"My account will soon be settled with my Maker," rejoined Fawkes; "and He will punish or reward me according to my deserts. I have acted according to my conscience, and can never repent that which I believe to be a righteous design."

"But do you not now see that you were mistaken?" returned Viviana—"do you not perceive that the sword which you raised against others has been turned against yourself? —and that the Great Power whom you serve and worship has declared himself against you?"

"You seek in vain to move me," replied Fawkes. "I am as insensible to your arguments as to the tortures of my enemies."

"Then Heaven have mercy upon your soul!" she rejoined.

"Look at me, Viviana," cried Fawkes, "and behold the wreck I am. What has supported me amid my tortures—in this dungeon—in the presence of my relentless foes?—what, but the consciousness of having acted rightly? And what will support me on the scaffold except the same conviction? If you love me, do not seek to shake my faith. But it is idle to talk thus. You cannot do so. Rest satisfied we shall meet again. Everything assures me of it. Wretched as I appear in this solitary cell, I am not wholly miserable, because I am buoyed up by the certainty that my actions are approved by Heaven."

"I will not attempt to destroy the delusion, since it is productive of happiness to you," replied Viviana. "But if my earnest, heartfelt prayers can conduce to your salvation, they shall not be wanting."

As she spoke, the door of the cell was opened by Jasper Ipgreve, who stepped towards her, and seized her roughly by the hand.

"Your time has expired, mistress," he said; "you must come with me.

"A minute longer," implored Fawkes.

"Not a second," replied Ipgreve.

"Shall we not meet again?" cried Viviana, distractedly.

"Ay, the day before your execution," rejoined Ipgreve. "I have good news for you," he added, pausing for a moment, and addressing Fawkes. "Mr. Tresham, who I told you has been brought to the Tower, has been taken suddenly and dangerously ill."

"If the traitor perishes before me, I shall die content," observed Fawkes.

"Then rest assured of it," said Viviana. "The task of vengeance is already fulfilled."

She was then forced away by Ipgreve, and delivered by him to the hooded officials outside, who hurried her back to her dungeon.

XII.

THE TRAITOR BETRAYED.

LORD MOUNTEAGLE arrived at the Tower shortly after Viviana, and repairing at once to the lieutenant's lodgings, had a brief conference with him, and informed him that he had a secret order to deliver to Jasper Ipgreve, from the Earl of Salisbury, touching the conspirators. Sir William Waad would have summoned the jailer; but Mounteagle preferred visiting him at the Well Tower, and accordingly proceeded thither.

He found Ipgreve with his wife and daughter, and telling him he desired a moment's private speech with him, the jailer dismissed them. Suspecting that the new-comer's errand related in some way to Viviana, Ruth contrived to place herself in such a situation that she could overhear what passed. A moment's scrutiny of Jasper's villanous countenance satisfied Mounteagle that the Earl of Salisbury was not mistaken in his man; and, as soon as he supposed they were alone, he unhesitatingly opened his plan to him. As he expected, Jasper exhibited no reluctance to undertake it; and, after some further discussion, it was agreed to put it in execution without delay.

"The sooner Mr. Tresham is silenced the better," said

Jasper; "for he threatens to make disclosures to the Council that will bring some noble persons" (with a significant look at Mounteagle), "into trouble."

"Where is he confined?" demanded the other.

"In the Beauchamp Tower, "replied Ipgreve.

"I will visit him at once," said Mounteagle; "and when I have conferred with him will call for wine. Bring two goblets, and in that which you give to Tresham place this powder."

Ipgreve nodded assent, and with a grim smile took the packet. Shortly after this they quitted the Well Tower together, and passing under the archway of the Bloody Tower, crossed the green, and entered the fortification in which the traitor was confined. Tresham was treated with far greater consideration than the other conspirators, being allowed the use of the large room on the upper floor of the Beauchamp Tower, which was seldom allotted to any persons except those of the highest distinction. When they entered, he was pacing to and fro within his chamber in great agitation; but he immediately stopped on seeing Mounteagle, and rushed towards him.

"You bring me my liberation?" he said.

"It is impossible to effect it at present," returned the other. "But make yourself perfectly easy. Your confinement will not be of long duration."

"I will not be trifled with," cried Tresham, furiously. "If I am examined by the Council, look to yourselves. As I hope for salvation, the truth shall out."

"Leave us," said Mounteagle, with a significant look at the jailer, who quitted the chamber.

"Hark'e, Mounteagle," said Tresham, as soon as they were alone, "I have been your tool thus far. But if you propose to lead me blindfold to the scaffold, you are greatly mistaken. You think that you have me safe within these walls; that my voice cannot be heard; and that I cannot betray you. But you are deceived—fearfully deceived, as you will find. I have your letters—the Earl of Salisbury's letters, proving that you were both aware of the plot—and that you employed me to watch its progress, and report it to you. I have also letters from Doctor Dee, the warden of Manchester, detailing his acquaintance with the conspiracy, and containing descriptions of the persons of Fawkes and Catesby, which I showed to the Earl of Salisbury.—These letters are now in my possession, and I will deliver them to the Council if I am not released."

"Deliver them to me, and I swear to you, you shall be set free," said Mounteagle.

"I will not trust you," rejoined Tresham. "Liberate me, and they are yours. But I will not rob myself of vengeance. I will confound you and the false Earl of Salisbury."

"You wrong us both by your unjust suspicions," said Mounteagle.

"Wrong you!" echoed Tresham, contemptuously. "Where is my promised reward? Why am I in this dungeon? Why am I treated like a traitor? If you meant me fairly, I should not be here, but, like yourself, at liberty, and in the enjoyment of the King's favour. But you have duped me, villain, and shall rue it. If I am led to the scaffold it shall be in your company."

"Compose yourself," rejoined Mounteagle, calmly. "Appearances, I own, are against us. But circumstances render it imperatively necessary that the Earl of Salisbury should *appear* to act against you. You have been charged by Guy Fawkes, when under the torture, of being a confederate in the design, and your arrest could not be avoided. I come hither to give you a solemn assurance that no harm shall befall you, but that you shall be delivered from your thraldom in a few days—perhaps in a few hours."

"You have no further design against me?" said Tresham, suspiciously.

"What motive could I have in coming hither, except to set your mind at rest?" rejoined Mounteagle.

"And I shall receive my reward?" demanded Tresham.

"You will receive your reward," returned Mounteagle, with significant emphasis. "I swear it. So make yourself easy."

"If I thought I might trust you, I should not heed my imprisonment, irksome though it be," rejoined Tresham.

"It cannot be avoided for the reasons I have just stated," replied Mounteagle. "But come, no more despondency. All will be well with you speedily. Let us drown care in a bumper. What ho! jailer," he added, opening the door, "a cup of wine!"

In a few minutes Ipgreve made his appearance, bearing two goblets filled with wine on a salver, one of which he presented to Mounteagle, and the other to Tresham.

"Here is to your speedy deliverance from captivity!" said Mounteagle, draining the goblet. "You will not refuse that pledge, Tresham?"

2 c

"Of a surety, not," replied the other. "To my speedy deliverance !"

And he emptied the cup, while Mounteagle and the jailer exchanged significant glances.

"And now, having fully discharged my errand, I must bid you farewell," said Mounteagle.

"You will not forget your promise ?" observed Tresham.

"Assuredly not," replied the other. "A week hence, and you will make no complaint against me.—Are you sure you did not give me the wrong goblet ?" he added to Ipgreve, as they descended the spiral staircase.

"Quite sure, my lord," returned the jailer with a grim smile.

Mounteagle immediately quitted the Tower, and, hastening to Whitehall, sought out the Earl of Salisbury, to whom he related what he had done. The Earl complimented him on his skilful management of the matter; and, congratulating each other upon having got rid of a dangerous and now useless instrument, they separated.

On the following day, Tresham was seized with a sudden illness, and, making known his symptoms to Ipgreve, the chirurgeon who attended the prison was sent for, and, on seeing him, pronounced him dangerously ill, though he was at a loss to explain the nature of his disorder. Every hour the sick man grew worse, and he was torn with racking pains. Connecting his sudden seizure with the visit of Lord Mounteagle, an idea of the truth flashed upon him, and he mentioned his suspicions to the chirurgeon, charging Jasper Ipgreve with being accessory to the deed. The jailer stoutly denied the accusation, and charged the prisoner in his turn with making a malicious statement to bring him into discredit.

"I will soon test the truth of his assertion," observed the chirurgeon, taking a small flat piece of the purest gold from his doublet. "Place this in your mouth."

Tresham obeyed, and Ipgreve watched the experiment with gloomy curiosity.

"You are a dead man," said the chirurgeon to Tresham, as he drew forth the piece of gold, and perceived that it was slightly tarnished. "Poison *has* been administered to you."

"Is there no remedy—no counter-poison ?" demanded Tresham, eagerly.

The chirurgeon shook his head.

"Then let the lieutenant be summoned," said Tresham; "I have an important confession to make to him. I charge this man," pointing to the jailer, "with giving poisoned wine to me. Do you hear what I say to you ?"

"I do," replied the chirurgeon.

"But he will never reveal it," said Ipgreve, with great unconcern. "I have a warrant from the Earl of Salisbury for what I have done."

"What!" cried Tresham, "can murder be committed here with impunity?"

"You have to thank your own indiscretion for what has happened," rejoined Ipgreve. "Had you kept a close tongue in your head, you would have been safe."

"Can nothing be done to save me?" cried the miserable man, with an imploring look at the chirurgeon.

"Nothing whatever," replied the person appealed to. "I would advise you to recommend your soul to God."

"Will you not inform the lieutenant that I desire to speak with him?" demanded Tresham.

The chirurgeon glanced at Ipgreve, and receiving a sign from him, gave a promise to that effect.

They then quitted the cell together, leaving Tresham in a state of indescribable agony both of mind and body. Half an hour afterwards the chirurgeon returned, and informed him that the lieutenant refused to visit him, or to hear his confession, and wholly discredited the fact of his being poisoned.

"I will take charge of your papers, if you choose to commit them to me," he said, "and will lay them before the Council."

"No," replied Tresham; "while life remains to me I will never part with them."

"I have brought you a mixture which, though it cannot heal you, will, at least, allay your sufferings," said the chirurgeon.

"I will not take it," groaned Tresham. "I distrust you as much as the others."

"I will leave it with you, at all events," rejoined the chirurgeon, setting down the phial.

The noise of the bolts shot into their sockets sounded to Tresham as if his tomb were closed upon him, and he uttered a cry of anguish. He would have laid violent hands upon himself, and accelerated his own end, but he wanted courage to do so, and continued to pace backwards and forwards across his chamber as long as his strength lasted. He was about to throw himself on the couch, from which he never expected to rise again, when his eyes fell upon the phial. "What if it should be poison!" he said, "it will end my sufferings the sooner."

And placing it to his lips, he swallowed its contents. As

2 c 2

the chirurgeon had foretold, it alleviated his sufferings, and throwing himself on the bed he sank into a troubled slumber, during which he dreamed that Catesby appeared to him with a vengeful countenance, and tried to drag him into a fathom-less abyss that yawned beneath their feet. Shrieking with agony, he awoke, and found two persons standing by his couch. One of them was the jailer, and the other appeared, from his garb, to be a priest; but a hood was drawn over his head so as to conceal his features.

"Are you come to witness my dying pangs, or to finish me?" demanded Tresham of the jailer.

"I am come for neither purpose," replied Ipgreve; "I pity your condition, and have brought you a priest of your own faith, who, like yourself, is a prisoner in the Tower. I will leave him with you, but he cannot remain long, so make the most of your time." And with these words he retired.

When he was gone, the supposed priest, who spoke in feeble and faltering accents, desired to hear Tresham's con-fession, and having listened to it, gave him absolution. The wretched man then drew from his bosom a small packet, and offered it to the confessor, who eagerly received it.

"This contains the letters of the Earl of Salisbury and Lord Mounteagle, which I have just mentioned," he said. "I pray you lay them before the Privy Council."

"I will not fail to do so," replied the confessor.

And reciting the prayer for one *in extremis* over the dying man, he departed.

"I have obtained the letters from him," said Mounteagle, throwing back his hood as he quitted the chamber, and addressing the jailer. "And now you need give yourself no further concern about him; he will be dead before morning."

Jasper Ipgreve locked the door upon the prisoner, and proceeded to the Well Tower. When he returned, he found Mounteagle's words had come to pass. Tresham was lying on the floor quite dead—his collapsed frame and distorted coun-tenance showing the agonies in which he must have expired.

XIII.

THE TRIAL.

THE trial of the conspirators, which had been delayed in order that full evidence might be procured against them, was, at length, appointed to take place in Westminster Hall, on Monday, the 27th of January, 1606. Early on the morning of this day, the eight surviving confederates (Garnet and Oldcorne being at this time secreted at Hendlip) were conveyed in two large covered wherries from the fortress to the place of trial. In spite of the severity of the weather,—it was snowing heavily, and the river was covered with sheets of ice,—they were attended by a vast number of boats filled with persons anxious to obtain a sight of them. Such was the abhorrence in which the actors in the conspiracy were held by the populace, that, not content with menaces and execrations, many of these persons hurled missiles against the wherries, and would have proceeded to further violence if they had not been restrained by the pikemen. When the prisoners landed, a tremendous and fearful shout was raised by the mob stationed at the head of the stairs, and it required the utmost efforts of the guard to protect them from injury. Two lines of soldiers, with calivers on their shoulders, were drawn out from the banks of the river to the entrance of the Hall, and between them the conspirators marched.

The melancholy procession was headed by Sir William Waad, who was followed by an officer of the guard and six halberdiers. Then came the executioner, carrying the gleaming implement of death with its edge turned from the prisoners. He was followed by Sir Everard Digby, whose noble figure and handsome countenance excited much sympathy among the beholders, and Ambrose Rookwood. Next came the two Winters, both of whom appeared greatly dejected. Next, John Grant and Robert Bates,—Catesby's servant, who had been captured at Holbeach. And lastly, Keyes and Fawkes.

Bitterly and justly incensed as were the multitude against the conspirators, their feelings underwent some change as they beheld the haggard countenance and shattered frame of Guy Fawkes. It was soon understood that he was the individual who had been found in the vault near the Parliament House, with the touchwood and matches in his belt ready to fire the train; and the greatest curiosity was exhibited to see him.

Just as the foremost of the conspirators reached the entrance of the Hall, a terrific yell, resembling nothing human, except the roar of a thousand tigers thirsting for blood, was uttered by the mob, and a tremendous but ineffectual attempt was made to break through the lines of the guard. Never before had so large an assemblage been collected on the spot. The whole of the space, extending on one hand from West-

minster Hall to the gates of Whitehall, and on the other
to the Abbey, was filled with spectators; and every roof,
window, and buttress were occupied.   Nor was the interior
of the Hall less crowded.   Not an inch of room was unoccu-
pied; and it was afterwards complained in Parliament, that
the members of the House had been so pressed and incom-
moded, that they could not hear what was said at the
arraignment.

The conspirators were first conveyed to the court of the
Star-Chamber, where they remained till the Lords Commissioners had arrived and taken their seats.   The commissioners
were the Earl of Nottingham, Lord High Admiral of England;
the Earl of Suffolk, Steward of the Household; the Earl of
Worcester, Master of the Horse; the Earl of Devonshire,
Master of the Ordnance; the Earl of Northampton, Warden
of the Cinque Ports; the Earl of Salisbury, Principal Secretary of State; Sir John Popham, Lord Chief Justice; Sir
Thomas Fleming, Lord Chief Baron of the Exchequer; and
Sir Thomas Walmisley and Sir Peter Warburton, Knights,
and both Justices of the Common Pleas.

Summoned by an usher, the conspirators were conducted
to a platform covered with black cloth, which had been
erected at the lower end of the Hall.   A murmur of indignation, vainly sought to be repressed by the grave looks of
the commissioners, burst from the immense assemblage, as
they one by one ascended the steps of the platform.   Guy
Fawkes was the last to mount, and his appearance was followed by a deep groan.   Supporting himself against the rail
of the scaffold, he surveyed the assemblage with a stern
and undaunted look.   As he gazed around, he could not help
marvelling at the vast multitude before him.   The whole of
the peers and all the members of the House of Commons
were present, while in a box on the left, though screened by
a lattice, sat the Queen and Prince Henry; and in another
on the right, and protected in the same way, the king and
his courtiers.

Silence being peremptorily commanded, the indictment was
read, wherein the prisoners were charged with conspiring to
blow up the King and the peers with gunpowder, and with
attempting to incite the Papists, and other persons, to open
rebellion; to which all the conspirators, to the no small surprise of those who heard them, and were aware that they had
subscribed their confessions, pleaded not guilty.

"How, sir?" cried the Lord Chief Justice, in a stern tone
to Fawkes.   "With what face can you pretend to deny the

indictment, when you were actually taken in the cellar with the powder, and have already confessed your treasonable intentions?"

"I do not mean to deny what I have confessed, my lord," replied Fawkes. "But this indictment contains many matters which I neither can nor will countenance by assent or silence. And I therefore deny it."

"It is well," replied the Lord Chief Justice. "Let the trial proceed."

The indictment being opened by Sir Edward Philips, serjeant-at-law, he was followed by Sir Edward Coke, the attorney-general, who in an eloquent and elaborate speech, which produced an extraordinay effect upon the assemblage, expatiated upon the monstrous nature of the plot, which he characterized as "the greatest treason that ever was plotted in England, and against the greatest king that ever reigned in England;" and after narrating the origin and progress of the conspiracy, concluded by desiring that the confessions of the prisoners should be openly read. This done, the jury were ordered by the Lord Chief Justice to retire, and the injunction being obeyed, they almost instantly returned with a verdict of guilty.

A deep, dread silence then prevailed throughout the Hall, and every eye was bent upon the conspirators, all of whom maintained a composed demeanour. They were then questioned by the Lord Chief Justice whether they had anything to say why judgment of death should not be pronounced against them."

"All I have to crave of your lordships," said Thomas Winter, "is, that being the chief offender of the two, I may die for my brother and myself."

"And I ask only that my brother's request may not be granted," said Robert Winter. "If he is condemned, I do not desire to live."

"I have nothing to solicit—not even pardon," said Keyes, carelessly. "My fortunes were always desperate, and are better now than they have ever been."

"I desire mercy," said Rookwood, "not from any fear of death, but because so shameful an ending will leave a perpetual stain upon my name and blood. I humbly submit myself to the King, and pray him to imitate our Supreme Judge, who sometimes punishes corporally, but not mortally."

"I have been guilty of a conspiracy, intended but never effected," said John Grant, "and solicit forgiveness on that plea."

"My crime has been fidelity to my master," said Bates. "If the king will let me live, I will serve him as faithfully as I did Mr. Catesby."

"I would not utter a word," said Fawkes, looking sternly round; "if I did not fear my silence might be misinterpreted. "I would not accept a pardon if it were offered me. I regard the project as a glorious one, and only lament its failure."

"Silence the vile traitor," said the Earl of Salisbury, rising.

And as he spoke two halberdiers sprang up the steps of the scaffold, and placing themselves on either side of Fawkes, prepared to gag him.

"I have done," he said, contemptuously regarding them.

"I have nothing to say, save this," said Sir Everard Digby, bowing to the judges. "If any of your lordships will tell me you forgive me, I shall go more cheerfully to the scaffold."

"Heaven forgive you, Sir Everard," said the Earl of Nottingham, returning his reverence, "as we do."

"I humbly thank your lordship," replied Digby.

Sentence was then passed upon the prisoners by Lord Chief Justice Popham, and they were removed from the platform.

As they issued from the Hall, and it became known to the assemblage without that they were condemned, a shout of fierce exultation rent the air, and they were so violently assailed on all sides, that they had great difficulty in reaching the wherries. The guard, however, succeeded, at length, in accomplishing their embarkation, and they were conveyed back in safety to the Tower.

XIV.

THE LAST MEETING OF FAWKES AND VIVIANA.

Up to this time, Viviana had not been allowed another interview with Guy Fawkes. She was twice interrogated by the Privy Council, but having confessed all she knew of the conspiracy, excepting what might implicate Garnet and Oldcorne, neither of whom she was aware had been apprehended, she was not again subjected to the torture. Her health, however, rapidly sank under her confinement, and she was soon reduced to such an extreme state of debility that she could not leave her bed. The chirurgeon, having been called in by Dame Ipgreve to attend her, reported her condition to

Sir William Waad, who directed that every means should be adopted for her restoration, and that Ruth Ipgreve should remain in constant attendance upon her.

Ascertaining all particulars relative to Guy Fawkes from the jailer's daughter, it was a sad satisfaction to Viviana to learn that he spent his whole time in devotion, and appeared completely resigned to his fate. It had been the Earl of Salisbury's purpose to bring Viviana to trial at the same time as the rest of the conspirators, but the chirurgeon reporting that her removal at this juncture would be attended with fatal consequences, he was compelled to defer it.

When the result of the trial was made known to Viviana by Ruth, though she had anticipated the condemnation of Guy Fawkes, she swooned away, and on her recovery, observed to Ruth, who was greatly alarmed at her looks, "I feel I am going fast. I should wish to see my husband once more before I die."

"I fear it is impossible, madam," replied Ruth; "but I will try to accomplish it."

"Do so," rejoined Viviana; "and my blessing shall rest ever on your head."

"Have you any valuable?" inquired Ruth. "My heart bleeds to make the demand at such a moment. But it is the only way to produce an effect on the avaricious nature of my father."

"I have nothing but this golden crucifix," said Viviana; "and I meant to give it to you."

"It will be better employed in this way," rejoined Ruth, taking it from her.

Quitting the cell, she hurried to the Well Tower, and found her father, who had just returned from locking up the conspirators in their different dungeons, sitting down to his evening meal.

"What is the matter with the wench?" he cried, staring at her. "You look quite distracted. Is Viviana Radcliffe dead?"

"No; but she is dying," replied Ruth.

"If that is the case I must go to her directly," observed Dame Ipgreve. "She may have some valuable about her which I must secure."

"You will be disappointed, mother," rejoined Ruth, with a look of irrepressible disgust. "She has nothing valuable left but this golden crucifix, which she has sent to my father, on condition of his allowing Guy Fawkes to see her before she dies."

"Give it me, wench," cried Jasper Ipgreve; "and let her die in peace."

"She will *not* die in peace unless she sees him," replied Ruth. "Nor shall you have it if you do not comply with her request."

"How!" exclaimed the father, "do you dare——"

"Think not to terrify me, father," interrupted Ruth; "I am resolute in this. Hear me," she cried, seizing his arm, and fixing a look upon him that seemed to pierce his soul— "hear me," she said, in a tone so low as to be inaudible to her mother; "she *shall* see him, or I will denounce you as the murderer of Tresham. Now will you comply?"

"Give me the cross," said Ipgreve.

"Not till you have earned it," replied his daughter.

"Well, well," he rejoined; "if it must be, it must. But I may get into trouble in the matter. I must consult Master Forsett, the gentleman jailer, who has the charge of Guy Fawkes, before I dare take him to her cell."

"Consult whom you please," rejoined Ruth, impatiently; "but lose no time, or you will be too late."

Muttering imprecations on his daughter, Ipgreve left the Well Tower, and Ruth hurried back to Viviana, whom she found anxiously expecting her, and related to her what she had done.

"Oh, that I may hold out till he comes!" cried Viviana; "but my strength is failing fast."

Ruth endeavoured to comfort her; but she was unequal to the effort, and bursting into tears, knelt down, and wept upon the pillow beside her. Half an hour had now elapsed. It seemed an age to the poor sufferers, and still the jailer came not, and even Ruth had given up all hope, when a heavy tread was heard in the passage; the door was opened; and Guy Fawkes appeared, attended by Ipgreve and Forsett.

"We will not interrupt your parting," said Forsett, who seemed to have a touch of humanity in his composition. And beckoning to Ruth to follow him, he quitted the cell with Ipgreve.

Guy Fawkes meanwhile had approached the couch, and gazed with an expression of intense anguish at Viviana. She returned his glance with a look of the utmost affection, and clasped his hand between her thin fingers.

"I am now standing on the brink of eternity," she said, in a solemn tone, "and I entreat you earnestly, as you hope to insure our meeting hereafter, to employ the few days left you in sincere and hearty repentance. You have sinned—sinned

deeply, but not beyond the power of redemption. Let me
feel that I have saved you, and my last moments will be
happy. Oh! by the love I have borne you—by the pangs I
have endured for you—by the death I am now dying for you
—let me implore you not to lose one moment, but to suppli-
cate a merciful Providence to pardon your offence."

"I will—I will," rejoined Fawkes, in broken accents.
"You have opened my eyes to my error, and I sincerely repent it."

"Saved! saved!" cried Viviana, raising herself in the bed.
Opening her arms, she strained him to her bosom; and for a
few moments they mingled their tears together.

"And now," she said, sinking backwards, "kneel by me—
pray for forgiveness—pray audibly, and I will join in your
prayer."

Guy Fawkes knelt by the bedside, and addressed the most
earnest supplications to Heaven for forgiveness. For awhile
he heard Viviana's gentle accents accompany him. They
grew fainter and fainter, until at last they totally ceased.
Filled with a dreadful apprehension, he sprang to his feet.
An angelic smile illumed her countenance; her gaze was
fixed on him for one moment—it then grew dim and dimmer,
until it was extinguished.

Guy Fawkes uttered a cry of the wildest despair, and fell
to the ground. Alarmed by the sound, Forsett and Ipgreve,
who were standing outside, rushed into the cell, and instantly
raised him. But he was now in a state of distraction, and
for the moment seemed endowed with all his former strength.
Striving to break from them, he cried, in a tone of the most
piercing anguish, "You shall not tear me from her! I will
die with her! Let me go, I say, or I will dash out my brains
against these flinty walls, and balk you of your prey."

But his struggles were in vain. They held him fast, and
calling for further assistance, conveyed him to his cell, where,
fearing he might do some violence to himself, they placed
him in irons.

Ruth entered the cell as soon as Fawkes and the others
had quitted it, and performed the last sad offices for the
departed. Alternately praying and weeping, she watched by
the body during the whole of the night. On the following
day, the remains of the unfortunate Viviana were interred in
the chapel of Saint Peter on the green, and the sole mourner
was the jailer's daughter.

"Peace be with her!" cried Ruth, as she turned away
from the grave. "Her sorrows at last are over."

XV.

GUY FAWKES was for some time wholly inconsolable. His stoical nature seemed completely subdued, and he wept like an infant. By degrees, however, the violence of his grief abated, and calling to mind the last injunctions of her whose loss he mourned, he addressed himself to prayer, and acknowledging his guilt, besought her intercession with Heaven for his forgiveness.

It will not seem strange, when his superstitious character is taken into consideration, that he should fancy he received an immediate proof that his prayers were heard. To his excited imagination it appeared that a soft unearthly strain of music floated in the air over his head; that an odour like that of Paradise filled his cell; while an invisible finger touched his brow. While in this entranced state, he was utterly insensible to his present miserable situation, and he seemed to have a foretaste of celestial happiness. He did not, however, desist from prayer, but continued his supplications throughout the day.

On that night he was visited by the lieutenant, who announced to him that the execution of four of the conspirators was fixed for Thursday (it was then Tuesday), while his own and that of the three others would not take place till the following day.

"As you are the greatest traitor of all, your execution will be reserved to the last," pursued Waad. "No part of the sentence will be omitted. You will be dragged to Old Palace Yard, over against the scene of your intended bloody and damnable action, at a horse's tail, and will be there turned off the gallows, and hanged, *but not till you are dead.* You will then be embowelled; your vile heart, which conceived this atrocious design, will be torn beating from your breast; and your quarters will be placed on the palace gates as an abhorrent spectacle in the eyes of men, and a terrible proof of the King's just vengeance."

Guy Fawkes heard the recapitulation of his dreadful sentence unmoved.

"The sole mercy I would have craved of his Majesty would have been permission to die first!" he said. "But Heaven's will be done! I deserve my doom."

"What! is your stubborn nature at length subdued?" cried the lieutenant, in surprise. "Do you repent of your offence?"

"Deeply and heartily," returned Fawkes.

"Make the sole amends in your power for it, then, and

disclose the names of all who have been connected with the atrocious design," rejoined Waad.

"I confess myself guilty," replied Fawkes, humbly. "But I accuse no others."

"Then you die impenitent," rejoined the lieutenant, "and cannot hope for mercy hereafter."

Guy Fawkes made no answer, but bowed his head upon his breast, and the lieutenant, darting a malignant look at him, quitted the cell.

On the following day the whole of the conspirators were taken to Saint John's Chapel in the White Tower, where a discourse was pronounced to them by Doctor Overall, Dean of Saint Paul's, who enlarged upon the enormity of their offence, and exhorted them to repentance. The discourse over, they were about to be removed, when two ladies, clad in mourning habits, entered the chapel. These were Lady Digby and Mrs. Rookwood, and they immediately flew to their husbands. The rest of the conspirators walked away, and averted their gaze from the painful scene. After an ineffectual attempt to speak, Lady Digby swooned away, and was committed by her husband, while in a state of insensibility, to the care of an attendant. Mrs. Rookwood, however, who was a woman of high spirit and great personal attractions, though the latter were now wasted by affliction, maintained her composure, and encouraging her husband to bear up manfully against his situation, tenderly embraced him and withdrew. The conspirators were then taken back to their cells.

At an early hour on the following morning the four miserable persons intended for death, namely Sir Everard Digby, the elder Winter, John Grant, and Bates, were conducted to the Beauchamp Tower. Bates would have stood aloof from his superiors; but Sir Everard Digby took him kindly by the hand, and drew him towards them.

"No distinctions must be observed now," he said. "We ought to beg pardon of thee, my poor fellow, for bringing thee into this strait."

"Think not of me, worshipful sir," replied Bates. "I loved Mr. Catesby so well, that I would have laid down my life for him at any time; and now I die cheerfully in his cause."

"Mr. Lieutenant," said Robert Winter to Sir William Waad, who stood near them with Forsett and Ipgreve, "I pray you commend me to my brother. Tell him I die in entire love of him, and if it is possible for the departed to watch over the living, I will be with him at his last hour."

At this moment, a trampling of horses was heard on the green, and the lieutenant proceeding to the grated window, saw four mounted troopers, each having a sledge and hurdle attached by ropes to his steed, drawn up before the door. While he was gazing at them, an officer entered the room, and informed him that all was in readiness. Sir William Waad then motioned the prisoners to follow him, and they descended the spiral staircase.

The green was thronged with horse and foot-soldiers, and as the conspirators issued from the arched door of the fortification, the bell of Saint Peter's Chapel began to toll. Sir Everard Digby was first bound to a hurdle, with his face towards the horse, and the others were quickly secured in the same manner. The melancholy cavalcade was then put into motion. A troop of horse-soldiers in their full accoutrements, and with calivers upon their shoulders, rode first; then came a band of halberdiers on foot; then the masked executioner, mounted on a led horse; then the four prisoners on the hurdles, one after the other; then the lieutenant on horseback; while another band of horse-soldiers, equipped like the first, brought up the rear. They were met by the recorder of London, Sir Henry Montague, and the sheriffs, at the gate of the Middle Tower, to the latter of whom the lieutenant, according to custom, delivered up the bodies of the prisoners. After a short delay, the train again set forward, and emerging from the Bulwark Gate, proceeded through an enormous concourse of spectators towards Tower-street.

Aware that a vast crowd would be assembled in the City, and apprehensive of some popular tumult, the Lord Mayor had issued precepts to the aldermen of every ward, commanding them "to cause one able and sufficient person, with a halberd in his hand, to stand at the door of every dwelling-house in the open street in the way that the traitors were to be drawn towards the place of execution, there to remain from seven in the morning until the return of the sheriffs." But these were not the whole of the arrangements made to preserve order. The cavalcade, it was fixed, was to proceed along Tower-street, Gracechurch-street, Lombard-street, Cheapside, and so on to the west end of Saint Paul's Cathedral, where the scaffold was erected. Along the whole road, on either side, a line of halberdiers was drawn up, while barriers were erected against the cross streets. Nor were these precautions needless. Such a vast concourse was collected, that nothing but the presence of a strong armed force could have prevented confusion and disorder. The roofs of all the houses, the towers of the churches, the steps of the crosses were covered with spectators, who groaned and hooted as the conspirators passed by.

The scaffold, as has just been stated, was erected in front of the great western entrance of the cathedral. The mighty valves of the sacred structure were thrown open, and disclosed its columned aisles crowded with spectators, as was its roof and central tower. The great bell, which had begun to toll when the melancholy procession came in sight, continued to pour forth its lugubrious sounds during the whole of the ceremonial. The rolling of muffled drums was likewise heard above the tumultuous murmurs of the impatient multitude. The whole area from the cathedral to Ludgate-hill was filled with spectators, but an open space was kept clear in front of the scaffold, in which the prisoners were one by one unbound from the hurdles.

During this awful pause, they had sufficient time to note the whole of the dreadful preparations. At a little distance from them was a large fire, on which boiled a caldron of pitch, destined to receive their dismembered limbs. A tall gallows, approached by a double ladder, sprung from the scaffold, on which the hangman was already mounted with the rope in his hand. At the foot of the ladder was the quartering-block, near which stood the masked executioner with a chopper in his hand, and two large sharp knives in his girdle. His arms were bared to the shoulder; and a leathern apron, soiled by gory stains, and tied round his waist, completed his butcherly appearance. Straw was scattered upon the scaffold near the block.

Sir Everard Digby was the first to receive the fatal summons. He mounted with a firm footstep, and his youth, his noble aspect, and undaunted demeanour, awakened, as before, the sympathy of the beholders. Looking round, he thus addressed the assemblage :

"Good people, I am here about to die, ye well know for what cause. Throughout the matter, I have acted according to the dictates of my conscience. They have led me to under-take this enterprise, which, in respect of my religion, I hold to be no offence, but in respect of the law a heinous offence, and I therefore ask forgiveness of God, of the King, and of the whole realm."

Crossing himself devoutly, he then knelt down, and recited his prayers in Latin, after which he arose, and again looking round, said in an earnest voice :

"I desire the prayers of all good Catholics, and of none other."

"Then none will pray for you," replied several voices from the crowd.

Heedless of the retort, Sir Everard surrendered himself to the executioner's assistant, who divested him of his cloak and doublet, and unfastened his collar. In this state he mounted the ladder, and the hangman fulfilled his office.

Robert Winter was next summoned, and ascended the scaffold with great firmness. Everything proclaimed the terrible tragedy that had just been enacted. The straw was sprinkled with blood, so was the block, so were the long knives of the executioner, whose hands and arms were dyed with the same crimson stain; while in one corner of the scaffold stood a basket, containing the dismembered limbs of the late unfortunate sufferer. But these dreadful sights produced no effect on Robert Winter. Declining to address the assemblage, he at once surrendered himself to the assistant, and shared the fate of his friend.

Grant was the next to follow. Undismayed as his predecessor, he looked round with a cheerful countenance, and said:

"I am about to suffer the death of a traitor, and am content to die so. But I am satisfied that our project was so far from being sinful, that I rely entirely on my merits in bearing a part in it, as an abundant satisfaction and expiation for all the sins I have at other times of my life committed."

This speech was received by a terrific yell from the multitude. Wholly unmoved, however, Grant uttered a few prayers, and then crossing himself, mounted the ladder, and was quickly despatched. The bloody business was completed by the slaughter of Bates, who died as resolutely as the others.

These executions, being conducted with the utmost deliberation, occupied nearly an hour. The crowd then separated to talk over the sight they had witnessed; and to keep holiday during the remainder of the day; rejoicing that an equally exciting spectacle was in store for them on the morrow.

XVI.

OLD PALACE YARD.

Guy Fawkes's tranquillity of mind did not desert him to the last. On the contrary, as his term of life drew near its close, he became more cheerful and resigned; his sole anxiety being that all should be speedily terminated. When Ipgreve took leave of him for the night, he threw himself on his couch and soon fell into a gentle slumber. His dreams were soothing, and he fancied that Viviana appeared to him clad in robes of snowy whiteness, and regarding him with a smiling

countenance, promised that the gates of eternal happiness
would be opened to him on the morrow.

Awaking about four o'clock, he passed the interval between
that time and his summons by the jailer in earnest prayer.
At six o'clock Ipgreve made his appearance. He was accompanied by his daughter, who had prevailed on him to allow
her to take leave of the prisoner. She acquainted Fawkes
with all particulars of the interment of Viviana, to which he
listened with tearful interest.

"Would my remains might be laid beside her!" he said.
"But fate forbids it!"

"Truly does it," observed Ipgreve, gruffly; "unless you
would have her body removed to the spikes of Whitehall gates."

Disregarding this brutal speech, which called a blush of
shame to the cheeks of Ruth, Fawkes affectionately pressed
her hand, and said:

"Do not forget me in your prayers, and sometimes visit
the grave of Viviana."

"Doubt it not," she replied, in accents half suffocated by grief.

Fawkes then bade her farewell, and followed the jailer
through various intricate passages, which brought them to a
door opening upon one of the lower chambers of the Beauchamp Tower. Unlocking it, Ipgreve led the way up the
circular staircase, and ushered his companion into the large
chamber, where Rookwood, Keyes, and Thomas Winter were
already assembled.

The morning was clear, but frosty, and bitterly cold; and
when the lieutenant appeared, Rookwood besought him to
allow them a fire as their last earthly indulgence. The request was peremptorily refused. A cup of hot spiced wine was,
however, offered them, and accepted by all except Fawkes.

At the same hour as on the previous day, the hurdles were
brought to the entrance of the fortification, and the prisoners
bound to them. The recorder and sheriffs met them at the
Middle Tower, as they had done the other conspirators, and
the cavalcade set forth. The crowd was even greater than
on the former occasion; and it required the utmost exertion
on the part of the guard to maintain order. Some little
delay occurred at Ludgate; and during this brief halt, Rookwood heard a cry, and looking up, perceived his wife at the
upper window of one of the habitations, waving her hand-
kerchief to him, and cheering him by her gestures. He endeavoured to answer her by signs; but his hands were fast
bound, and the next moment the cavalcade moved on.

At Temple Bar another halt occurred; and as the train moved slowly forward, an immense crowd, like a swollen stream, swept after it. The two gates at Whitehall, then barring the road to Westminster, were opened as the train approached, and a certain portion of the concourse allowed to pass through. The scaffold, which had been removed from Saint Paul's, was erected in the middle of Old Palace Yard, in front of the House of Lords. Around it were circled a band of halberdiers, outside whom stood a dense throng. The buttresses and pinnacles of the Abbey were covered with spectators; so was the roof of the Parliament House, and the gallery over the entrance.

The bell of the Abbey began to toll as the train passed through the gates of Whitehall, and its deep booming filled the air. Just as the conspirators were released from the hurdles, Topcliffe, who had evidently from his disordered attire, arrived from a long journey, rode up, and dismounted.

"I am just in time," he cried, with an exulting glance at the conspirators; this is not the last execution I shall witness. Fathers Garnet and Oldcorne are prisoners, and on their way to London. I was a long time in unearthing the priestly foxes, but I succeeded at last."

At this moment an officer approached, and summoned Thomas Winter to mount the scaffold. He obeyed, and exhibited no symptom of quailing, except that his complexion suddenly turned to a livid colour. Being told of this by the lieutenant, he tried to account for it by saying that he thought he saw his brother precede him up the steps. He made a brief address, protesting he died a true Catholic, and in that faith, notwithstanding his offences, hoped to be saved.

Rookwood followed him, and indulged in a somewhat longer oration, "I confess my offence to God," he said, "in seeking to shed blood, and implore his mercy. I likewise confess my offence to the King, of whose majesty I humbly ask forgiveness; and I further confess my offence to the whole State, of whom in general I entreat pardon. May the Almighty bless the King, the Queen, and all their royal progeny, and grant them a long and happy reign! May He turn their hearts to the Catholic faith, so that heresy may be wholly extirpated from the kingdom!"

The first part of this speech was well received by the assemblage, but the latter was drowned in groans and hootings, amid which Rookwood was launched into eternity.

Keyes came next, and eyeing the assemblage disdainfully, went up the ladder, and threw himself off with such force that he broke the rope, and was instantly despatched by the executioner and his assistants.

Guy Fawkes now alone remained, and he slowly mounted the scaffold. His foot slipped on the blood-stained boards, and he would have fallen, if Topcliffe, who stood near him, had not caught his hand. A deep silence prevailed as he looked around, and uttered the following words in a clear and distinct voice :

"I ask forgiveness of the King and the State for my criminal intention, and trust that my death will wash out my offence."

He then crossed himself and knelt down to pray, after which his cloak and doublet were removed by the executioner's assistant and placed with those of the other conspirators. He made an effort to mount the ladder, but his stiffened limbs refused their office.

"Your courage fails you," sneered Topcliffe, laying his hand upon his shoulder.

"My strength does," replied Fawkes, sternly regarding him. "Help me up the ladder, and you shall see whether I am afraid to die."

Seeing how matters stood, the executioner who stood by, leaning upon his chopper, tendered him his blood-stained hand. But Fawkes rejected it with disgust, and exerting all his strength, forced himself up the ladder.

As the hangman adjusted the rope, he observed a singular smile illumine the features of his victim.

"You seem happy," he said.

"I *am* so," replied Fawkes, earnestly,—"I see the form of her I loved beckoning me to unfading happiness."

With this, he stretched out his arms and sprang from the ladder. Before his frame was exposed to the executioner's knife, life was totally extinct.

XVII.

THE LAST EXECUTION.

LITTLE more remains to be told, and that little is of an equally painful nature with the tragical events just related.

Fathers Garnet and Oldcorne, together with Mr. Abingdon and their servants, arrived in London on the 12th of February, about a fortnight after the execution of the other conspirators. They were first taken to the Gate-house at West-

minster, and were examined on the following day by the Earl
of Salisbury and the Privy Council at the Star-Chamber.
Nothing could be elicited from them, and Garnet answered
the Earl's interrogatories with infinite subtlety and address.
The examination over, they were ordered to be removed to
the Tower.

Topcliffe accompanied them to the stairs. As they proceeded thither, he called Garnet's attention to a ghastly
object stuck on a spike over the palace gates.

"Do you recognise those features?" he asked.

"No," replied Garnet, shudderingly averting his gaze.

"I am surprised to hear it," rejoined Topcliffe, "for they
were once well known to you. It is the head of Guy Fawkes.
Of all the conspirators," he added, with a bitter laugh, "he
was the only one who died truly penitent. It is reported that
this happy change was wrought in him by Viviana Radcliffe."

"Heaven have mercy upon his soul!" muttered Garnet.

"I will tell you a strange tale about Catesby," pursued
Topcliffe. "He was buried in the garden at Holbeach with
Percy, but an order was sent down by the Earl of Salisbury to
have their bodies disinterred and quartered. When Catesby's
head was severed from the trunk, to be set on the gates of
Warwick, fresh blood spouted forth, as if life were in the veins."

"You do not expect me to believe this idle story?" said
Garnet, incredulously.

"Believe it or not, as you please," returned Topcliffe,
angrily.

On arriving at the fortress, Garnet was lodged in the large
chamber of the Beauchamp Tower, and allowed the attendance of his servant, Nicholas Owen, while Oldcorne was
equally well accommodated in the Constable Tower. This
leniency was the result of the policy of the Earl of Salisbury,
who hoped to obtain disclosures from the two Jesuit priests
which would enable him to strike the decisive blow he meditated against the Papists. But he was unsuccessful. They
refused to make any confessions which would criminate themselves or implicate others; and as none of the conspirators,
not even Tresham, had admitted their connexion with the
plot, it was difficult to find proof against them. Garnet
underwent daily examinations from the Earl of Salisbury and
the commissioners, but he baffled all their inquiries.

"If we cannot wring the truth from you by fair means, Mr.
Garnet," said Salisbury, "we must have recourse to torture."

"*Minare ista pueris,*" replied Garnet, contemptuously.

"Leave these two priests to me, my lord," observed Sir

William Waad, who was present at the examination, which took place at the council-chamber in his lodgings,—"leave them to me," he said in a low voice to the Earl, "and I will engage to procure a full confession from their own lips, without resorting to torture."

"You will render the State an important service by doing so," replied Salisbury, in the same tone. "I place the matter entirely in your hands."

The lieutenant set to work without loss of time. By his directions, Garnet and Oldcorne were removed from their present places of confinement to two subterranean cells immediately adjoining each other, but between which a secret recess, contrived in the thickness of the wall, and built for the purpose it was subsequently put to, existed. Two days after they had been so immured, Ipgreve, who had received his instructions, loitered for a moment in Oldcorne's cell, and with affected hesitation informed him that for a trifling reward he would enable him to hold unreserved communication with his fellow-prisoner.

Oldcorne eagerly caught at the bait, but required to be satisfied that the jailer could make good his words. Ipgreve immediately proceeded to the side of the cell, and holding a lamp to the wall, showed him a small iron knob.

"Touch this spring," he said, "and a stone will fall from its place, and enable you to converse with Father Garnet, who is in the next cell. But you must take care to replace the stone when any one approaches."

Promising to observe the utmost caution, and totally unsuspicious of the deceit practised upon him, Oldcorne gave Ipgreve the reward, and as soon as he was gone, touched the spring, and found it act precisely as the jailer had stated.

Garnet was greatly surprised to hear the other's voice, and on learning how the communication was managed, was at first suspicious of some stratagem, but by degrees his fears wore off, and he became unreserved in his discourse with his companion, discussing the fate of the conspirators, their own share in the plot, the probability of their acquittal, and the best means of baffling their examiners. All these interlocutions were overheard and taken down by the lieutenant and two other witnesses, Forsett and Lockerson, private secretary to the Earl of Salisbury, who were concealed in the recess. Having obtained all the information he desired, Sir William Waad laid his notes before the Council, and their own confessions being read to the priests, they were both greatly confused, though neither would admit their authenticity.

Meanwhile their two servants, Owen and Chambers, had been repeatedly examined, and refusing to confess, were at last suspended from a beam by the thumbs. But this producing no result, they were told that on the following day they would be placed on the rack. Chambers then offered to make a full confession, but Owen, continuing obstinate, was conveyed back to his cell. Ipgreve brought him his food as usual in the evening, and on this occasion it consisted of broth and a small allowance of meat. It was the custom of the jailer to bring with him a small blunt-pointed knife, with which he allowed the prisoner to cut his victuals. Having got possession of the knife, Owen tasted the broth, and complaining that it was quite cold, he implored the jailer to get it warmed for him, as he felt extremely unwell. Somewhat moved by his entreaties and more by his appearance, Ipgreve complied. On his return, he found the unfortunate man lying in one corner of the cell, partially covered by a heap of straw which ordinarily formed his bed.

"Here is your broth," he said. "Take it while it is hot. I shall have myself no further trouble about you."

"It will not be needed," gasped Owen.

Alarmed by the sound of his voice, Ipgreve held the light towards him, and perceived that his face was pale as death. At the same time he remarked that the floor was covered with blood. Instantly divining the truth, the jailer rushed towards the wretched man, and dragging away the blood-stained straw, found he had inflicted a frightful wound upon himself with the knife, which he still held in his grasp.

"Fool that I was to trust you with the weapon!" cried Ipgreve. "But who would have thought it could inflict a mortal wound?"

"Any weapon will serve him who is resolved to die," rejoined Owen. "You cannot put me on the rack now." And with a ghastly expression of triumph he expired.

Soon after this, Oldcorne and Abingdon were sent down to Worcester, where the former was tried and executed. Stephen Littleton suffered death at the same time.

On Friday, the 23rd of March, full proofs being obtained against him, Garnet was arraigned of high treason at Guildhall. The trial, which excited extraordinary interest, was attended by the King, by the most distinguished personages, male and female, of his court, and by all the foreign ambassadors. Garnet conducted himself throughout his arrraignment, which lasted for thirteen hours, with the same courage and address which he had displayed on his examinations before the commissioners. But his subtlety availed him little. He was found guilty and condemned.

The execution of the sentence was for some time deferred, it being hoped that a complete admission of his guilt would be obtained from him, together with disclosures relative to the designs of the Jesuit party. With this view the examinations were still continued, but the rigour with which he had been latterly treated was relaxed. A few days before his execution, he was visited by several eminent Protestant Divines,—Doctor Montague, Dean of the Chapel Royal; Doctor Neile, Dean of Westminster; and Doctor Overall, Dean of Saint Paul's,—with whom he had a long disputation on points of faith and other spiritual matters.

At the close of this discussion, Doctor Overall remarked— "I suppose you expect, Mr. Garnet, that after your death, the Church of Rome will declare you a martyr?"

"I a martyr!" exclaimed Garnet, sorrowfully. "O, what a martyr I should be! If, indeed, I were really about to suffer death for the Catholic religion, and had never known of this project except by means of sacramental confession, I might perhaps be accounted worthy the honour of martyrdom, and might deservedly be glorified in the opinion of our Church. As it is, I acknowledge myself to have sinned in this respect, and deny not the justice of the sentence passed upon me."

Satisfied, at length, that no further disclosures could be obtained from him, the King signed the warrant for his execution on the 2nd of May.

The scaffold was erected at the west end of Saint Paul's Cathedral, on the spot where Digby and the other conspirators had suffered. A vast assemblage was collected as on the former occasion, and similar precautions were taken to prevent tumult and disturbance. The unfortunate man's torture was cruelly and unnecessarily prolonged by a series of questions proposed to him on the scaffold by Doctor Overall and the Dean of Westminster, all of which he answered very collectedly and clearly. He maintained his fortitude to the last. When fully prepared, he mounted the ladder, and thus addressed the assemblage:

"I commend myself to all good Catholics. I grieve that I have offended the King by not revealing the design entertained against him, and that I did not use more diligence in preventing the execution of the plot. I commend myself most humbly to the Lords of his Majesty's Council, and entreat them not to judge too hardly by me. I beseech all men that Catholics may not fare the worse for my sake, and

I exhort all Catholics to take care not to mix themselves with seditious or traitorous designs against the King's Majesty, whom God preserve!"

Making the sign of the cross upon his forehead and breast, he continued:

"*In nomine Patris, Filii, et Spiritûs Sancti! Jesus Maria! Maria, mater gratiæ! mater misericordiæ! Tu me ab hoste protege, et horâ mortis suscipe! In manus tuas, Domine, commendo spiritum meum, quia tu redemisti me, Domine, Deus veritatis.*" Again crossing himself, he added,—"*Per crucis hoc signum fugiat procul omne malignum! Infige crucem tuam, Domine, in corde meo!*"

And with this last pathetic ejaculation he threw himself from the ladder.

Garnet obtained, after death, the distinction he had disclaimed while living. He was enrolled, together with Oldcorne, among the list of Catholic martyrs. Several miracles are affirmed by the Jesuits to have been performed in his behalf. Father More relates that on the lawn at Hendlip, where he and Oldcorne last set foot, "a new and hitherto unknown species of grass sprang up into the exact shape of an imperial crown, and remained for a long time without being trodden down by the feet of passengers, or eaten up by the cattle." It was further asserted that a spring of oil burst forth at the west end of Saint Paul's Cathedral on the precise spot where he suffered. But the most singular prodigy is that recounted by Endæmon Joannes, who affirms that in a straw which had been sprinkled with Garnet's blood, a human countenance, strangely resembling that of the martyr, was discovered. This legend of the Miraculous Straw, having received many embellishments and improvements as it travelled abroad, obtained universal credence, and was conceived to fully establish Garnet's innocence.

Anne Vaux, the Jesuits' devoted friend, retired with her sister, Mrs. Brooksby, to a nunnery in Flanders, where she ended her days.

So terminated the memorable and never-to-be-forgotten Gunpowder Treason, for deliverance from which our Church still offers thanksgivings, and in remembrance of which, on the anniversary of its discovery, faggots are collected, and bonfires lighted, to consume the effigy of the arch-conspirator, GUY FAWKES.

THE END.

LONDON: C. WHITING, BEAUFORT HOUSE, DUKE STREET, LINCOLN'S-INN-FIELDS.

ajj